BLACK+DECKER™

The Complete Guide to

BATHROOMS

Updated 5th Edition

Dazzling Upgrades & Hardworking Improvements
You Can Do Yourself

COOL SPRINGS PRESS

Inspiring | Educating | Creating | Entertaining

Brimming with creative inspiration, how-to projects, and useful information to enrich your everyday life, Quarto Knows is a favorite destination for those pursuing their interests and passions. Visit our site and dig deeper with our books into your area of interest: Quarto Creates, Quarto Cooks, Quarto Homes, Quarto Lives, Quarto Drives, Quarto Explores, Quarto Gifts, or Quarto Kids.

First published in 2018 by Cool Springs Press, an imprint of The Quarto Group, 401 Second Avenue North, Suite 310, Minneapolis, MN 55401 USA. T (612) 344-8100 F (612) 344-8692 www.QuartoKnows.com

Cool Springs Press titles are also available at discount for retail, wholesale, promotional, and bulk purchase. For details, contact the Special Sales Manager by email at specialsales@quarto.com or by mail at The Quarto Group, Attn: Special Sales Manager, 401 Second Avenue North, Suite 310, Minneapolis, MN 55401 USA.

10 9 8 7 6 5 4 3 2

ISBN: 978-0-7603-6130-6

Digital edition published in 2018
eISBN: 978-0-7603-6131-3

Library of Congress Cataloging-in-Publication Data

Names: Cool Springs Press, author. | Black & Decker Corporation (Towson, Md.), consultant.
Title: Black & Decker the complete guide to bathrooms : design, update, remodel, improve, do it yourself / by editors of Cool Springs Press.
Other titles: Complete guide to bathrooms
Description: 5th edition. | Minneapolis, Minnesota : Quarto Publishing Group USA Inc., Cool Springs Press, 2017. | Includes index.
Identifiers: LCCN 2017047189 | ISBN 9780760361306 (sc)
Subjects: LCSH: Bathrooms--Remodeling--Amateurs' manuals.
Classification: LCC TH4816.3.B37 C66 2017 | DDC 643/.52--dc23
LC record available at https://lccn.loc.gov/2017047189

Acquiring Editor: Mark Johanson
Edition Editor: Chris Peterson
Editor: Bryan Trandem
Project Manager: Jordan Wiklund
Art Director: Brad Springer
Cover Designer: Brad Springer
Layout: Danielle Smith-Boldt
New Photography:
Photographer: Rich Fleischman
Photo Assistant: Erik Sateren

Printed in China

MIX
Paper from responsible sources
FSC® C008047
www.fsc.org

NOTICE TO READERS

For safety, use caution, care, and good judgment when following the procedures described in this book. The publisher and BLACK+DECKER cannot assume responsibility for any damage to property or injury to persons as a result of misuse of the information provided.

The techniques shown in this book are general techniques for various applications. In some instances, additional techniques not shown in this book may be required. Always follow manufacturers' instructions included with products, since deviating from the directions may void warranties. The projects in this book vary widely as to skill levels required: some may not be appropriate for all do-it-yourselfers, and some may require professional help.

Consult your local building department for information on building permits, codes, and other laws as they apply to your project.

The Complete Guide to Bathrooms **5th Edition**

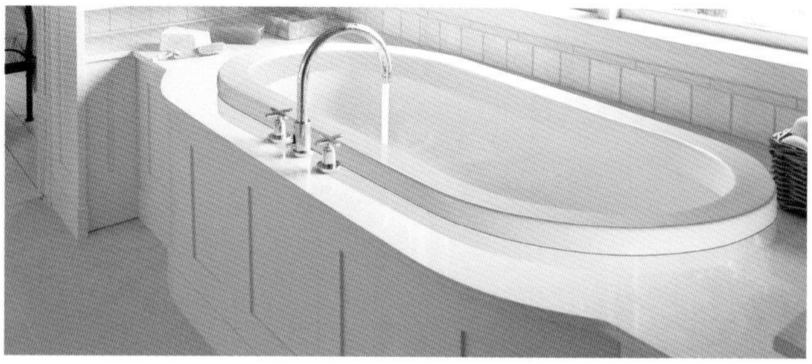

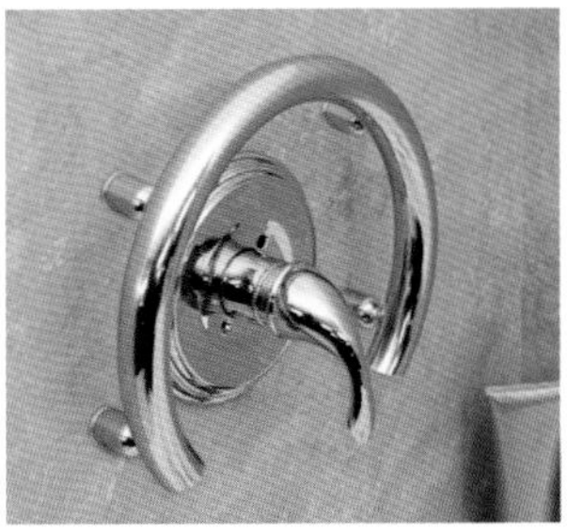

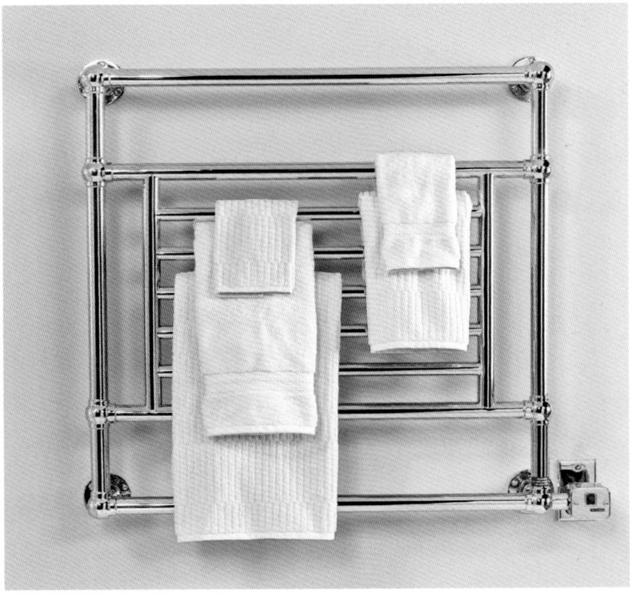

Introduction

Want to increase the value of your home? Remodel your bathroom. Renovating and updating a bathroom continues to be one of the best investments you can make in improving a home, in terms of resale price. But even more than the objective value, you'll be making your life immeasurably more pleasant by adding comfort, efficiency, and a pleasing appearance to a room most homeowners use multiple times a day.

Although trends in bathroom design come and go more frequently than they do in any other room in the house, indicators of style and luxury remain the same. Even though the trend in tiles is toward more ornate, hand-painted surfaces, tiles themselves remain a go-to material in bathroom renovations. They are easy to install and easy to keep clean, look fantastic, and offer a mind-boggling number of options. Pick just about any color or pattern you can dream up, and choose a size that complements the room itself.

And tiles are just the tip of the iceberg of bathroom-design options.

These days, you can choose mirrors with built-in LED lighting (see page 190) and shower and bath fixtures that continue to evolve in both function and form.

Function—especially function in service of comfort and convenience—is an ongoing focus of bathroom design. New showerheads with more comfortable grip handles are now widely offered in every finish and style that faucets are. You'll even find showerheads with built-in colored LED lights, to change up the look of the shower and indulge users in beneficial chromatherapy.

The story of bathroom design is not written in game-changing technological advances, but is more about modest improvements. Fairly recent innovations such as hands-free faucets are growing in popularity and subsequently being refined in design and function. The basic low-flow, water-conserving toilet remains the same, but you will find incremental changes that make your life easier, such as new self-cleaning toilets.

Nowhere are small changes having a bigger impact than in the growth and refinement of universal design elements. **Universal design** is all about accessibility for everyone, including the elderly, young children, and especially anyone with mobility and balance issues or disabilities. It used to be that features such as safety grab bars or a walk-in bath looked sterile and clinical. It was hard to find universal design accessories that had any real style. That's no longer the case.

In today's marketplace, you'll find many beautiful walk-in tubs. These are designed to be right at home in a luxury bathroom and give the homeowner a chance to build universal design elements into an upscale bathroom renovation. Put in an eye-catching walk-in soaking tub while you're young and agile, and the tub may well serve you right through your golden years. You can also pick from a range of grab bars in distinctive finishes to match just about any bathroom style, with flair that will complement other fixtures in the room.

All this adds up to one reality: these days, you can have exactly the bathroom function you want, in exactly the look you crave. Current bathroom fixtures, features, finishes, and accessories provide a perfect meeting of seamless, convenient function and beautiful, stylish form. All that's left is to sift through the options in the chapters that follow and get started on your own spa-worthy, accessible, and delightful new bathroom design.

PLANNING & DESIGNING YOUR BATHROOM

Gallery of Bathrooms

This is the golden age of mix-and-match elements in the bathroom. The range and selection of different features and fixtures for home bathrooms has never been greater. All those options present exciting design—and function—alternatives for any homeowner who is looking to update his or her bathroom. But they can also represent a daunting number of confusing choices.

The gallery in the pages that follow will help you cut through the choices and hone down to just the features, appearances, and styles that make the most sense for you, your family, and your home. But more than that, this is a dream guide. Never considered the "library look" for your master bath? Now you can, without committing to the high-dollar cabinetry and dark colors it takes to create that look. Think a walk-in shower stall might be a better alternative to the cramped, shallow, four-foot bathtub in the guest bathroom? The pictures in the pages that follow should give a clear idea of how a walk-in shower stall could look in your space.

Even as you peruse some of the flashier fixtures in these photos, pay attention to the small details. Maybe you're not ready for a full-blown bathroom remodel, but you can still find the perfect faucet, mirror, or shelf to accent your current bathroom. After all, changing a bathroom's look doesn't necessarily mean gutting the room and starting from scratch.

Whatever the case, the diversity of styles, room sizes, features, and fixtures presented here should give you a wonderful starting point for planning your bathroom project. Then, it's just a matter of rolling up your sleeves and getting to work.

Create a custom-built appearance with carefully selected cabinetry. The cabinets here are manufacturer produced, but with the inset door panels and incredible cove molding, they look like the work of a master craftsman. The gray color and marble vanity top are the perfect complements to the elegant and sophisticated storage features.

Combine functionality with sleek, streamlined, clutter-free panache by choosing European-styled fixtures and design elements. The blond flooring and wall-mounted vanity scream Scandinavia, and the urbane, upscale toilet and vessel sink reinforce that impression. Both the toilet and the vanity-sink combo can be mounted at a custom height to better accommodate a wheelchair user.

Let your bathroom shout "sophisticated" with a seductively stylish vessel sink. The range of materials and styles has never been greater, including unusual offerings such as this volcanic-rock sink with a fired-on finish that won't chip, fade, or stain.

Match curves to curves. A tray vessel sink (below) is not unusual in today's contemporary bathroom, but an oval version is. The shape of this lovely sink mirrors the shape of the bathtub, creating a repetition that helps guide the eye through the room's design.

Rely on simplicity for timeless style. The uncomplicated traditional style of this toilet is coupled with a cutting-edge self-cleaning technology (using a set-it-and-forget-it tank cartridge), and the look marries perfectly with the basic contemporary tub and unfussy floating double-sink vanity. Because the elements all feature uncomplicated designs, the room will appear as fresh years from now as it does today.

Play it safe with matching fixtures. You can please the eye and streamline your fixture shopping by buying a suite of fixtures from the same family, such as the showerhead, controls, and faucets in this bathroom. The brushed-nickel finish is easier to keep clean than chrome, and it adds a sophisticated aspect to the look of the room.

Add grace with a gooseneck. Metal wall tiles and a stainless-steel undermount sink are sophisticated but could be a bit stark and cold. Adding a gooseneck faucet softens the look a bit and provides a counterpoint to the strong linear look of the wall.

Save space with a console sink. Most console sinks are modest in size, usually featuring only the sink and supporting structure. This one features the added bonus of a shelf between the legs, offering a place for towels or other small-item storage.

Incorporate small touches that deliver big comfort. A towel drawer built into this cabinet tower is a discreet yet extravagant addition, one that adds a lot to the daily use of this bathroom.

Walk into luxury. Today's walk-in tubs are more than just pragmatic accessibility features for bathers with mobility issues. Manufacturers now outfit walk-in tubs with luxury features, such as the jets and chrome fixtures shown here.

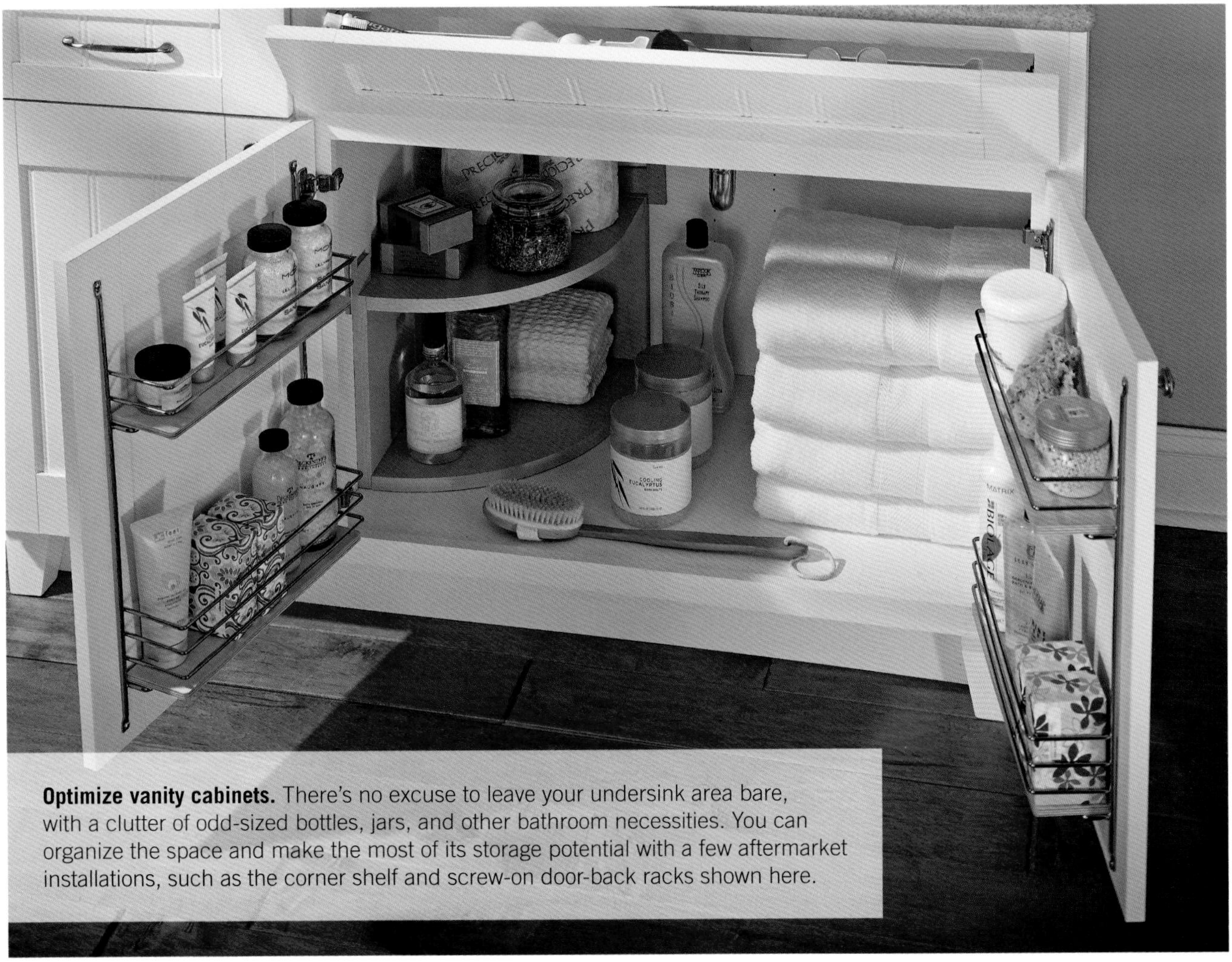

Optimize vanity cabinets. There's no excuse to leave your undersink area bare, with a clutter of odd-sized bottles, jars, and other bathroom necessities. You can organize the space and make the most of its storage potential with a few aftermarket installations, such as the corner shelf and screw-on door-back racks shown here.

Style and accessibility can go hand in hand, as this stunning shower illustrates. A chic trench drain ensures no water from this curbless shower makes it onto the floor outside, and a seat and handheld shower wand on a sliding bar make showering as easy for people with mobility issues as it is for anyone else in the house.

Steam your cares away. Among the many luxury features that have become available for home bathrooms, a steam shower is one of the most high impact. The steam unit in this room fits nicely under the sink in a modern vanity, and it services a wonderful shower enclosure with built-in, flip-down seat.

Focus on faucet flair. Where a bathroom has a calming color scheme and cool and elegant features such as the white solid-surface sink shown here, it only makes sense to go a bit wild with the choice of faucet. This elegant example is a beautiful addition that stands out from its understated surroundings and makes a statement that justifies the cost of the faucet.

Noon on the Third Day

Bathroom Elements

The number of styles and materials used in bathroom fixtures and surfaces continues to grow. As design options multiply, manufacturers are also answering the need for usable (and often code-required) safety features; water-conserving faucets, toilets, and showers; and essentials that are ADA (Americans with Disabilities Act) compliant.

You'll find choices from the plain and simple to over-the-top luxurious. In fact, the biggest chore you'll usually face in remodeling a bathroom is whittling down all those choices.

Even when you're working with a fairly tight budget, consider splurging where the money will have the biggest impact. Love a long, leisurely bath? A jetted tub, or a deep soaking unit, may be the ideal luxury. Is there a gang of kids constantly using the guest bathroom? A stylish hands-free faucet with built-in water timer might be the answer to your prayers.

Whatever feature you're shopping for, bring along measurements of the current space, a measuring tape, and a notebook and pen. You'll probably be surprised by the options you find, and you'll want to make sure anything that catches your fancy will fit where it needs to go.

In this chapter:

Bathtubs & Jetted Tubs

Although you can find bathtubs in a wide variety of sizes and shapes, your existing bathroom floorplan usually dictates exactly what size you should buy. But if you don't mind moving some plumbing, or you are building an all-new bathroom, your options expand dramatically.

Tubs are categorized first by the method used to install them. The three basic installation styles are alcove, deck-mounted, and freestanding.

Alcove tubs are the most common. They are often enclosed on three sides, which is why they are also called "recessed tubs." One-piece tub-and-shower combination fixtures are also available to fit standard-size alcoves. Custom sizes can be made for odd-size alcoves.

Deck-mounted tubs and whirlpools, also called drop-in tubs, generally rest directly on the subfloor or in a thinset mortar base. They are surrounded by custom-built decks or platforms. Typically, these tubs have a larger capacity than attached-apron tubs. The cost of making the deck can cause these tubs to be more expensive than other types, but the design possibilities are nearly limitless.

Freestanding tubs are available in an amazing range of styles and materials. The two basic types of freestanding tub are *footed* and *pedestal*, but within those two groups are a large number of interpretations that range from the classic clawfoot tub to ultramodern units that are almost works of art. In any case, these are most often fabricated from enameled iron, polymer, or, on the high side, marble or other stone surfaces. They are meant to hold up to abuse because they lack the protective structure of an apron or deck. The plumbing is most often exposed, and the hardware presents even more design possibilities.

Corner tubs are becoming increasingly popular, not only because they allow homeowners to make use of what is often dead space in the bathroom, but because they are now often designed to include a surprising amount of room for bathers.

Semiattached tubs are butted to a wall, essentially giving the appearance of a freestanding tub while conveniently exploiting a plumbed wall in the same way as an alcove tub. Semiattached tubs are an interesting variation that allows the homeowner to add a design element with the choice of the three-sided apron (for which manufacturers often offer interchangeable options).

A deck-mounted tub can be customized to fit your space and your bathroom's design. This deck was built to blend, and it complements the vanity, walls, and floor. The side-mounted faucet and controls allow bathers to recline completely in either direction without bumping up against the hardware. The jets inside the tub ensure a spa-like bathing experience that turns an everyday ritual into something special.

A clawfoot tub is an iconic bathroom fixture. The original models made of cast iron with an enameled porcelain finish can be found through architectural-salvage companies, although the supply is dwindling and the prices are climbing. Reproductions of this style are made with lighter-weight composites and polymers.

Traditional one-piece alcove tubs remain one of the most popular choices among homeowners. The tub lends itself to accents such as high-end surround tile and distinctive fixtures and hardware.

Match your tub to the sink and toilet by purchasing all at once as part of a suite. The freestanding tub in this room is a spectacular addition only made better with the inclusion of a sleek toilet and matching vanity-top sink. It's a stunning look that makes the room stand out.

Tub Materials

Tubs are manufactured from many different materials, each with its own pros and cons.

Fiberglass is an inexpensive, lightweight material that can be finished in a variety of colors. It is easily molded, so fiberglass tubs can have seats, grab bars, soap dishes, and shampoo shelves molded into the sides. Though fiberglass has many benefits, its surface can scratch easily, and its color will fade.

Acrylic, like fiberglass, can be molded into just about any size and shape. Unlike fiberglass, however, the color runs through the entire substance, making it less likely to show scratches or to fade.

Enameled steel tubs are pressed from sheets of steel and coated with a baked-on enamel similar to that of cast-iron tubs, but the enamel layer is thin and susceptible to chipping. It doesn't retain heat well and tends to be noisy.

Cast iron is the most durable material available for tubs. Iron is cast into a tub shape, then coated with a baked-on enamel that is relatively thick (1⁄16 inch), resulting in a richly colored finish. The enamel is strong, durable, and resistant to chips, scratches, and stains.

Cast iron is just about indestructible, but it's also extremely heavy. In some cases, the floor framing must be reinforced to support the additional weight. Cast iron is used most commonly for clawfoot and other standalone bathtubs.

Polymer can be cast into just about any tub shape and is a solid color throughout, making it impervious to scratches. The finish can be made to mimic quality surfaces such as marble or granite. Polymer also retains heat well, although the gel coat used on polymer breaks down over time.

Solid-surface tubs are gaining popularity. As with solid-surface countertops, the tubs can be made in one piece of resin or quartz and formed into many different shapes—including some with built-in features such as soap dishes. The materials retain heat well, come in many surface looks, and are durable.

Specialty Tubs

Soaking tubs are deeper and have higher sides than other styles. Traditional Japanese versions feature sides as high as 4 feet, but contemporary American soaking tubs usually have walls from 20 to 36 inches high. Traditional soaking tubs are tall enough that bathers may sit, rather than recline, although the shallowest modern models are soaking tubs only to the extent that they will allow an adult to be covered completely with water when reclined. The experience is luxurious and meditative.

Large deck-mounted tubs offer options when it comes to locating the spout and valve handles. In many cases this means you can position the spout near the tub center so you can lean back against either end of the tub without hitting any hardware.

Jetted tubs circulate heated water that's mixed with air through jets mounted in the body of the tub. The pumps move as much as 50 gallons of water per minute to create a massaging effect that relieves stress and muscle pain. Better-quality jets can be adjusted to alter both the streams' direction and the proportion of air and water (more air means a more vigorous massage).

Jetted tubs are almost always made of acrylic, and sizes and shapes vary tremendously. Prices also vary—they can range from $700 to $10,000 and up before installation. Price is determined by the number of jets (from four to 10 or more), the size of the water pump, and options such as an inline heater.

You'll find a variety of accessories for jetted tubs. A multispeed motor allows you to choose various settings from a gentle, relaxing soak to a vigorous massage. An inline heater maintains the water temperature. Grab bars, mood lights, pillows, timers, mirrors, and touch-pad controls are all available for added convenience and comfort.

Before you invest in a jetted tub, review the maintenance requirements. Some demand extensive upkeep of pumps, timers, and controls, and many roomy models require an extra-large water heater.

A jetted tub can be installed by a skilled homeowner familiar with the basic techniques of carpentry, plumbing, and tile setting. Some are small enough to fit in the alcove used for standard bathtubs, though most models require the construction of a surrounding deck or platform.

A tub platform can be tucked into a corner or even an alcove. If you add tile or another moisture-resistant wall covering on the corner walls, you may consider adding a handheld shower near the corner. Handheld showers are not a good idea for island tubs.

Install a curved-front alcove tub to enjoy maximum bathing space in a limited footprint. A model with the faucet and controls offset increases the usable interior space even more.

Showers

Tub-and-shower combos remain the most common bathing setup, largely because the combination crams the most function into the least amount of space. They also allow users to bathe either way, making them ideal in a bathroom used by more than one person. However, most combination units are not luxurious baths or showers.

For luxury, you'll want a dedicated bathing structure. And, in fact, more and more homeowners are abandoning tubs for full-featured walk-in shower enclosures. Within the modest footprint taken up by an alcove bathtub, it's quite possible, and within most homeowners' budgets, to install an upscale shower with frameless glass panels, custom tile work, a sleek curbless shower pan, and multiple showerheads.

The most common shower in homes across America is the one that fits inside an existing alcove tub. It's a simple setup, especially when paired with a shower curtain rather than a sliding glass door.

One-piece alcove shower enclosures can be simple and modest or incredibly upscale and detailed, such as the oversized unit shown here.

If budget is a concern, you can find all-in-one shower-enclosure kits that include a base, three-wall surrounds, and the hardware and fixtures you'll need. Increasingly, these prefab products can be fairly upscale as well, featuring inset tile columns, multiple showerheads, stylish grab bars, and molded-in shelves and recesses for body-care products.

One-piece enclosures are widely available for the DIYer. Seamless stalls are molded from fiberglass or acrylic, making this option easy to clean and maintain. A wide range of sizes and styles are available. Some include seats, linear drains, steam units, and other chic features.

Neo-angle showers are designed to fit into corners. Made of acrylic or fiberglass, they are completely self-contained with integrated shower bases, walls, and doors.

Shower-surround panels are used to construct simple, inexpensive shower enclosures. They are built above a preformed shower pan. Three individual panels are bonded to the walls of the framed alcove, and the seams are sealed.

Freestanding showers are complete units unattached to walls. These are the least common option and range from sheetmetal or fiberglass units to elaborate glass-block enclosures.

Custom shower stalls can be designed to fit into odd or unusually shaped spaces. The walls can be finished with the surface material of your choosing, such as ceramic or stone tile, glass block, or even solid-surface material to do away with grout lines. Specialized options, such as benches, steam-bath fixtures, shelves, and soap dishes, can be incorporated into the design.

Curbless showers are designed for physically challenged users. The shower entrance has no curb at all, providing easy access to the shower. One-piece molded units are available, or barrier-free showers can be custom-built. Most have built-in shower seats and grab bars. See pages 92 to 103 for more information on curbless showers.

Shower doors and curtains are usually purchased separately from the shower itself. Options range from simple plastic curtains costing a few dollars to custom-made tempered-glass doors.

Multiple showerheads, shower towers, and steam showers can create a more luxurious shower. Steam showers require extra plumbing, wiring, and a shower stall with doors that seal tightly.

SHOWER LIGHTS

An overhead light ensures safety in the shower. Make sure that any light installed in a shower area is moisture resistant. Some shower lights include a heating element.

Prefab shower trays come in a variety of styles, including sleek features like the concealed trench drain in this unit.

A simple shower enclosure using off-the-shelf pan, hardware, fixtures, and frameless glass panels can create a stunning centerpiece to an already stunning bathroom.

Custom shower enclosures are limited only by imagination and can include, as this one does, a wood-slat floor over a curbless drain pan, marble walls, and multiple showerheads for a sumptuous experience.

Sinks

The variety of sinks available today practically guarantees that you can find a lavatory sink to match your space, budget, and taste. The most significant difference between the major sink types is the manner in which they are installed: wall mounted, pedestal or console, and countertop.

Wall-mounted sinks hang directly from the wall, taking up little space and offering easy access to plumbing hookups. Basic wall-mounted sinks are good options for utility bathrooms or half baths, where exposed plumbing and lack of storage space are not serious drawbacks. Designer wall-mounted styles feature attached aprons that hide plumbing. These are also accessibility features, allowing people in wheelchairs to roll under the sink for easy use.

Pedestal sinks and **console sinks** are wall-mounted styles that rest on a pedestal or legs that may or may not provide actual support to the sink bowl. A decorative pedestal may conceal plumbing and can be a smart choice for a small guest bathroom or powder room where floorspace is particularly scarce. Console sinks have legs supporting the front two corners and often feature an apron to mask plumbing connections. The advantage of a console sink over a pedestal model is that small baskets or a modest, simple shelving unit can be placed underneath for additional storage.

Self-rimming sinks drop into a cutout in the countertop, with the rim overlapping the cutout's edges.

Integral sinks, usually made of solid-surface material or cultured marble, are molded into countertops and are easy to install and maintain.

Undermounted sinks are attached with clips beneath a cutout in a solid-surface, stone, or concrete countertop.

A pedestal sink has visual appeal and an efficient footprint but lacks any storage.

A solid-surface sink and countertop are the perfect match for a modern single-handle faucet and chic wall-mounted vanity.

Vessel sinks sit on top of a countertop, with only a small cutout for the drain.

Sinks can be made of a number of materials. **Cultured marble** is an inexpensive material often used to create integral sink-and-countertop combinations to fit standard vanity sizes.

Porcelain (vitreous china) may be used for self-rimming sinks. It has a durable glossy surface that is nonporous and easy to clean. Porcelain sinks are readily available in white and almond, and you can special order other colors. For a truly unique addition to your bathroom décor, consider a hand-painted porcelain sink in a floral or other one-of-a-kind design.

Solid-surface material is long lasting and easy to clean; scratches can be buffed or sanded out. It is one of the more expensive choices for bathroom sinks, but its durability and ease of care help justify the price. Solid-surface sinks are available in self-rimming, undermounted, and integral models, with a variety of colors and patterns to choose from.

Stainless steel brings a high-tech look and durability to bathroom sinks. It is available in either a satin or mirror finish. Price varies according to thickness, or gauge—the lower the gauge number, the thicker the steel. Look for 18-gauge material with a noise-reducing undercoating. Because they are lightweight, stainless-steel sinks are often used for undermounting.

Composite and acrylic sinks are less common because they aren't ideal in high-traffic areas. However, where the sinks won't see a lot of use, these can be low-cost, attractive alternatives to more durable materials.

Tempered glass is used to create stylish vessel sinks for bathrooms. Undermounted styles can be lit from underneath to create a mood-setting glow. Art-glass sinks continue to grow in popularity, and, if crafted properly, a cast or fused-glass sink can be every bit as durable and safe as tempered glass—with a nearly infinite number of possible designs and colors.

Other materials, such as concrete, copper, carved stone, and wood, can be used to create more stylized bathrooms. Enameled cast iron is extremely durable but available in limited shapes and colors, which is why it is used less often than other options. Volcanic rock is a relatively new material, but one that comes in a range of bold and subtle colors and appearances and is amazingly durable. Before you select a sink made of an unusual material, consider the shipping time, installation procedures, maintenance, and cost.

Self-rimming sinks (also called drop-ins) fit into a cutout in a countertop and usually are secured with mounting clips from below.

Undermount sinks have a very contemporary appearance and offer some clean-up advantages, but they can only be installed in countertops that have a contiguous waterproof composition (such as solid surface or poured concrete).

These artistic sinks are crafted from volcanic rock, as is the counter they rest on. The material offers a unique and incredibly durable surface.

Toilets & Bidets

The toilet is the essential centerpiece fixture in a bathroom—the room is not really a bathroom without one. If you're of a European bent, the bidet may be a necessary partner to the toilet. Although the bidet as a personal hygiene fixture and bathroom standard has yet to become commonplace in America, it can be a wonderful addition to the right bathroom and for the right occupants.

In this country, though, the biggest advances have occurred in toilet design. Not only are there more designs than ever before, but there is also a lot of variation in actual types of new toilets—not to mention that there are even new cleaning technologies that can change your life for the better. Chief among these is the self-cleaning toilet, a unit that keeps the bowl clean with the help of a special cartridge full of cleaning fluid. Periodically change the cartridge, and you may never have to scrub a toilet bowl again.

Beyond the technology, you'll need to decide on a form for any new toilet you buy. That can be a complicated decision. The standard two-piece tank toilet now shares the market with unibody models and streamlined, tankless, wall-mounted versions. All are high-efficiency fixtures, as mandated by law, so the choice is usually just a preference of design style and weighing the pros and cons of each type. A wall-mounted model saves floor space and gives you the option of seating heights, but it requires more fabrication work than replacing a standard toilet with another standard model. Other toilet variations may completely conceal plumbing pipes for a more elegant appearance.

Of course, the real choice for most homeowners is in the look of the toilet or bidet. Thankfully, you won't hurt for options, and all are fairly easy to install. To make things even easier, you can select a toilet as part of a bathroom suite, comprising a matching bathtub, toilet, and sink.

Today's toilets are wonderful style statements all on their own but ultimately should complement the tub if there is one and the sink if possible. Integrating the toilet in this way makes for a unified design; the comfort is already built right into modern toilets.

Fixture Types

Two-piece toilets have a separate tank and bowl, and they account for the vast majority of toilets in homes today. Their main advantage is low cost.

Wall-mounted toilets are space-saving options that offer other advantages as well.

Flushing mechanisms are changing rapidly to keep pace with the demand for greater water economy. One common technology is the dual-flush design, which has a light flush option for liquid waste only that can save 20% on water usage over standard 1.6-gallon models.

Bidets are a companion to the toilet, meant for basic washing and hygiene. They aren't common in America and require extra space and plumbing in the bathroom, but they will give your bathroom a worldly, cosmopolitan feel if you choose to install one.

Cabinets & Vanities

Storage will always be at a premium in most bathrooms. A major reason for remodeling bathrooms is to add storage that better serves the people who use the room. Storage options can be broken down into two basic categories: cabinets and shelves. However, within these categories, you'll find a head-spinning number of variations and options. For instance, both cabinets and shelves are offered as freestanding units, attached and affixed models, and custom storage units that you build into the bathroom remodel.

Wall cabinets are often shallow, but they are incredibly useful concealed storage in the bathroom because they can be put just about anywhere in the room—including over the door. Cabinets come in many different configurations designed specifically for the confines of the bathroom, from shallow, tall, and thin wall-mounted units to deeper freestanding cabinets meant to accent vanity storage.

Vanity cabinets are incredibly adaptable. You can use the traditional enclosed vanity for a maximum of interior storage space or pick up a legged variety with a lower shelf that supplements the hidden cabinet storage. Vanity cabinets range from the miniscule to the mammoth, and they come in every design style you can imagine for your bathroom.

Wall-mounted storage, like the contemporary vanity and matching cabinet here, can be a space-saving solution—one that allows for cleaning underneath while still supplying handy, accessible storage space.

Medicine chests are classic cabinets used in all manner of bathrooms. Although usually shallow, the storage is quick access and provides a place to keep certain items, such as medicines, out of the reach of children. Where medicine chests were once outfitted just with glass or plastic shelves, today you can buy a model that includes a power strip for charging battery-operated personal care devices and specialized storage for grooming equipment. In any case, the chests can be surface mounted or recessed into the wall for a sleeker look. Many upscale versions also include integral lighting.

Standalone cabinets, often called "linen cabinets," are usually tall and narrow. The shape takes advantage of the available vertical space in most bathrooms. These are handy not only for towel storage but also for supplies such as toilet-paper rolls, extra boxes of tissue, and more.

Tall, thin cabinets are often excellent choices for additional storage in a bathroom. The shape takes up a modest amount of space and provides abundant storage. Combining open shelving with enclosed cabinetry in a unit such as this ensures that just about anything you might need to store in the room has a proper place to go.

Vanities with legs lend an open and airy feeling to the bathroom and provide an option for useful shelving underneath. The hardware on this vanity was selected to match the brushed finish of the chic faucet and shower fixtures, creating a very unified look.

Cabinets come in many shapes and sizes, but the basic choice you'll have to make at the beginning of your search for the perfect bathroom cabinets is whether to buy what's available at retail or build (or have built) custom cabinets that fit the space and your needs like a glove.

Stock cabinets are mass-produced in convenient, standardized sizes. Most of these are created from medium-density fiberboard (MDF) carcasses with veneer or laminate surfaces, although several manufacturers do produce wood cabinets. Prices vary widely depending on craftsmanship and detailing, but stock cabinets are inevitably less expensive than full custom units.

Custom cabinets are built to suit the size and shape of the area you have available, in the material of your choosing. You can have custom cabinets built by a craftsman, but some manufacturers offer custom cabinetry services—you simply provide measurements and select from a menu of materials and details, and they produce and deliver the cabinets to be installed by a local installer (or you). In either case, the lead time is usually much greater for custom cabinets than it is for stock units.

Shelves can be a useful and flexible addition to any bathroom, and they are wonderful complements to cabinetry. The selection of shelves available for bathrooms is astounding, and, as with cabinets, you can custom-build shelves to suit your precise needs. Keep in mind that any shelves you install are decorative elements as well as useful storage.

Medicine-chest designs have evolved right along with the look and function of most other bathroom features. This sleek unit represents a significant departure from the traditional swing-out-door medicine chest. The mirror slides up to allow access to the shelving inside, eliminating the door-swing arc that can be an awkward nuisance in the ever-space-challenged bathroom. Notice that in keeping with the sophisticated technology, the mirror is frameless, offering an appealingly streamlined and modern look.

A linen cabinet is a freestanding furnishing, but it can take on a built-in appearance if you integrate it with other cabinets and wall trim. Linen cabinets and linen closets can be made more efficient by customizing with features such as door-back shelves and pull-out laundry bins.

Slide-out storage racks are especially useful in base cabinets. Functioning basically as drawers, slide-out racks can be included at the time of purchase or added later.

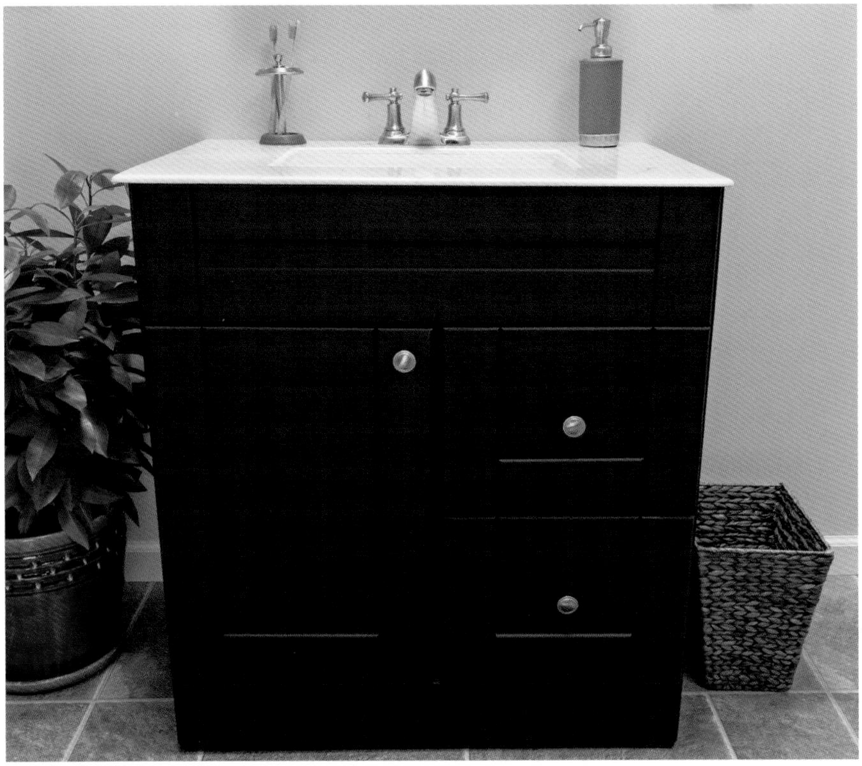

Drawers are on the rise. Even in small to medium vanity cabinets, where cabinet drawers traditionally expose only sink traps, supply tubes, and dark, unfriendly space, cabinetmakers are finding ways to design a small drawer or two to provide discreet, clean storage space. The combination of a cabinet door to access plumbing and two small drawers breaks with the symmetry of a traditional vanity cabinet as well, providing a small design surprise.

Lighting

Lighting can set the mood of any room. Dim lights and lit candles are perfect for a leisurely soak in the tub. When it comes to shaving or applying makeup, though, bright lights are best.

As with the rest of the house, the bathroom is best served by a combination of general, task, and accent lighting to ensure personal safety, provide ambience, and permit various uses of the space.

General lighting usually involves an overhead fixture or fixtures that illuminate the whole room. Natural lighting is considered part of your general lighting.

Task lighting provides directed light for specific activities, such as applying makeup or shaving.

Accent lighting can be used to highlight decorative points of interest, such as architectural details or artwork.

Surface-mounted fixtures are easy to install and available in a variety of styles. Just be sure that all fixtures you choose are moisture-proof and meant for use in a bathroom environment.

Recessed ceiling fixtures are set into canisters and have trim kits that are mounted flush with the surface of the ceiling, and some include adjustable heads that allow you to direct the light one way or another. This improves headroom in a small bath.

Wall-mount fixtures are common in bathrooms and provide ideal lighting for personal grooming, especially when placed on both sides of a mirror, as well as above.

Ceiling-mount fixtures are excellent overall light sources in the small spaces of most bathrooms.

Never lose sight of the fact that the right bathroom lighting not only supplies illumination, it can also be a decorative accent.

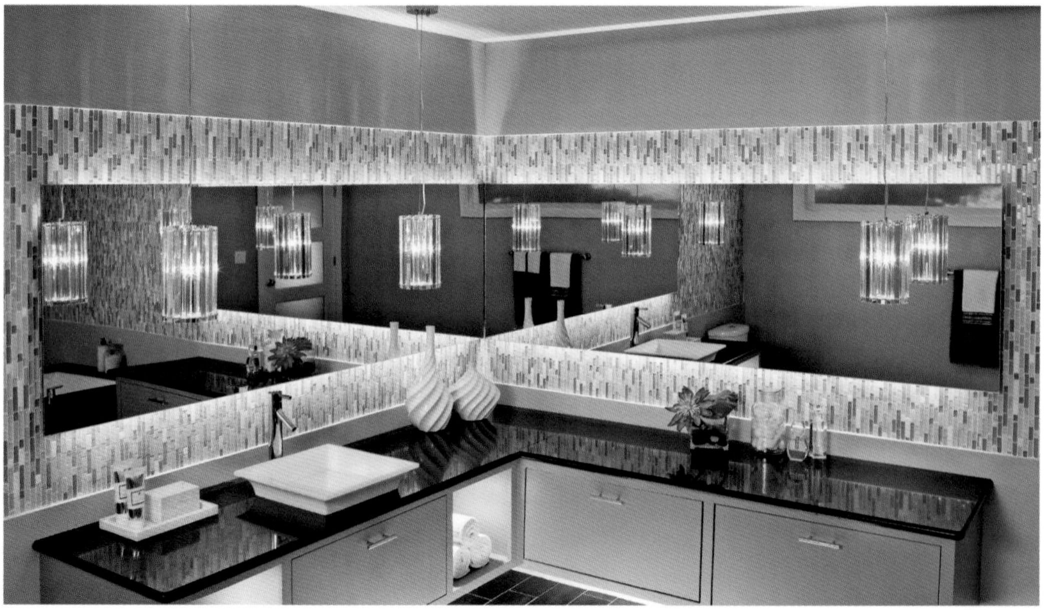

Some new medicine cabinet models come equipped with integral lighting, such as the side-mounted tube fixtures on these units. Medicine-chest lighting is developed to create the most realistic and accurate image in the mirror.

Heating & Ventilation

Consider room size, the number of windows, and the type of heat in the rest of the house when making decisions about your bathroom heating system. Consult a professional before making final decisions. If your primary heat system is inadequate, you have three basic choices for auxiliary heat in bathrooms.

Electric heaters are mounted either by themselves or as part of light, vent, or heating units.

Heat lamps use infrared light bulbs to provide radiant heat.

DIY radiant-heat floor systems are electric mats installed beneath floor coverings to warm your feet and heat your room.

Light and vent combinations serve the dual purpose of lighting the room and reducing moisture and odors. Some contain an infrared heating element for a third function (inset).

Radiant floor-heating systems are installed beneath the flooring and circulate either hot water or electricity.

Good ventilation protects surfaces from moisture damage, deters mold and mildew, and keeps air fresh. Vents with electric fans (pages 196 to 199) are required by code in any bathroom without windows. The vent must exhaust moist air directly outdoors, not into attics or wall cavities.

Purchase a vent fan that's rated at least 5 cubic feet per minute higher than the square footage of your bathroom. Local building codes may have specific requirements, so check with your building inspector or HVAC contractor before selecting a ventilation unit.

Walls & Ceilings

If you add, move, replace, or resurface walls in your bathroom, use the best materials for the job. Options include the following.

Drywall is adequate for most bathrooms, except for the area around tubs and showers.

Greenboard is a drywall with waterproof facing. It has fallen out of usage in recent years.

Cementboard is used primarily as an underlayment for ceramic tile.

Glass block is a decorative building block that has great visual appeal but can't bear loads.

You'll want the wall and ceiling finishes to be easy to maintain. Wall finishes for tub and shower surrounds and behind sinks and toilets should be waterproof.

A marble-tiled wall is a classic upscale look, and a matching marble counter and vessel sink on top of a wall-hung vanity are a space-saving update to that look.

Solid-surface panels, such as this black quartz accent surface that matches the tub deck, can make ideal waterproof bathroom wall surfaces.

Paint finishes range from flat to glossy (enamel). Glossy finishes are best for areas that will be cleaned often. Latex (water-based) paints are more environmentally friendly than oil-based paints.

Wallpaper should be treated to withstand moisture. Choose smooth-textured, solid vinyl or vinyl-coated wallpaper in a bathroom.

Wall tiles are durable, easy to clean, and available in hundreds of styles, colors, and materials, including stone, ceramic, glass, and—if you want a really unusual look—metals.

Solid-surface material is often used to fashion walls in tub and shower surrounds.

Bathroom ceilings need moisture-resistant finishes. Avoid textured ceilings, which peel in humid conditions and are difficult to clean, repair, or paint.

Flooring

Bathroom floors should stand up to daily use, frequent cleaning, and moisture.

Resilient sheet flooring is inexpensive but is seldom the first choice of professional designers. It is simple to install, easy to clean, seamless, and available in a vast number of colors, patterns, and styles. Resilient sheet products include linoleum, which is incredibly eco-friendly, and vinyl, which is far less so.

Resilient tile and planks made of vinyl are easy to install. The latest versions are made to stand up to even the most demanding bathroom conditions. These products are easier to install than ever and include marmoleum, a very green option.

Ceramic tile is available in three main types: glazed ceramic tile, quarry tile, and water-resistant porcelain tile. Although cleaning issues are created by the grout lines, mosaic sheets of ceramic tile are highly popular.

Natural stone tile is a premium flooring material. Granite, marble, and slate are the most common stone products for bathroom floors.

A faux-wood laminate floor provides an ideal durable stage. The star on that stage is a dramatic and luxurious jetted tub tucked in an alcove with a view.

A dramatic black marble tile floor helps a simple, elegant, deep freestanding tub pop in this chic bathroom.

Larger ceramic tiles are ideal for more modest bathrooms. Choose a subtle color to complement other surfaces, like the sharp and refined quartz countertops and bathtub half wall here.

Hardwood floors are difficult to totally waterproof, so they should be limited to half baths, where moisture will not be a big problem.

Laminates offer an easy-to-install flooring option that is water resistant, durable, and available in an amazing selection of surface appearances, from stone tiles to wide wood planks.

The condition of your floor structure may affect the cost of installing new flooring. If the subfloor must be replaced or repaired, more time and money will be required. Consult a professional to assess the state of your subfloor.

Getting Started

A great bathroom provides a comfortable, attractive, and convenient setting. It is a private retreat where you can tend to your needs in a relaxed and pleasant fashion.

When designing a new bathroom or renovating an existing one, style can be as big a consideration as function. From the choice of materials to the layout of fixtures, the space should reflect your individual sense of style through the use of particular colors, textures, and patterns.

And yet, a bathroom does have to be functional. Without a strong foundation on which to express your style, you may spend money and time creating your new bath, but it may not turn out as you'd hoped. So the first step is to determine your needs and budget and draw up some plans.

In this chapter:

- Determining Your Needs
- Designing for Accessibility
- Design Standards
- Drawing Plans
- Removal & Demolition: Toilets
- Removal & Demolition: Sinks & Cabinets
- Removal & Demolition: Showers & Tubs
- Building a Wet Wall

Determining Your Needs

A typical bathroom is divided into three activity areas: the toilet, the sink, and the shower or tub. To create a successful bath design, you need to consider the relationship of these areas, allowing for accessibility and safety. This relationship varies depending on the type of bathroom being renovated: half bath, family bath, or master bath.

Half baths, also called powder rooms, are small rooms near common areas of the home. They are designed largely for visitors to use. They can be as small as 20 square feet and are often located near entrances or entertainment areas of a home. It's best to have their doors open into hallways.

Half baths typically feature a toilet and a vanity or pedestal sink finished with smaller fixtures and finer materials. When designed as a guest bath that includes a shower, these rooms require more space and are called "three-quarter baths."

The family bath is usually located near the sleeping areas in a home. It is used by more than one family member, and it should provide storage for toiletries, towels, laundry, and cleaning supplies. It features at least one sink, one toilet, and a shower and tub or tub-shower combination.

A larger bathroom allows space for extra features, such as double sinks or separate shower and tub areas. A small family bath may conserve space by combining the tub and shower, incorporating recessed shelving, and featuring space-efficient fixtures and storage cabinets. Finishes and fixtures should be low maintenance and highly durable, such as ceramic tile and enameled fixtures.

Bathrooms for children must be safe for them to use unsupervised and should be easy to adapt as the children grow. Features that make daily hygiene easier and safer for children include single-handle faucets with antiscald guards, adjustable showerheads, safety plugs in receptacles, grab bars, smaller toilets, lowered sinks, and vanities with built-in step stools.

The master bath is usually connected to the master bedroom and is a sanctuary for the owners of the house. It is typically quite large and may have separate activity centers containing features such as a jetted tub, shower, toilet partition, and multiple sinks and vanities. It may even feature a sauna or steam room. The fixtures and finishing materials generally feature ceramic, stone, or marble tiles; custom cabinets; and upscale accessories.

A half bath need not lack drama. This small space includes the basics, using a compact wall-mounted vanity to save space. But the inclusion of sumptuous wall materials, high-end flooring, and near-theatrical lighting around a stunning mirror make it a showpiece space in the home.

There's no rule that says a modest family bath needs to be less than opulent. You can fit a lot into a small space, like this skylight-lit, simple, elegant, and deep drop-in tub.

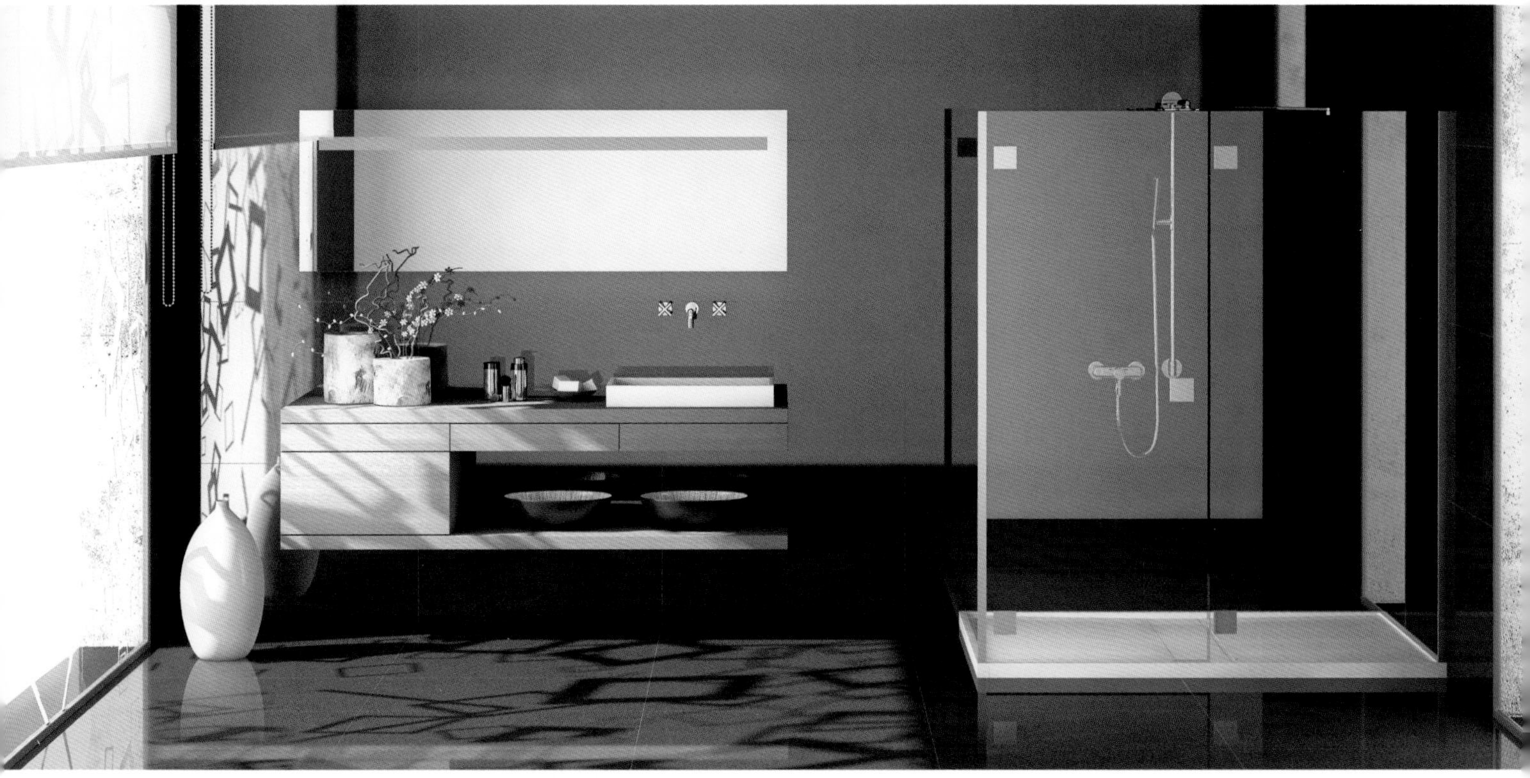

A master bathroom is the place to splurge, especially when modern is your style. The floors and walls in this room are beautiful and waterproof quartz composite; every feature in the room combines luxurious comfort and astounding sculptural beauty.

Designing for Accessibility

Accessibility has become a key issue not only in the codes that regulate residential bathroom construction but with almost every feature designed for bathrooms. From toilets to faucets to lighting and beyond, manufacturers are responding to an aging population and the need to accommodate all potential users of a home's bathroom.

Designing bathrooms to accommodate the needs of any individual—including those with mobility limitations and even the severely disabled—is at the heart of what is known as universal design. The term was coined by disabled architect Ronald Mace. The goal? In Mace's words, "the design of products and environments to be usable by all people to the greatest extent possible, without the need for adaptation or specialized design." In practice, that translates to turnkey fixtures that work for able-bodied individuals and those who use a wheelchair or walker alike.

More recently, a focus has been placed on accommodating the 78 million baby boomers who are rapidly aging into an incredibly large elderly population. Studies show that these people want to stay in their homes and remain independent as long as possible. The aging-in-place movement has sprung up to facilitate that and to set guidelines for bathroom design specifically to suit elderly users. But in reality, aging in place is a subset of universal design, and it is a difference largely without a distinction. If you take the steps outlined here and select fixtures and features designed for maximum accessibility, your bathroom will be welcoming and user friendly now and as you age, and for anyone who might need to use it.

Aging-in-place bathroom design often deals with remodeling existing spaces to better suit users with age-related mobility issues. Those who can't stand for the span of a shower can take one while sitting in this specially adapted stool. They can use the ergonomic handheld showerhead with a handle that clips onto a nearby grab bar. Even the toilet-paper holder has been replaced with one that has a grab bar built in.

Universal Design Standards

Bathroom elements that meet the mandates of universal design are continually being refined by manufacturers as they respond to legislation such as the Americans with Disabilities Act (ADA) and the needs of an aging population. Design style is inevitably a part of the process. Utilitarian features such as grab bars are increasingly crafted with stunning looks and finishes that make them easy to integrate into even the most sophisticated bathroom style.

Grab bars. The new rule for grab bars is "dual purpose." Towel racks, toilet-paper holders, and bathroom shelving are all being crafted with integrated grab bars. Not only does this mean buying and installing one fixture in place of two, it means the grab bars are a blended part of the overall look of the bathroom. Even grab bars for showers are seeing style upgrades, with molded finger grips and the same selection of surface finishes found in other fixtures, such as showerheads and faucets.

Toilets. The key to making this essential fixture comfortable for every potential user lies in seat height. Manufacturers have come up with a multitude of solutions, including power-lift toilet seats, height adapters, higher-than-normal traditional toilets and those that can be adjusted, and wall-mounted toilets that can installed at any height. Grab bars are essential to assist movement on and off any toilet, so it's fortunate that you can find attractive toilet paper holder–grab bar combinations.

Faucets. The first step in making faucets accessible was the use of paddle handles and single-handle faucets that could easily be manipulated by those lacking dexterity or motor skills. Nowadays, technology is aiding people with coordination and hand-strength difficulties in the form of motion-activated and touch-activated faucets. These make using the faucet as easy as moving a hand. They are also a breeze to install (see page 166).

Bathtubs. The standard bathtub-shower combination can be retrofitted to accommodate limited-mobility users with the addition of special stools and handheld showerheads with ergonomic grips. Better yet, consider replacing an existing tub with a walk-in model equipped with a door. These tubs typically have seats at chair height to make the transition into the tub easier. Many also feature jets and heaters to create a luxurious experience. When shopping for a walk-in tub, pay close attention to the contours of the seat and back support. These will be key to how comfortable and supportive the tub is over the course of a nice long soak. Choose a door style that best accommodates the user's preference; available styles open in or out, up or down. The lower the threshold, the better, and the door handle should be easy for the intended user to operate.

Other types of tubs can be made easier to use by locating the controls on the outside edge of the tub or tub deck. This allows the user to fill the tub without leaning over and possibly losing balance.

UNDERSTANDING AGING IN PLACE

The aging-in-place movement shares much with the general universal design trend, the key difference being the focus on the needs of the elderly. As we age, we lose strength in our hands, arms, and legs and often have to deal with nagging chronic injuries associated with aging—arthritis and limited flexibility and mobility chief among those complaints. Many aging-in-place changes are focused on accommodating those conditions and preventing any injury that could short-circuit independence.

Lighting. Older people often deal with diminished vision, so effective lighting is key to making aging-in-place bathrooms safer and more user friendly. This entails a combination of undercabinet and undercounter lighting, baseboard or cove lighting, special shower lights, and more powerful ambient lights on the wall and ceiling to dispel any visually confusing shadows.

Nonslip surfaces. Falls are the number-one cause of elderly immobilization and can have serious health ramifications. It's essential that tubs, floors, and shower stalls have truly nonslip surfaces that maintain traction even when wet. This means a slip-resistant glaze or texture on any bathroom flooring, and decals or slip-preventing strips in bathtub-shower combinations.

Showers. The two areas of continuing development in terms of universal-design showers are the shower pan and the fixtures. Low-threshold, walk-in showers were the ideal a few years ago (often equipped with ramps for wheelchairs), allowing anyone with strength and balance issues to easily step into a shower stall. That idea has evolved into true curbless showers that are on the same level as the surrounding floor. Although installing a curbless shower was once a major custom construction project, you can now buy a kit with a relatively streamlined and simple installation process (see page 92). Grab bars remain an essential addition to any shower enclosure, and the increasing variety of designs and finishes virtually guarantees you can match grab-bar finish to that of the shower controls and showerhead.

Showerheads themselves have been made more accessible by mounting handheld styles on slide bars so that the height can be adjusted to suit any user, and the showerhead itself can be removed as needed. Nonslip ergonomic grips are making handheld showerheads even easier to use for people with motor-skill and grip limitations.

Most modern shower enclosures—whether one-piece prefab units or those built from the shower pan up—include some sort of seat. Fold-down seats are easy to retrofit into an existing shower, but many showers now include built-in or molded shower seats. Either way, the seat should be 18 inches high and at least 15 inches deep. Shower antiscald devices are also a wise addition to any shower to protect all users from burns.

Sinks and vanities. More and more wall-mounted sinks and vanities are being offered at retail. These ensure that bathroom users with wheelchairs can roll under the sink to wash their hands or brush their teeth. Many wall-mounted sinks come with attractive aprons to conceal plumbing. Roll-out vanity cabinets can be used as storage accents, replacing the undersink space in traditional vanities.

Doors and doorways. Bathroom doorways should be 32 to 36 inches wide to allow passage of a wheelchair. Shower doors should open out, or both ways, to ensure user safety.

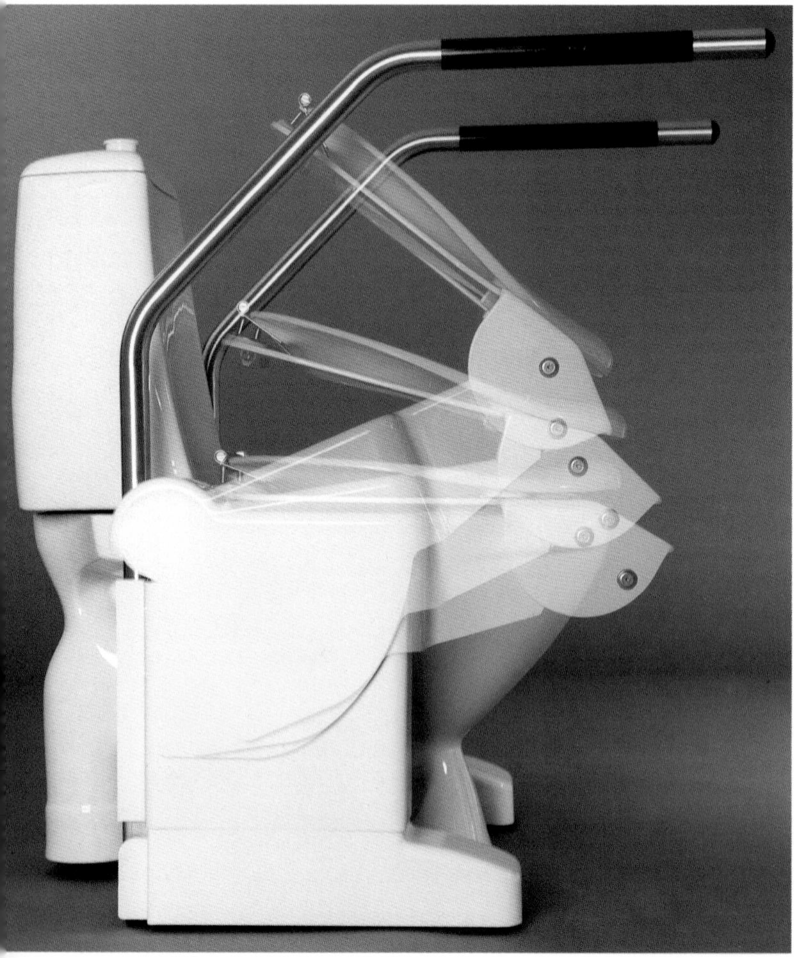

Power lifts make toilet use easier for people with limited leg or joint strength.

A side-mounted faucet is easier to reach on this wheelchair-accessible, roll-under, wall-mounted sink.

A motion-sensing faucet is not only easier for the elderly and children to use but helps stop the spread of disease.

This bathroom sacrifices nothing to style but is completely accessible, with a roll-in curbless shower, roll-under sink with handy side ledges, and sturdy grab bars everywhere they might be needed.

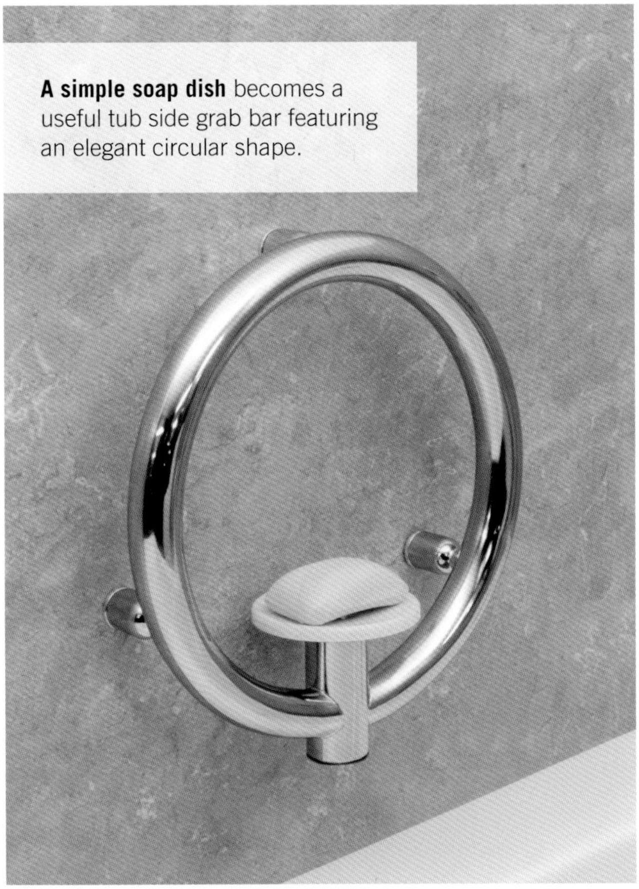

A simple soap dish becomes a useful tub side grab bar featuring an elegant circular shape.

This innovative grab bar uses suction to hold to just about any bathroom surface, and it can be released and repositioned as needed with a click of the gray release tabs on either end.

This alcove tub features a chair-height seat and a slide-down front wall. To take a bath, the user simply sits on the seat, swings their legs over, and pulls the wall up. The tub offers many amenities, including simple-to-use controls, a heater, and jets.

Design Standards

Once you've drawn up your plan and created a materials list, you'll need to have them reviewed by your local building department. Getting approval early in the process can save you time and expense later. To help ensure success, here are some design standards for you to follow.

The National Kitchen and Bath Association (NKBA) publishes a list of bathroom design standards to help people plan rooms that are safe and accessible to all users (see Resources, page 251).

Your bathroom probably won't conform to all of the recommended standards, but they can help guide your overall plan. What your plan must include is everything prescribed by the local building codes, including plumbing and wiring codes (see pages 246 to 249).

BATHROOM DESIGN STANDARDS

Codes and permits are necessary to ensure safety in any remodel. They're not the most fun to focus on—not like choosing just the right floor covering or deciding between granite and marble countertops—but they are important.

- Plan doorways with a clear floor space equal to the door's width on the push side and greater than the door's width on the pull side.
- Design toilet enclosures with at least 36" × 66" of space; include a pocket door or a door that swings out toward the rest of the bathroom.
- Install toilet-paper holders approximately 26" above the floor, toward the front of the toilet bowl if possible.
- Place fixtures so faucets are accessible from outside the tub or shower. Add antiscald devices to tub and sink faucets (they are required for shower faucets).
- Avoid steps around showers and tubs, if possible.
- Fit showers and tubs with safety rails and grab bars.
- Install shower doors so they swing open into the bathroom, not the shower.
- Use tempered glass or another type of safety glass for all glass doors and partitions.
- Include storage for soap, towels, and other items near the shower, located 15" to 48" above the floor. These should be accessible to a person in the shower or tub.
- Provide natural-light openings equal to at least 10% of the floor area in the room.

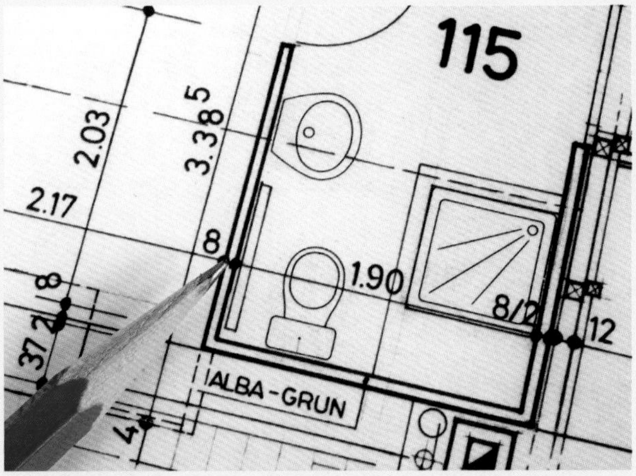

- Illuminate all activity centers in the bathroom with task and ambient lighting.
- Provide a minimum clearance of 15" from the centerline of sinks to any sidewalls. Double-bowl sinks should have 30" clearance between bowls from centerline to centerline.
- Provide access panels for all electrical, plumbing, and HVAC systems connections.
- Include a ventilation fan that exchanges air at a rate of 8 air changes per hour.
- Choose countertops and other surfaces with edges that are smoothed, clipped, or radiused.

NOTE: Clear floor spaces within the bathroom can overlap.

RECOMMENDED CLEARANCES

A bathroom should be planned with enough approach space and clearance room to allow a wheelchair or walker user to enter and turn around easily. The guidelines for approach spaces (patterned areas) and clearances shown here include some ADA guidelines and recommendations from universal-design specialists.

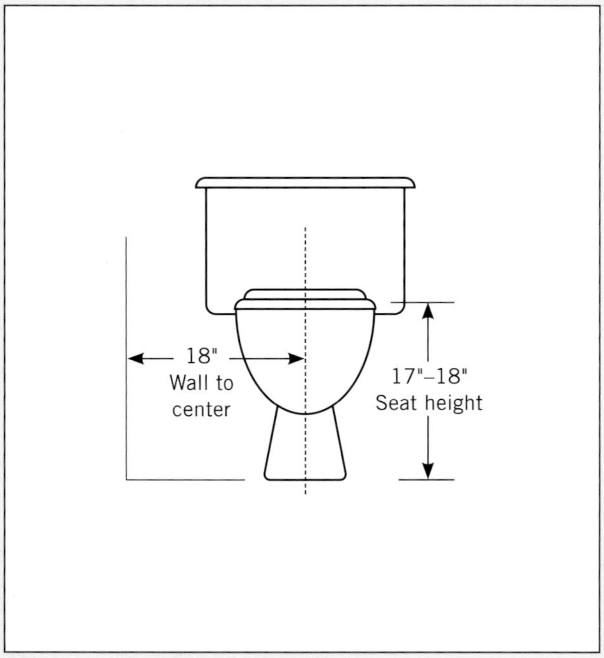

Toilet

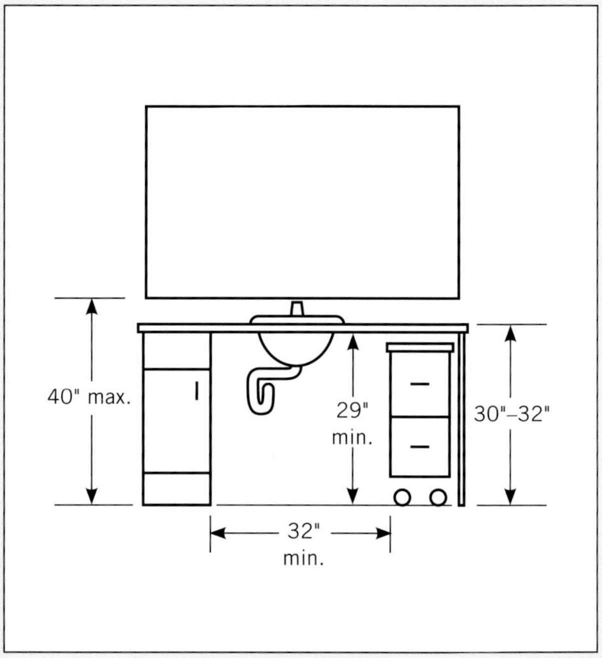

Sink & Vanity

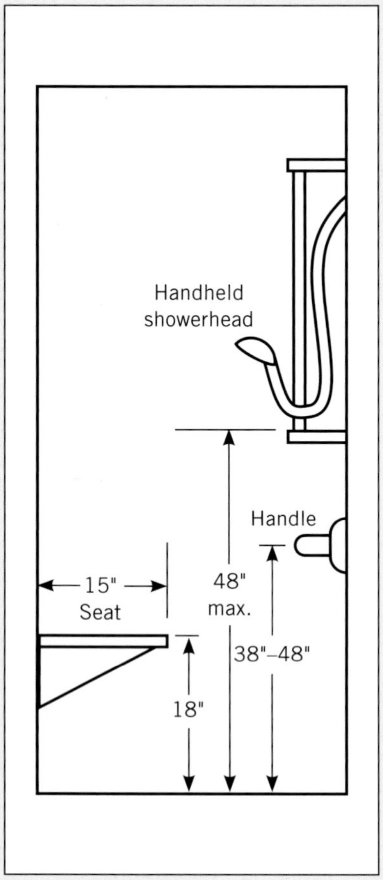

Shower

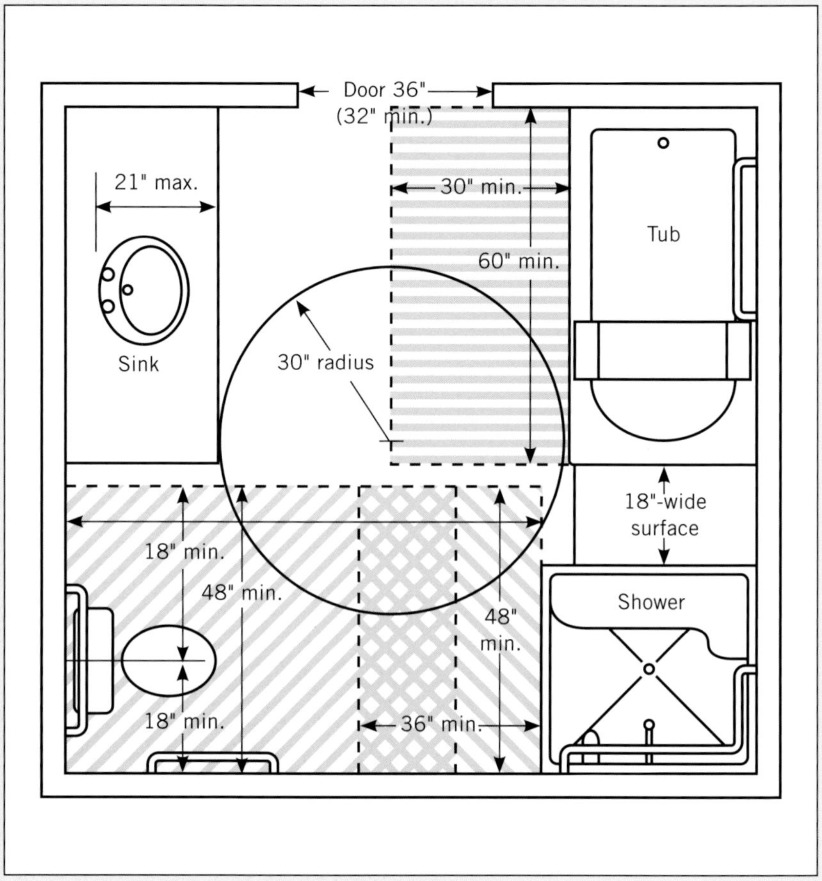

Floor Plan

BUILDING CODES FOR BATHROOMS

The following are some of the most common building codes for bathrooms. Contact your local building department for a list of all codes enforced in your area.

- The minimum ceiling height in bathrooms is 7'. (Minimum floor area is determined by clearances around fixtures.)
- Sinks must be at least 4" from side walls and have 21" of clearance in front.
- Sinks must be spaced 4" away from neighboring sinks and toilets and 2" away from bathtubs.
- Toilets must be centered 15" from side walls and tubs, with 21" clearance in front.
- New and replacement toilets must be low-flow models (no more than 1.6 gal. per flush).
- Shower stalls must be at least 30" × 30", with 24" of clearance in front of shower openings.
- Faucets for showers and combination tub-showers must be equipped with antiscald devices.
- Supply lines that are ½" in diameter can supply a single fixture or one sink and one toilet.
- A ¾"-diameter supply line must be used to supply two or more fixtures.
- Waste and drain lines must slope ¼" per foot toward the main DWV stack to aid flow and prevent blockage.
- Each bathroom must be wired with at least one 20-amp circuit for GFCI-protected receptacles and one 15-amp (minimum) circuit for light fixtures and vent fans without heating elements.
- All receptacles must be GFCI protected.
- There must be at least one permanent light fixture controlled by a wall switch.
- Wall switches must be at least 60" away from bathtubs and showers.
- Toilet, shower, vanity, and other bathroom compartments must have adequate lighting.
- Light fixtures over bathtubs and showers must be vaporproof, with a UL rating for wet areas.
- Vanity light fixtures with built-in electrical receptacles are prohibited.
- Whirlpool motors must be powered by dedicated GFCI-protected circuits.
- Bathroom vent ducts must terminate no less than 10' horizontally or 3' vertically above skylights.

***NOTE:** Codes for accessible bathrooms may differ.

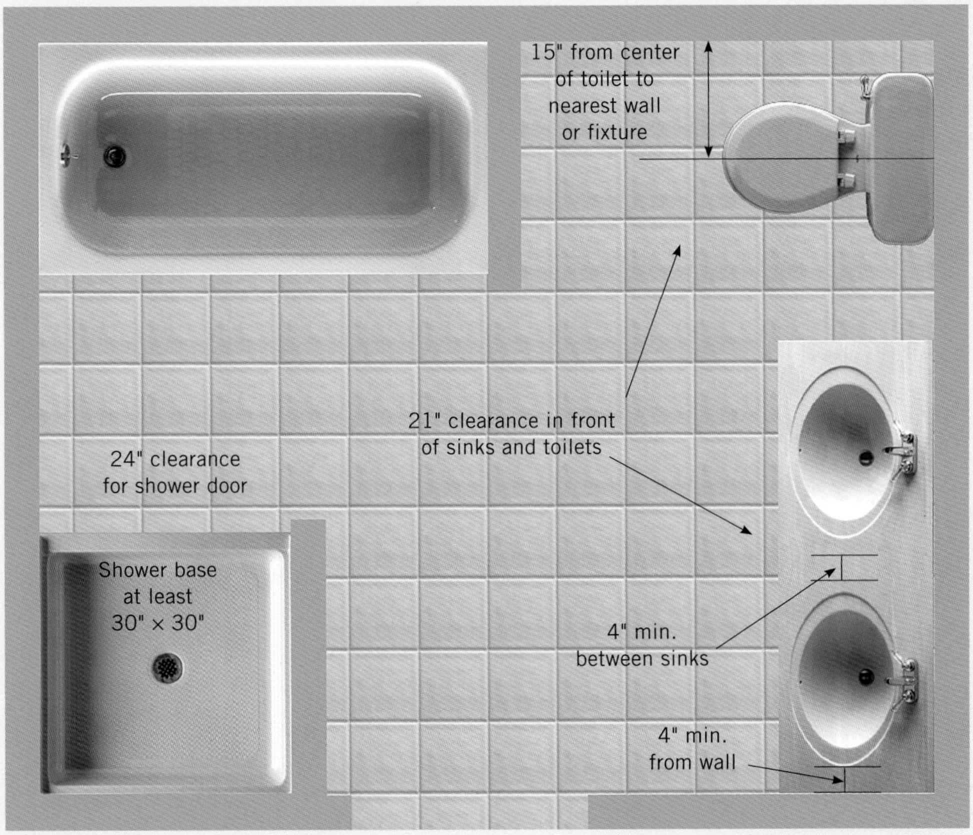

Follow minimum clearance and size guidelines when planning locations of bathroom fixtures. Easy access to fixtures is fundamental to creating a bathroom that is comfortable, safe, and easy to use.

Drawing Plans

If your new bathroom involves a layout change or expansion, you'll find it helpful to create floor plans and elevation drawings. A floor plan illustrates an overhead view, while an elevation drawing illustrates a face-on view. Your drawings will be the basis for obtaining permits, negotiating contracts with tradespeople, and ordering products.

To begin, make a rough sketch of the existing floor plan. Measure and record the size and location of all existing fixtures and mechanicals from a fixed point. Sketch an elevation of each wall.

Use these rough sketches to draft a precise scale drawing of your existing floor plan. You can now sketch variations of your new bathroom using the scale drawing of the floor plan as a guide.

Use the overall dimensions of your new floor plan to sketch elevation options. In the end, the elevations and floor plans must agree.

A scale drawing shows everything in accurate proportion. After measuring the dimensions of your existing bathroom, draft a floor plan, including any adjoining space that could be used for expansion of the layout (such as the storage closet shown on next page). The normal scale for bathroom plans is ½" = 1'.

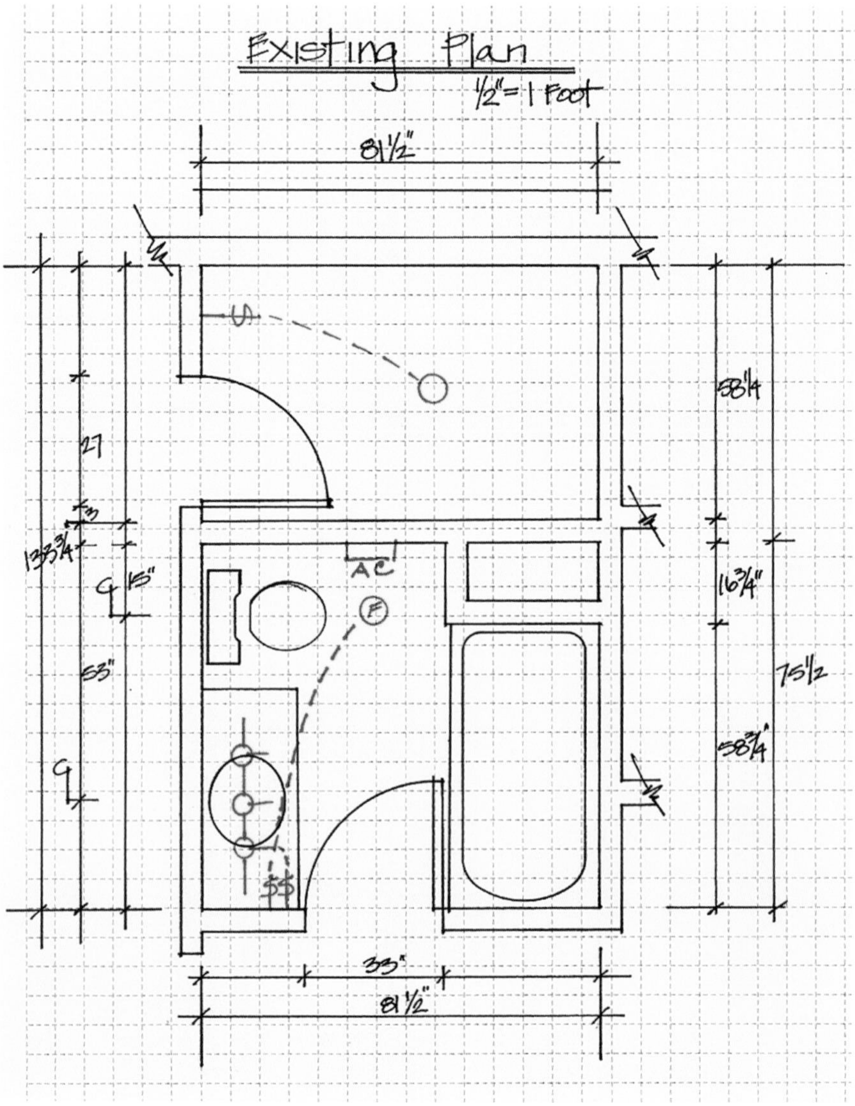

The existing-floor-plan draft should contain dimension lines noting the accurate measurements of the space, including the location of all existing fixtures. This draft also shows the location of electrical circuits. It is the starting point for your remodeled bathroom plan.

NEW BATHROOM FLOOR-PLAN SAMPLES

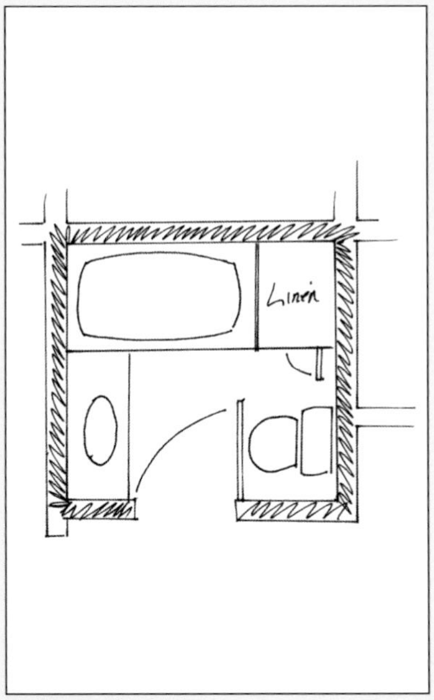

Option A: This floor-plan option of the draft on the opposite page shows a layout change within the existing space. The sink and vanity stay in the same place, but the tub and toilet have been switched. There is room to add a linen cabinet, but the space is still very cramped.

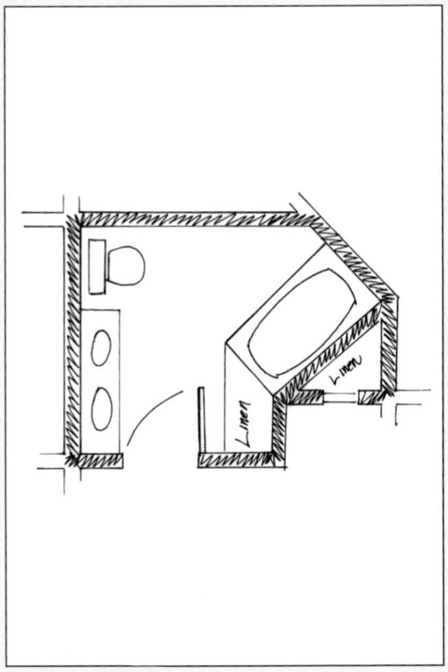

Option B: This option explores expanding the room and experimenting with some interesting angles. There is now plenty of floor space for two people, plus room for a double vanity and a large linen cabinet for increased storage.

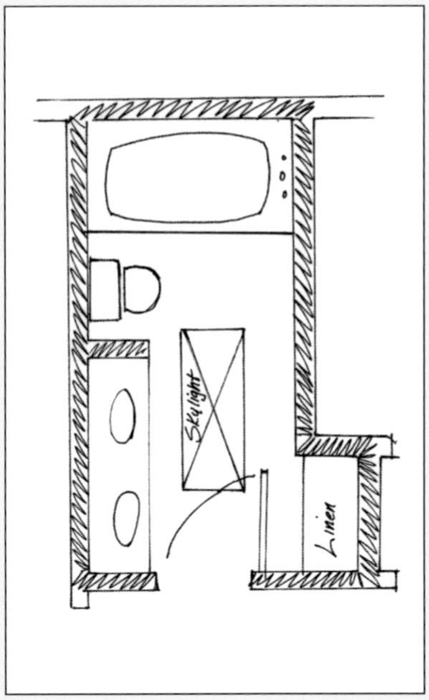

Option C: The existing room is expanded by annexing the adjacent closet. There's plenty of floor space, a double vanity, and a built-in linen cabinet. This plan has the practical benefits of Option B but is less expensive to build.

BATHROOM ELEVATION OPTIONS

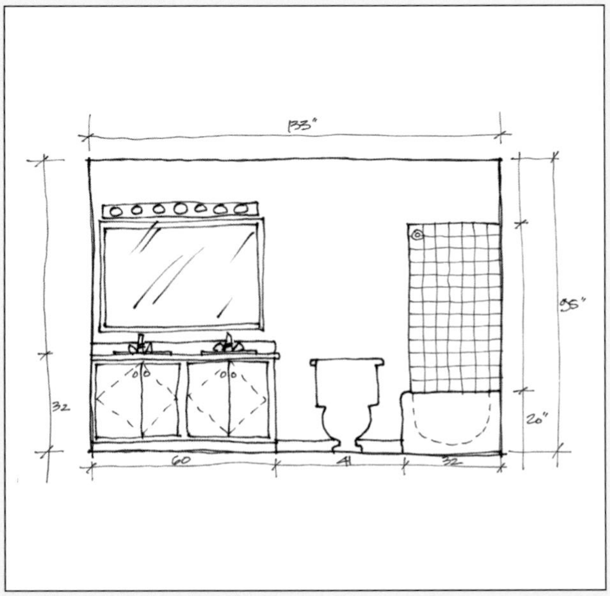

Option A: This elevation shows a simple arrangement with a standard mirror and light fixture. It also shows ceramic tile in the shower area, ending just above the shower curtain.

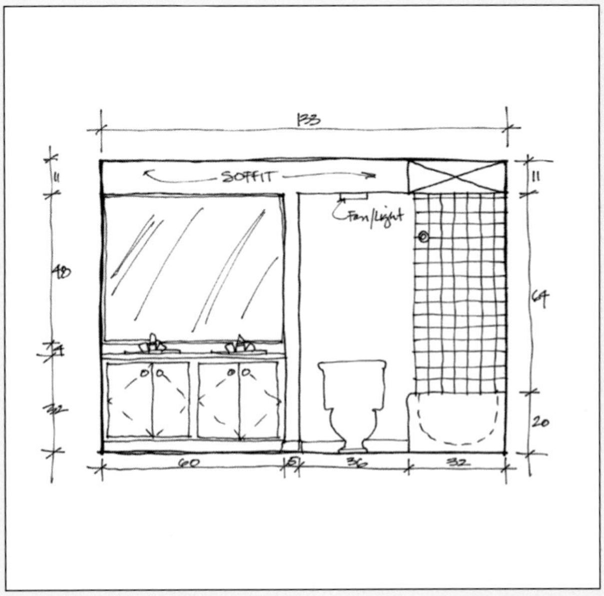

Option B: This variation shows a custom mirror framed in by a partition wall and a soffit that runs above the vanity, toilet, and tub. Lights are recessed in the soffit.

Removal & Demolition: Toilets

The toilet is the first fixture to be removed in most remodeling projects. Loosening corroded or rusted nuts and bolts is the most difficult part of the process.

Old toilets that will not be reinstalled may be broken up into small, easily managed pieces using a sledgehammer. Disconnect the toilet and cover it with a heavy blanket before breaking it. Wear eye protection, long sleeves, and heavy gloves during the demolition.

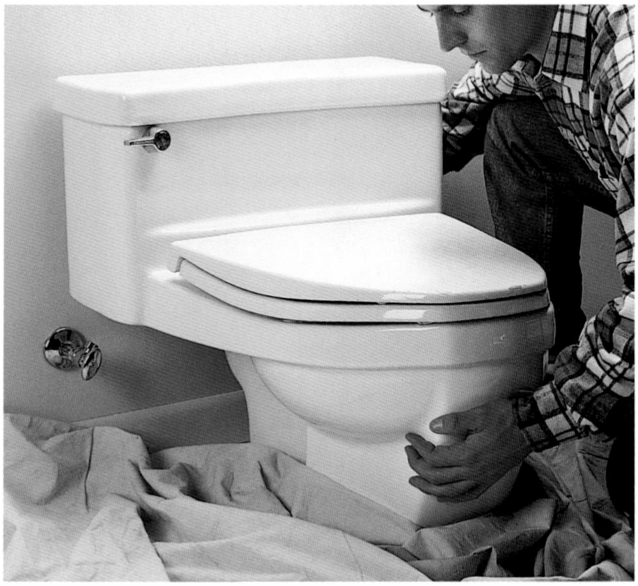

Most toilets are fragile and should be removed during full remodeling projects, even if you do not plan to replace them. Always use care when handling any fixture made of china or porcelain.

TOOLS & MATERIALS

Adjustable wrench	Sponge
Ratchet wrench and sockets	Rag
Screwdriver	Drop cloth
Putty knife	Eye and ear protection
Basin wrench	Work gloves

TIPS FOR REMOVING TOILETS

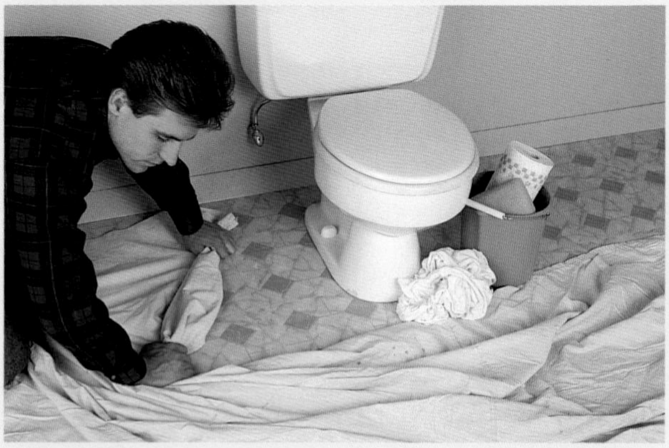

Protect your floor with a drop cloth when removing the toilet if you plan to keep the original floor covering. Residue from the wax ring seal between the bottom of the toilet and the toilet flange is very difficult to remove from floor coverings.

Disconnect any pipes between a wall-mounted toilet tank and the bowl after turning off the water supply and emptying the tank. Older toilets often have a metal elbow that connects the tank to the bowl. Set 2 × 4 braces below the tank before detaching it from the wall.

How to Remove a Toilet & Wax Ring

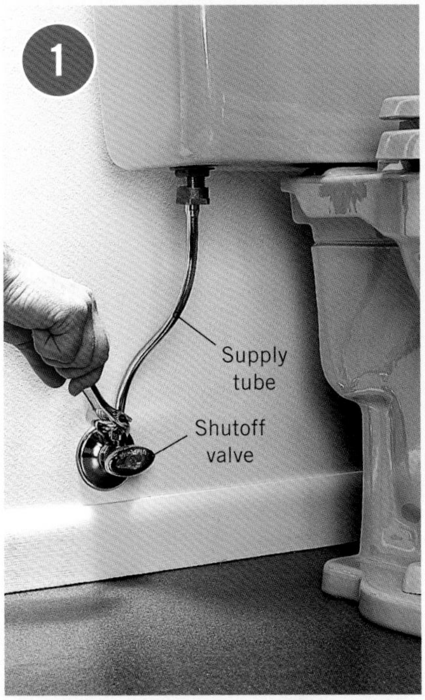

Turn off the water, then flush the toilet to empty the tank. Use a sponge to remove the remaining water in the tank and bowl. Disconnect the supply tube with an adjustable wrench.

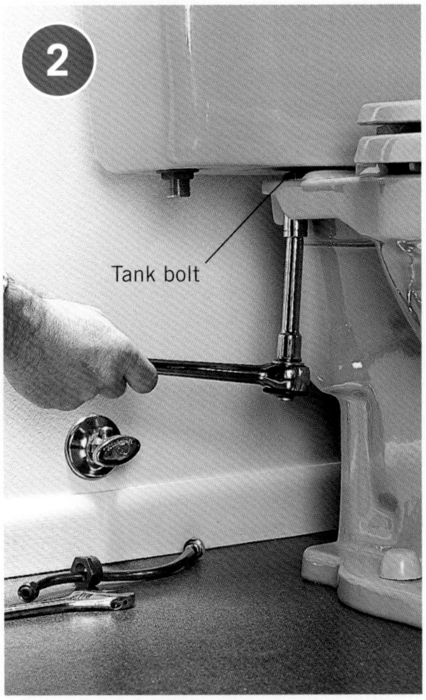

Remove the nuts from the tank bolts with a ratchet wrench. Carefully remove the tank and set it aside.

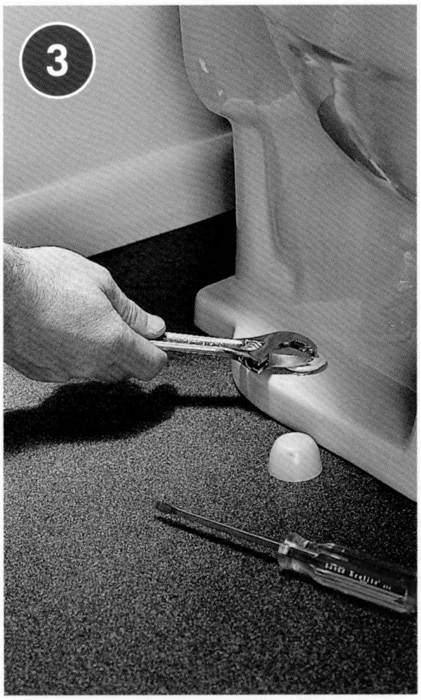

Pry off the floor-bolt trim caps at the base of the toilet, then remove the floor nuts with an adjustable wrench.

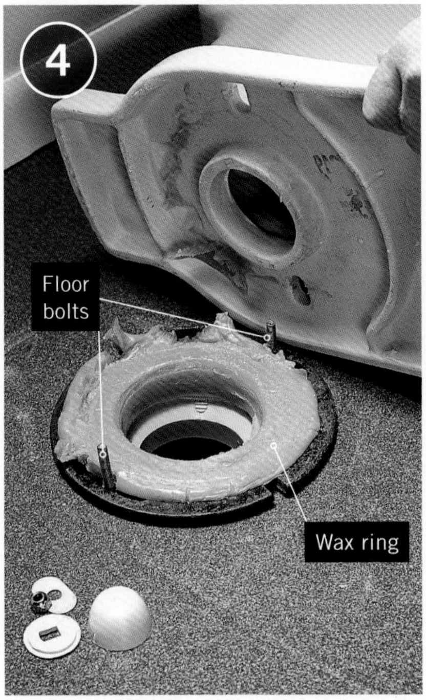

Straddle the toilet and rock the bowl from side to side until the seal breaks. Carefully lift the toilet off the floor bolts and set it on its side. A small amount of water may spill from the toilet trap.

Remove the old wax from the toilet flange in the floor. Plug the drain opening with a damp rag to prevent sewer gases from rising into the house.

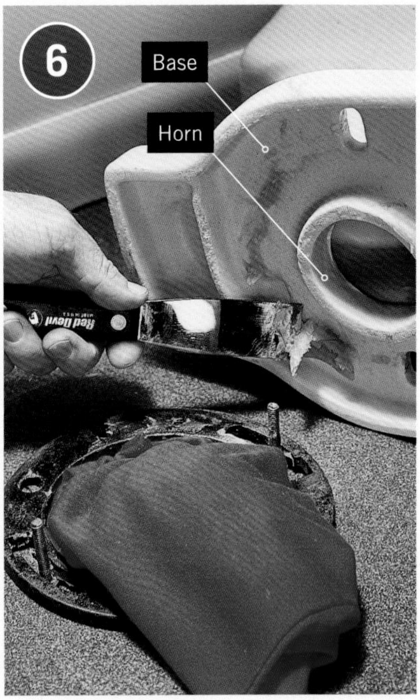

If the old toilet will be reused, clean the old wax and putty from the horn and the base of the toilet.

Removal & Demolition: Sinks & Cabinets

Replacing bathroom sinks, countertops, and cabinets is a quick and relatively inexpensive way to give your bathroom a fresh, new look.

First, disconnect the plumbing, then remove the sink basin or integral sink-countertop unit. Next, take out any remaining countertops. Finally, remove the cabinets and vanities.

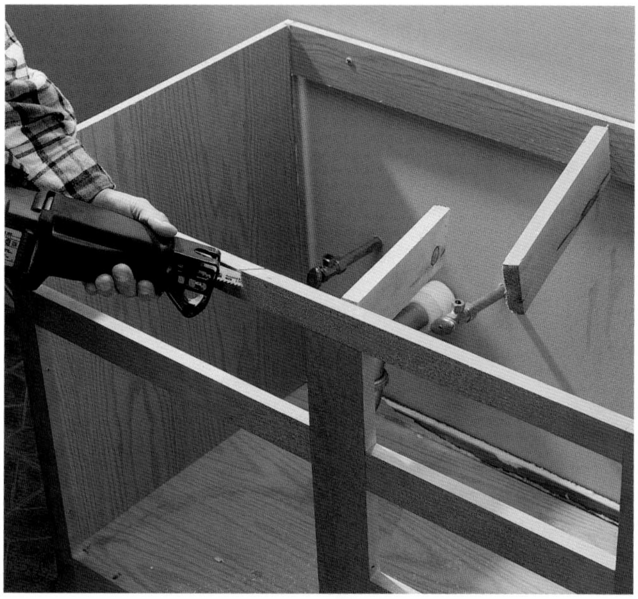

Cut apart cabinets and vanities to simplify their removal and disposal. A reciprocating saw or jigsaw works well for this job. Wear eye protection.

TOOLS & MATERIALS

Bucket	Screwdriver	Adjustable wrench	Reciprocating saw	Flat pry bar	Eye and ear protection
Utility knife	Basin wrench	Channel-type pliers	Hacksaw or pipe cutter	Work gloves	

How to Disconnect Sink Plumbing

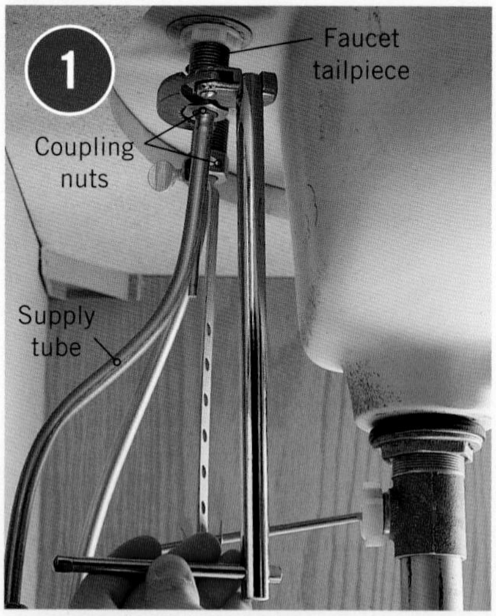

Turn off the shutoff valves, then remove the coupling nuts that connect the supply tube to the faucet tailpieces using a basin wrench. If the supply tubes are soldered, cut them above the shutoff valves.

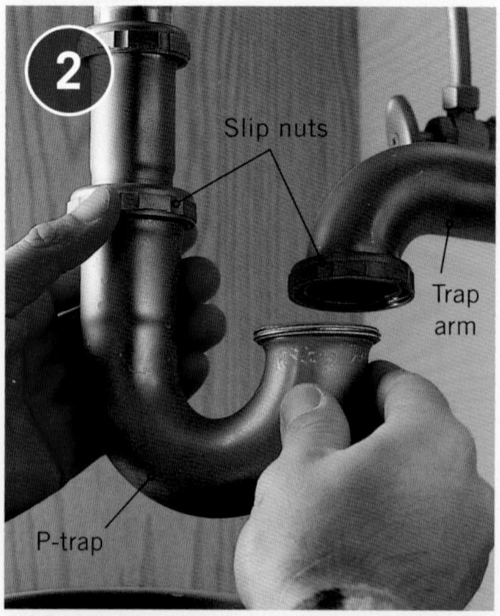

With a bucket beneath, remove the P-trap by loosening the slip nuts at both ends. If the nuts will not turn, cut out the drain trap with a hacksaw. When prying or cutting, take care to avoid damaging the trap arm that runs into the wall.

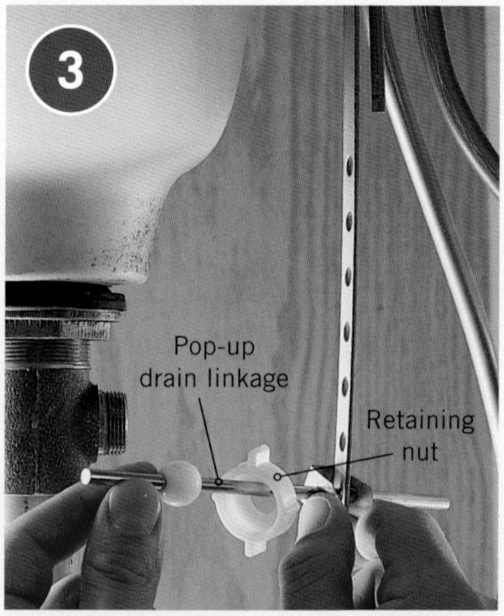

Disconnect the pop-up drain linkage from the tailpiece of the sink drain by unscrewing the retaining nut.

TIPS FOR REMOVING SINKS

Self-rimming sink: Disconnect the plumbing, then slice through any caulking or sealant between the sink rim and the countertop using a utility knife. Lift the sink off the countertop.

Undermount sink: Disconnect the plumbing, including the drain tailpiece. To support the sink, tie wire around a piece of scrap wood and set the wood across the sink opening. Thread the wire down through the drain hole and attach it to another scrap of wood. Twist the wire until taut, then detach the mounting clips. Slice through any caulking, slowly loosen the wire, then remove the sink.

Wall-mounted sink: Disconnect the plumbing, slice through any caulk or sealant, then lift the sink off the wall brackets. For models attached with lag screws, wedge 2 × 4s between the sink and floor to support it while the screws are removed.

Pedestal sink: Disconnect the plumbing. If the sink and pedestal are bolted together, disconnect them. Remove the pedestal first, supporting the sink from below with 2 × 4s. Lift the sink off the wall brackets (photo, left).

Integral sink-countertop: Disconnect the plumbing, then detach the mounting hardware underneath the countertop. Slice through any caulk or sealant between the countertop and wall and between the countertop and vanity. Lift the sink-countertop unit off the vanity.

Removal & Demolition: Showers & Tubs

Bathtubs and showers are heavy and bulky fixtures, so they pose special problems for removal. Unless the tub or shower has unique salvage value, cut or break the unit into pieces for easy removal and disposal. This technique allows one person to handle most of the disposal chores. Always wear eye protection and heavy gloves when cutting or breaking apart fixtures.

For most tubs and showers, you need to remove at least 6 inches of wall surface around the tub or shower pan to gain access to fasteners holding it to the wall studs. Maneuvering a tub out of an alcove is also easier when the wall surfaces are removed. If you are replacing the entire wall surface, do all the demolition work before removing the tub.

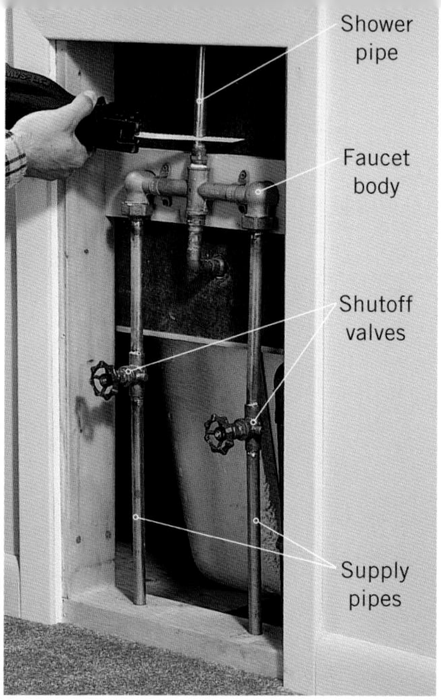

Disconnect the faucet through the access panel, usually located on the wall surface behind or next to the tub faucet and drain. (If the tub does not have an access panel, add one.) Turn off the shutoff valves, then cut the shower pipe above the faucet body. Disconnect or cut off the supply pipes above the shutoff valves.

TOOLS & MATERIALS

Reciprocating saw	Hacksaw	Wrecking bar	Wire cutter	2 × 4 or 1 × 4 lumber
Channel-type pliers	Adjustable wrench	Hammer	Eye and ear protection	Rag
Screwdriver	Flat pry bar	Masonry chisel	Utility knife	Work gloves

How to Remove Handles & Spouts

Shut off the water supply, then remove the faucet handles by prying off the covers and unscrewing the mounting screws.

Remove the tub spout by inserting a screwdriver into the spout and twisting counterclockwise until it unscrews from the stub-out that extends from the wall plumbing.

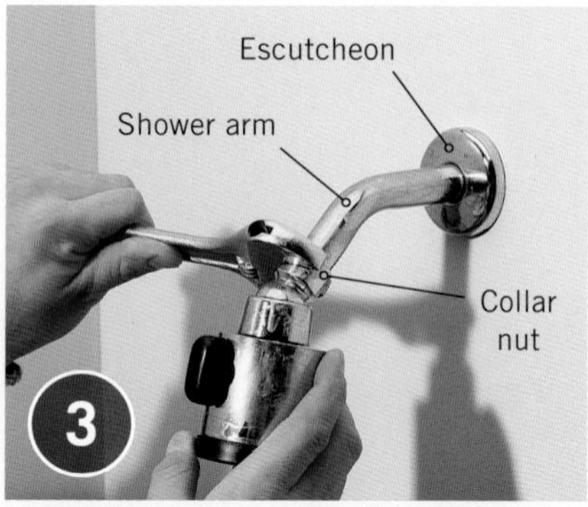

Unscrew the collar nut to remove the showerhead. Loosen the escutcheon, then twist the shower arm counterclockwise to unscrew it from the wall plumbing.

How to Disconnect Drain Plumbing

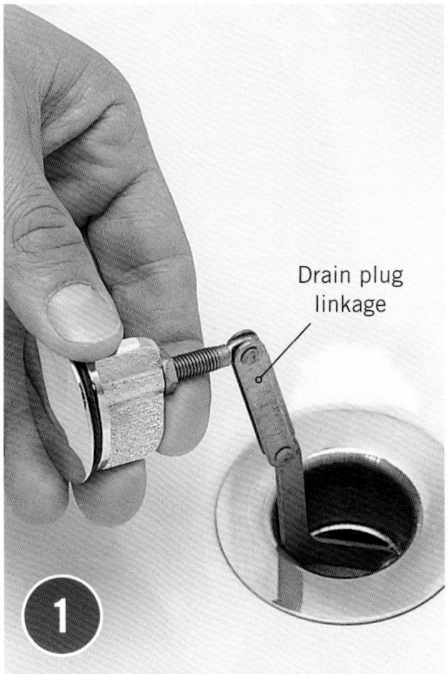

Remove the drain plug. Most bathtub plugs are connected to drain-plug linkage that is lifted out along with the plug.

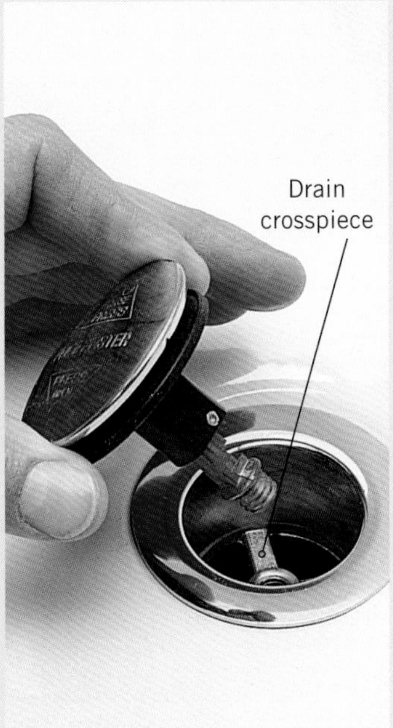

Spring-mounted drain plugs: Remove the plug by unscrewing it from the drain crosspiece.

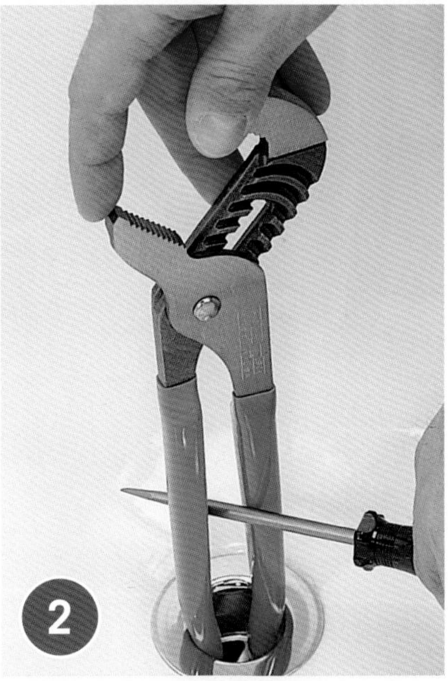

Disconnect the drain assembly from the tub by inserting a pair of pliers into the drain opening and turning the crosspiece counterclockwise. Insert a long screwdriver between the handles and use it to twist the pliers.

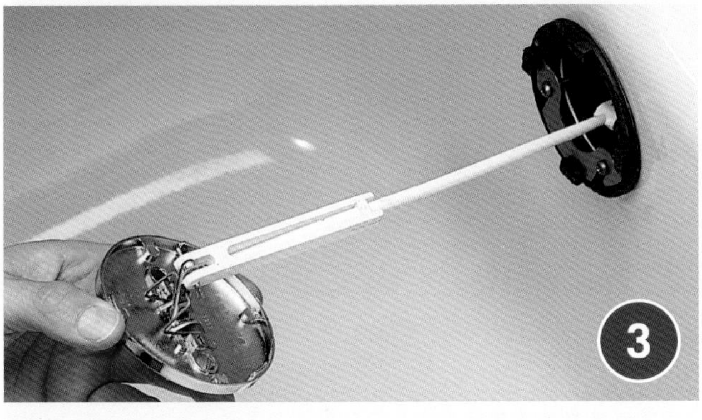

Remove the screws in the overflow coverplate (top photo). Remove the coverplate along with any attached drain plug (bottom photo).

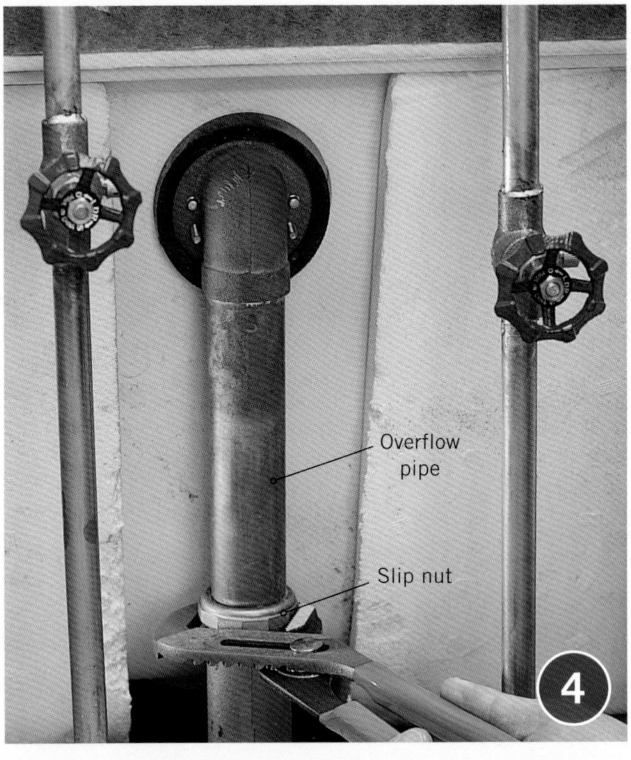

Remove the overflow pipe by unscrewing the slip nut that holds it to the rest of the drain assembly, then lift out the pipe. Stuff a rag into the waste pipe after the overflow pipe is removed to keep debris from entering the trap.

How to Remove a Shower Stall

After disconnecting the faucet handles, spout, and showerhead, remove the shower curtain rod or shower door, molding or trim, and any other accessories.

Slice the caulking around each shower panel using a utility knife. Remove any screws holding the panels together.

Pry shower panels away from the wall using a flat pry bar. If the panels are still intact, cut them into small pieces for easier disposal using a jigsaw or a sharp utility knife.

Fabricated shower bases (fiberglass or plastic): Slice the caulking between the base and the floor, then unscrew any fasteners holding the base to the wall studs. Pry the base from the floor with a wrecking bar.

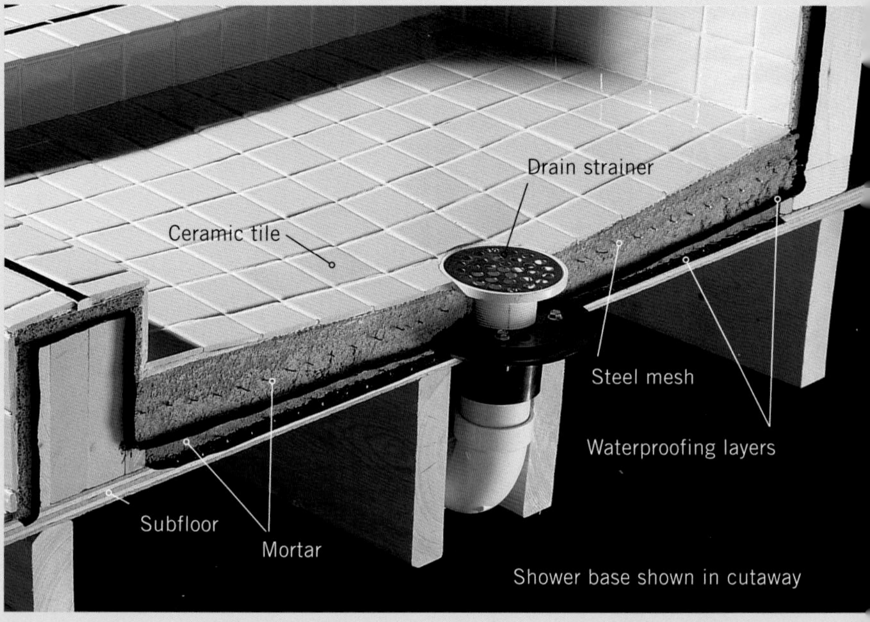

Ceramic-tile shower base: Remove the drain strainer, and then stuff a rag into the drain opening. Wearing protective equipment, break apart a section of tile with a hammer and masonry chisel. Cut through any steel-mesh reinforcement using a wire cutter. Continue knocking tile and mortar loose until the waterproofing layers are exposed, then scrape off the layers with a long-handled floor scraper.

How to Remove a Bathtub

Use a reciprocating saw to cut away at least 6" of the wall surface above the tub on all sides. Before cutting into a wall, be sure faucet handles, spouts, and drains are all disconnected.

Remove the fasteners that hold the tub flanges to the wall studs, then use a wrecking bar or a piece of 2 × 4 to pry the bathtub loose.

Lift the edge of the bathtub and slip a pair of 1 × 4 runners beneath the tub apron. Pull the tub away from the wall using the runners as skids. Have helpers when removing steel and cast-iron tubs.

Cut or break the bathtub into small pieces for easy disposal. Fiberglass, reinforced polymer, and pressed-steel tubs can be cut with a reciprocating saw. Cast-iron and steel tubs should be carried out.

Building a Wet Wall

A wet wall is simply a wall that contains plumbing for water supply and drainage. To accommodate the drain and vent pipes, which range from 1½ to 3 inches in diameter for branch lines, the wall framing needs to be built with 2 × 6 or larger dimensional lumber. You can also attach furring strips (usually 2 × 2) to existing 2 × 4 framing members to increase wall thickness. The chart on the next page describes how deeply you are allowed to notch wall-framing members under various load conditions, as well as the maximum-diameter holes you may drill for running plumbing and wiring.

Building a new wet wall or converting an existing wall to house new plumbing requires a building permit and an onsite inspection once all of the hookups are made. Do not install any wall coverings until after your plumbing and wiring have been inspected and approved.

TOOLS & MATERIALS

- Circular saw
- Wrecking bar or pry bar
- Drill/driver
- Caulk gun
- Adhesive
- Hammer
- 8d finish or casing nails
- Masking tape
- Hole saw
- Jigsaw
- Basic plumbing tools
- Reciprocating saw
- Protective plates
- Plumbing pipes and hangers
- Dust mask
- Eye and ear protection
- Work gloves

MAXIMUM HOLE & NOTCH CHART

FRAMING MEMBER	MAXIMUM HOLE SIZE	MAXIMUM NOTCH SIZE
2 × 4 load-bearing stud	1⁷⁄₁₆" diameter	⅞" deep
2 × 4 nonload-bearing stud	2½" diameter	1⁷⁄₁₆" deep
2 × 6 load-bearing stud	2¼" diameter	1⅜" deep
2 × 6 nonload-bearing stud	3⁵⁄₁₆" diameter	2³⁄₁₆" deep
2 × 6 joists	1½" diameter	⅞" deep
2 × 8 joists	2⅜" diameter	1¼" deep
2 × 10 joists	3¹⁄₁₆" diameter	1½" deep
2 × 12 joists	3¾" diameter	1⅞" deep

This framing-member chart shows the maximum sizes for holes and notches that can be cut into studs and joists when running pipes. Where possible, use notches rather than bored holes, because pipe installation is usually easier. When boring holes, there must be at least ⅝" of wood between the edge of a stud and the hole and at least 2" between the edge of a joist and the hole. Joists can be notched only in the end ⅓ of the overall span, never in the middle ⅓ of the joist. When two pipes are run through a stud, the pipes should be stacked one over the other, never side by side.

SIZING FOR WATER-DISTRIBUTION PIPES

FIXTURE	UNIT RATING
Toilet	3
Vanity sink	1
Shower	2
Bathtub	2
Dishwasher	2
Kitchen sink	2
Clothes washer	2
Utility sink	2
Sillcock	3

SIZE OF SERVICE PIPE FROM STREET	SIZE OF DISTRIBUTION PIPE FROM WATER METER	MAXIMUM LENGTH (FT.)—TOTAL FIXTURE UNITS					
		40	60	80	100	150	200
¾"	½"	9	8	7	6	5	4
¾"	¾"	27	23	19	17	14	11
¾"	1"	44	40	36	33	28	23
1"	1"	60	47	41	36	30	25
1"	1¼"	102	87	76	67	52	44

Water-distribution pipes are the main pipes extending from the water meter throughout the house, supplying water to the branch pipes leading to individual fixtures. To determine the size of the distribution pipes, you must first calculate the total demand in "fixture units" (above, left) and the overall length of the water-supply lines, from the street hookup through the water meter and to the most distant fixture in the house. Then, use the second table (above, right) to calculate the minimum size for the water-distribution pipes.

SIZING FOR BRANCH PIPES & SUPPLY TUBES

FIXTURE	MIN. BRANCH-PIPE SIZE	MIN. SUPPLY-TUBE SIZE
Toilet	½"	⅜"
Vanity sink	½"	⅜"
Shower	½"	½"
Bathtub	½"	½"
Dishwasher	½"	½"
Kitchen sink	½"	½"
Clothes washer	½"	½"
Utility sink	½"	½"
Sillcock	¾"	NA
Water heater	¾"	NA

Branch pipes are the water-supply lines that run from the distribution pipes toward the individual fixtures. Supply tubes are the vinyl, chromed copper, or braided tubes that carry water from the branch pipes to the fixtures.

PIPE SUPPORT INTERVALS

TYPE OF PIPE	VERTICAL-RUN SUPPORT INTERVAL	HORIZONTAL-RUN SUPPORT INTERVAL
Copper	10'	6'
PEX	5'	3'
CPVC	10'	3'
PVC	10'	4'
Steel	12'	10'
Iron	15'	5'

Minimum intervals for supporting pipes are determined by the type of pipe and its orientation in the system. Remember that the measurements shown above are minimum requirements.

How to Build & Plumb a Wet Wall

Clear the work area. If you are remodeling an existing wall to contain plumbing for a new bathroom, you'll need to completely remove the wall coverings so you can fur out the wall studs. This project requires a building permit and at least one onsite inspection. Shut off power at the main service panel before cutting into walls.

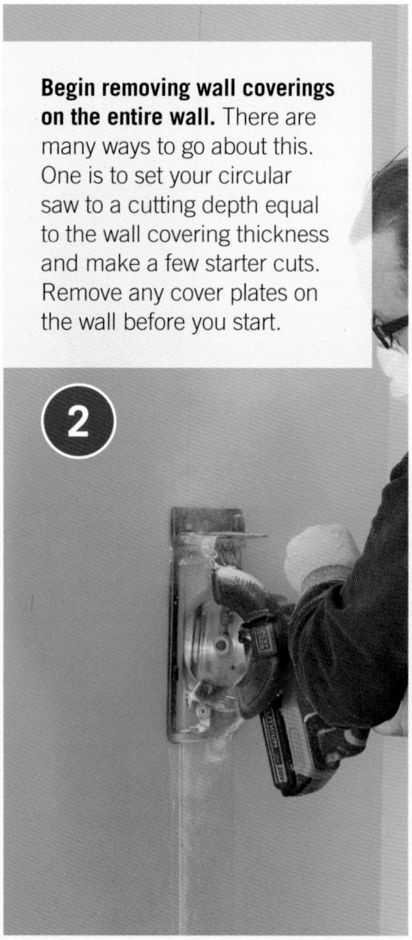

Begin removing wall coverings on the entire wall. There are many ways to go about this. One is to set your circular saw to a cutting depth equal to the wall covering thickness and make a few starter cuts. Remove any cover plates on the wall before you start.

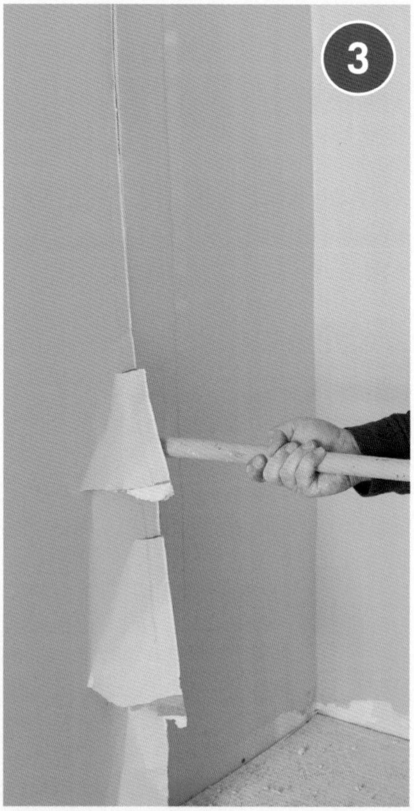

Next, use a wrecking bar to pry the wallcovering loose. Work in sections that are large, but manageable. Discard the material you remove immediately.

Remove old drywall screws or nails that remain in the wall-framing members.

Cut 2 × 2 furring strips to length. Start with the sole plate of the wall. Apply a bead of construction adhesive to the 2 × 2.

Attach the furring strips to the wall-framing members with 8d finish or casing nails. Drive a nail every 12 to 16".

Install the vertical furring strips next, using nails and construction adhesive. Finally, attach furring strips to the wall cap plate. Reroute wiring in the wall according to your plan. If you are keeping receptacles or switches in the same place, you'll still need to move the boxes forward in the wall cavity so the edges will be flush with the new wall surface.

If you are installing a drain for a tub or shower, mark out the location of the drain on the subfloor. Remove floor coverings first. Mark a centerpoint for the drainage pipe onto the sole plate. The pipe should align with the location for the drain trap. If your plan calls for it, drill additional holes for fixture drains, such as the wall sink stub-out being installed in this wall.

Drill holes for the drain pipes using a hole saw that's slightly larger than the outside diameter of the new pipe. In most cases, a 2"-diameter pipe is adequate for this type of branch drain, so a 2½" hole saw is a good choice.

Feed sections of drain pipe up through the holes in the sole plate and floor (if you are tying in to the plumbing on the floor below—the easiest way to tap into the existing plumbing system). Connect the drain line to a drainage stack, maintaining a slope of at least ¼" per 1' It is always a good idea to include a cleanout on the new branch line.

(continued)

Cut notches in the wall-framing members to hold the horizontal plumbing in the drain lines. See chart on page 61. Cut no deeper than needed to hold the pipes.

Cut the horizontal lines to length and set them into the notches. You can hold them in place with tape if they don't stay put.

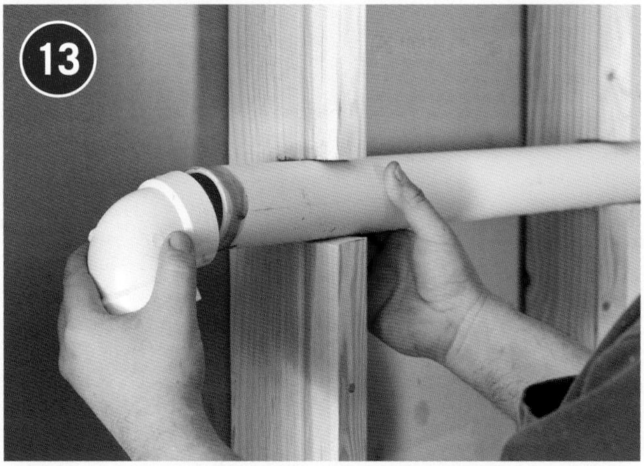

Attach a 90° elbow to the end of the new horizontal line so it aligns with the drain pipe coming up through the floor. The other end of horizontal pipe is fitted with a T-fitting so the vent line can be extended up through the cap plate and ceiling.

With the drain pipes seated in the fitting below the floor (but not cemented), mark the free ends of the vertical pipes for cutting at the points where they will join the fittings on the horizontal line. Dry-fit this union. Do not cement yet.

Remove the subfloor in the section you've laid out for the drain. Cut with a jigsaw, using a starter hole if you need to. If you've planned the drain location wisely it will not fall over a floor joist.

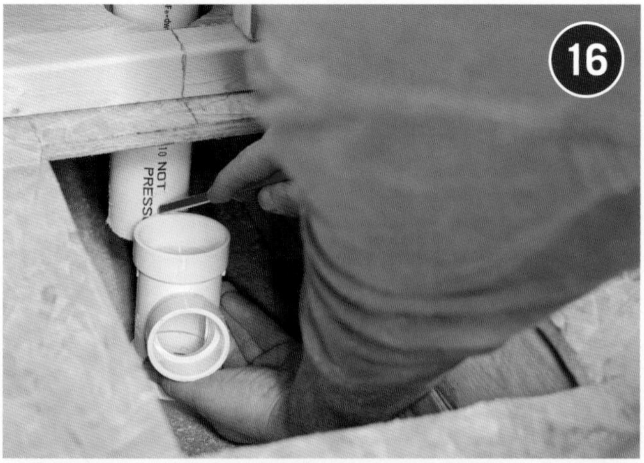

Reach into the hole in the subfloor and mark the vertical pipe for cutting to accept a T-fitting. The tee should have a slight sweep downward. Normally, the open end of the tee is sized for a 1½"-diameter drain tube to run from the vertical drain line to the drain trap.

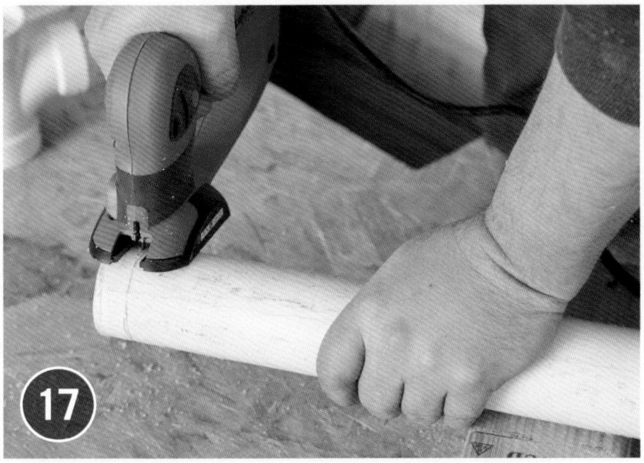

Remove the drain pipes and cut them to the lengths you've marked.

Cement the reducing tee into the drain line for the tub, making sure to orient the sweep correctly and to align the opening with the drain-trap location.

Cement a reducing tee into the drain line for the sink stub-out.

Cement the drain lines into the drain fittings from below. Solvent-cement the branch drain line components on the floor below, tying the line into the main drain stack or another large branch drain.

Connect the vent pipe from the wet wall with another vent line in the attic or, if you prefer, run it out through the roof and flash and cover it according to your local plumbing codes.

Install cold and hot water-supply lines, connecting from the floor below.

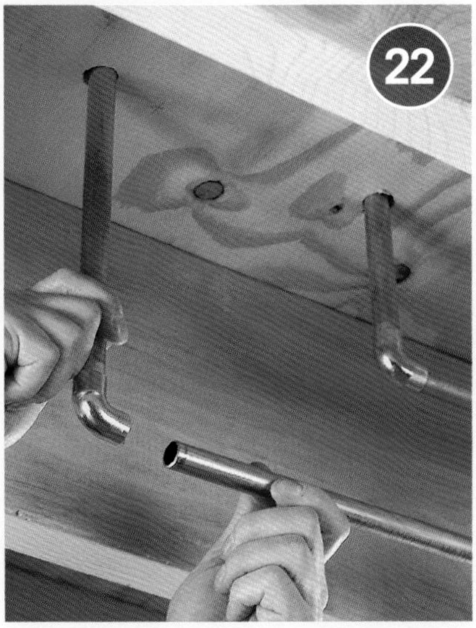

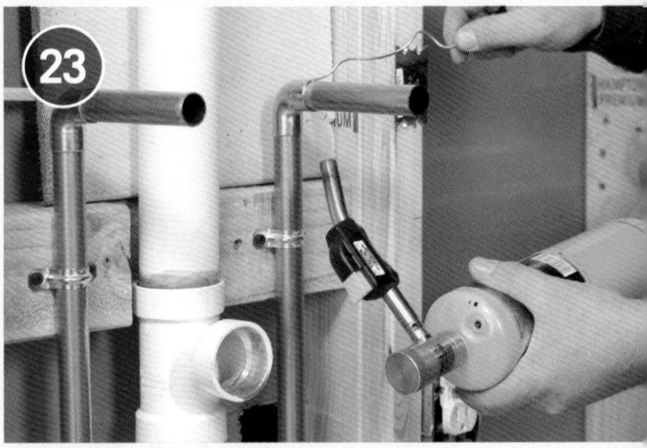

Solder supply stub-outs onto the new water lines. Install protective metal plates on the wall studs to cover pipe (and electrical cable) penetrations. Have your work inspected and, when approved, you may go ahead and install wall coverings.

BATHROOM REMODELING PROJECTS

Showers, Tubs & Whirlpools

These days, bathtubs and showers can be put just about anywhere. You can locate a freestanding tub center stage in your bathroom, put a neo shower in a dead-space corner, butt a semifreestanding jetted tub up against a wall, or make the whole bathroom a wet room, confusing the boundaries of tub and shower. The options go on and on.

The downside to all those possibilities is that they require creative plumbing. Not only do you have to run plumbing to exactly where it needs to go (which sometimes may be the middle of the floor), but if you've included jets or a heater with your tub—or a steam feature or special lights in a shower enclosure—you'll also need to run power to the location.

However, it's always best to start with the basics—how showers are constructed; how different types of tubs are positioned, set up, and used; and how any excess water will be handled in the case of either tubs or showers. You'll find information on all that and more in this chapter.

In this chapter:

- Installing Showers
- Shower Enclosure Kits
- Glass-Wall Shower
- Curbed Shower Base
- Wet Rooms & Curbless Showers
- Alcove Bathtubs
- 3-Piece Tub Surrounds
- Drop-In Tubs
- Freestanding Tubs
- Sliding Tub Doors
- Air-Jet Tubs
- Tub & Shower Fittings
- Adding a Shower to a Bathtub

Installing Showers

You can build a shower just about anywhere there's a 30-inch square spot of real estate in the bathroom. The main decision is always going to be whether you want to use a completely prefabricated enclosure or build one from the base up. In either case, making the enclosure watertight will be your prime consideration. Water-resistant drywall is the standard for prefab panels and enclosures, but manufacturers sometimes recommend specific products be used. Local building codes may also designate different techniques, such as using a waterproof membrane between the studs and the backer material.

The type of shower pan or base is an even more complicated issue. These days, many homeowners are opting for linear "trench" drains that sit level with the floor. They allow you to install a completely curbless shower floor, although most current installations still involve a curbed base. However, wet rooms are becoming increasingly popular. A wet room is a bathroom with no barriers between the shower and the rest of the room. It can alleviate the need for an actual enclosure, although the surfaces in the room all need to be watertight.

Ceramic tile for custom showers is installed the same way as in other applications. Ceramic shower accessories, such as a soap dish, are mortared in place during the tile installation.

Antiscald Valves

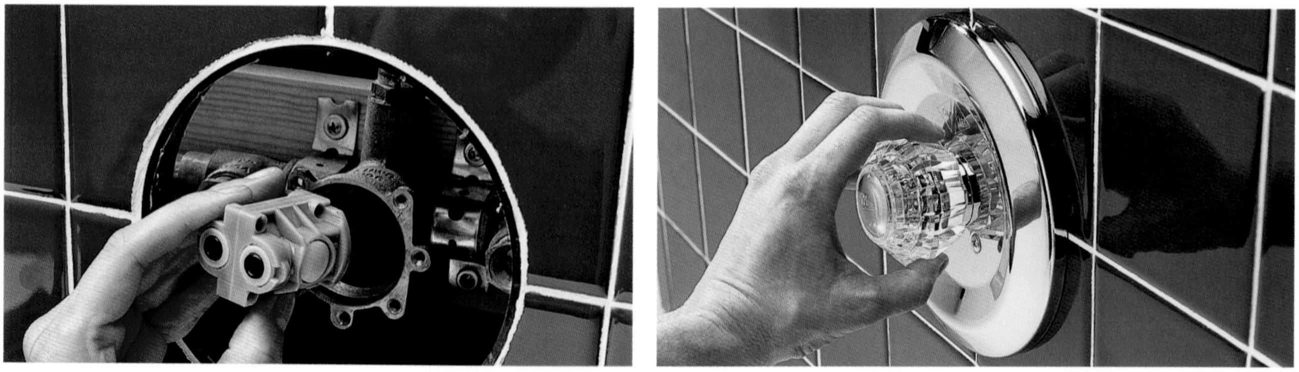

Antiscald valves are safety devices that protect against sudden water temperature changes. They are required by most building codes for faucets in showers and combination tub-showers. Once installed, faucets with antiscald valves look like standard faucets.

Anatomy of a Shower

Shower stalls are available in many different sizes and styles, but the basic elements are the same. Most shower stalls have a shower alcove, a supply system, and a drain system.

Shower alcove: The alcove is the frame for the stall, with 2 × 4 walls built to fit around a shower pan and blocking to secure the plumbing. The pan—in most cases—sets into a mortar bed for support, and water-resistant drywall or cementboard covers the alcove walls.

The supply system: The shower arm extends from the wall, where an elbow fitting connects it to the shower pipe. The pipe runs up from the faucet, which is fed by the hot and cold water supplies.

The drain system: The drain cover attaches to the drain tailpiece. A rubber gasket on the tailpiece slips over the drain pipe, leading to the P-trap and the branch drain.

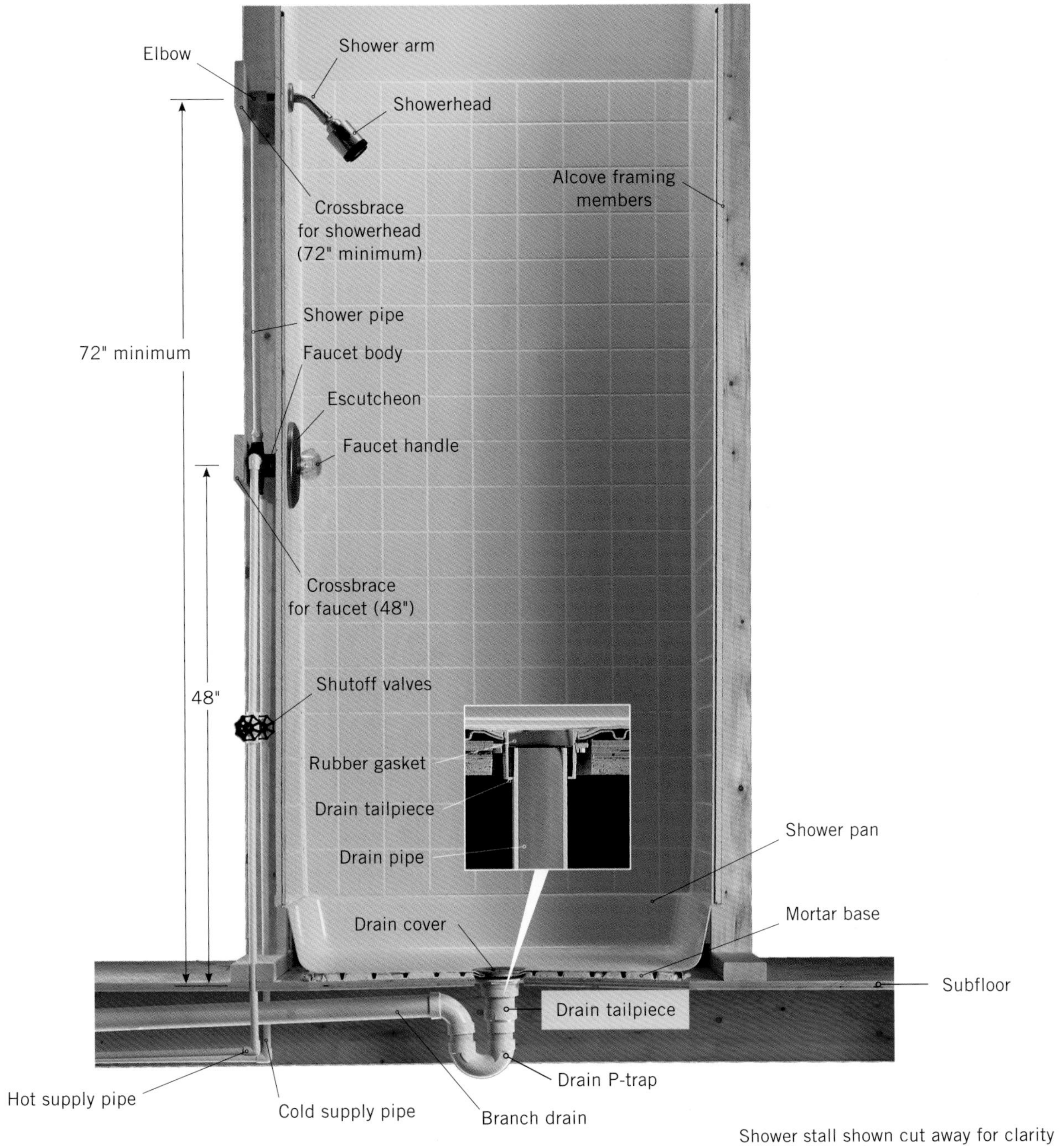

Shower stall shown cut away for clarity

Shower-Enclosure Kits

TOOLS & MATERIALS

Tape measure	Hacksaw
Pencil	Masking tape
Hammer	Slicone caulk
Carpenter's square	Caulk gun
Screwdrivers	Panel adhesive
Deck screws	Silicone sealant
Pipe wrench	Thinset mortar
Level	Trowel
Strap wrench	Lumber
Adjustable wrench	Shower enclosure kit
Pliers	Shower door
Drill/driver	Showerhead
Center punch	Faucet
File	Plumbing supplies
Utility knife	Eye and ear protection
Jigsaw or hole saw	Work gloves

The fastest and easiest way to create a new shower in your bathroom is to frame in the stall area with lumber and wallboard and then install a shower-enclosure kit. Typically consisting of three fiberglass or plastic walls, these enclosure kits snap together at the corners and nestle inside the flanges of the shower pan to create nearly foolproof mechanical seals. Often the walls are formed with shelves, soap holders, and other conveniences.

If you are on a tight budget, you can find extremely inexpensive enclosure kits to keep costs down. You can even create your own custom enclosure using waterproof beadboard panels and snap-together connectors. Or, you can invest in a higher-grade kit made from thicker material that will last much longer. Some kits are sold with the receptor (and perhaps even the door) included. The kit shown here is designed to be attached directly to wall studs, but others require a backer wall for support. The panels are attached to the backer with high-tack panel adhesive.

Paneled shower surrounds are inexpensive and easy to install. Designed for alcove installations, they often are sold with matching shower pans (called receptors). Some include molded-in accessories, such as shelves or soap dishes. High-end versions include tiled sections, faux tile, and faux stone panels, and some even include matching fixtures, controls, and built-in grab bars.

How to Install a Shower Enclosure

Mark out the location of the shower, including any new walls, on the floor and walls. Most kits can be installed over wallboard, but you can usually achieve a more professional-looking wall finish if you remove the wall covering and floor covering in the installation area. Dispose of the materials immediately and thoroughly clean the area.

If you are adding a wall to create the alcove, lay out the locations for the studs and plumbing on the new wood sill plate. Also lay out the stud locations on the cap plate that will be attached to the ceiling. Refer to the enclosure-kit instructions for exact locations and dimensions of studs. Attach the sill plate to the floor with deck screws and panel adhesive, making sure it is square to the back wall and the correct distance from the side wall.

Align a straight 2 × 4 right next to the sill plate and make a mark on the ceiling. Use a level to extend that line directly above the sill plate. Attach the cap plate at that point.

Install the 2 × 4 studs at the outlined locations. Check with a level to make sure each stud is plumb and then attach them by driving deck screws toenail style into the sill plate and cap plate.

(continued)

Cut an access hole in the floor for the drain, according to the installation-manual instructions. Drill openings in the sill plate of the wet wall (the new wall in this project) for the supply pipes, also according to the instructions.

Install a drain pipe and branch line and then trim the drain pipe flush with the floor. If you are not experienced with plumbing, hire a plumber to install the new drain line.

Install new supply risers as directed in the instruction manual (again, have a plumber do this if necessary). Also install crossbraces between the studs in the wet wall for mounting the faucet body and shower arm.

NOTE: Some local codes require that you use gate valve shutoffs, not ball valves.

If the supply plumbing is located in a wall (old or new) that is accessible from the non-shower side, install framing for a removable access panel.

Attach the drain tailpiece that came with your shower pan to the underside of the unit, following the manufacturer's instructions precisely. Here, an adjustable spud wrench is being used to tighten the tailpiece.

OPTION: To stabilize the pan, especially if the floor is uneven, pour or trowel a layer of thinset mortar into the installation area, taking care to keep the mortar out of the drain access hole. Do not apply mortar in areas where the pan has feet that are intended to make full contact with the floor.

Set the pan in place, check to make sure it is level, and shim it if necessary. Secure the pan with large-head roofing nails driven into the wall stud so the heads pin the flange against the stud. Do not overdrive the nails.

Lay out the locations for the valve hole or holes in the end wall panel that will be installed on the wet wall. Check your installation instructions. Some kits come with a template marked on the packaging carton. Cut the access hole with a hole saw and drill or with a jigsaw and fine-tooth blade. If using a jigsaw, orient the panel so the good surface is facing down. *(continued)*

Position the back wall so there is a slight gap (about $\frac{1}{32}$") between the bottom of the panel and the rim of the pan—set a few small spacers on the rim if need be. Tack a pair of roofing nails above the top of the back panel to hold it in place (or use duct tape). Position both end walls and test the fits. Make clip connections between panels (inset) if your kit uses them.

Remove the end walls so you can prepare the installation area for them. If your kit recommends panel adhesive, apply it to the wall or studs. In the kit shown here, only a small bead of silicone sealant on the pan flange is required.

Reinstall the end panels, permanently clipping them to the back panel according to the kit manufacturer's instructions. Make sure the front edges of the end panels are flush with the front of the pan.

Once the panels are positioned correctly and snapped together, fasten them to the wall studs. If the panels have predrilled nail holes, drive roofing nails through them at each stud at the panel tops and every 4 to 6" along vertical surfaces.

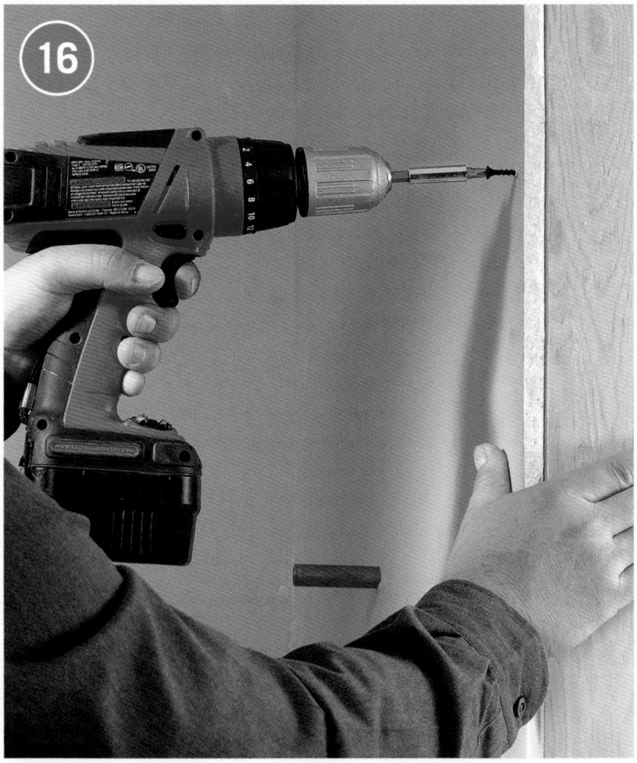

Install wall-covering material above the enclosure panels and anywhere else it is needed. Use moisture-resistant materials, and maintain a gap of ¼" between the shoulders of the top panel flanges and the wall covering.

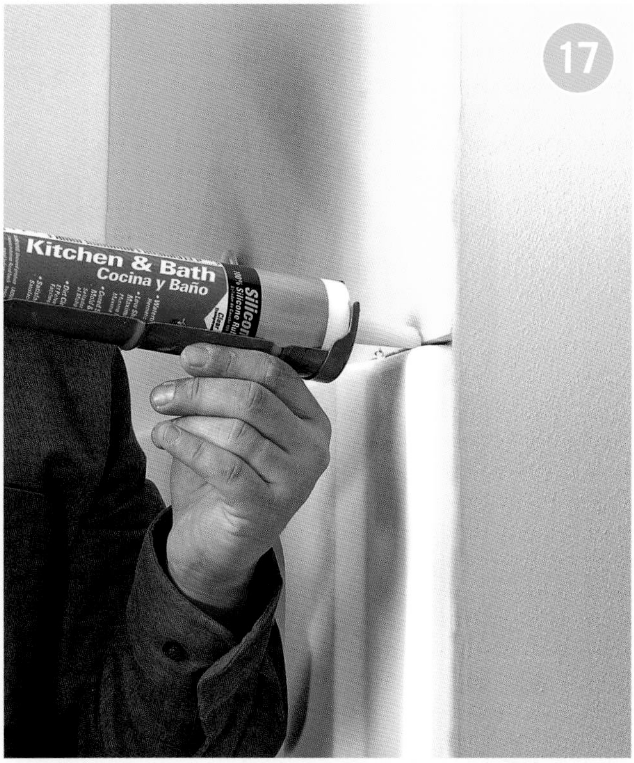

Finish the walls and then caulk between the enclosure panels and the wall coverings with silicone caulk.

Install the faucet handles and escutcheon and caulk around the escutcheon plate. Install the shower-arm escutcheon and showerhead. Add a shower door.

Make an access panel and attach it at the framed opening created in step 8. A piece of ¼" plywood framed with mitered case molding and painted to match the wall is one idea for access-panel covers.

Glass-Wall Shower

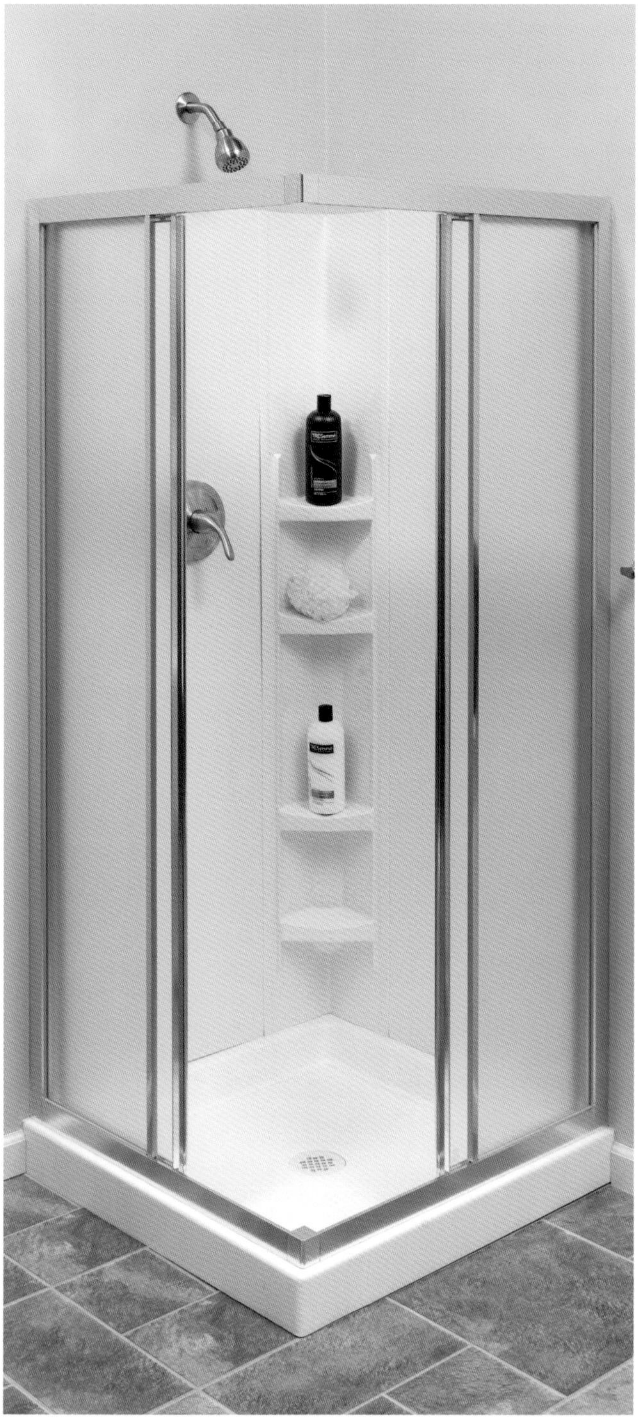

One method for creating a quick shower stall is with a glass-wall kit, ideal for small bathrooms. It tucks neatly into the corner of your bathroom and can make use of either a custom-built shower pan (page 84) or a prefabricated shower pan like that commonly used in framed-in alcoves (page 72). Many such showers come with the base pan as part of the kit, while with others you will need to buy or build a separate shower pan.

The kit we've used to demonstrate a glass-wall shower installation includes the shower pan, three wall pieces (two flat panels and a corner shelf/ connector unit), and the glass panels and frames for the sliding door. All connectors and hardware are included, but this isn't the case with all such kits. Always buy your shower kit, examine the components, and read the instruction carefully to see if additional parts and materials are needed.

The key to smooth installation with a wall-kit shower is making sure the wall panels, frames, and shower pan fit squarely in the corners and against the existing walls. Walls that are out of square or not perfectly flat can complicate this job, so spending some time to correct faulty walls is time well spent if you're installing a glass-wall shower.

Any shower kit will require very diligent and careful sealing of the joints using siliconized latex caulk and silicone sealant. Do not rush this step, as it is crucial to achieving a workable, leak-free shower.

TOOLS & MATERIALS

- Glass-wall shower kit with shower pan
- Tape measure
- Pencil or marker
- 4' level
- Drill with bits and hole saw
- Straightedge
- Utility knife
- Silicone sealant
- Wall (panel) adhesive
- Siliconized latex caulk
- Caulk gun
- Carpenter's square
- Hammer
- Center punch
- Phillips screwdriver
- Masking tape
- Mineral spirits
- Clean cloths
- Plastic wall anchors
- Ear and eye protection
- Work gloves

How to Install a Glass-Wall Shower

Prepare the floor drain and install a prefabricated shower pan in the corner of the room, following the instructions on steps 5 to 10 on pages 74 to 75. Make sure the outside diameter of the drain pipe matches the requirements of the shower pan (ours required a 2⅜" outside diameter for the drain pipe). The shower pan must sit perfectly level on the floor and tight against the wall studs on the two adjoining walls for the installation to proceed smoothly.

Draw centerlines along the top of the outer thresholds of the shower pan. Position one of the metal wall channels vertically against the wall, so the bottom edge is centered on the centerline. Use a level to adjust the wall channel for plumb, then mark the mounting-hole locations on the wall through the holes in the wall channel.

Drill holes and drive plastic wall anchors for the metal shower channels. The plastic wall anchors are included in most shower kits.

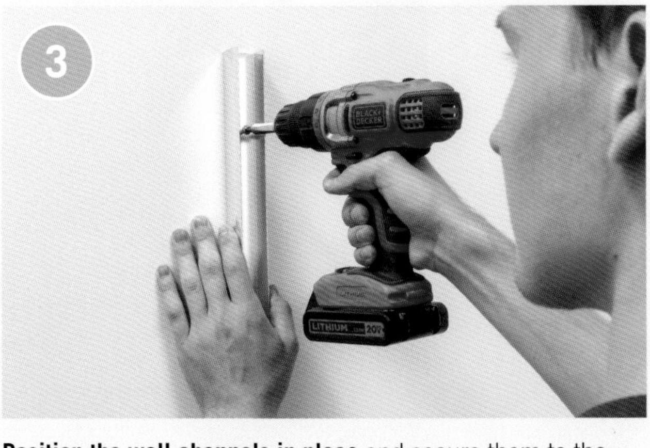

Position the wall channels in place and secure them to the wall with mounting screws driven through the mounting holes and into the wall anchors.

Fill the gaps between the shower base and the wall with siliconized latex caulk. Install the other wall channel in the same way, and seal the remaining gap between the shower pan and the wall. Lightly sand the top face of the shower pan curbs with the sandpaper included in the kit. This will create a better bonding surface when you seal the pan at the end of the project. *(continued)*

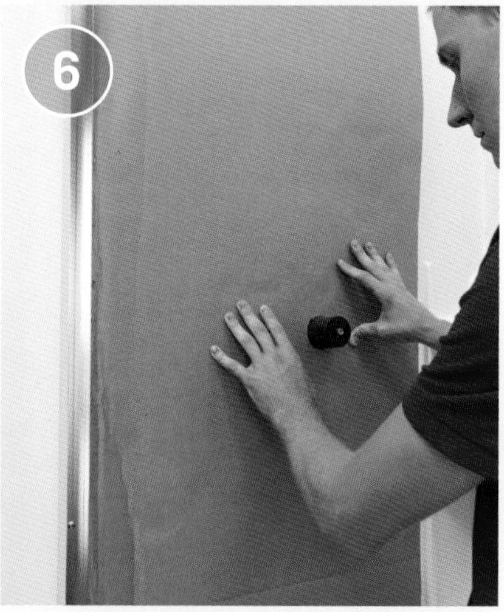

Prepare the walls in whatever manner recommended by the kit instructions. Test-fit the side panels and the corner panel by taping them in place temporarily with masking tape, with the shiny side of the panels facing out. The wall panels should butt against the wall channels and rest flat against the shower-pan curbs. If the wall panels don't line up correctly, it indicates that the wall channels are out of plumb or the shower pan is not level. The corner panel should slightly overlap the side wall panels, by about ½". Some trimming may be necessary if the overlap is greater.

To prepare the side wall that will contain the plumbing fixtures, cut a cardboard template to the same size as the wall panel and place the template against the wall. Mark the location of the shower and faucet on the template. Make an X against this side of the cardboard for reference. Remove the cardboard template, then use a utility knife to cut away openings for the plumbing stub-outs on the template. Test-fit the cardboard template against the wall, making sure the plumbing pipes fit correctly.

Use the template to mark the opening on the wall panel that will hold the shower plumbing fixtures, then use an appropriately sized hole saw to cut openings in the wall panel. Make sure to align the wall panel correctly when marking: the shiny side will face into the shower.

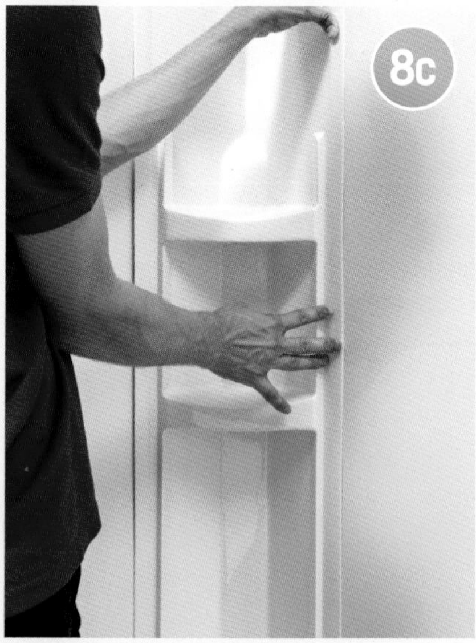

Beginning with the panel without plumbing cutouts, spread a continuous ¼" bead of panel adhesive along the four edges of the back of the wall panel, no closer than 2" to the edges. Leave gaps at the ends, so air can escape when pressing the panels against the wall. Also apply an S-shaped continuous bead to the center of the panel. Position the panel against the wall so the bottom rests firmly against the shower-pan curb and side edges are against the wall channel and the corner of the room. Press the panel against the wall firmly, and smooth it with even hand pressure until the panel is perfectly flat. Repeat with the wall that has plumbing cutouts, making sure to apply a bead of panel adhesive around the cutouts. Finally, apply panel adhesive to the back of the corner panel and press it into place. (Some shower models may have connecting rod that joins the corner panel to the shower-pan unit.) If any excess adhesive has squeezed out around the edges of the panel, clean it away with a rag moistened with mineral spirits.

Following the kit instructions, begin assembling the doorframes. With our kit, the first step is to attach the center guide to the bottom rail using the screws included with the kit.

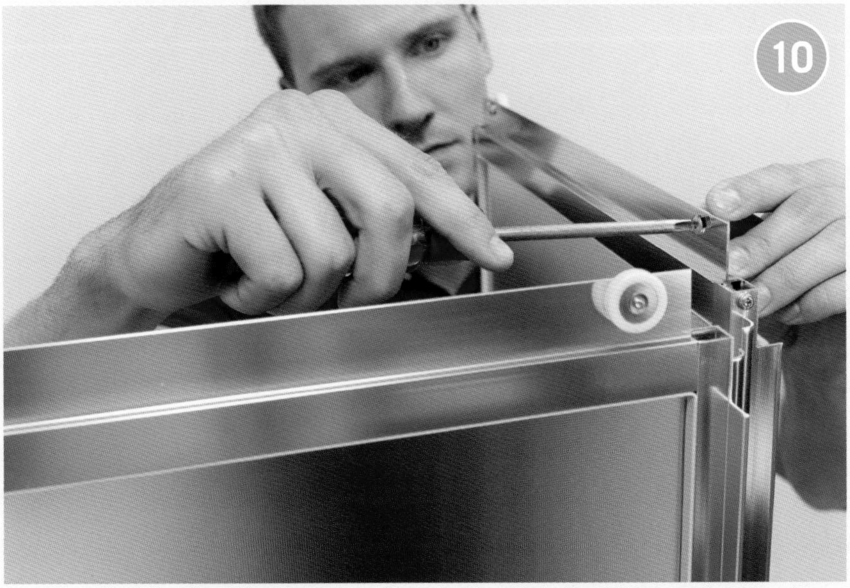

Stand the sliding door panels upright so the hanging brackets are at the top. Install the rollers on the same side of the door panels as the door stops.

Most shower kits have both stationary glass panels and sliding panels. Begin by installing the first stationary panel by inserting it into the wall channel so the roller channel at the side of the top rail is facing inside the shower stall. Now insert the sliding door panel on this side, so that the rollers engage the roller channel inside the top rail. Repeat this step with the opposite-side stationary panel and sliding door panel. Secure the top and bottom rails of the glass panels to the side channels and to one another using the corner connectors included with the kit.

(continued)

Install the seal strips on the back of both sliding door panels, as per the kit instructions. These pliable strips will allow the door to form a watertight seal against the stationary panels.

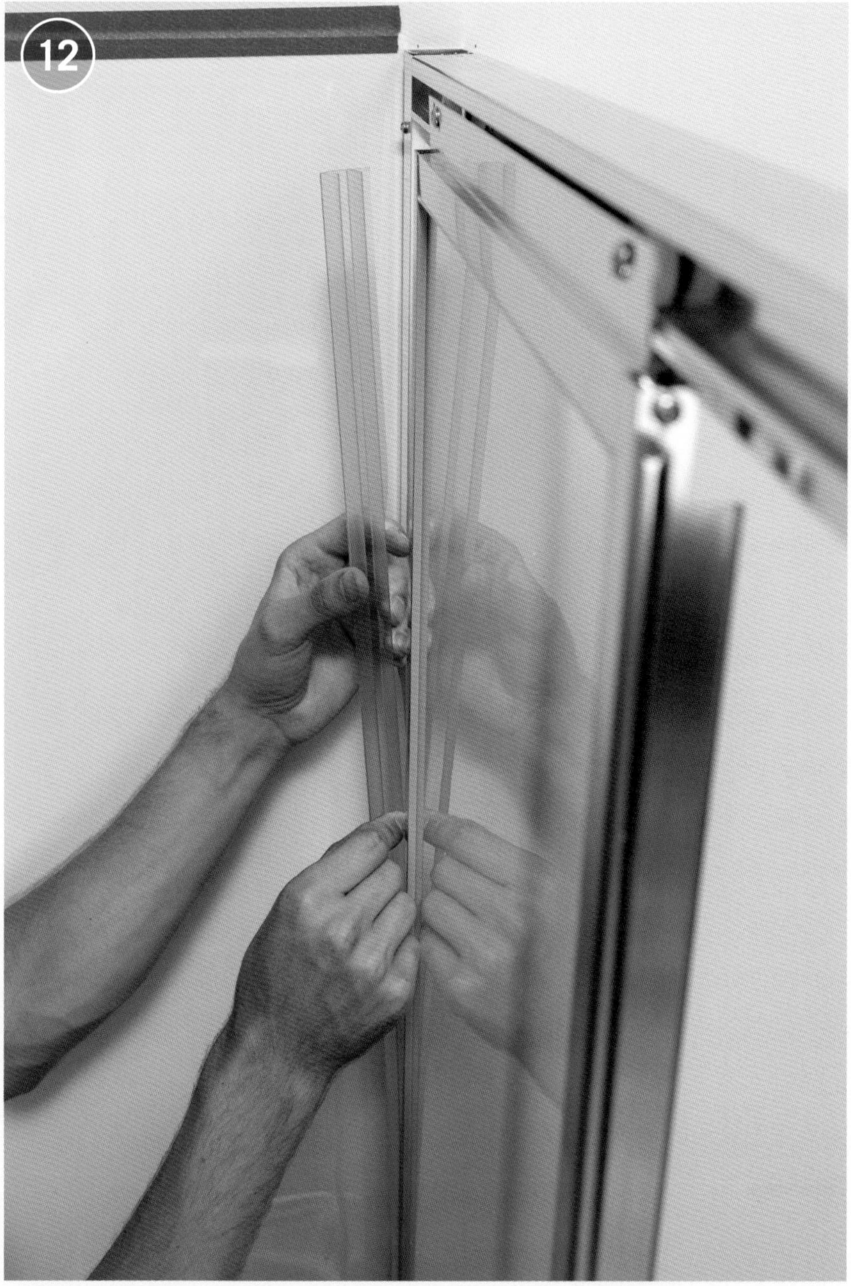

Make small adjustments to the entire assembly to center it on the top face of the shower pan curbs. Once positioned correctly, so that the entire unit is plumb and the bottoms of the stationary panels are flat and level on the shower pan, drill holes in the frame through the adjustment holes in the glass frames, and secure the unit to the wall channels with the provided screws. Test the doors and, if necessary, make small adjustments by loosening and then reattaching the roller screws at the top of the doors. Allow the shower unit to sit in place for 12 hours before beginning the waterproofing step.

14

Waterproofing the shower will require the use of two different but similar-sounding products: siliconized latex caulk and silicone sealant. First, apply siliconized caulk to the seams between the wall panels and corner panel, between the wall panels and the metal wall channels, the seam where the wall panels and corner panel meet the shower pan, and along the tops of the wall panels. Apply silicone sealant to the heads of all screws in the upright panel frames. From inside of the shower, apply silicone sealant along the seams where the bottom rails lay on the shower pan curb and along the bottoms of the wall channels and glass panel upright frames. Also apply silicone sealant around the center guide. Apply silicone sealant around the joint where the bottom rails butt up against the bottom connector. Finally, apply sealant to the heads of any exposed screws.

15

Let the caulked and sealed seams dry completely. To complete your shower, make the plumbing hookups of the shower faucet spray head and the shower valve. Test the shower to check for leaks.

Curbed Shower Base

Building a custom-tiled shower base lets you choose the shape and size of your shower rather than having its dimensions dictated by available products. Building the base is quite simple, though it does require time and some knowledge of basic masonry techniques because the base is formed primarily using mortar. What you get for your time and trouble can be spectacular.

Before designing a shower base, contact your local building department regarding code restrictions and to secure the necessary permits. Most codes require water controls to be accessible from outside the shower and describe acceptable door positions and operation. Requirements such as these influence the size and position of the base.

Choosing the tile before finalizing the design lets you size the base to require mostly full tile. Showers are among the most frequently used amenities in the average home, so it really makes sense to build one that is comfortable and pleasing to your senses. Consider using small tile and gradating the color from top to bottom or in a sweep across the walls. Or, use trim tile and listellos on the walls to create an interesting focal point.

Whatever tile you choose, remember to seal the grout in your new shower and to maintain it carefully over the years. Water-resistant grout protects the structure of the shower and prolongs its useful life.

TOOLS & MATERIALS

- Tape measure
- Circular saw
- Hammer
- Utility knife
- Stapler
- 2' level
- Mortar mixing box
- Trowel
- Wood float
- Grout tile
- Felt-tip marker
- Ratchet wrench
- Tin snips
- Torpedo level
- Tools for installing tile
- Framing lumber (1×, 2 × 4, 2 × 10)
- 16d galvanized common nails
- 15# building paper
- Staples
- 3-piece shower drain
- PVC cement
- Galvanized-metal lath
- Thick-bed floor mortar ("deck mud")
- Latex mortar additive
- Thinset mortar
- CPE waterproof membrane and preformed dam corners
- CPE membrane solvent glue
- CPE membrane sealant
- Cementboard and materials for installing cementboard
- Materials for installing tile
- Builder's sand
- Portland cement
- Masonry hoe
- Work gloves
- Dust mask or respirator
- Straightedge
- ¼" wood shims
- Thinset mortar
- Tile spacers
- Balloon tester
- Silicone caulk
- Caulk gun
- Eye and ear protection

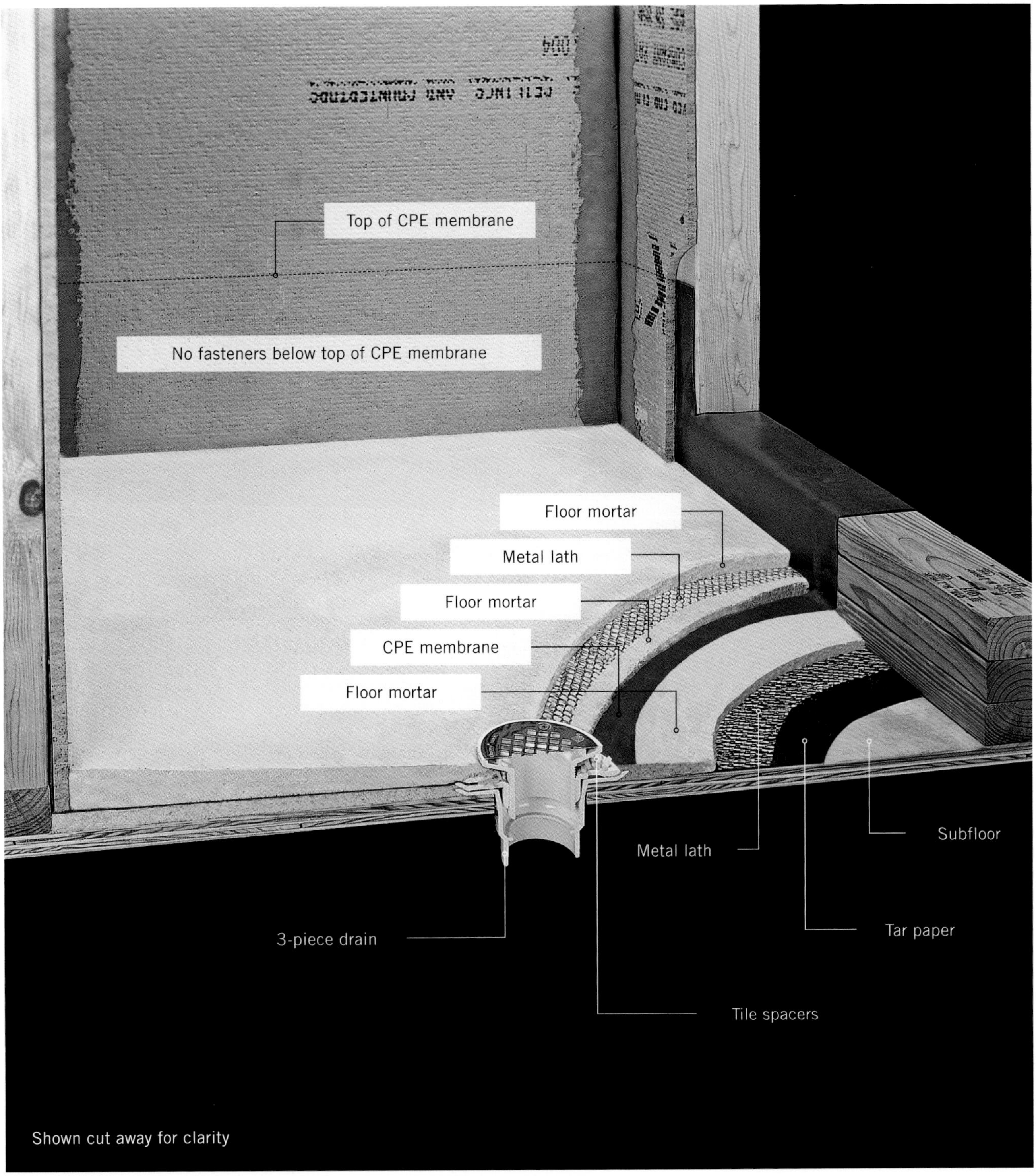

TIPS FOR BUILDING A CUSTOM SHOWER BASE

A custom-tiled shower base is built in three layers to ensure proper water drainage: the prepan, the shower pan, and the shower floor. A mortar prepan is first built on top of the subfloor, establishing a slope toward the drain of ¼" for every 12" of shower floor. Next, a waterproof chlorinated polyethylene (CPE) membrane forms the shower pan, providing a watertight seal for the shower base. Finally, a second mortar bed reinforced with wire mesh is installed for the shower floor, providing a surface for tile installation. If water penetrates the tiled shower floor, the shower pan and sloped prepan will direct it to the weep holes of the 3-piece drain. One of the most important steps in building a custom-tiled shower base is testing the shower pan after installation (step 13). This allows you to locate and fix any leaks to prevent costly damage.

MIXING DECK MUD

Mortar beds for laying tile are made from deck mud, a simple mortar consisting of a proportioned mixture of builder's sand and Portland cement with a little water added to bind the particles together. Sometimes referred to as dry-pack mortar or floor mud, it can be purchased in prepackaged blends or you can easily make it yourself. It can be set in thicker layers than ordinary thinset mortar.

Deck mud is made with a ratio of four to six parts of builder's sand to one part of Portland cement. The higher the proportion of Portland cement in the mixture, the richer it is considered to be. Leaner mortars contain a lower proportion of Portland cement. A mortar bed 1¼" thick (a common thickness for a shower receptor base) requires approximately 12 pounds of dry sand per square foot of application. Add an additional 3 pounds of sand per square foot for each additional ¼" of mortar thickness desired. The amount of Portland cement required will depend on the mixing ratio and the total volume of sand required to complete the job. A richer blend that uses a 4:1 ratio is suitable for small areas, such as shower-pan mortar beds.

The ingredients for making your own mortar-bed "mud" are minimal. You'll need sharp sand (also called builder's sand), Portland cement, and water. The proportions vary by application.

How to Mix Deck Mud

Add the dry ingredients (builder's sand and Portland cement) to a mortar box in the correct ratio. For general purposes, 4 parts sand to 1 part mortar mix (by volume) works. Don't mix more mud than you can use in a half hour or so.

Add small amounts of clean water to the dry mixture and blend to an evenly moist consistency using a masonry hoe. Be sure to wear gloves and a dust mask or respirator.

Check the consistency. A squeezed clump of deck mud should hold its shape without sagging or falling apart.

How to Build a Curbed Shower Base

Remove building materials to expose subfloor and stud walls. Cut three 2 × 4s for the curb and fasten them to the floor joists and the studs at the shower threshold with 16d galvanized common nails. Also cut 2 × 10 lumber to size and install in the stud bays around the perimeter of the shower base.

Staple 15# building paper to the subfloor of the shower base. Disassemble the 3-piece shower drain and glue the bottom piece to the drain pipe with PVC cement. Partially screw the drain bolts into the drain piece, and stuff a rag into the drain pipe to prevent mortar from falling into the drain.

Mark the height of the bottom drain piece on the wall farthest from the center of the drain. Measure from the center of the drain straight across to that wall, then raise the height mark ¼" for every 12" of shower floor to slope the pre-pan toward the drain. Trace a reference line at the height mark around the perimeter of the entire alcove using a level.

Staple galvanized-metal lath over the building paper; cut a hole in the lath ½" from the drain. Mix floor mortar (or "deck mud") to a fairly dry consistency using a latex additive for strength; mortar should hold its shape when squeezed (inset). Trowel the mortar onto the subfloor, building the prepan from the flange of the drain piece to the height line on the perimeter of the walls. *(continued)*

Continue using the trowel to form the prepan, checking the slope using a level and filling any low spots with mortar. Finish the surface of the prepan with a wood float until it is even and smooth. Allow the mortar to cure overnight.

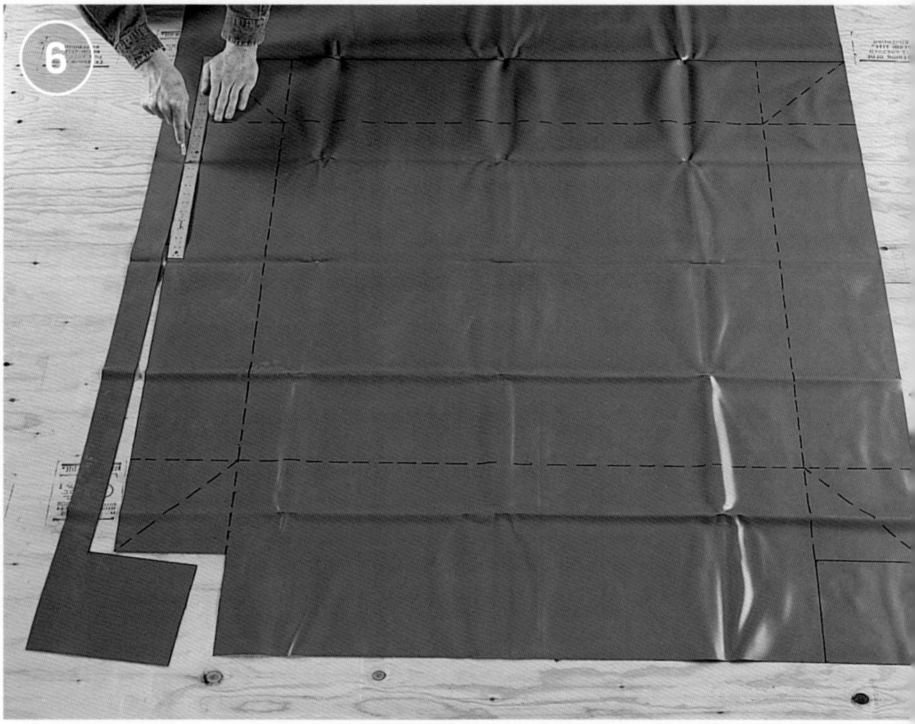

Measure the dimensions of the shower floor and mark them out on a sheet of CPE waterproof membrane using a felt-tipped marker. From the floor outline, measure out and mark an additional 8" for each wall and 16" for the curb end. Cut the membrane to size using a utility knife and straightedge. Be careful to cut on a clean, smooth surface to prevent puncturing the membrane. Lay the membrane onto the shower pan.

Measure to find the exact location of the drain and mark it on the membrane, outlining the outer diameter of the drain flange. Cut a circular piece of CPE membrane roughly 2" larger than the drain flange, then use CPE membrane solvent glue to weld it into place and reinforce the seal at the drain.

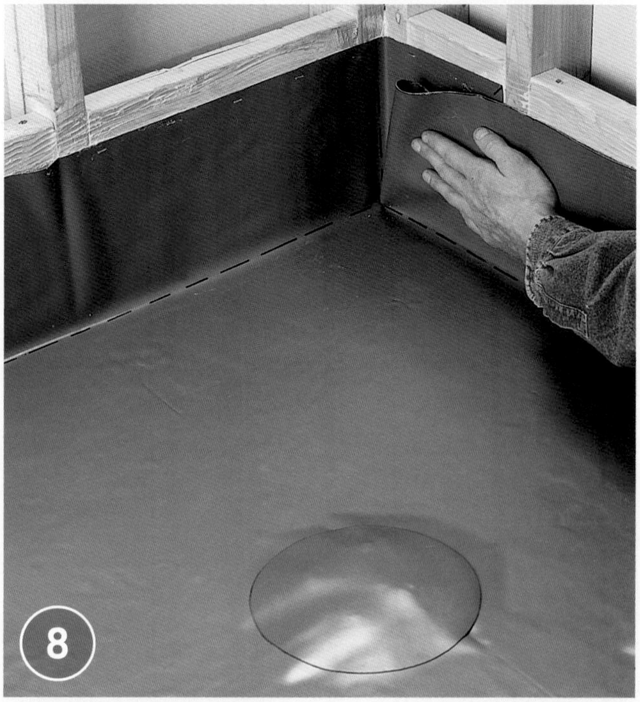

Apply CPE sealant around the drain. Fold the membrane along the floor outline. Set the membrane over the pre-pan so the reinforced drain seal is centered over the drain bolts. Working from the drain to the walls, carefully tuck the membrane tightly into each corner, folding the extra material into triangular flaps.

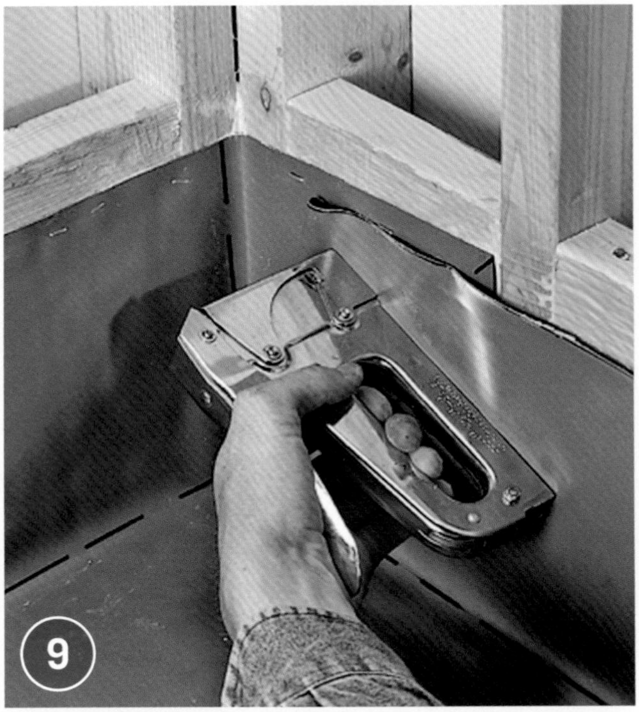

Apply CPE solvent glue to one side, press the flap flat, then staple it in place. Staple only the top edge of the membrane to the blocking; do not staple below the top of the curb or on the curb itself.

At the shower curb, cut the membrane along the studs so it can be folded over the curb. Solvent-glue a dam corner at each inside corner of the curb. Do not fasten the dam corners with staples.

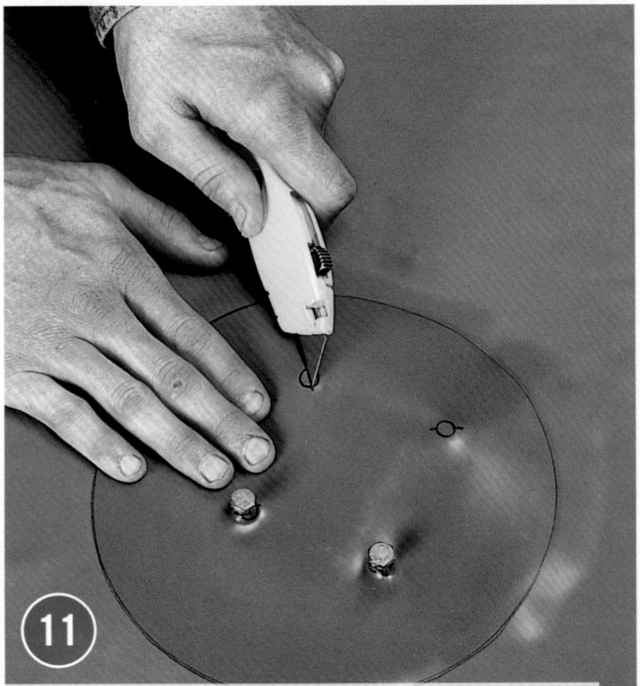

At the reinforced drain seal on the membrane, locate and mark the drain bolts. Press the membrane down around the bolts, then use a utility knife to carefully cut a slit just large enough for the bolts to poke through. Push the membrane down over the bolts.

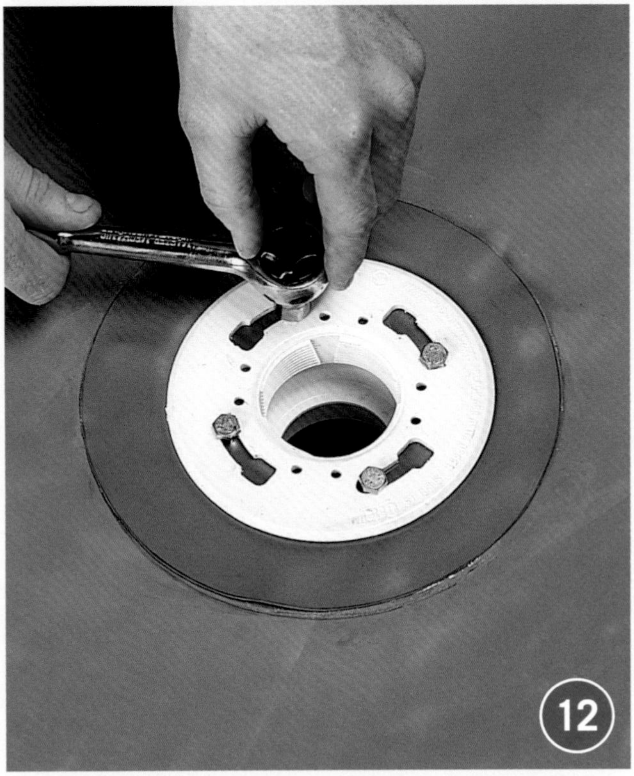

Use a utility knife to carefully cut away only enough of the membrane to expose the drain and allow the middle drain piece to fit in place. Remove the drain bolts, then position the middle drain piece over the bolt holes. Reinstall the bolts, tightening them evenly and firmly to create a watertight seal. *(continued)*

Test the shower pan for leaks overnight. Place a balloon tester in the drain below the weep holes, and fill the pan with water to 1" below the top of the curb. Mark the water level and let the water sit overnight. If the water level remains the same, the pan holds water. If the level is lower, locate and fix leaks in the pan using patches of membrane and CPE solvent.

Install cementboard on the alcove walls, using ¼" wood shims to lift the bottom edge off the CPE membrane. To prevent puncturing the membrane, do not use fasteners in the lower 8" of the cementboard. Cut a piece of metal lath to fit around the three sides of the curb. Bend the lath so it tightly conforms to the curb. Pressing the lath against the top of the curb, staple it to the outside face of the curb. Mix enough mortar for the two sides of the curb.

Overhang the front edge of the curb with a straight 1× board, so it is flush with the outer wall material. Apply mortar to the mesh with a trowel, building to the edge of the board. Clear away excess mortar, then use a torpedo level to check for plumb, making adjustments as needed. Repeat for the inside face of the curb. Allow the mortar to cure overnight.

NOTE: The top of the curb will be finished after tile is installed (step 19).

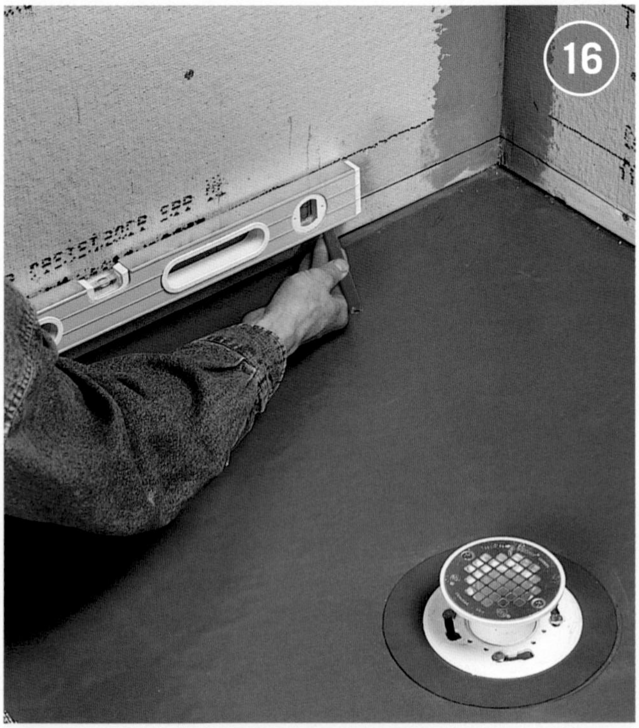

Attach the drain strainer piece to the drain, adjusting it to a minimum of 1½" above the shower pan. On one wall, mark 1½" up from the shower pan, then use a level to draw a reference line around the perimeter of the shower base. Because the prepan establishes the ¼" per foot slope, this measurement will maintain that slope.

Spread tile spacers over the weep holes of the drain to prevent mortar from plugging the holes. Mix the floor mortar, then build up the shower floor to roughly half the thickness of the base. Cut metal lath to cover the mortar bed, keeping it ½" from the drain (see photo in step 18).

Continue to add mortar, building the floor to the reference line on the walls. Use a level to check the slope, and pack mortar into low spots with a trowel. Leave space at the drain for the thickness of the tile. Float the surface using a wood float until it is smooth and slopes evenly to the drain. When finished, allow the mortar to cure overnight before installing the tiles.

After the floor has cured, draw reference lines and establish the tile layout, then mix a batch of thinset mortar and install the floor tile. At the curb, cut the tiles for the inside to protrude ½" above the unfinished top of the curb and the tiles for the outside to protrude ⅝" above the top, establishing a ⅛" slope so water drains back into the shower. Use a level to check the tops of the tiles for level as you work.

Mix enough floor mortar to cover the unfinished top of the curb, then pack it in place between the tiles using a trowel. Screed off the excess mortar flush with the tops of the side tiles. Allow the mortar to cure, then install bullnose cap tile. Install the wall tile, then grout, clean, and seal all the tile. After the grout has cured fully, run a bead of silicone caulk around all inside corners to create control joints.

Wet Rooms & Curbless Showers

Wet rooms—bathrooms in which all surfaces are waterproof—have long been a popular choice for upscale remodeling projects and new construction in the United Kingdom. But now, thanks to the increasing focus on universal design and an ongoing desire for sophisticated bathroom looks, wet rooms are becoming a popular option for American homeowners.

The idea behind a wet room is that moisture doesn't need to be contained in any single area of the room because the whole room is as waterproof as a shower stall. This alleviates the need for divider walls and enclosures, freeing up space and giving a wet room a seamless, streamlined look. Because of the space-saving aspects, wet rooms are particularly well suited for smaller bathrooms.

Installing a wet room involves laying down layers that work together to provide an impermeable barrier to water, a process called "tanking." That process is made easy with the use of special rubberized waterproof tape and waterproofing compound that is simply rolled onto wall and floor surfaces. Some companies even provide complete wet-room kits (see Resources, page 251). The finished surface can be traditional tile (the most common choice), solid panels such as the quartz composite surfaces used in contemporary vanity countertops, or sheet flooring, such as vinyl or linoleum.

In practice, the preliminary work is a lot like taping and skim-coating a newly drywalled room. The more challenging aspects of wet-room installation are making sure all the openings—from drains to water-supply inlets—are properly sealed with special membrane, and correctly sloping the floor to a central drain. Normally, a wet room floor is sloped from all four corners for this purpose, but you can opt for a sleeker look with the use of a concealed linear "trench" drain along one edge of the room. This type of drain requires that the floor be sloped in one direction only.

A curbless shower is a natural part of a wet room. A single wall-surface material is commonly used on all walls for ease of installation and to unify the look.

Regardless of the drain used, wet rooms normally include a curbless shower, because there is no need to contain runoff water. Curbless showers present a sleek and sophisticated look, which is why homeowners are choosing to include them in many different bathrooms—including those that are not true wet rooms. Properly installed within an enclosure, a curbless shower can serve a traditional bathroom every bit as well as a raised-pan shower would.

Installing a curbless shower has become a feasible project for even modestly skilled home DIYers thanks to well-thought-out kits that include all the materials you'll need (see page 94). Wet rooms, on the other hand, usually require professional installation to ensure that the leaks never become a problem and all applicable building codes are met.

TYPICAL WET-ROOM CONSTRUCTION

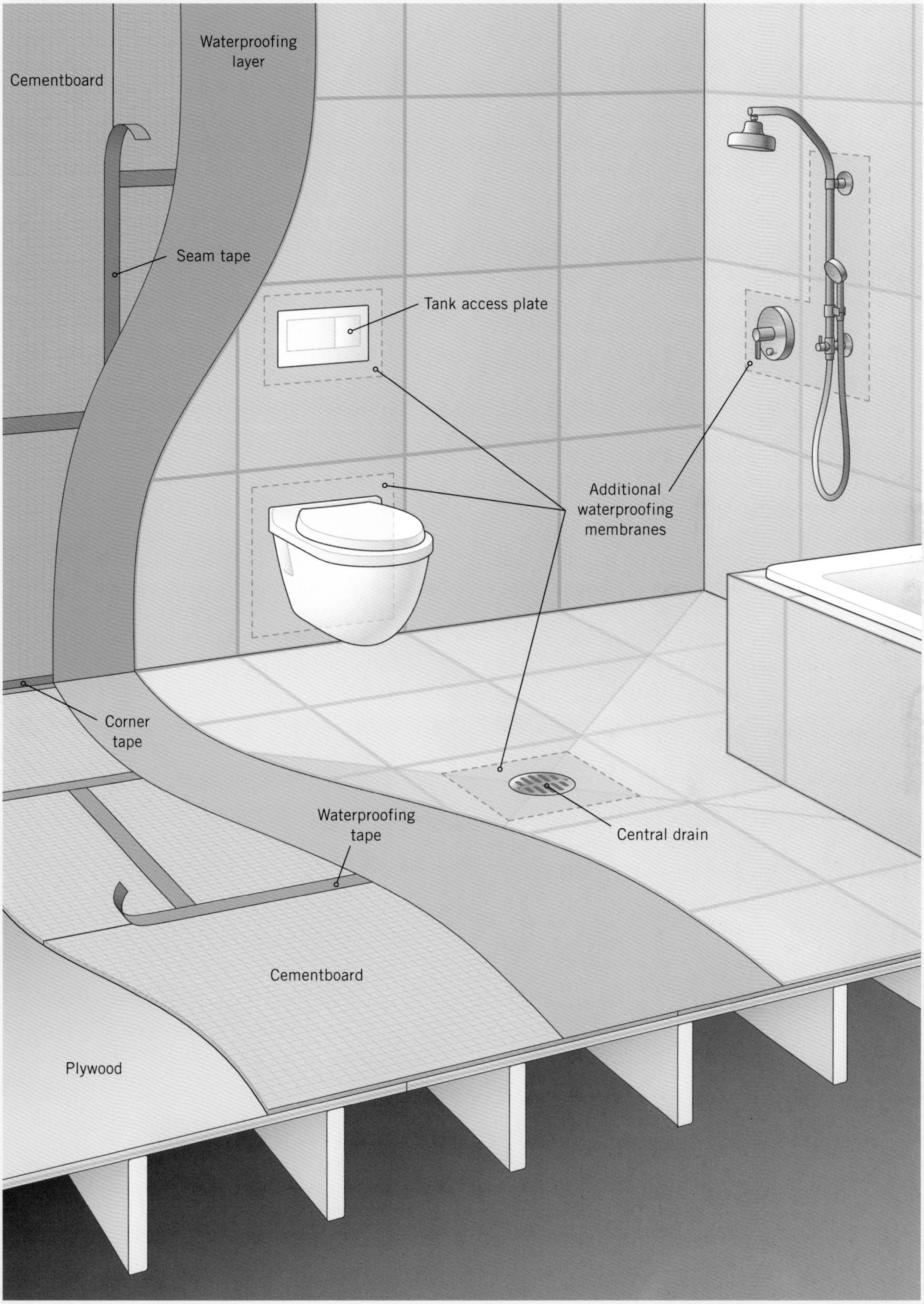

Installing a Curbless Shower

Whether it's part of a complete wet room or installed as a standalone feature, a curbless shower combines easy access for those with limited mobility, convenience for other users, and a look that is trendy, sophisticated, and attractive. The trick to installing one of these water features is to ensure the moisture stays inside the shower.

Once upon a time, creating a reliably waterproof enclosure for a curbless shower was no small chore. It meant putting a lot of work into creating a custom shower pan. This kind of project was usually above the skill level or desire of the weekend DIYer, and it generally meant hiring a contractor.

Now you can buy curbless shower-pan kits that make installation a breeze. The manufacturers have thought through all the issues that can arise and have developed the kits and shower pans to be as foolproof as possible, while also meeting prevailing codes and best standards and practices. Installing a curbless shower using one of these kits is a realistic project for any home handyperson with even moderate DIY skills and a weekend to spare.

These pans come with preconfigured slopes to ensure optimal drainage away from the shower's edges. The product we used for this project, the Tuff Form kit from Access Reliability Center (See Resources, page 251), includes an offset drain hole that offers the option of rotating the pan in the event of a joist or mechanicals that are in the way. This product is offered in nine different sizes and can be cut with a circular saw to just about any shape—including more unusual, curvy shapes for a truly custom look.

Curbless shower-pan manufacturers also sell pans with trench drains for an even sleeker look. The pan we used for this project is typical of the prefab curbless pan construction; it can support 1,100 pounds even though the pan itself weighs less than 70 pounds. It sits right on floor joists, with the addition of blocking to support the area around the drain, and to provide nailing surfaces around the edges.

Kits like these offer advantages beyond the ease of installation and a thoughtful configuration of parts. Usually, the plumbing can be completely adjusted and connected from above, so you won't need to work in the basement or a crawl space, or open up a first-floor ceiling to install a second-floor shower. The kits themselves generally include almost everything you'll need for the installation.

TOOLS & MATERIALS

- Curbless shower kit
- Circular saw
- Jigsaw or handsaw
- Caulk gun
- Torpedo level
- Cordless drill and bits
- PVC cement and brush
- Screwdriver
- Speed square
- Putty knife
- Palm sander and 120-grit pad
- Scissors
- Rubber gloves
- Synthetic paintbrush
- Roller and roller handle
- Caulk/construction adhesive
- Blocking
- Sealant
- Waterproofing tape
- Membrane
- Ear and eye protection
- Work gloves

A curbless shower kit includes almost everything you need. All you have to supply are some basic tools, the tile, and a little elbow grease.

WET ROOMS AND UNIVERSAL DESIGN

Because a wet room allows the bathroom to be designed with fewer barriers and a single-level floor surface, these rooms are natural partners to a universal design approach. If you're thinking about converting a bathroom to a wet room, it's worthwhile to consider a little extra effort to make the space as accessible as possible for the maximum number of users.

Walls. Where codes allow it, consider using thick plywood rather than cementboard for the wall subsurfaces. Plywood allows for direct installation of grab bars without the need for blocking or locating studs. If you're set on using cementboard, plan out locations for grab bars near toilets, behind and alongside bathtubs, and in showers. Most codes specify that grab bars must be able to support up to 200 pounds—which usually means adding blocking in the walls behind the grab bars.

Shower stall. One of the benefits to adding a curbless shower is easy wheelchair (or walker) access. For maximum accessibility, the shower area should be at least 60" wide by at least 36" deep (60" by 60" is preferable). This allows a wheelchair user to occupy the stall with a helper. And, although the idea is a wide-open shower space, it's always a good idea to add a fold-down seat. This allows for transfer from a wheelchair or a place for someone with limited leg strength and endurance to sit.

How to Install a Waterproof Sub-Base for a Curbless Shower

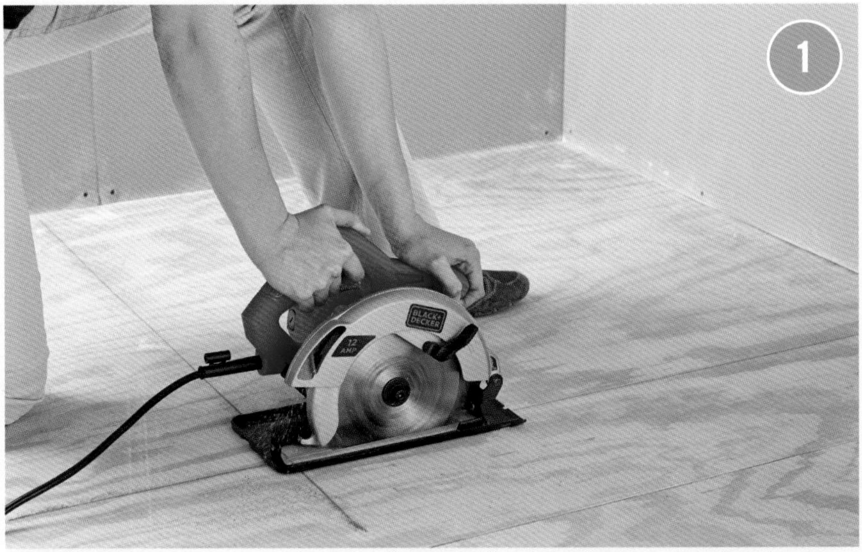

Remove the existing flooring material in the area of the shower pan (if you're remodeling an existing bathroom). Use a circular saw to cut out and remove the subfloor in the exact dimensions of the shower pan. Finish the cuts with a jigsaw or handsaw.

Reinforce the floor with blocking between joists as necessary. Toenail bridge blocking in on either side of the drain waste-pipe location, and between joists anywhere you'll need a nailing surface along the edges of the shower pan. If trusses or joists are spaced more than 16" on center, add bridge blocking to adequately support the pan.

(continued)

Set the pan in the opening to make sure it fits and is level. If it is not level, screw shims to the tops of any low joists and check again; repeat if necessary until the pan is perfectly level in all directions.

Install or relocate drain pipes as needed. Check with your local building department: if the drain and trap are not accessible from below you may need to have an onsite inspection before you cover up the plumbing.

Check the height of the drain pipe. Its top should be exactly 2⅜" from the bottom of the pan—measure down from the top of the joist. If the drain pipe is too high, remove it and trim with a tubing cutter. If it is too low, replace the assembly with a new assembly that has a longer tailpiece.

Lay a thick bead of construction adhesive along the contact areas on all joists, nailing surfaces, and blocking.

Set the pan in place and screw it down using at least 2 screws along each side. Do not overtighten the screws. If you've cut off the screwing flange on one or more sides to accommodate an unusual shape, drill ⅛" pilot holes in the cut edges at joist or blocking locations and drive the screws through the holes.

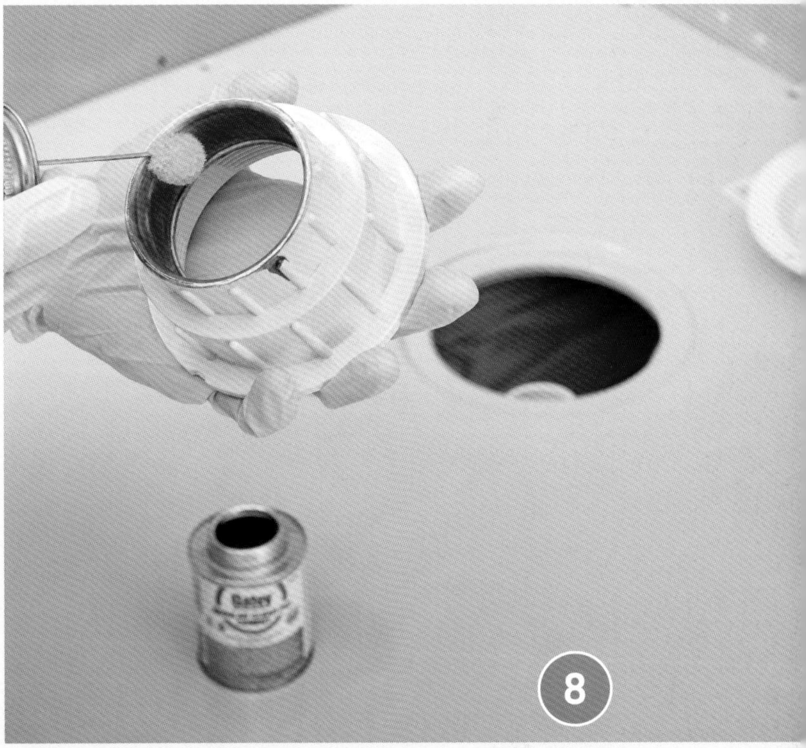

Disassemble the supplied drain assembly. Be careful not to lose any of the screws. Place the drain tailpiece on the waste pipe under where the pan's drainhole will be located and measure to check that it sits at the correct level. Solvent-glue the tailpiece to the end of the waste pipe.

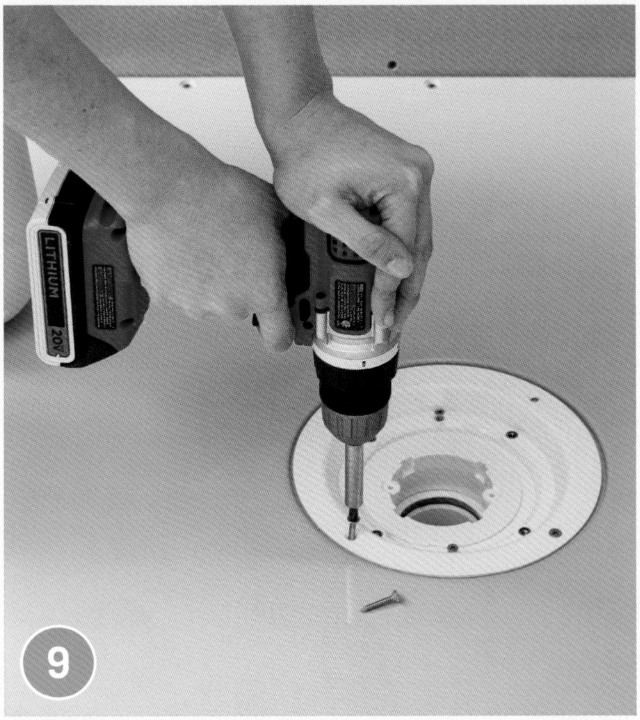

Position the supplied gaskets on top of the tailpiece (check the manufacturer's instructions; the gaskets usually need to be layered in the correct order). Set the drain flange piece on top of the tail and into the drain hole in the pan. Drill ⅛" pilot holes through the flange and into the pan. Screw the flange to the pan.

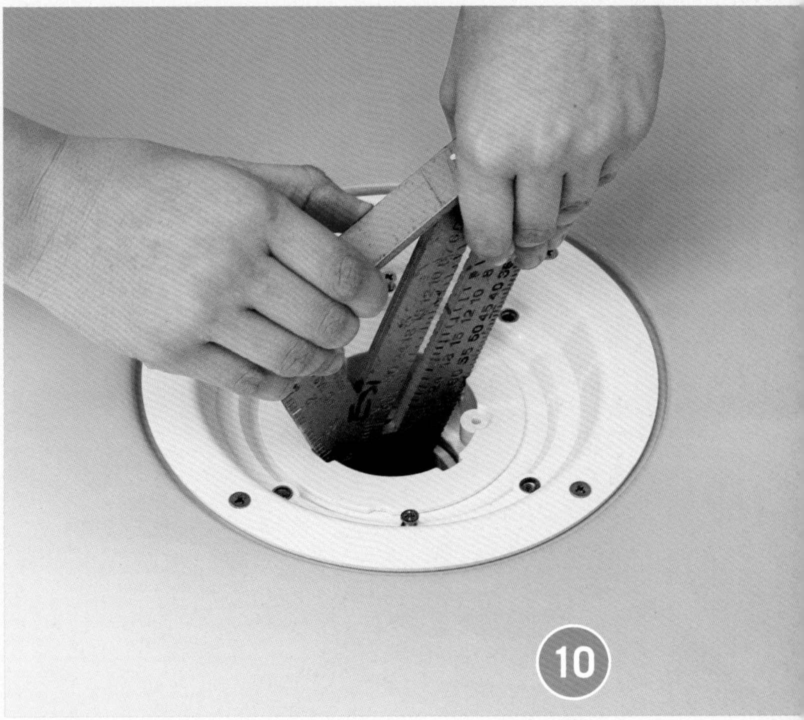

Thread the tail top piece into the tail through the drain flange. Use a speed square or other lever, such as spread-channel lock pliers, to snugly tighten the tail top piece in place.

(continued)

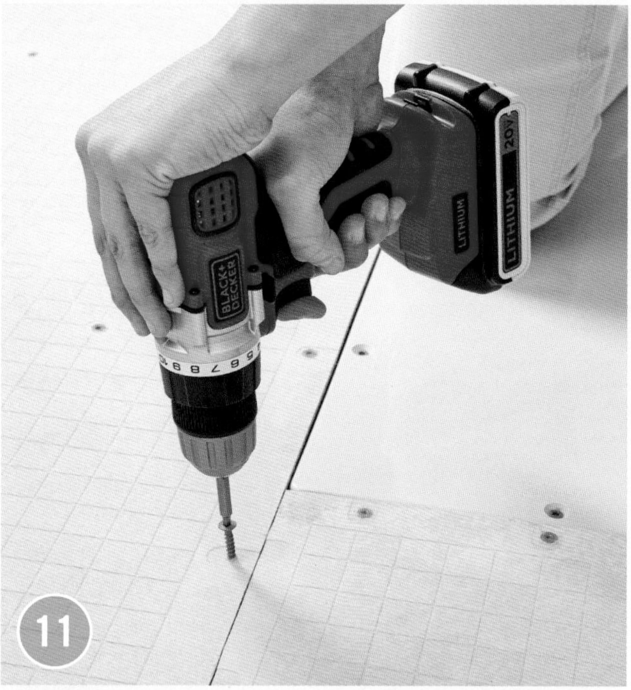

Install tile underlayment for the rest of the project area. If the underlayment is higher than the top of the pan once it is installed, you'll have to sand it to level, gradually tapering away from the pan.

Scrape any stickers or other blemishes off the pan with a putty knife. Lightly sand the entire surface of the pan using 120-grit sandpaper to help the sealant adhere. After you're done sanding, wipe down the sanded pan with a damp sponge. Make sure the entire area is clean.

Seal the edge seams at the wall and between the pan and subfloor with waterproof latex sealant. Caulk any pan screw holes that were not used.

Cut strips of waterproofing tape to cover all seams in the tile underlayment (both walls and floor). Also cut strips for the joints where walls and floor meet. Open the pail of liquid waterproofing membrane and mix the liquid thoroughly. Beginning at the top and working down, brush a bed of waterproofing liquid over the seams. Before it dries, set the tape firmly into the waterproofing. Press and smooth the tape. Then brush a layer of waterproofing compound over the tape.

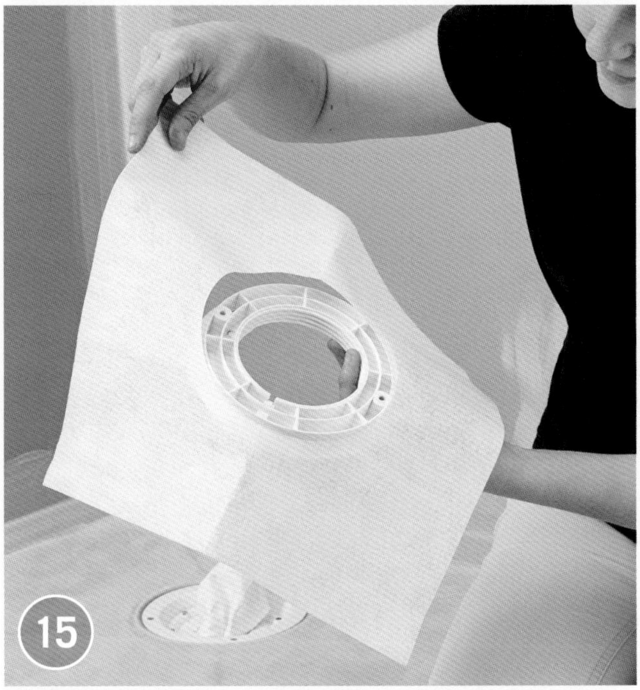

Trace a hole in the center of the waterproof drain gasket using the bottom of the drain clamping donut. Cut the hole out using scissors. Be careful cutting the gasket because it is a crucial part of the drain waterproofing. Check the fit with the gasket against the underside of the clamping donut top flange.

Apply a thin coat of the waterproofing compound around the drain hole and to the back of the drain gasket. Don't apply too much; if the waterproofing is too thick under the gasket, it may not dry correctly.

Put the gasket in place and brush a coat of the waterproofing over the gasket. Screw the clamping donut in place on the top of the drain and over the membrane. Hand-tighten the bolts and then cover the clamping donut with the waterproofing compound (avoid covering the slide lock for the drain grate).

Use a roller to roll waterproofing compound across the walls and over the entire pan surface. The ideal is 4mm thick (about the thickness of a credit card). Allow this first coat to dry for 2 hours, then cover with a second coat. This should conclude the waterproofing phase of the project, and you're ready to begin laying tile once the waterproofing compound has dried thoroughly.

How to Install Tile for a Curbless Shower

TOOLS & MATERIALS

Ear and eye protection
Work gloves
Tile
Spacers
Thinset tile adhesive
Trowel
Pencil
Tile saw or nippers
Grout
Towel
Sponge

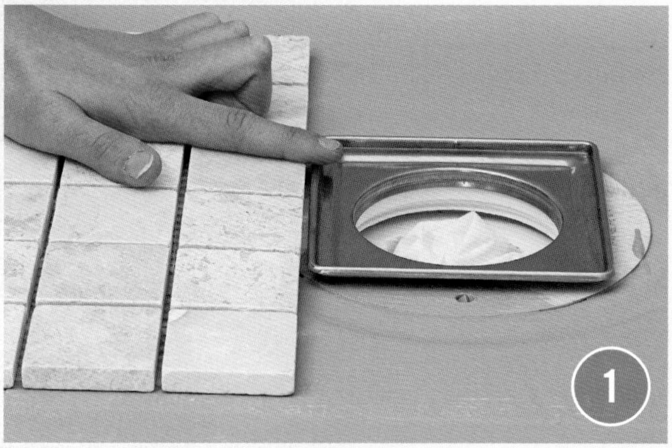

Set the floor tile first. Begin by placing a sample of the floor tile directly next to the drain so you can set the drain grate height to match. The adjustable mounting plate for the grate should be flush with the tops of the tile.

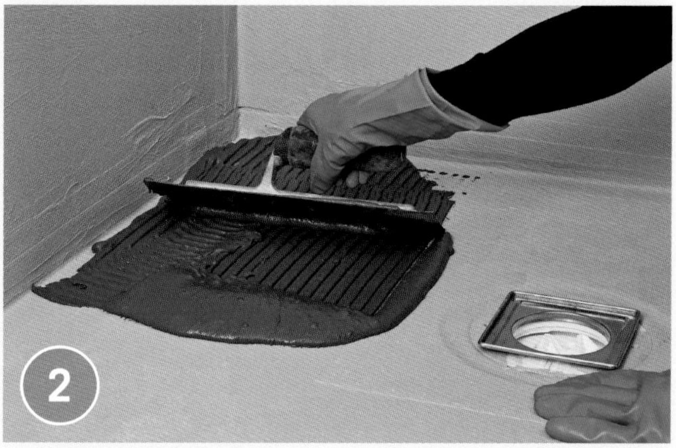

Begin laying floor tile in the corner of the shower. Lay a bed of thinset tile adhesive, using a notched trowel. The thinset container should specify the notch size (⅜" square notch is common).

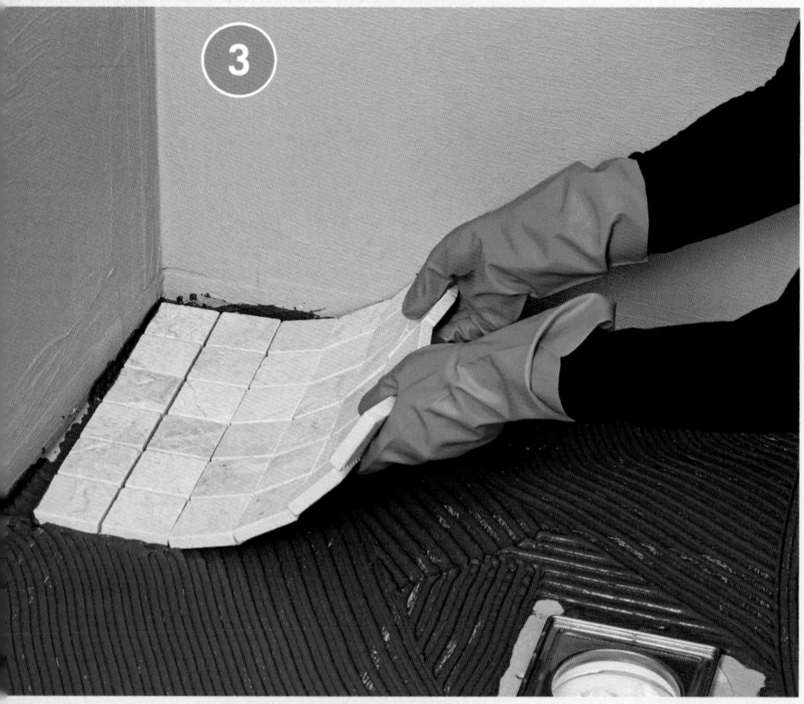

Place the corner tile into the bed of thinset and press it to set it. Don't press down too hard or you will displace too much of the material. Continue laying tile, fanning out from the corner toward the drain opening. Leave space around the drain opening as it is likely you'll need to cut tiles to fit.

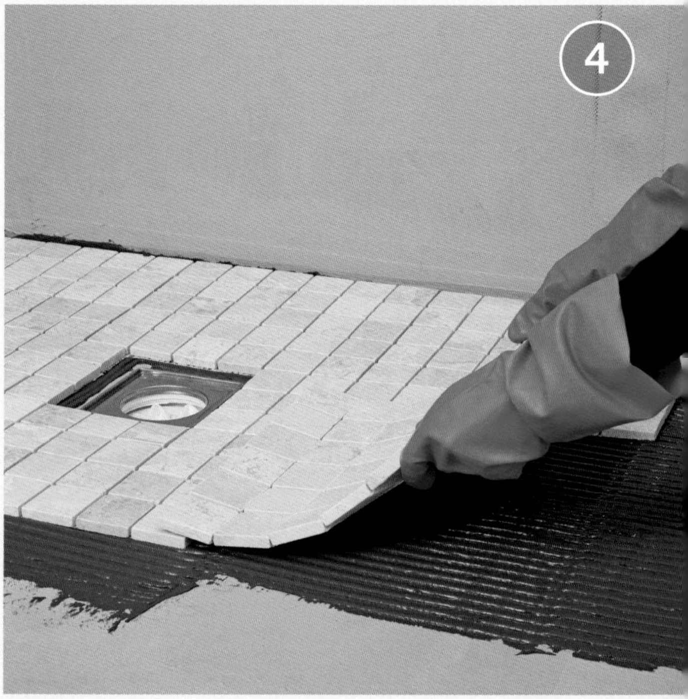

Install tile so a small square of untiled area is left around the drain opening (which, in the system seen here, is square, making for an easier cutting job).

Mark the tiles that surround the drain opening for cutting. Leave a small gap between the tiles next to the drain-grate mounting plate.

Cut the tiles along the trim lines using a tile saw. If you are not comfortable using a tile saw, score the tiles and cut them with tile nippers.

Apply thinset onto the shower pan, taking care not to get any on the drain-grate mounting plate. You may need to use a small trowel or a putty knife to get into small gaps.

Set the cut tiles around the drain opening, doing your best to maintain even gaps that match the gaps in the rest of the floor. Once you've finished tiling around the drain, finish setting floor tile in the rest of the project area. *(continued)*

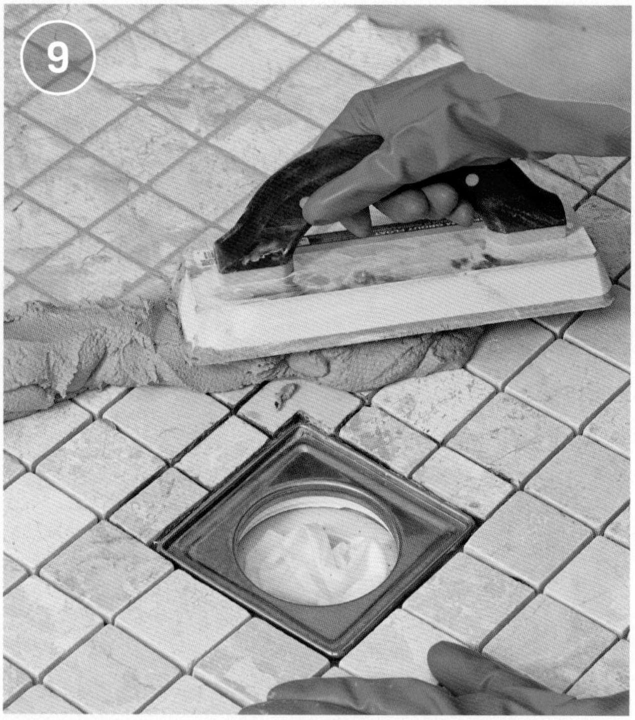

Let the floor tile set overnight and then apply grout. Using a grout sponge, wipe the grout over the gaps so all gaps are filled evenly. After the grout dries, buff the floor with a towel to wipe up excess residue.

Snap the grate cover into the cover mounting plate (if you've stuffed a rag into the drain opening to keep debris out, be sure to remove it first). The grate cover seen here locks in with a small key that should be saved in case you need to remove the grate cover.

Begin setting the wall tile. Generally, it's easiest if you start at the bottom and work upward. Instead of thinset adhesive, an adhesive mat is being used here. This relatively new product is designed for walls and is rated for waterproof applications. It is a good idea to use a spacer (¼" thick or so) to get an even border at the bottoms of the first tiles.

In the design used here, a border of the same mosaic tile used in the floor is installed all around the shower area to make the first course. Dark-brown accent tiles are installed in a single vertical column running upward, centered on the line formed by the shower faucet and showerhead. This vertical column is installed after the bottom border.

Next, another vertical column of accent tiles is installed on each side of the large, dark tiles. These columns are also laid using the floor tile, which connects the walls and floor visually in an effective way.

Finally, larger field tiles that match the floor tile used outside the shower area are installed up to the corner and outward from the shower area. Starting at the bottom, set a thin spacer on top of the border tiles to ensure even gaps.

Grout the gaps in the wall tiles. It's usually a good idea to protect any fittings, such as the shower faucet handle escutcheon, with painter's tape prior to grouting. If you wish, a clear surround may be installed to visually define the shower area, as in the photo to the right, but because the shower pan is pitched toward the drain it really is not necessary.

Alcove Bathtubs

TOOLS & MATERIALS

- Channel-type pliers
- Hacksaw
- Carpenter's level
- Pencil
- Tape measure
- Saw
- Screwdriver
- Drill
- Adjustable wrench
- Trowel
- Shims
- Galvanized deck screws
- Drain-waste-overflow kit
- 1 × 3, 1 × 4, and 2 × 4 lumber
- Galvanized roofing nails
- Galvanized roof flashing
- Thinset mortar
- Tub and tile caulk
- Propane torch
- Eye and ear protection
- Work gloves

Most homes are equipped with an alcove tub that includes a tub surround and shower. By combining the tub and the shower in one fixture, you conserve precious bathroom floor space and simplify the initial installation. Plus, you only have one bathing fixture that needs cleaning.

But because tub-showers are so efficient, they do get a lot of use and tend to have fairly limited lifespans. The fact that the most inexpensive tubs on the market are designed for alcove use also reduces the average lifespan. Pressed-steel tubs have enamel finishes that crack and craze; plastic and fiberglass tubs get grimy and stained; and even acrylic and composite tubs show wear eventually (and as with other fixtures, styles and colors change too).

Plumbing an alcove tub is a relatively difficult job because getting access to the drain lines attached to the tub and into the floor is often very awkward. Although an access panel is required by most codes, the truth is that many tubs were installed without them or with panels that are too small or hard to reach to be of much use. If you are contemplating replacing your tub, the first step in the decision process should be to find the access panel and determine if it is sufficient. If it is not (or there is no panel at all), consider how you might enlarge it. Often, this means cutting a hole in the wall on the adjoining room and also in the ceiling below. This creates more work, of course, but compared to the damage caused by a leaky drain from a subpar installation, making an access opening is little inconvenience.

A tub alcove is sized to accept a standard bathtub, usually 5' long in most of North America. A tub with an apron is typical, but you can build out the front instead if you choose.

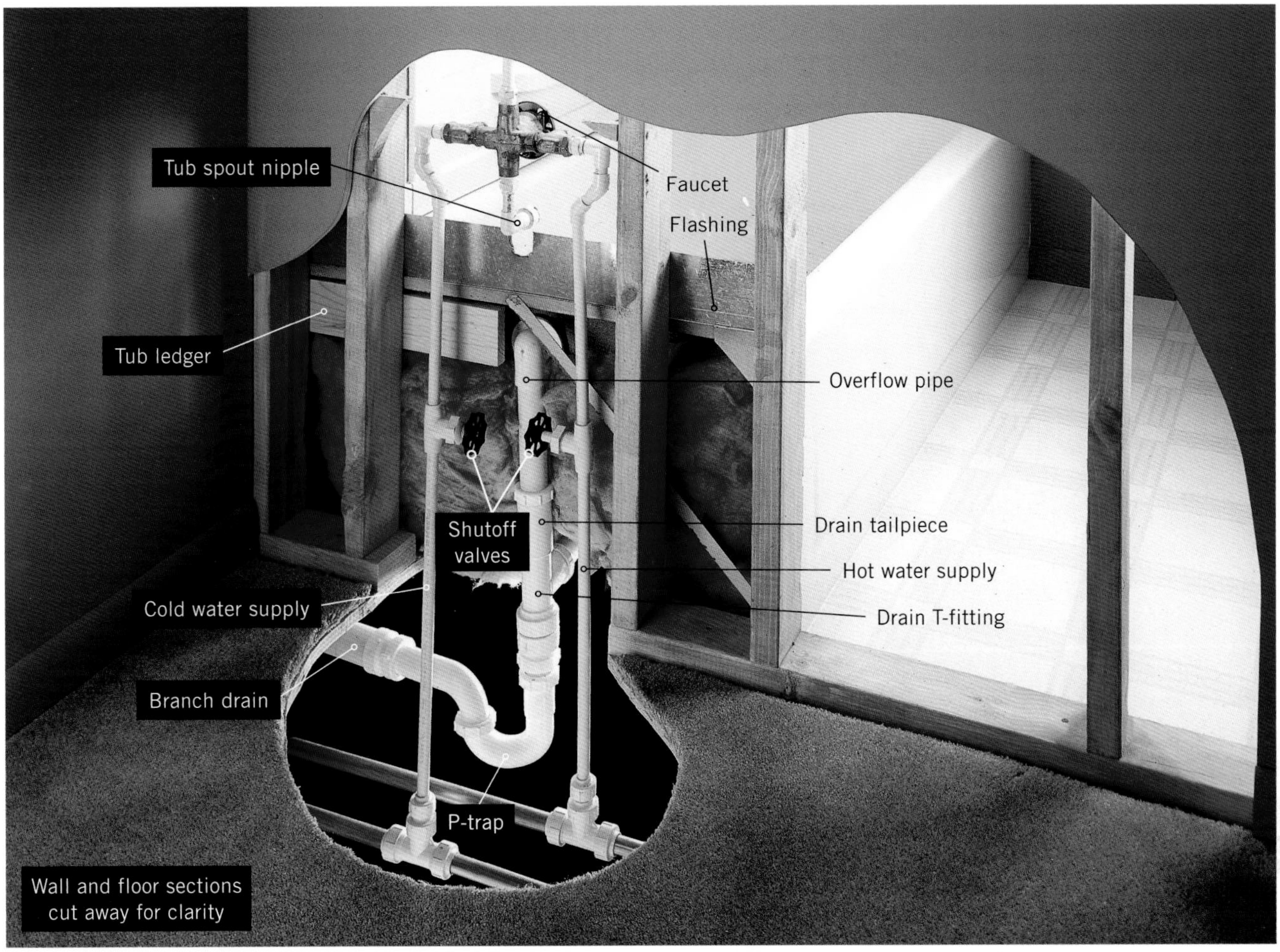

The plumbing for a bathtub includes hot and cold supply pipes, shutoff valves, a faucet, and a spout. Supply connections can be made before or after the tub is installed. The drain-waste-overflow system for a bathtub includes the overflow pipe, drain T-fitting, P-trap, and branch drain. The overflow pipe assembly is attached to the tub before installation.

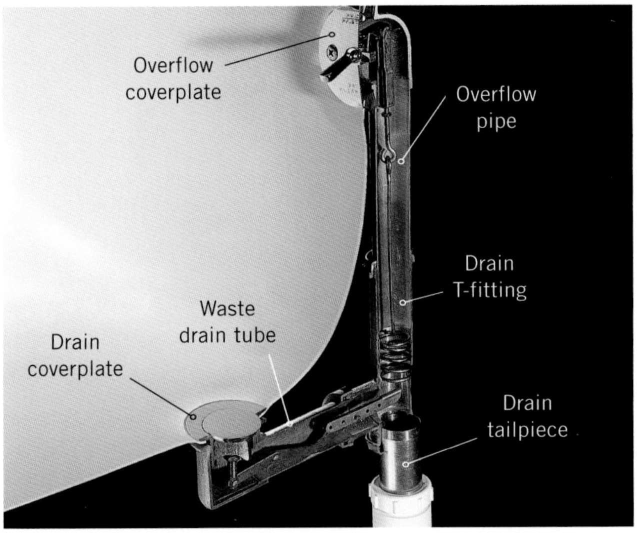

A drain-waste-overflow kit with a stopper mechanism must be attached to the tub before it is installed. Available in both brass and plastic types, most kits include an overflow coverplate, a height-adjustable overflow pipe, a drain T-fitting and tailpiece, a waste drain tube, and a drain coverplate that screws into the drain tube.

Add fiberglass insulation around the body of a steel bathtub to reduce noise and conserve heat. Before setting the tub in position, wrap unfaced batting around the tub and secure it with string or twine. For showers, deck-mounted whirlpools, and saunas, insulate between the framing members.

How to Install a New Alcove Tub

Prepare for the new tub. Inspect and remove old or deteriorated wall surfaces or framing members in the tub area. With today's mold-resistant wallboard products, it makes extra sense to go ahead and strip off the old alcove wall coverings and ceiling down to the studs so you can replace them. This also allows you to inspect for hidden damage in the wall and ceiling cavities.

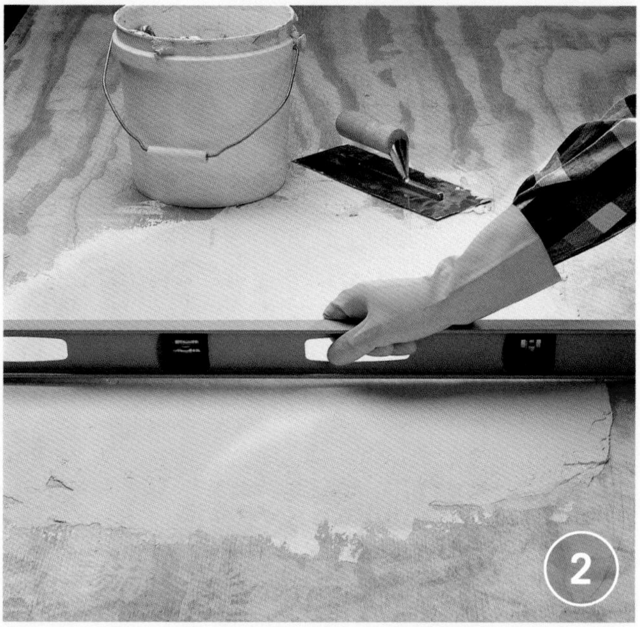

Check the subfloor for level—if it is not level, use pour-on floor leveler compound to correct it (ask at your local home center). Make sure the supply and drain pipes and the shutoff valves are in good repair and correct any problems you encounter. If you have no bath fan in the alcove, now is the perfect time to add one.

Check the height of the crossbraces for the faucet body and the showerhead. If your family members needed to stoop to use the old shower, consider raising the brace for the showerhead. Read the instructions for your new faucet/diverter and check to see that the brace for the faucet body will conform to the requirements (this includes distance from the surround wall as well as height). Adjust the brace locations as needed.

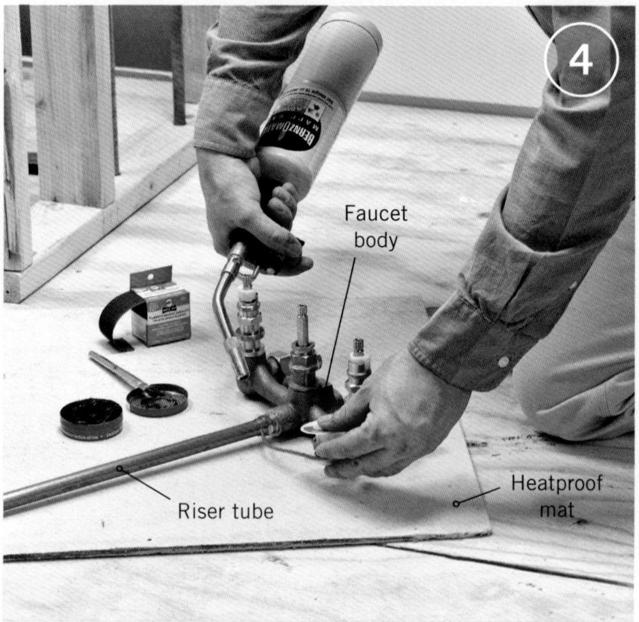

Begin by installing the new water-supply plumbing. Measure to determine the required height of your shower-riser tube and cut it to length. Attach the bottom of the riser to the faucet body and the top to the shower elbow.

Attach the faucet body to the crossbrace with pipe-hanger straps. Then, attach supply tubing from the stop valves to the faucet body, making sure to attach the hot water to the left port and cold to the right port. Also secure the shower elbow to its crossbrace with a pipe strap. Do not attach the shower arm yet.

Slide the bathtub into the alcove. Make sure the tub is flat on the floor and pressed flush against the back wall. If your tub did not come with a tub protector, cut a piece of cardboard to line the tub bottom, and tape pieces of cardboard around the rim to protect the finish from damage.

Mark locations for ledger boards. To do this, trace the height of the top of the tub's nailing flange onto the wall studs in the alcove. Then remove the tub and measure the height of the nailing flange. Measure down this same amount from your flange lines and mark new ledger-board locations.

Install 1 × 4 ledger boards. Drive two or three 3" galvanized deck screws through the ledger board at each stud. All three walls should receive a ledger. Leave an open space in the wet wall to allow clearance for the drain-waste-overflow (DWO) kit.

(continued)

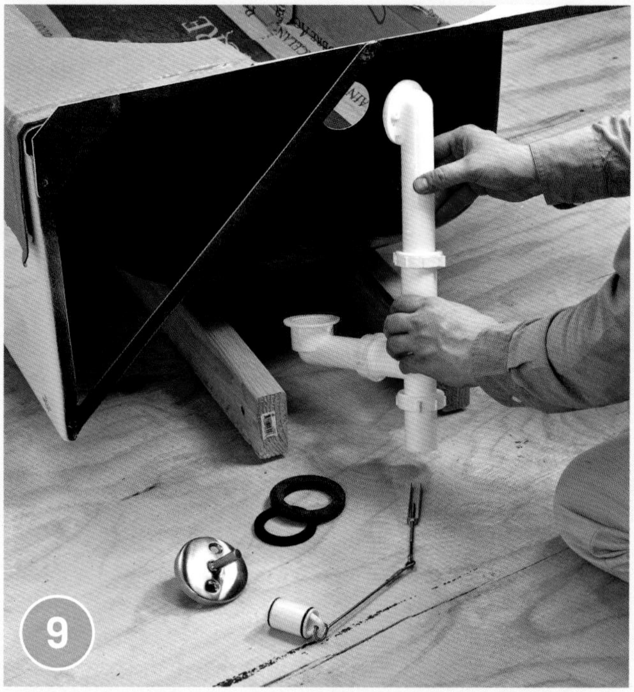

Install the drain-waste-overflow (DWO) pipes before you install the tub. Make sure to get a good seal on the slip nuts at the pipe joints. Follow the manufacturer's instructions to make sure the pop-up drain linkage is connected properly. Make sure rubber gaskets are positioned correctly at the openings on the outside of the tub.

Thread the male-threaded drain strainer into the female-threaded drain-waste elbow. Wrap a coil of plumber's putty around the drain outlet underneath the plug rim first. Hand-tighten only.

Attach the overflow coverplate, making sure the pop-up drain controls are in the correct position. Tighten the mounting screws that connect to the mounting plate to sandwich the rubber gasket snugly between the overflow pipe flange and the tub wall. Then, finish tightening the drain strainer against the waste elbow by inserting the handle of a pair of pliers into the strainer body and turning.

Place the tub back into the alcove, taking care not to bump the DWO assembly and disturb the connections. You definitely will want a helper for this job. If the drain outlet of the DWO assembly is not directly over the drain pipe when the tub is in position, you'll need to remove it and adjust the drain line location.

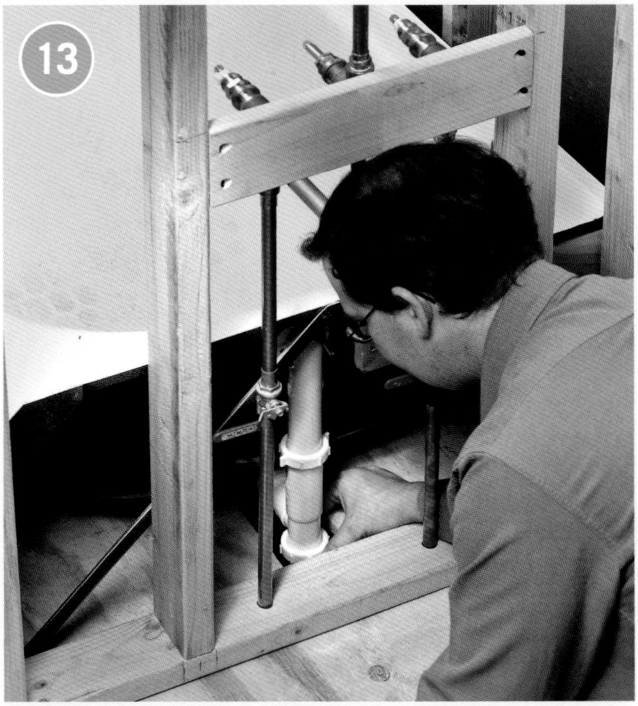

Attach the drain outlet from the DWO assembly to the drain P-trap. If your alcove walls are covered, you will appreciate that you spent the time to create a roomy access panel for the tub plumbing. Test the drain and overflow to make sure they don't leak. Also test the water-supply plumbing, temporarily attaching the handles, spout, and shower arm so you can operate the faucet and the diverter.

Drive a 1½" galvanized roofing nail at each stud location, just over the top of the tub's nailing flange (inset). The nail head should pin the flange to the stud. For extra protection against moisture penetration, nail strips of metal flashing to the studs so they cover the tub flange.

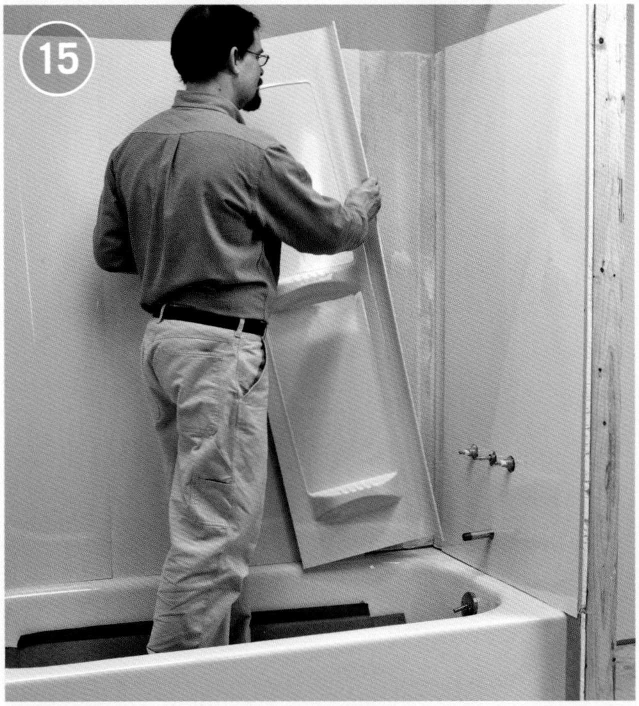

Install the wall coverings and tub surround (see pages 110 to 113 for a 3-piece surround installation). You can also make a custom surround from tileboard or cementboard and tile.

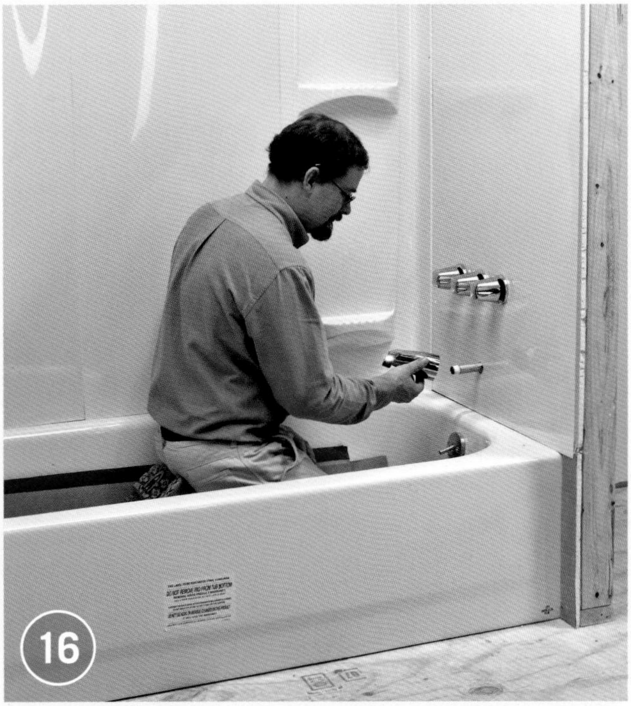

Install fittings. First, thread the shower arm into the shower elbow and attach the spout nipple to the valve assembly. Also attach the shower head and escutcheon, the faucet handle/diverter with escutcheon, and the tub spout. Use thread lubricant on all parts.

Three-Piece Tub Surrounds

No one wants bathroom fixtures that are aging or yellowed from years of use. A shiny new tub surround can add sparkle and freshness to your dream bath.

Tub surrounds come in many different styles, materials, and price ranges. Choose the features you want and measure your existing bathtub surround for sizing. Surrounds typically come in three or five pieces. A three-panel surround is being installed here, but the process is similar for five-panel systems.

Surface preparation is important for good glue adhesion. Plastic tiles and wallpaper must be removed and textured plaster must be sanded smooth. Surrounds can be installed over ceramic tile that is well attached and in good condition, but it must be sanded and primed. All surfaces must be primed with a water-based primer.

TOOLS & MATERIALS

- Jigsaw
- Hole saw
- Drill
- Measuring tape
- Level
- Caulk gun
- Caulk
- Adhesive
- Screwdriver
- Adjustable wrench
- Pry bar
- Hammer
- 3-piece tub surround
- Paint roller and sleeve (optional)
- Primer (optional)
- Ear and eye protection
- Work gloves

Three-piece tub surrounds are inexpensive and come in many colors and styles. The typical unit has two end panels and a back panel that overlap in the corners to form a watertight seal. They are formed from fiberglass, PVC, acrylic, or proprietary resin-based polymers. Five-piece versions are also available and typically have more features, such as integral soap shelves and even cabinets.

How to Install a Three-Piece Tub Surround

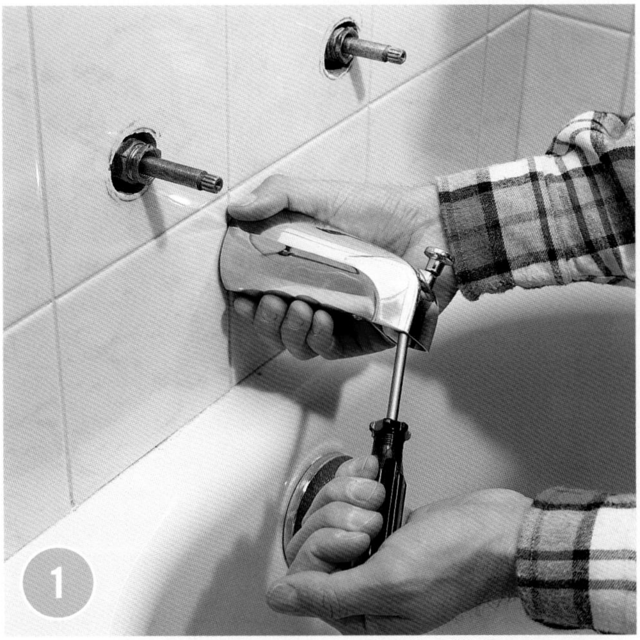

Remove the old plumbing fixtures and wall coverings in the tub area. In some cases you can attach surround panels to old tileboard or even tile, but it is generally best to remove the wall coverings down to the studs if you can, so you may inspect for leaks or damage.

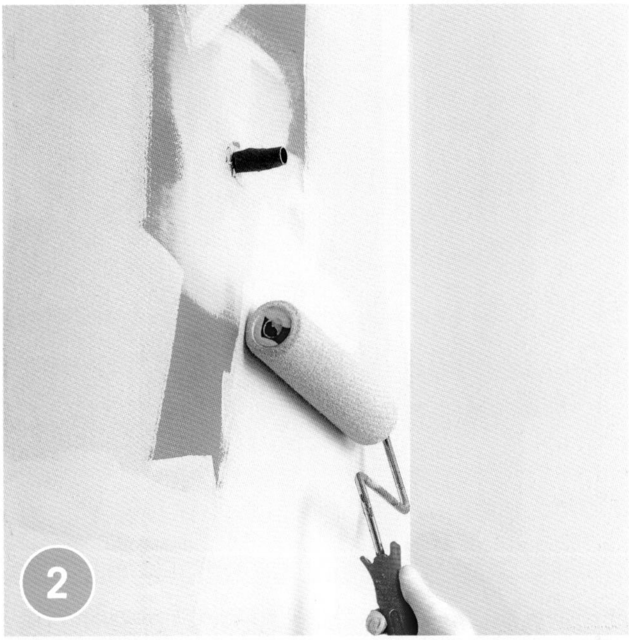

Replace the wall coverings with appropriate materials, such as water- and mold-resistant wallboard or cementboard (for ceramic-tile installations). Make sure the new wall surfaces are smooth and flat. Some surround-kit manufacturers recommend that you apply a coat of primer to sheet goods such as greenboard to create a better bonding surface for the panel adhesive.

Test-fit the panels before you start; the tub may have settled unevenly or the walls may be out of plumb. Check the manufacturer's directions for distinguishing right and left panels. Place a panel in position on the tub ledge. Use a level across the top of the panel to determine if it is level. Create a vertical reference line to mark the edge of the panel on the plumbing end.

TEST-FITTING

Ensure a perfect fit by taping the surround panels to the walls in the tub area. Make sure the tops are level when the overlap seams are aligned and that you have a consistent gap between the panel bottoms and the tub flange. Mark the panels for cutting if necessary and, once the panels have been removed, make any adjustments to the walls that are needed.

(continued)

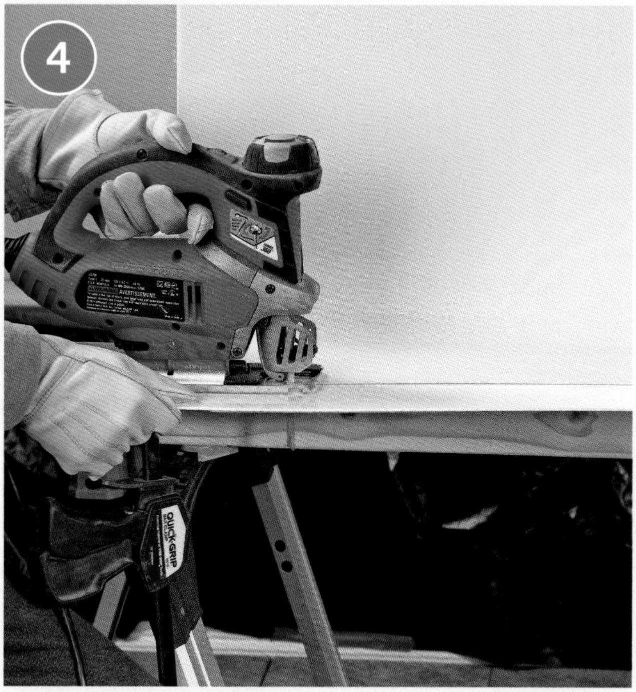

After performing the test fit, check the fitting instructions to see if you need to trim any of the pieces. Follow the manufacturer's instructions for cutting. Here, we had to cut the corner panels because the instructions advise not to overlap the back or side panel over the corner panels by more than 3". Cut panels using a jigsaw and a fine-tooth blade that is appropriate for cutting fiberglass or acrylic tileboard.

Lay out the locations of the faucets, spout, and shower arm. Measure in from the vertical reference line (made in step 3) and up from the top of the tub ledge. Remeasure for accuracy, as any cuts to the surround are final. Place the panel face-up on a sheet of plywood. Mark the location of the holes. Cut the holes ½" larger than the pipe diameter. If your faucet has a recessed trim plate, cut the hole to fit the recess. Using a hole saw or a jigsaw, cut out the plumbing access holes.

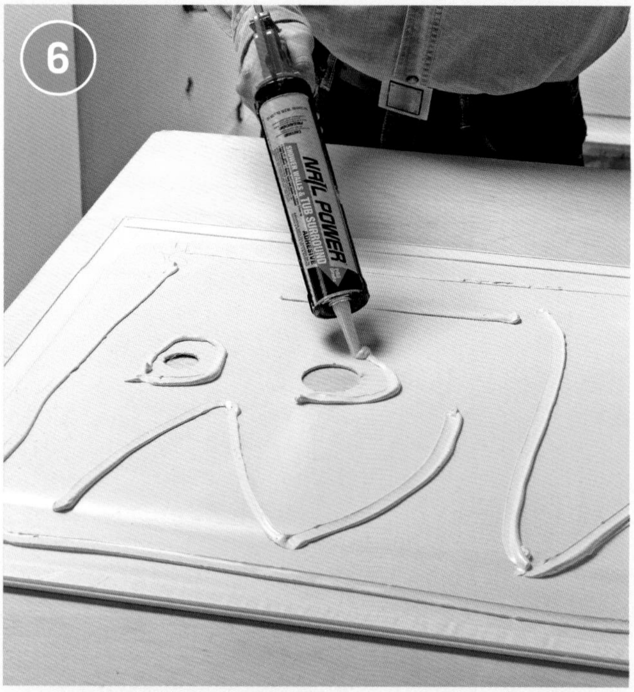

Apply the panel adhesive to the back of an end plumbing panel. Circle the plumbing outlet holes 1" from the edge. Follow the manufacturer's application pattern. Do not apply adhesive closer than 1" to the double-sided tape or the bottom edge of the panel.

Remove the protective backing from the tape. Carefully lift the panel by the edges and place against the corner and top of the tub ledge. Press firmly from top to bottom in the corner, then throughout the panel.

Test-fit the opposite end panel and make any necessary adjustments. Apply the adhesive, remove the protective backing from the tape, and put in place. Apply pressure to the corner first from top to bottom, and then apply pressure throughout.

Apply adhesive to the back panel following the manufacturer's instructions. Maintain a 1" space between adhesive tape and the bottom of the panel. Remove protective backing from the tape. Lift the panel by the edges and carefully center between the two end panels. When positioned, firmly press in place from top to bottom.

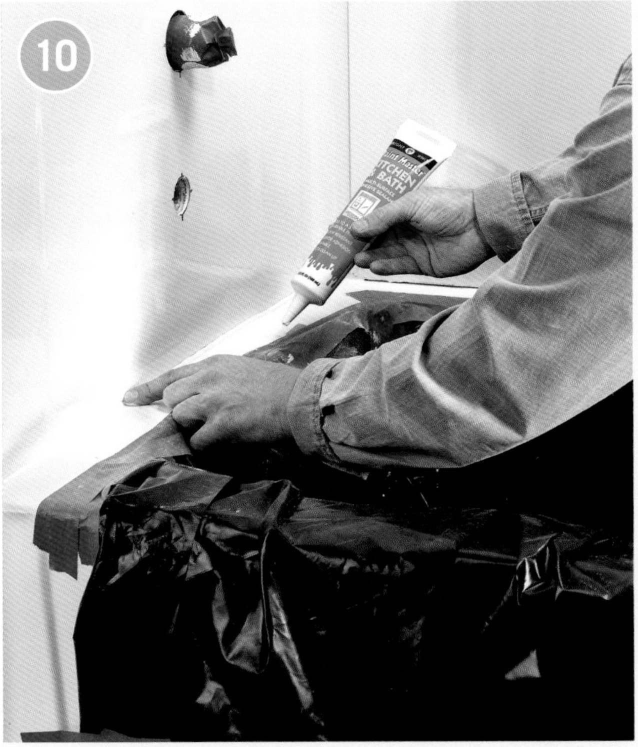

Apply caulk to the bottom and top edges of the panels and at panel joints. Dip your fingertip in water and use it to smooth the caulk to a uniform bead.

Apply silicone caulk to escutcheons or trim plates and reinstall them. Allow a minimum of 24 hours for caulk and adhesive to cure thoroughly before using the shower or tub.

Drop-In Tubs

Drop-in tubs are some of the most adaptable and interesting fixtures you can add to a bathroom. Not only does the interior size lend itself to a luxurious soaking experience, but many drop-in tubs are jetted because the supporting structure can easily make room for a pump, heater, water-supply lines, and electrical connections. Even a plain drop-in tub can serve the same role as a traditional Japanese soaking tub, helping melt your stresses and tensions away.

These tubs are manufactured with a lip, which is often embellished to become a decorative feature in and of itself. However, the supporting structure is the greater opportunity to make a big design statement.

Drop-in tubs are usually deep but not necessarily wide. That makes them ideal for the long, narrow spaces that are so common in home bathrooms. They are especially effective when placed under windows, as this one has been. This tub has been set into a modest platform, but the tub itself adds big luxury in what amounts to a small footprint.

TOOLS & MATERIALS

- Plumbing tools and supplies
- Tape measure
- Drill
- Hammer
- 4' level
- Utility knife
- 2 × 4 lumber
- 2" screws
- 1¼" cementboard screws
- Notched trowel
- Grout sponge
- CDX plywood
- Cementboard
- Hacksaw
- Circular saw
- Torpedo level
- Thinset mortar
- Silicone caulk
- Deck-mount faucet set
- Drop-in tub
- Tile mortar
- Tile grout
- Grout float
- Ceramic tile (field and bullnose)
- Plumb bob
- Framing square
- Drywall
- Rag
- Eye and ear protection
- Work gloves

Depending on the floor space you have available, you can isolate a drop-in tub platform in the middle of the room, like an island, or position it in the more common location, along a wall. In any case, the tops and sides are canvases for your creativity.

The supporting structure also serves a pragmatic purpose. The top surface is a place to put hair- and body-care products; rest a drink or two; sit candles for an evocative, restful spa experience; or just store extra towels.

The platform built for this project is 22 inches high with a 14-inch-wide ledge, which comfortably accommodates someone sitting around the tub. The tub itself is 24 inches high, with a 2-inch-high lip. If your tub features an undistinguished lip, you can always build your platform so that the lip sits flush with the top surface of the platform, but keep in mind that a pronounced lip keeps towels and other items from sliding into the water.

ACCESS PANELS

Making the supply and drain hookups on a bathtub usually requires access from below or behind the installation area. When installing a drop-in tub in a framed deck platform, you can gain access through the platform apron area, too. If you are hooking up the drain with a slip connection, the Universal Plumbing Code requires that you install a permanent access panel (see page 77) in the wall behind the tub or in the floor and ceiling below. But regardless of codes, you should make a point of creating permanent access to the plumbing hookups whenever possible. In the tub installation seen here, a removable access panel on the opposite side of the wet wall provides access to both the drain and supply hookups. This allows the platform deck and apron to be tiled in a contiguous manner. Because the faucet plumbing is readily accessible, each supply tube is connected to a shutoff valve next to the fixture and supply risers are used to bring water to the faucet valve.

How to Install a Drop-In Tub with Platform

Place the tub in position on the subfloor. The tub should be 14½" from the two corner walls, measured from the underside of the tub lip—where the inside edge of the platform deck will run—to the wall studs. This allows for a ½"-thick wall surface. Shim as necessary to level the tub both ways, or adjust self-leveling feet if tub has them. Hang a plumb bob from the underside of the lip at each corner of tub and mark the subfloor. Check that marks on adjacent corners are the same distance from the wall.

Measure from under the lip edge to the subfloor. This will be the height of the platform wall framing, minus the CDX plywood decking, ½" cementboard, and tile.

Remove the tub and hammer a nail in at each corner point. Snap chalk lines to represent the inside lines of the inner platform wall. Measure, cut, and align the 2 × 4 sole plates with the chalk lines. Screw all four sole plates for the inside platform wall into position. Check diagonal measurements or use a framing square to ensure the sole plates are square.

Measure and mark 13½" from the inside edge of the open side sole plates at several points along the plates. These marks will serve as guide points for placing the sole plates of the outside platform walls. Line up the outside edge of the two outer-wall sole plates and screw them in place to the subfloor. Measure again to ensure the sole plates are positioned correctly.

Measure and cut studs to create the proper platform height. Install studs for both inside and outside platform walls, spacing them every 16". Use L configurations at corners so that the top plates intersect opposite the sole plates. Cut crossbraces and screw them in place, staggering with the stud placement.

Route supply lines from the wet wall to the location of the deck-mount faucet. The connections will depend on what type of deck-mount faucet you've chosen. Follow the manufacturer's instructions for securing the hot and cold connections for the faucet. If you're unsure of how to plumb the faucet, hire a plumber.

Measure and cut CDX plywood for the platform deck (the deck for the two open sides should overhang the outside wall edge by ½" to cover the cementboard that will be used on the walls). Screw the decking into position. If you will be mounting the faucet on the deck, cut holes for the valve handles and spout before screwing down that portion of the deck.

Measure and cut the deck cementboard to cover the plywood. Cut to the same overhang as the plywood and drill holes for the faucet if it will be deck mounted (the one seen here is mounted to the tub deck). Screw cementboard to the plywood deck over the top rail and crossbraces. Also attach cementboard to the platform aprons. *(continued)*

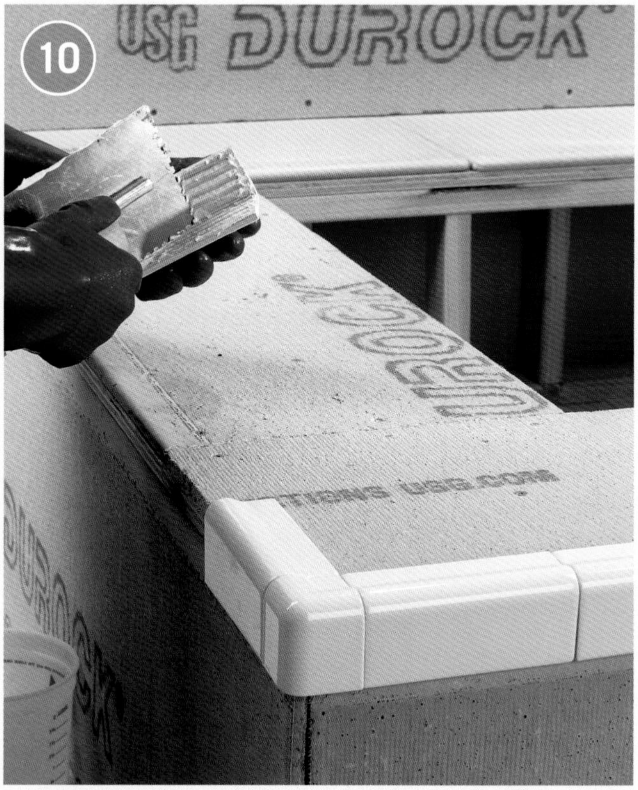

Attach wall coverings in the installation area. Here, six courses of wall tile will be installed on the walls above the tub deck. A strip of cementboard the same width as the total tile height is attached to the wall as a backer for the tile. Then, water-resistant drywall is installed to span from the cementboard to the ceiling to create a smooth, paintable wall surface.

Lay tile over the deck surface and the platform aprons using bullnose tile around the two outside edges. Tile on the inside edge of the platform does not need to be finished—it will be covered by the tub lip. Also install wall tiles.

Grout the platform and walls with sanded grout. Buff off excess grout with a coarse rag. Apply a grout sealing product after the grout has dried for several days (this may be done after the tub is installed if you do not want to wait).

Install the tub. Attach the drain-waste-overflow connection to the tub. Trowel a ½" bed of mortar on the subfloor where the tub bottom will sit (unless manufacturer's directions state otherwise). Set the tub in place in the platform opening, press down into the mortar, and check for level. There should be a very slight gap between the tub lip's bottom edge and the top of the tile.

Let the mortar bed dry and, working through the open walls and under the platform deck, connect the drain tailpiece to the trap. A large access panel lets you get at both the supply and drain hookups.

Apply a bead of tub-and-tile caulk in the seam between the tub lip and the tiled deck surface. Wet your finger and smooth the bead for a finished look.

Freestanding Tubs

Freestanding tubs offer maximum versatility in bathroom design because, theoretically, they can be placed anywhere in the bathroom. They can even be installed in an alcove, in place of an alcove tub. However, because they are attractive from all sides, and one of the key benefits is total access, most homeowners install freestanding tubs with some measure of floor space all around the tub.

Another selling point is the amazing variety among freestanding tubs. Options include the vast array of clawfoot tubs and pedestal tubs in styles from modern to classical. Rolltop freestanding tubs feature a rolled top lip that makes getting into and out of the tub easy. These are often egg shaped and deep, offering a comfortable soak after a long day. Slipper tubs offer a more dramatic shape, like Cinderella's ball slipper, with a high, sloped back that allows the bather to recline in ultimate comfort.

Clawfoot tubs are a category all their own. Although cast iron is the traditional material for clawfoots, manufacturers also offer easier-to-move acrylic and polymer options. You can pick from many different foot styles, including ball feet, ornamental feet, and, of course, the traditional claw feet. You can also outfit a clawfoot tub with a shower extension on the faucet body, a direct-spray "rainwater" head, and a shower ring from which a shower curtain can be hung (see pages 124 to 125).

The clawfoot tub in this project is a salvaged, cast-iron rolltop tub. Although the supply of vintage tubs is dwindling, they are still not hard to find, and in many cases you can get one for the price of hauling it away (no easy task). Often, the porcelain enamel finish needs refurbishing, which is a job best done by a tub-reglazing specialist. The installation process is a fairly simple one. The hardest part is usually running new drain and supply lines under the floor, so if you can place the tub over existing lines, you greatly simplify the installation process.

Regardless of the tub you choose, check with your local building inspector to help you determine whether your floor has adequate structural strength to safely support a freestanding tub. The inspector may suggest (or require) that you have the potential location evaluated by a qualified structural engineer.

TOOLS & MATERIALS

- Adjustable wrench
- Plumber's putty or silicone plumber's grease
- Teflon tape
- Power drill and bits
- Carpenter's level
- Hole saw
- Eye and ear protection
- Work gloves

PREPPING FOR A CLAWFOOT TUB

The actual installation of a clawfoot tub is fairly basic. Success, though, relies on proper preparation so that the tub is positioned just where you want it and the supply and drain lines are correctly aligned with the tub. Place the tub roughly where you want it and use a stud finder or other method to isolate the floor joists. Determine the location for connections under the floor (new tubs usually come with a template) and mark them by drilling pilot holes all the way through the subflooring. Install new drain and supply plumbing (this is a good time to call in a professional plumber). Finally, lay the finish flooring, if it is not already in place, before installing the tub. Make sure the floor is as level as possible.

How to Install a Clawfoot Tub

Position the tub exactly where you'd like it to rest, ideally over existing supply and drain lines. Install the feet first if they were not preattached (inset photo).

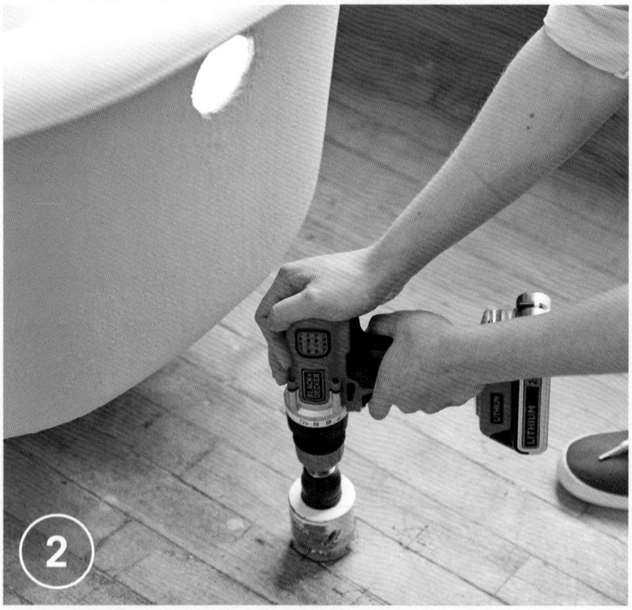

Mark locations for supply risers and drain tailpipe on the floor. Drill starter holes and double-check below the floor to make sure floor joists will not be directly under the access holes. Use a hole saw slightly wider than each pipe to drill access holes. Install supply lines and drain line.

Install the drain-waste-overflow assembly according to the manufacturer's instructions. With a freestanding tub, it is often easiest to join the assembly parts working upward from the drain-pipe connection in the floor. Install the drain flange in the tub, fastening it from the top into the drain shoe. Make the connection to the drain pipe in the floor—if the kit comes with a floor escutcheon that covers the drain connection, make sure it is in place before you attach the tailpipe to the T.

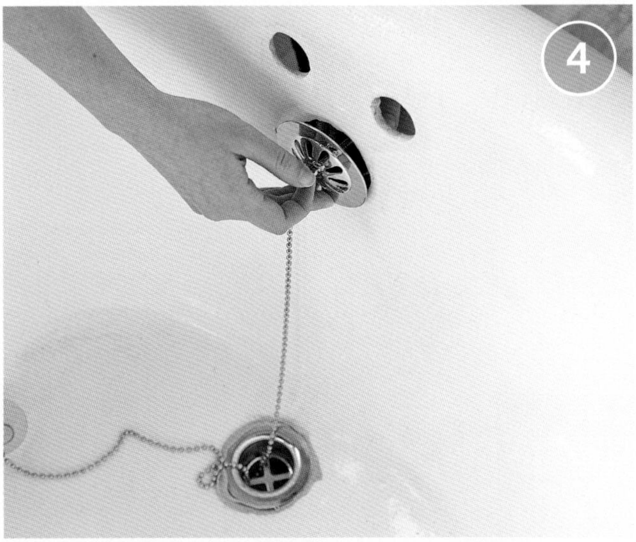

Fasten the overflow cover to the overflow receiver with the bolt or bolts that are provided. Be sure to position the rubber gasket that came with the drain kit so it fits neatly against the tub wall. Do not overtighten the fasteners.

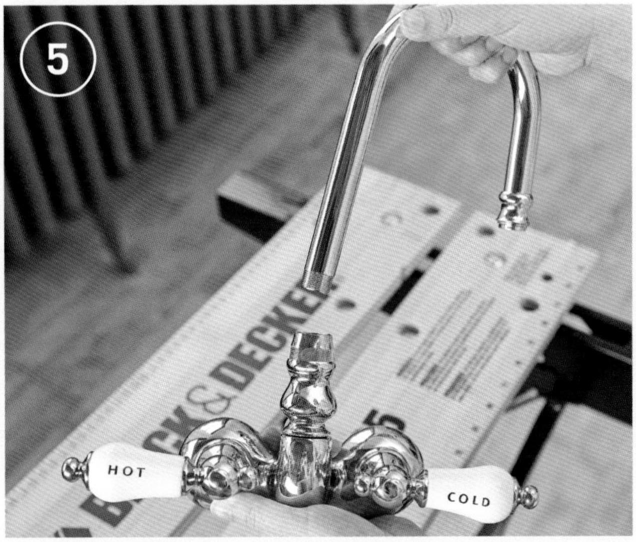

Assemble the faucet according to the manufacturer's instructions. Most older clawfoot tubs have a 2-valve faucet with a gooseneck spigot that mounts directly to the wall of the tub at the foot end. Many newer freestanding tubs utilize a wall-mounted faucet.

Mount the faucet body to the tub wall with the retainer nuts that thread onto the faucet valve stems.

Attach the supply risers to the valve inlets for the faucet. Put the supply-pipe base escutcheons in place on the floor over the supply-line connections. Secure the risers into the supply connections below the floor. Turn on the water supply and test to make sure there are no leaks in any of the pipes or fitting connections, including the drain and overflow.

FEET FIRST

Despite their great weight, it is always a good idea to anchor cast-iron tubs—even a small shift in position can cause the drain or supply connections to fail. Older tubs often have screw holes in the bottoms of the feet so they may be fastened to the floor once the hookups are made. Newer lighter-weight tubs generally use floor pins to stabilize the tub. Some manufacturers recommend using rubber pads and epoxy under each foot, in conjunction with dowels or mounting studs. Some tubs have self-leveling feet, with integral adjustment posts—check and follow the manufacturer's installation instructions.

Adding a Shower to a Freestanding Tub

Complete kits for converting a freestanding tub to a shower are widely available through plumbing-supply retailers. A quick online search will give you an idea of what's out there (use key phrases such as "clawfoot tub to shower," "clawfoot tub shower set," or "shower enclosure"). Kits include a special faucet with a built-in diverter, a riser pipe (extending from the faucet to the showerhead), and a rectangular shower-curtain frame that mounts to the ceiling and wall. Prices range from less than $100 to more than $500, depending on the style of the faucet and showerhead and the quality of the materials.

Examine your faucet and its water hookups carefully before ordering a kit. Measure the distance between the faucet tailpieces and the length and offset of the water-supply risers. The new faucet must fit into the existing holes in your tub. You may need to buy new supply risers to connect to the faucet.

A spout with a diverter, some metal supply tubing, and a shower-curtain frame can add showering capacity to a standalone tub.

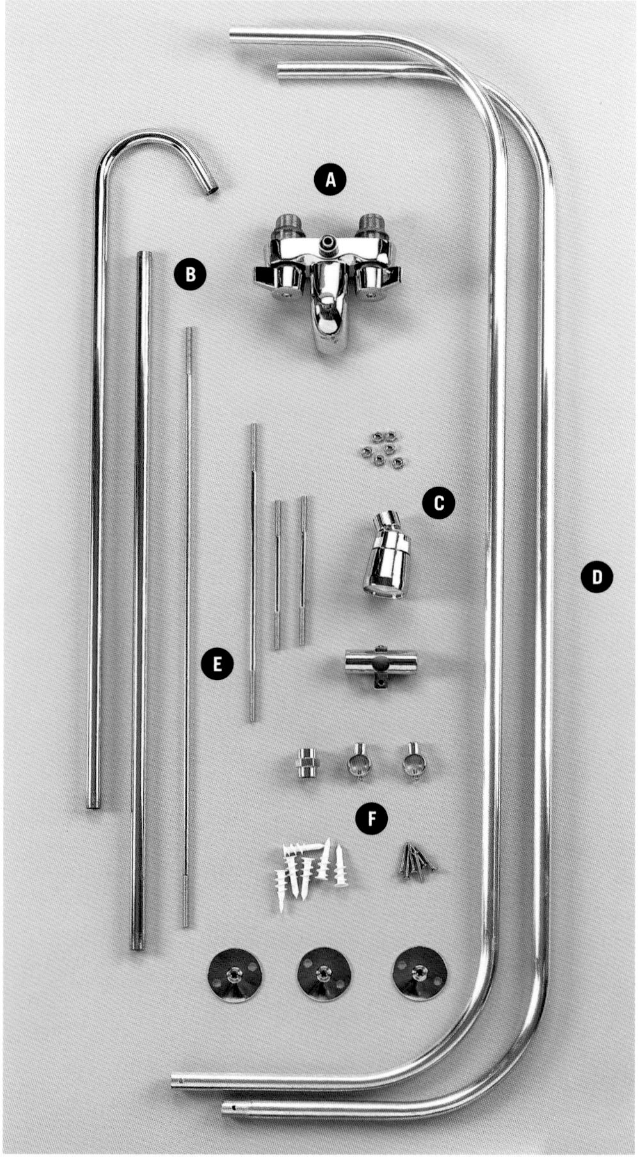

A packaged kit for adding a shower to your tub features a faucet with diverter (A), shower-riser plumbing (B), showerhead (C), a frame for the shower curtain (D) that mounts on the wall and ceiling with threaded rods (E), and fasteners and fittings (F).

TOOLS & MATERIALS

- Adjustable wrench
- Plumber's putty or silicone plumber's grease
- Teflon tape
- Power drill and bits
- Shower-conversion kit
- Tubing cutter
- Ear and eye protection
- Work gloves

How to Install a Shower-Conversion Kit

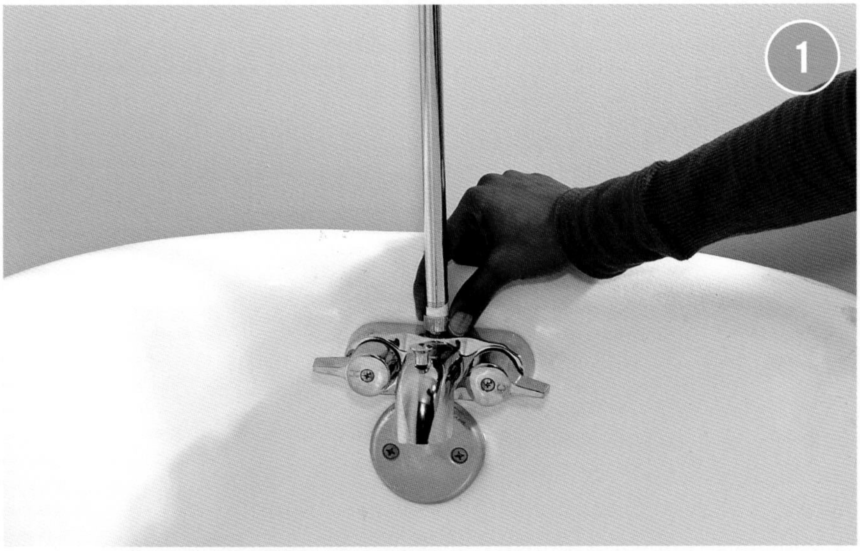

Remove the old tub faucet and replace it with the new diverter-type faucet from the kit. Fit the assembled shower riser into the top of the faucet and hand-tighten. Apply Teflon tape to the threads before making the connection. This assembly includes one straight and one curved section, joined by a coupling. The top, curved pipe includes a connector to a wall brace. Shorten the straight section using a tubing cutter, to lower the showerhead height, if desired. Slip the compression nut and washer onto the bottom end of the shower riser, and attach the riser to the top of the faucet, hand-tightening for the time being.

Assemble the curtain frame with a helper, securing it with setscrews. Hold the frame level and measure to the ceiling to determine the ceiling-brace pipe length. Cut the pipe and complete the ceiling-brace assembly. Set the shower riser to the desired height and connect the brace to the wall (ensure strong connections by driving the mounting screws into a wall stud and ceiling joist, if possible).

After the curtain frame is completely assembled and secured, tighten the faucet connection with a wrench. Full-size shower kits require one shower curtain on each side of the curtain frame. The hooks seen here feature roller bearings on the tops so they can be operated very smoothly with minimal resistance.

Sliding Tub Doors

Curtains on your bathtub shower are a hassle. If you forget to tuck them inside the tub, water flows freely onto your bathroom floor. If you forget to slide them closed, mildew sets up shop in the folds. And every time you brush against them they stick to your skin. Shower curtains certainly don't add much elegance or charm to a dream bath. Neither does a deteriorated door. Clean up the look of your bathroom, and even give it an extra touch of elegance with a new sliding tub door.

When shopping for a sliding tub door, you have a choice of framed or frameless. A framed door is edged in metal. The metal framing is typically aluminum but is available in many finishes, including those that resemble gold, brass, or chrome. Glass options are also plentiful. You can choose between frosted or pebbled, clear, mirrored, tinted, or patterned glass. Doors can be installed on ceramic-tile walls or through a fiberglass tub surround.

TOOLS & MATERIALS

- Measuring tape
- Pencil and marker
- Hacksaw
- Miter box
- Level
- Drill
- Center punch
- Masonry bit for tile wall
- Phillips screwdriver
- Caulk gun
- Masking tape
- Silicone sealant
- Tub-door kit
- Eye and ear protection
- Work gloves

A sliding tub door in a metal frame gives the room a sleek, clean look and is just one of the available options.

How to Install Sliding Tub Doors

Remove the existing door and inspect the walls. Use a razor blade to cut sealant from tile and metal surfaces. Do not use a razor blade on fiberglass surfaces. Remove remaining sealant by scraping or pulling. Use a silicone sealant remover to remove all residue. Remove shower-curtain rods, if present. Check the walls and tub ledge for plumb and level.

Measure the distance between the finished walls along the top of the tub ledge. Refer to the manufacturer's instructions for figuring the track dimensions. For the product seen here, $3/16$" is subtracted from the measurement to calculate the track dimensions.

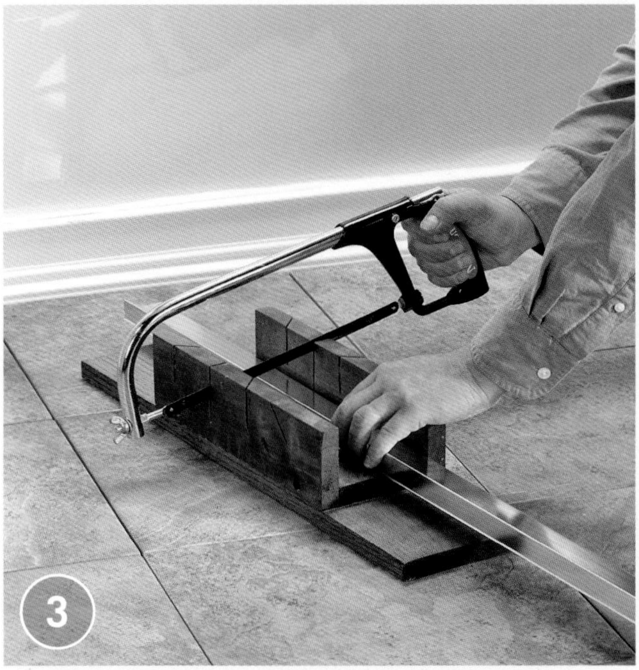

Using a hacksaw and a miter box, carefully cut the track to the proper dimension. Center the track on the bathtub ledge with the taller side out and so the gaps are even at each end. Tape into position with masking tape.

Place a wall channel against the wall with the longer side out and slide into place over the track so they overlap. Use a level to check the channel for plumb, and then mark the locations of the mounting holes on the wall with a marker. Repeat for the other wall channel. Remove the track. *(continued)*

Drill mounting holes for the wall channel at the marked locations. In ceramic tile, nick the surface of the tile with a center punch, use a ¼" masonry bit to drill the hole, and then insert the included wall anchors. For fiberglass surrounds, use a ⅛" drill bit; wall anchors are not necessary.

Apply a bead of silicone sealant along the joint between the tub and the wall at the ends of the track. Apply a minimum ¼" bead of sealant along the outside leg of the track underside.

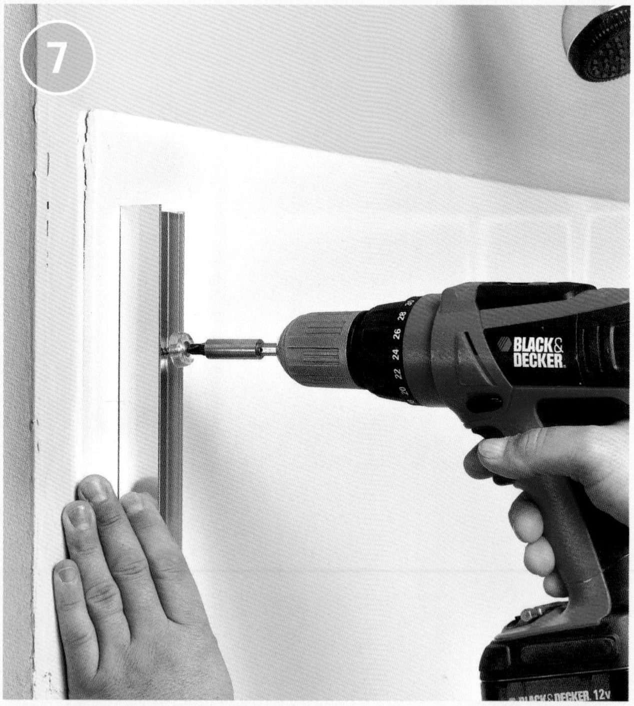

Position the track on the tub ledge and against the wall. Attach the wall channels using the provided screws. Do not use caulk on the wall channels at this time.

At a location above the tops of the wall channels, measure the distance between the walls. Refer to the manufacturer's instructions for calculating the header dimensions. For the doors seen here, the header dimension is the distance between the walls minus 1⁄16". Measure the header and carefully cut it to length using a hacksaw and a miter box. Slide the header down on top of the wall channels until seated.

Mount the rollers in the roller-mounting holes. To begin, use the roller-mounting holes second from the top. Follow the manufacturer's instructions for spacer or washer placement and direction.

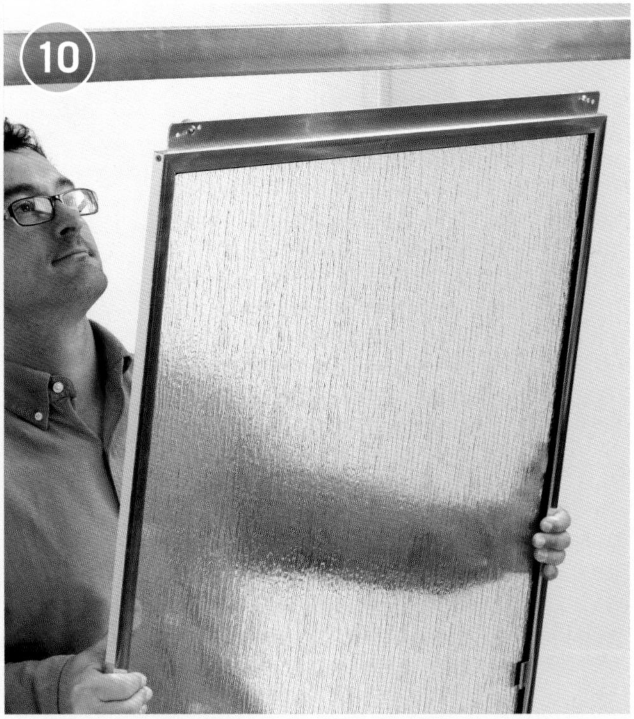

Carefully lift the inner panel by the sides and place the rollers on the inner roller track. Roll the door toward the shower end of the tub. The edge of the panel should touch both rubber bumpers. If it doesn't, remove the door and move the rollers to different holes. Drive the screws by hand to prevent overtightening.

Lift the outer panel by the sides with the towel bar facing out from the tub. Place the outer rollers over the outer roller track. Slide the door to the end opposite the shower end of the tub. If the door does not contact both bumpers, remove the door and move the rollers to different mounting holes.

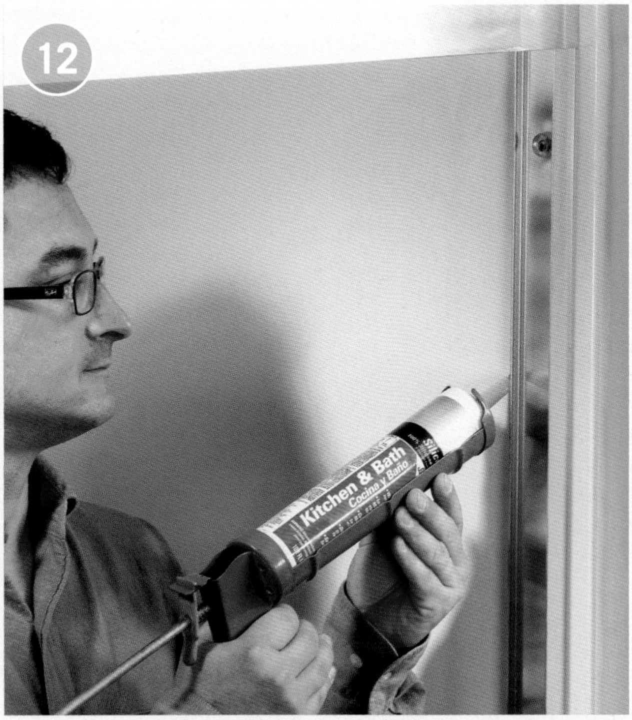

Apply a bead of silicone sealant to the inside seam of the wall and wall channel at both ends and to the U-shaped joint of the track and wall channels. Smooth the sealant with a fingertip dipped in water.

Air-Jet Tubs

TOOLS & MATERIALS

Plumbing tools and supplies	Drain-waste-overflow assembly
Utility knife	Shims
4' level	1 × 4 lumber
Square-edge trowel	Deck screws
Drill or power driver	Roofing nails
Channel-type pliers	Plumber's putty
Hacksaw	Dry-set mortar
Pencil	Trowel
Level	Silicone caulk
Circular saw	Jetted tub
Screwdriver	Faucet set
Adjustable wrench	Eye and ear protection
	Work gloves

A jetted tub is basically a bathtub that recirculates water, air, or a combination of the two to create an effect known as hydromassage. Hydromassage increases blood flow, relieves pressure on joints and muscles, and relieves tension. Indoor hydromassage tubs usually have a water pump that blows a mixture of air and water through jets located in the tub body. Many include an integral water heater.

The product you'll see installed on these pages is a bit different. It is an air-jet tub: a relatively new entry in the jetted-spa market that circulates only warm air, not water. This technology makes it safe to use bath oils, bubble bath, and bath salts in the spa. A model with no heater requires only a single 120-volt dedicated circuit. Models with heaters normally require either multiple dedicated 120-volt circuits or a 240-volt circuit.

Like normal bathtubs, jetted tubs can be installed in a variety of ways. Here, we install a drop-in tub (no nailing flange) in a three-wall alcove. This may require the construction of a new stub wall, like the short wall we plumbed as the wet wall for this installation. Unless you have a lot of wiring and plumbing experience, consider hiring professionals for all or parts of the project.

Air-jet tubs create a relaxing massage action, agitating the water with air. The air jets eliminate concerns about stagnant water and bacteria that can be a problem in the pipes of water-jet tubs.

WHIRLPOOL TUBS

Installing a whirlpool tub is similar to installing any other bathtub, once the rough-in is complete. Finishing a rough-in for a whirlpool tub requires that you install a separate GFCI-protected electrical circuit for the pump motor. Some building codes specify that a licensed electrician must do the wiring for a whirlpool tub, so check with your local building inspector.

Select your tub before you do the rough-in work, because exact measurements will differ from model to model. Select your faucet to match the trim kit that comes with the tub (although some tubs include faucet and controls). When choosing a faucet, make sure the spout is large enough to reach over the tub rim. Most whirlpool tubs use widespread faucets, because the handles and spout are separate and can be positioned however you like—even on opposite sides of the tub, if you want. Most building centers carry flex tubes in a variety of lengths for the connecting the faucet handles and spout.

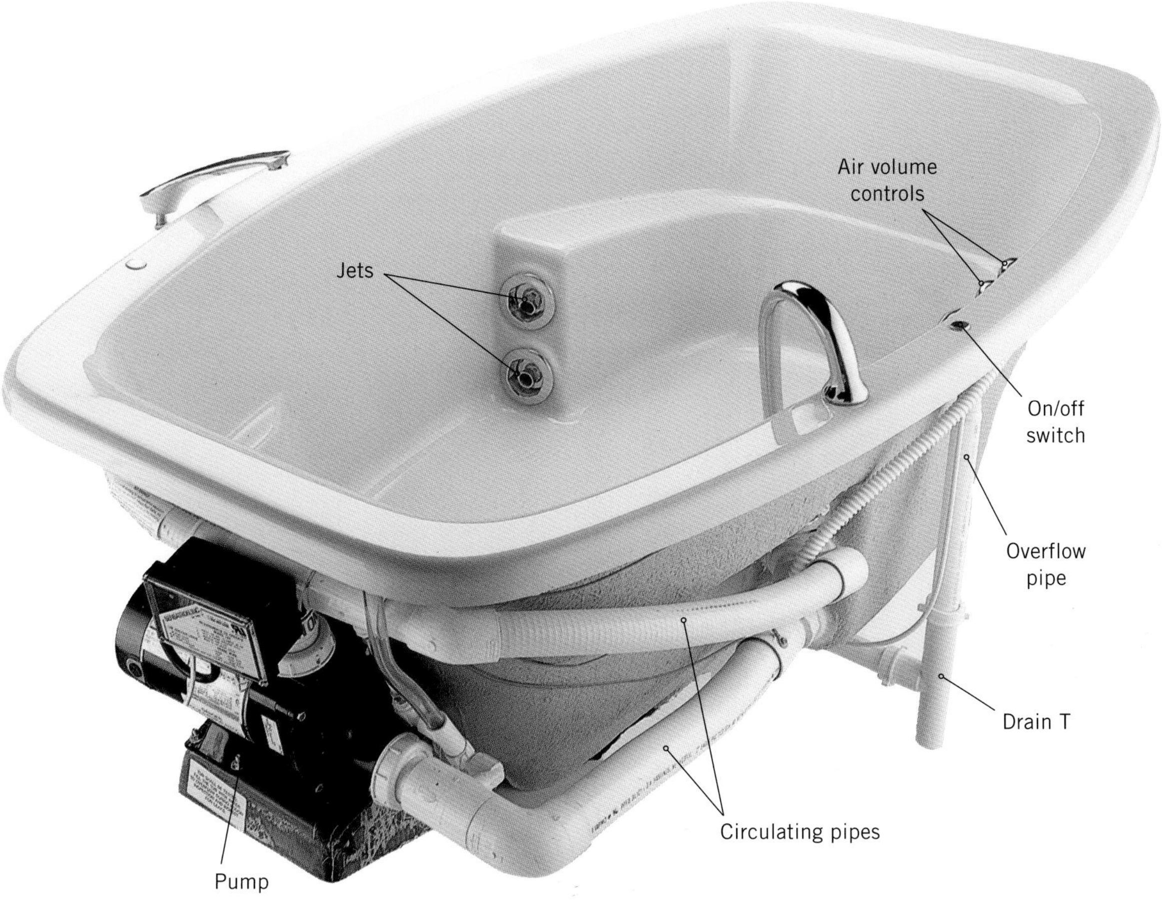

A whirlpool tub circulates aerated water through jets mounted in the body of the tub. Whirlpool pumps move as much as 50 gallons of water per minute to create a relaxing hydromassage effect. The pump, pipes, jets, and most of the controls are installed at the factory, making the actual hookup in your home quite simple.

How to Install a Jetted Tub

Prepare the site for the installation. Remove wall coverings in the installation area to expose bare studs. Provide a dedicated electrical circuit or circuits to the tub area according to the specifications in your installation manual (hire an electrician if you are not comfortable with wiring). This model plugs into a GFCI-protected receptacle on a dedicated 120-volt, 20-amp circuit.

Make framing improvements such as adding 1 × 4 bracing at supply risers and faucet-body locations. For drop-in tubs that do not have nailing flanges, you may need to add short stub walls to provide a stable resting point. Here, a short stub wall was installed at one end to serve as the tub wet wall.

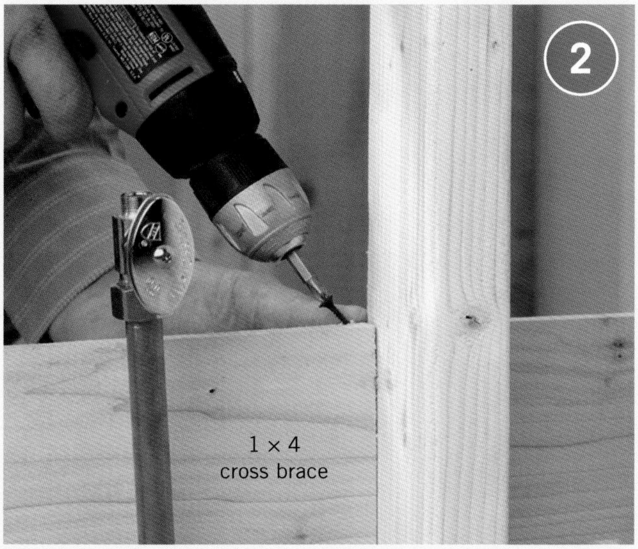

REQUIREMENTS FOR MAKING ELECTRICAL HOOKUPS

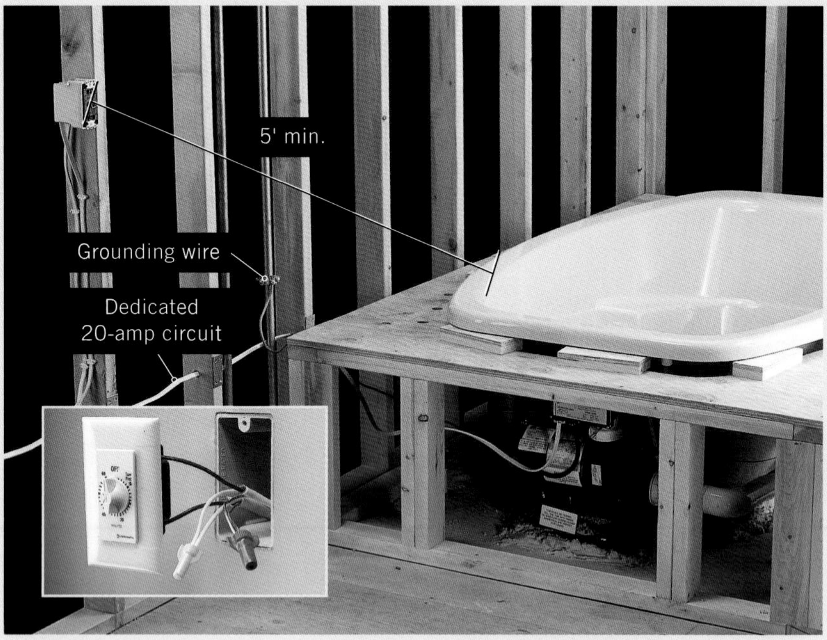

The electrical service for a whirlpool tub should be a dedicated 115- to 120-volt, 20-amp circuit. The pump motor should be grounded separately, normally to a metal cold-water supply pipe. Most tub motors are wired with 12/2 NM cable, but some local codes require the use of conduit. Remote timer switches (inset), located at least 5' from the tub, are required by some codes, even for a tub with a built-in timer.

A GFCI circuit breaker at the main service panel is required with jetted-tub installations. Hire an electrician to connect new circuits at your service panel if you are uncomfortable installing circuit cables on your own.

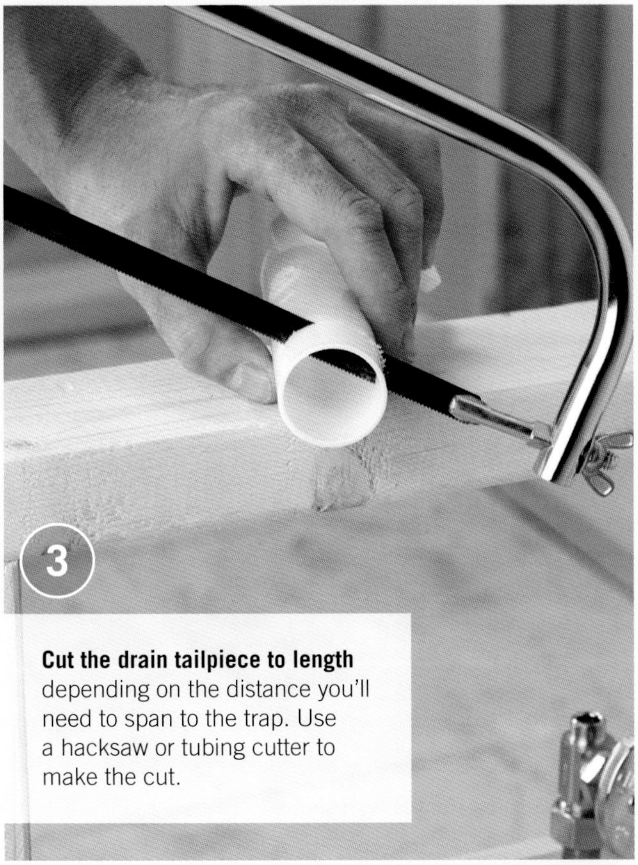

Cut the drain tailpiece to length depending on the distance you'll need to span to the trap. Use a hacksaw or tubing cutter to make the cut.

Prepare the floor or subfloor. Check with a level and fill any dips with floor leveling compound or mortar. If there is a joint in the subfloor in the installation area, make sure the sides are level. (The floor has to be level in order to support the weight of the tub, the water, and bathers.) Also make sure there is no rot or weakness in the structural elements.

Test the tub fit. First, cut a piece of the shipping carton to fit inside the tub and protect its surface. Have someone help you slide the tub into the installation area, flush against the wall studs, so you can check the fit.

TIP: Lay a pair of 1 × 4s perpendicular to the tub opening and use them as skids to make it easier to slide the tub in. Remove the skids and lower the tub on the floor.

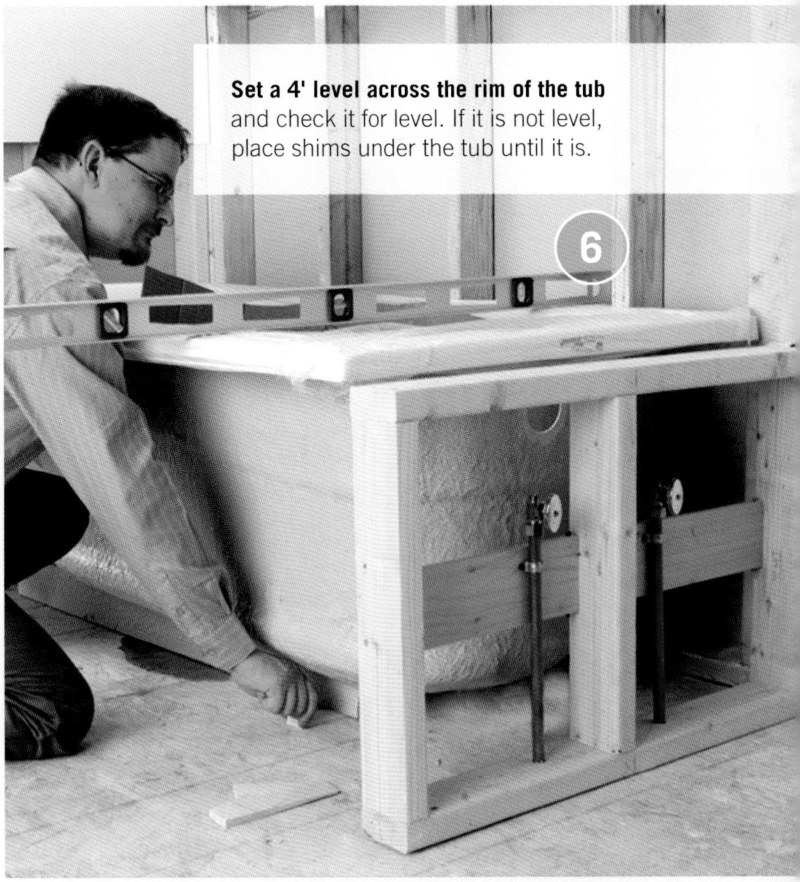

Set a 4' level across the rim of the tub and check it for level. If it is not level, place shims under the tub until it is.

(continued)

Mark the top of the tub's rim or nailing flange at each stud as a reference for installing additional supports or ledgers. Remove the tub from the alcove.

Add support frames or ledgers as directed by the manufacturer and secure them in the installation area so the top of the tub or nailing flange will be at the height you scribed in step 7.

Assemble the drain-waste-overflow kit to fit the drain and overflow openings, following the tub manufacturer's directions. Install the DWO kit (it is virtually impossible to attach it once the tub is in place).

Fasten the threaded parts of the drain assembly. A ring of plumber's putty between the drain coverplate and the tub will help create a good seal. If you will be installing a pop-up drain, install it now as well.

Attach the overflow coverplate so it conceals the overflow opening. Adjust the pop-up drain-plug linkage as directed by the manufacturer.

Begin the actual installation. For some tubs, it is recommended that you trowel a layer of thinset mortar in the installation area. But read your instructions carefully. Many tubs feature integral feet that are meant to rest directly on the floor.

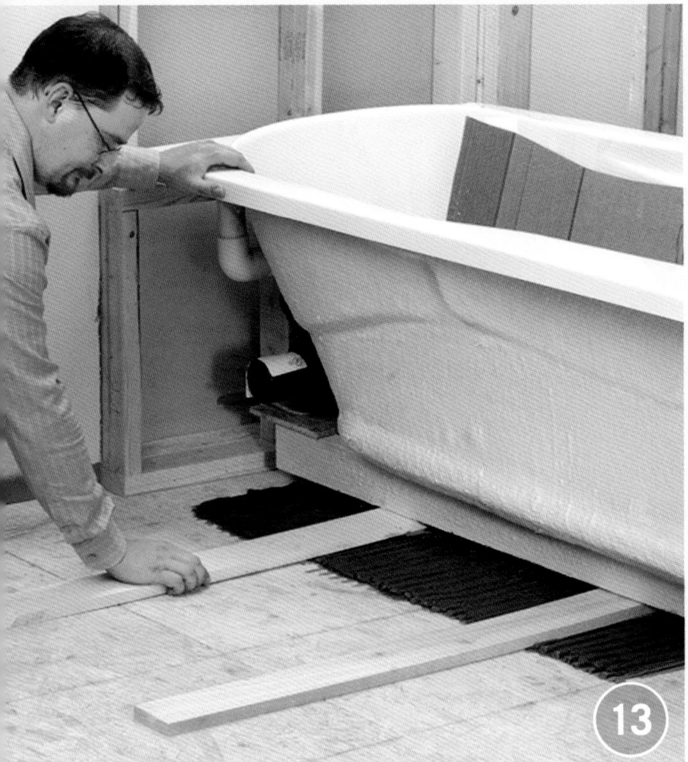

Slide the tub back into the opening. Remove the skids, if you are using them. Press down evenly on the tub rims until they make solid contact with the ledgers or frames.

Provide support for the tub on the open side if it does not have a structural skirt. Here, a 2 × 4 stub wall is built to the exact height of the underside of the rim and then attached in place. Screw it to both end walls and to the floor. *(continued)*

DRAIN HOOKUPS

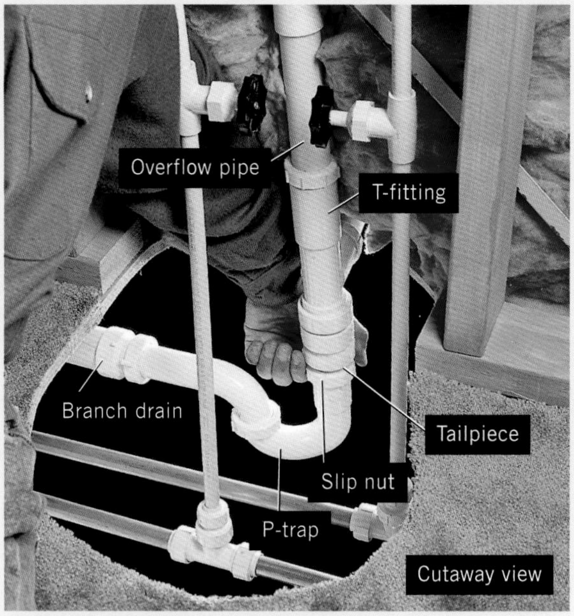

Make the plumbing drain connections before you proceed further. To connect the drain tailpiece to the trap, you will need access either from below or from an access panel. The photo above shows a typical tub drain configuration seen cutaway through the floor.

Cover the gaps in the wall coverings around the tub. Here, cementboard is installed in preparation for a tile backsplash. If your tub has nailing flanges, attach strips of metal flashing to the wall so they extend down to within about ¼" of the tub rim. If your tub has a removable apron, install it.

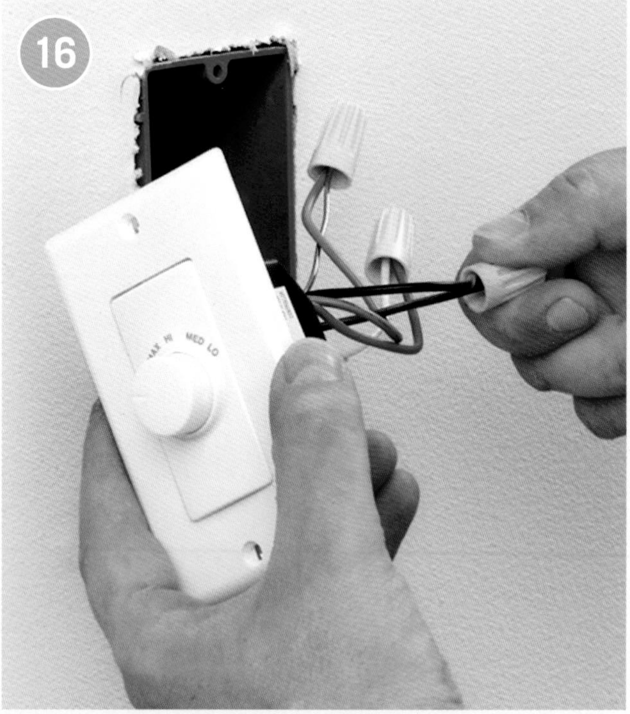

Make wiring connections according to the tub manufacturer's instructions. The requirements vary greatly among jetted tubs. Some municipalities may require that a licensed professional do this work. Here, the airflow regulator is being wired. Note that most codes have a safety requirement that the on/off switch must be located so it cannot be reached by a bather in the tub.

Test the operation of the tub before you finish the walls or deck in case there is a hidden problem. Fill it with a hose if you have not installed the faucet (the faucet normally is installed after the wall surfaces, unless you are deck-mounting the faucet on the tub rim). Run the tub. If it works, go ahead and drain the water.

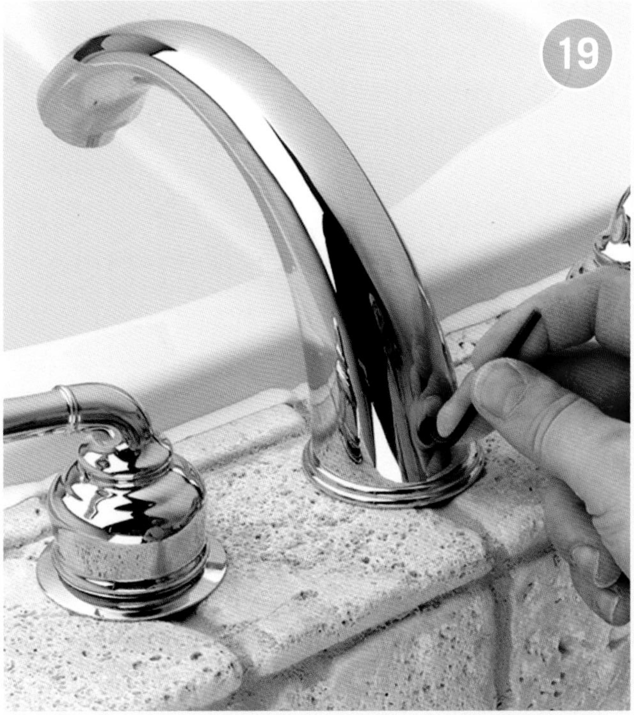

Finish the wall surfaces. Here, a tile surround and backsplash are being installed over the cementboard backer. The wall covering at the front of the wet wall is installed so it is easy to remove for plumbing access.

Hook up the faucet to the water supply plumbing according to the manufacturer's directions (or have your plumber do the job). Remove the aerator from the tip of the spout and run water through it to clear out any debris. Attach the aerator, fill the tub, and have yourself a nice, relaxing soak.

OPTIONAL ACCESSORIES

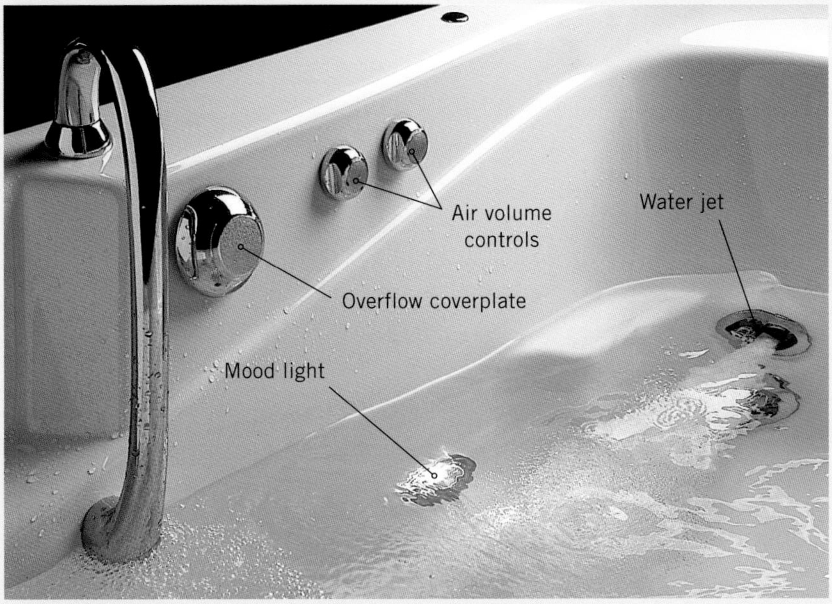

Mood lights are sold as factory-installed accessories by many manufacturers. Most are available with several filters to let you adjust the color to suit your mood. Mood lights are low-voltage fixtures wired through 12-volt transformers. Do not wire mood lights or other accessories into the electrical circuit that supplies the pump motor.

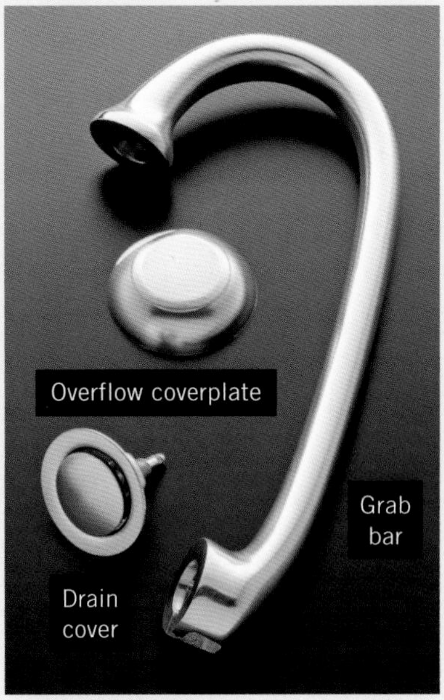

Trim kits for jetted tubs are ordered at the time of purchase. Available in a variety of finishes, all of the trim pieces except the grab bar and overflow coverplate are normally installed at the factory.

Tub & Shower Fittings

In many situations, replacing a bathtub spout can be almost as easy as hooking up a garden hose to an outdoor spigot. There are some situations where it is a bit more difficult, but still pretty simple. The only time it's a real problem is when the spout is attached to a plain copper supply nipple, rather than a threaded nipple. You'll know this is the case if the spout has a setscrew on the underside where it meets the wall. Many bathtub spouts are sold in kits with a matching showerhead and handle or handles. But for a simple one-for-one replacement, spouts are sold separately. You just need to make sure the new spout is compatible with the existing nipple (see page 142).

Tub-spout assemblies can be relatively complicated plumbing fittings, often performing three or four important functions. The spout itself is simple enough, since its only function is to deliver bathwater to the tub. But the diverter network and pop-up drain contain multiple moving parts that require precise adjustment and occasional repair or replacement (see photo, next page). The diverter is basically a stop valve that's activated by a lever or knob to block flow of water from the spout, forcing it up to a showerhead or out through a handheld showerhead, as seen here.

In many bathtub-shower plumbing systems, the spout has the important job of housing the diverter—a gate inside the spout that is operated by a lever with a knob. An open gate allows water to come out of the spout when the faucet is turned on. When the diverter is pulled shut, the water is redirected up a riser pipe and to the showerhead. Failure of the diverter is one of the most common reasons for replacing a spout.

Tub & Shower Combination Faucets

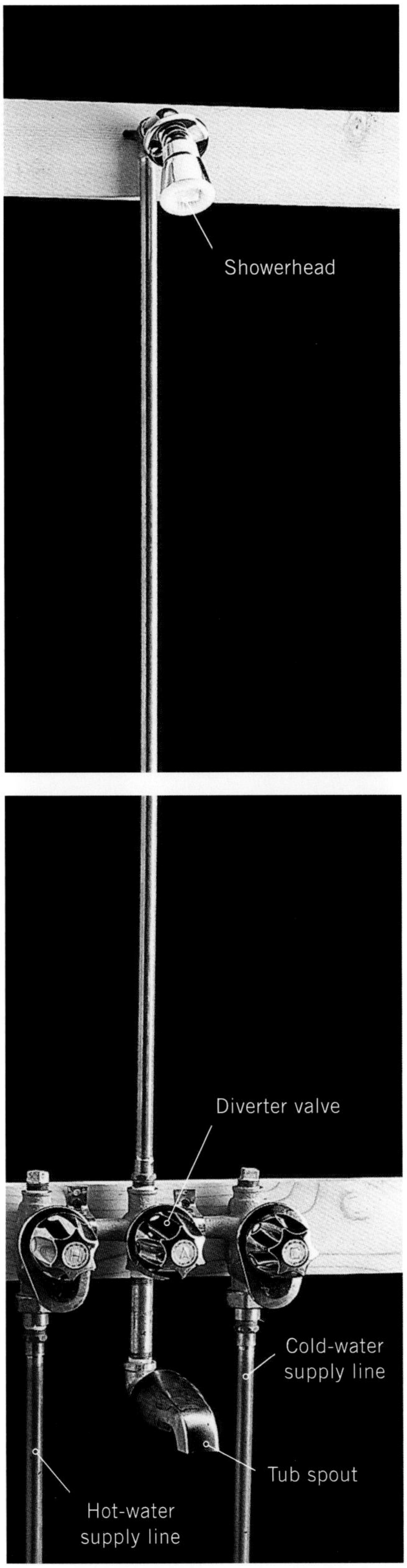

A 3-handle faucet has valves that are either compression or cartridge design.

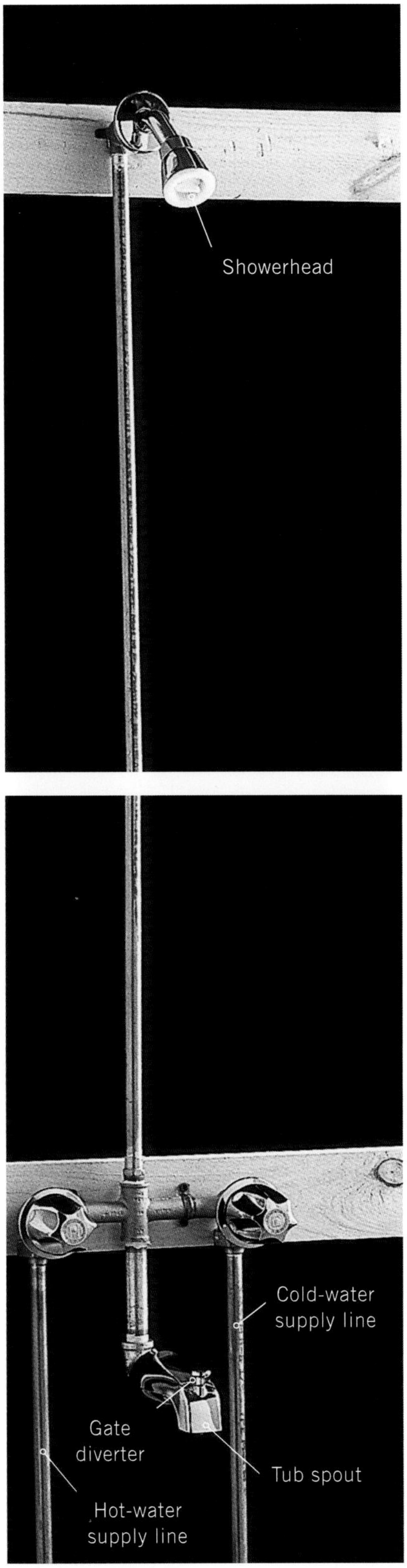

A 2-handle faucet has valves that are either compression or cartridge design.

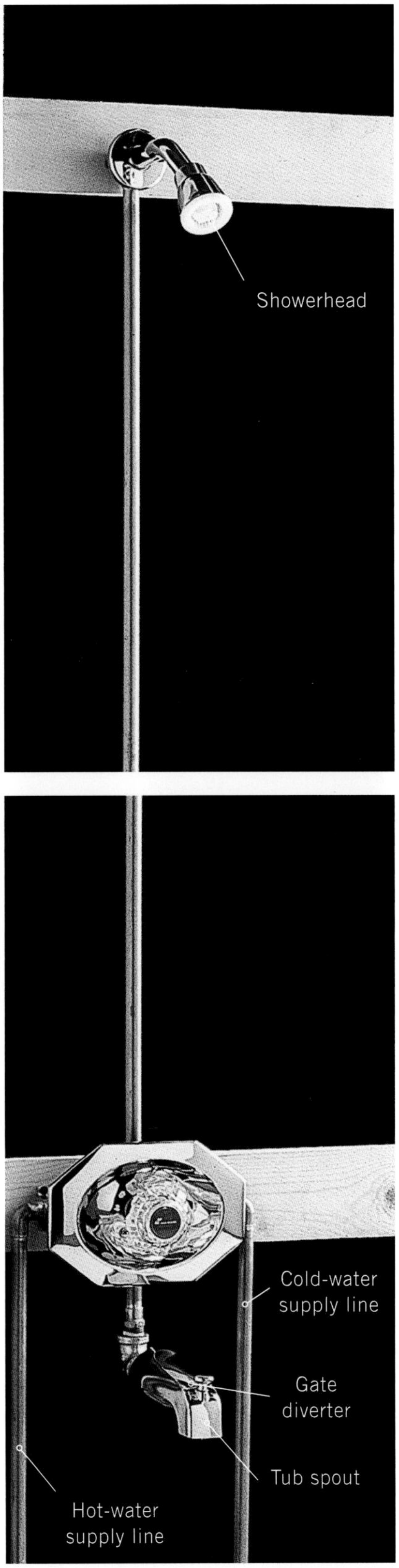

A single-handle faucet has valves that are cartridge, ball-type, or disc design.

How to Install a Slip-Fit Spout

Slip fitting: Check underneath the tub spout to look for an access slot or cutout, which indicates the spout is a slip-fit style that is held in place with a setscrew and mounted on a copper supply nipple. Loosen the screw with a hex (Allen) wrench. Pull off the spout.

Clean the copper nipple with steel wool. If you find any sharp edges where the nipple was cut, smooth them out with emery paper. Then, insert the O-ring that comes with the spout onto the nipple (see the manufacturer's instructions) and slide the spout body over the nipple in an upside-down position.

With the spout upside down for ease of access, tighten the setscrews on the clamp, working through the access slot or cutout, until you feel resistance.

Spin the spout so it's right-side up, then tighten the setscrew from below, making sure the wall end of the spout is flush against the wall. Do not overtighten the setscrew.

How to Install a Threaded Spout

If you see no setscrew or slot on the underside of the spout, it is attached to a threaded nipple. Unscrew the tub spout by inserting a heavy-duty flat screwdriver into the spout opening and spinning it counterclockwise.

OPTION: Grip the spout with a padded pipe wrench or channel-type pliers. Buy a compatible replacement spout at a home center or hardware store.

Wrap several courses of Teflon tape clockwise onto the pipe threads of the nipple. Using extra Teflon tape on the threads creates resistance if the spout tip points past 6 o'clock when tight.

Twist the new spout onto the nipple until it is flush against the wall and the spout is oriented properly. If the spout falls short of 6 o'clock, you may protect the finish of the spout with tape and twist it a little beyond hand tight with your channel-type pliers—but don't overdo it; the fitting can crack.

Adding a Shower to a Bathtub

Your dream bath remodel may include adding a shower to your old built-in bathtub—finally you will be able to enjoy the ease of waking up and hopping into a steamy shower. All you need to do is remove the spout and replace it with one equipped with an adapter hose outlet to which you can screw a flexible shower hose. Then you need to install a mounting bracket so you can hang the showerhead and free your hands. Add a telescoping shower curtain rod and a shower curtain and your new shower stall is ready for duty.

A

¾" x 3"

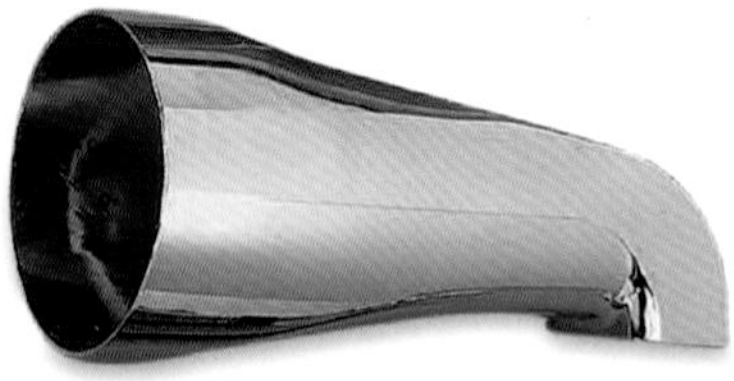

B

½" x 3"

C

¾" x 1½"

The appearance of the spout gives good clues as to which kind of nipple it is connected to. A spout with no diverter (A) is probably connected to a 3"-long threaded nipple. To install a diverter spout you'll need to replace the 3" threaded nipple with a shorter threaded nipple that sticks out no more than ½" from the wall—not too big of a job. If the spout has a small setscrew in a slot on the underside (B), it is probably attached with a slip fitting to a ½" copper supply nipple. Unless you are able to solder a new transition fitting onto the old pipe after cutting it, call a plumber to install the new spout here. Spouts with outlets for shower adapters (C) require a short threaded nipple (or comparable union) that sticks out from the wall no more than ¾".

Converting a plain bathtub into a tub-shower is a relatively easy task when you use a flexible shower adapter that fits onto a special replacement tub spout.

TOOLS & MATERIALS

- Pipe wrench
- Drill
- Glass and tile drill bit
- Measuring tape
- Screwdriver
- Marker
- Teflon tape
- Brass nipple
- Spout with diverter outlet
- Hand-held mountable showerhead with flexible hose
- Mounting hardware
- Eye and ear protection
- Work gloves

How to Add a Shower to a Bathtub

Make sure the old spout is not held in place with a setscrew (see previous page) and then remove it by wrapping it with a cloth and turning the spout with channel-type pliers or a pipe wrench.

If you have a long iron or brass nipple like this, you need to replace it with a short one. Threaded nipples have threads at each end, so you can usually unscrew the old one. Mark the nipple at the face of the wall and write "front" on your side. Unscrew it counterclockwise with a pipe wrench. Get a threaded brass nipple of the same diameter that is about ½" longer than the distance from the back of your old nipple to your line.

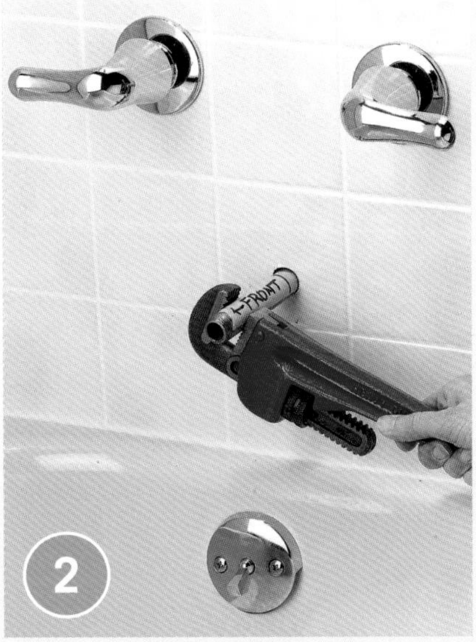

Wrap 6 layers of Teflon tape clockwise on the nipple and thread into the wall. Thread the reducing bushing onto the nipple. Thread the adapter spout on. Tighten farther with a screwdriver or dowel to orient the spout correctly.

Attach a flexible shower hose to the adapter hose outlet. Tighten with an adjustable wrench.

Determine the location of the showerhead bracket. Use the hose length as a guide, and make sure the showerhead can be lifted off the bracket with ease.

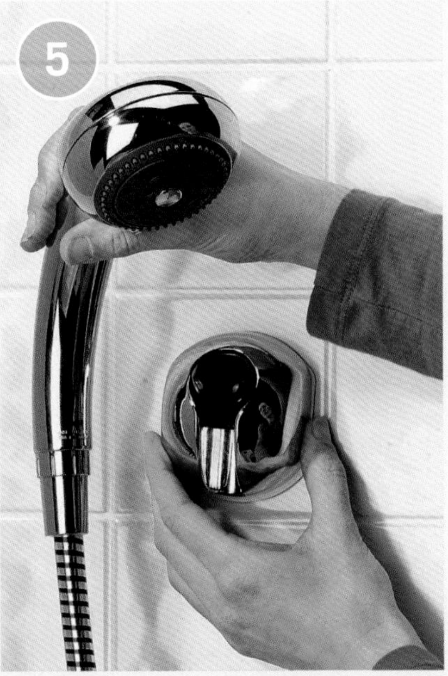

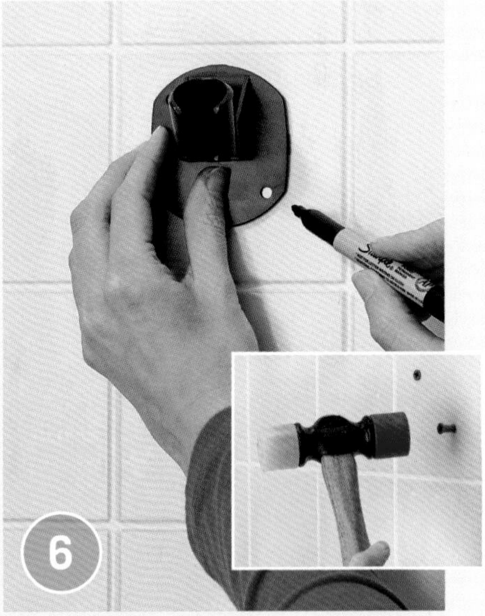

Mark the hole locations. Use a glass-and-tile bit in the size recommended by the manufacturer. Wear eye protection, and drill holes in the tile at the marks. Insert anchors and tap them in place with a wooden mallet. Screw the showerhead bracket to the wall.

Sinks & Vanities

Sinks and vanities are focal points in any bathroom's décor. You can choose from a vast array of materials and styles, but your decision will most likely be driven first and foremost by practicality.

If storage is a key requirement, pedestal, console, and most wall-mounted sinks will be crossed off your list before you even begin shopping. That doesn't mean you'll lack for options: vanities come in designs and finishes to match any look. Select a traditional wood unit with abundant undersink storage or go for a more contemporary look with a wall-hung unit featuring a drawer.

Sinks involve even more decision making. Vessel sinks are a unique look, while more traditional undermount or drop-in sinks are simple to install and provide a more conventional appearance. The counter under (or around, or part of) the sink is yet another factor in your choice. It must accommodate both the sink and the vanity choice.

These days, though, the conversation about sinks and vanities inevitably turns to aging-in-place and universal-design options. That's why we've included options that are not only convenient but, in some cases, ADA compliant.

In this chapter:

Pedestal & Console Sinks

TOOLS & MATERIALS

Pedestal sink	Water-resistant drywall
Silicone caulk	Pencil
Stud finder	Drill
Ratchet wrench	Eye and ear protection
Basin wrench	Work gloves
Lag screws	
2 × 4 lumber	

Pedestal and console sinks move in and out of popularity more frequently than other types, but even during the times that they aren't particularly trendy they still find a place in many remodels because of their classic and adaptable styling. You'll find them most frequently in small half baths or powder rooms, where their modest footprints make them space-efficient options. Designers are also increasingly using these styles as his-and-her sinks for bathrooms in which the sinks are meant to visually dominate the design.

The primary drawback to pedestal sinks is that they don't offer any storage. Their chief practical benefit is that they conceal plumbing some homeowners would prefer to keep out of sight. Console sinks, with their two front legs, offer some space underneath for rolling shelf units or a towel basket.

Pedestal sinks are mounted in one of two ways. Most inexpensive models are hung in much the same way as wall-mounted sinks are. The pedestal is actually installed after the sink is hung, and its purpose is purely decorative. But other, higher-end pedestal sinks have structural pedestals that bear the weight of the sink. All console sinks are mounted to the wall, although the front legs offer additional support and resistance to users leaning on the front of the sink.

A console bathroom sink is a wall-mounted lavatory with two front legs that provide backup support. Many have a narrow apron to conceal the drain trap.

A pedestal sink typically is hung on the wall. The primary function of the pedestal is to conceal plumbing and provide visual appeal.

How to Install a Pedestal Sink

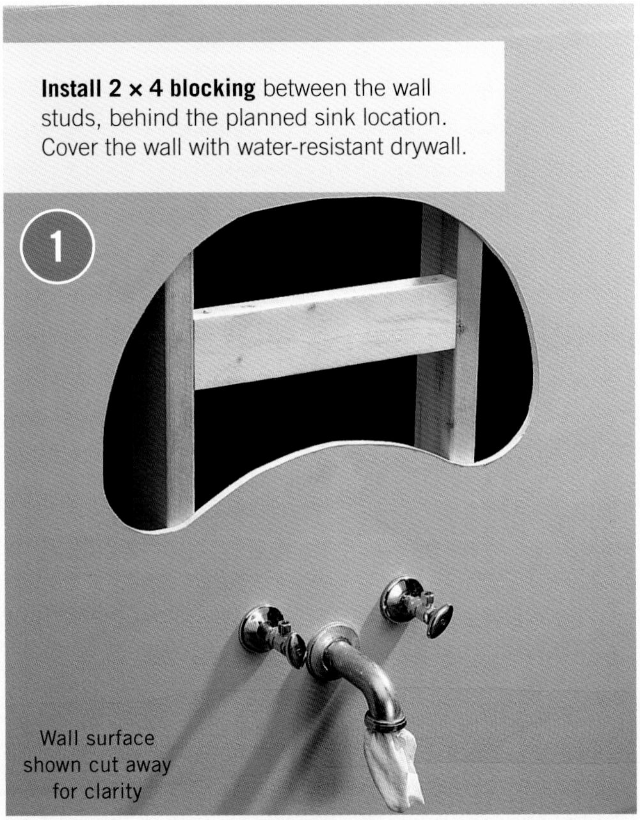

Install 2 × 4 blocking between the wall studs, behind the planned sink location. Cover the wall with water-resistant drywall.

Set the basin and pedestal in position and brace them with 2 × 4s. Outline the top of the basin on the wall, and mark the base of the pedestal on the floor. Mark reference points on the wall and floor through the mounting holes found on the back of the sink and the bottom of the pedestal.

Set aside the basin and pedestal. Drill pilot holes in the wall and floor at the reference points, then reposition the pedestal. Anchor the pedestal to the floor with lag screws.

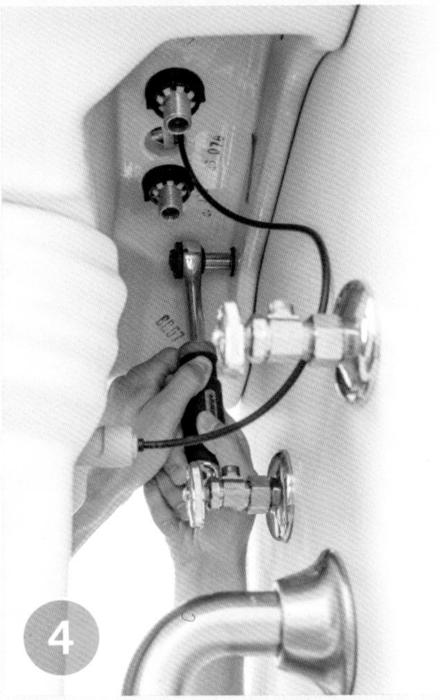

Attach the faucet set to the sink, then set the sink onto the pedestal. Align the holes on the back flange of the sink with the pilot holes drilled in the wall, then drive lag screws with washers into the wall brace using a ratchet wrench. Attach the sink-stopper mechanism to the sink drain.

Hook up the drain and supply fittings. Caulk between the back of the sink and the wall when installation is finished.

Wall-Mounted Sinks

TOOLS & MATERIALS

Carpenter's level	Basin wrench
Adjustable wrench	Tape measure
Pipe wrench	Hacksaw
Channel-type pliers	2 × 8 lumber
Power drill and bits	Drywall
Tubing cutting	Masking tape
Phillips screwdriver	Pencil or marker
Standard screwdriver	Eye and ear protection
Jigsaw	Work gloves

There are many benefits to a wall-mounted sink that, depending on your situation and needs, will offset the inherent lack of storage space. In contrast to the footprint of a traditional vanity-mounted sink, wall-mounted units can save space on the sides and in front of the fixture. More importantly, they are an essential addition to a universal-design bathroom where wheelchair accessibility is a key consideration. It's why these particular fixtures are sometimes called "roll-under" sinks.

All that practicality aside, early models at the lower end of the price spectrum were somewhat unattractive because their designs simply left the drain tailpiece, trap, and supply shutoff valves in plain sight. But there's no need for you to settle for a less-than-handsome wall-mounted sink. Manufacturers have developed two solutions to the problem of exposed plumbing. Some are designed with a bowl that conceals supply-line shutoffs, replacing the trap with sleekly designed tailpieces and squared-off trap bends. The other solution, and one more widely available, is a wall-mounted pedestal that covers the plumbing. Sinks with this feature are sometimes called "semipedestal."

We've opted to illustrate the installation of just such a sink in the instructions that follow. Keep in mind that different manufacturers sometimes use very different mounting procedures. In any case, the idea remains the same: strongly secure the sink to studs or blocking, so that it is completely stable and will not fall.

The most involved part of the installation process is usually rerouting water-supply and drain lines as necessary. You should hire a licensed plumber for this if you're not comfortable with the work. Once the plumbing is in place, the installation is quick and easy.

Although a wall-mounted sink offers many benefits—accessibility to wheelchair users among them—there's no need to sacrifice chic style for that functionality.

How to Install a Wall-Mounted Sink

Remove the existing sink if any. Remove wall coverings as necessary to install blocking for mounting the sink. Reroute water-supply and drain lines as necessary, according to the sink manufacturer's directions. The sink in this project required the centerpoints of the waste pipe be 21" and the supply lines 24¾" up from the finished floor. If you're unsure of your plumbing skills or code requirements, hire a professional plumber for this part of the project. Install blocking between the studs for attaching the mounting bracket for the sink. A doubled 2 × 8 is installed here. Have your plumbing inspected, if required by your municipality, before you install the drywall and finished wall surface.

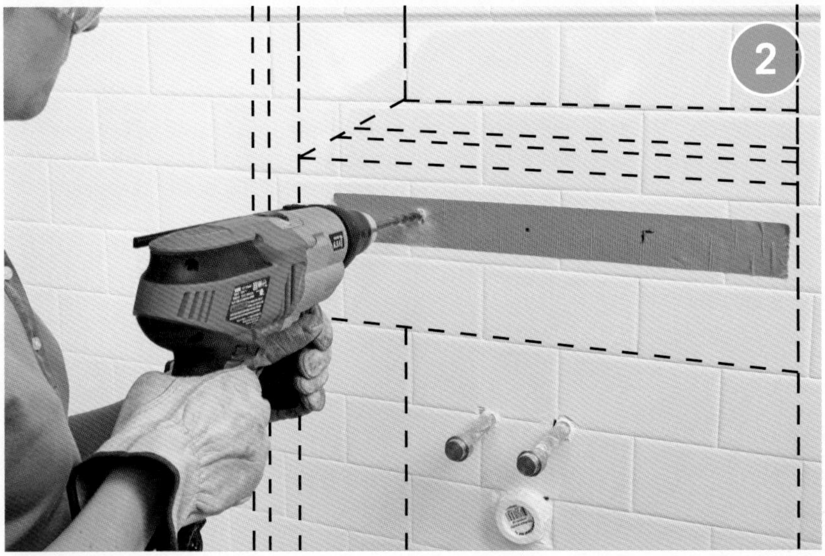

Drill guide holes for the mounting bolts if your sink is a direct-mount model, as this one is. Some wall-hung sinks are hung from a mounting bracket. The bolts used to hang this sink are threaded like lag screws on one end, with a bolt end that projects from the wall. The guide holes should be spaced exactly as the manufacturer specifies so they align with the mounting holes in the back mounting flange on the sink.

TIP: Protect tile surfaces with masking tape in the drilling areas to avoid chip-out.

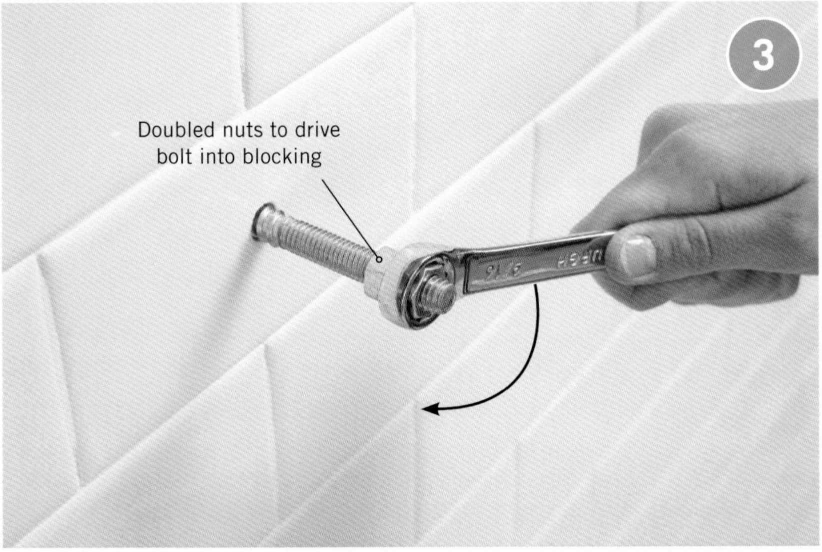

Drive the threaded mounting bolts (screw end first) into the guide holes. There should be pilot holes (smaller than the guide holes) driven into the blocking. To drive this hardware, spin a pair of nuts onto the bolt end and turn the bolt closest to you with a wrench. Drive the mounting bolt until the end is projecting out from the wall by a little more than 1½". Remove the nuts. Install the pop-up drain in the sink and then slide the sink over the ends of the mounting bolts so the mounting flange is flush against the wall. You'll want help for this. Thread the washers and nuts onto the ends of the mounting bolts and hand-tighten. Check to make sure the sink is level and then tighten the nuts with a socket or wrench, reaching up into the void between the basin and the flange. Don't overtighten—you could crack the sink flange. *(continued)*

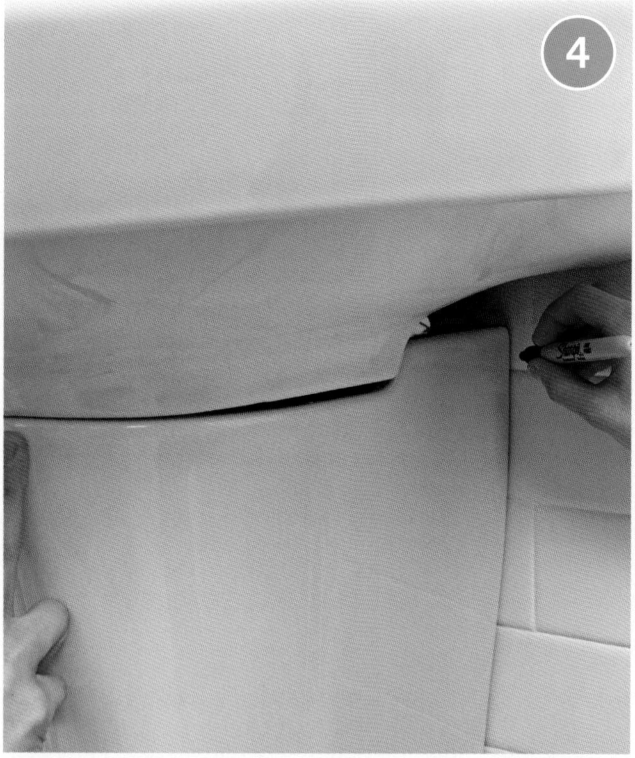

Have a helper hold the sink pedestal (in this model, a half pedestal) in position against the underside of the sink. Mark the edges of the pedestal on the wall covering as reference for installing the pedestal-mounting hardware.

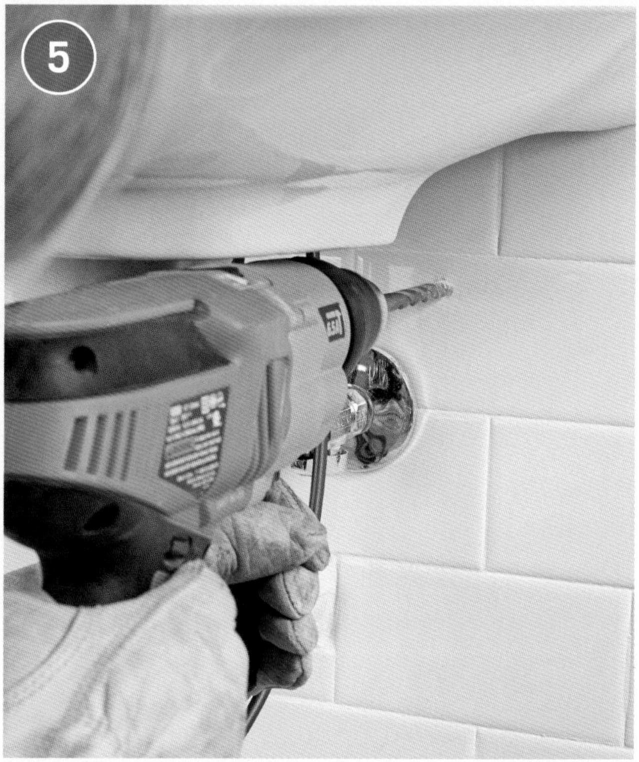

Remove the pedestal and drill the pilot holes for the pedestal-mounting bolts, which work in much the same way as the sink-mounting bolts. Drill guide and pilot holes, then drive the mounting bolts, leaving about 1¼" of the bolt end exposed.

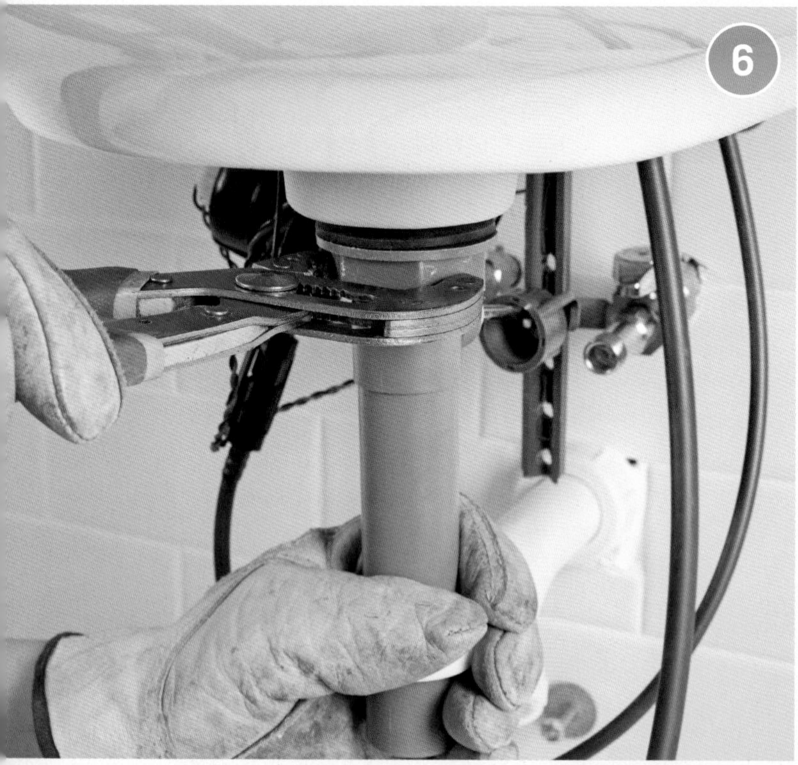

Install the drain and drain tailpiece on the sink. Also mount the faucet body to the sink deck if you have not done so already. Also attach the drain-trap arm to the drain stub-out in the wall and attach shutoff valves to the drain-supply lines.

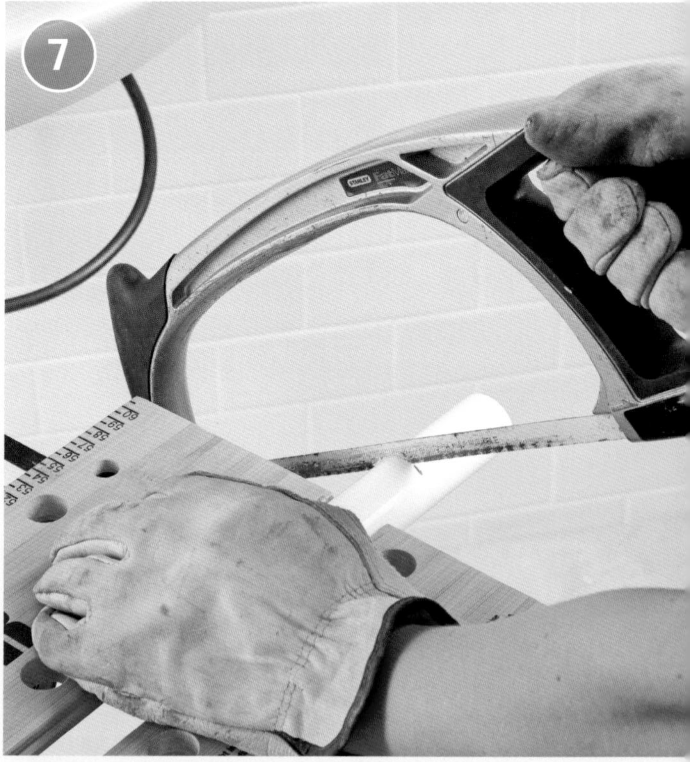

Complete the drain connection by installing a P-trap assembly that connects the tailpiece and the trap arm. Also connect the drain pop-up rod that projects out of the tailpiece to the pop-up plunger mechanism you've already installed.

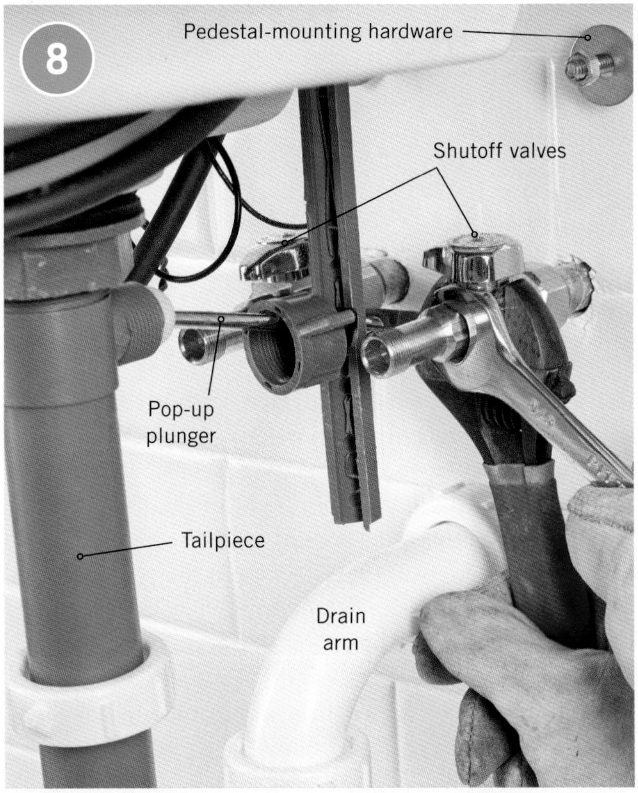

Make sure the shutoff valve fittings are tight and oriented correctly, and then hook up the faucet supply risers to the shutoff valves. Turn on the water supply and test.

LEAK FINDER

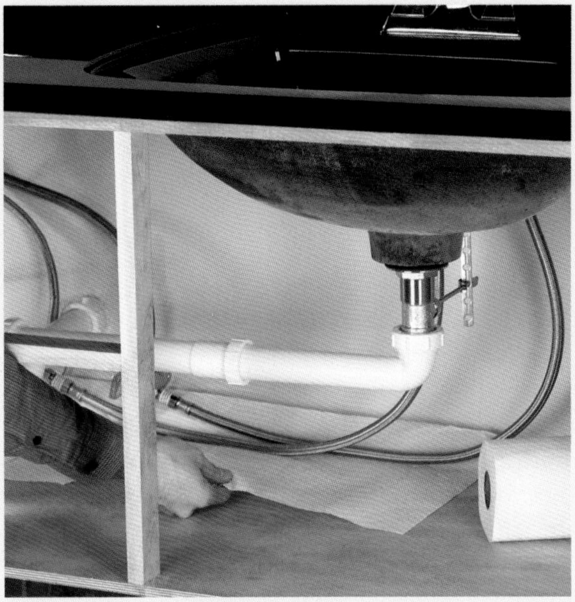

To quickly and easily find an undersink leak, lay bright white paper or paper towels under the pipes and drain connections. Open the water supply valves and run water in the sinks. It should be clear exactly where the water dripped from by the location of the drip on the paper.

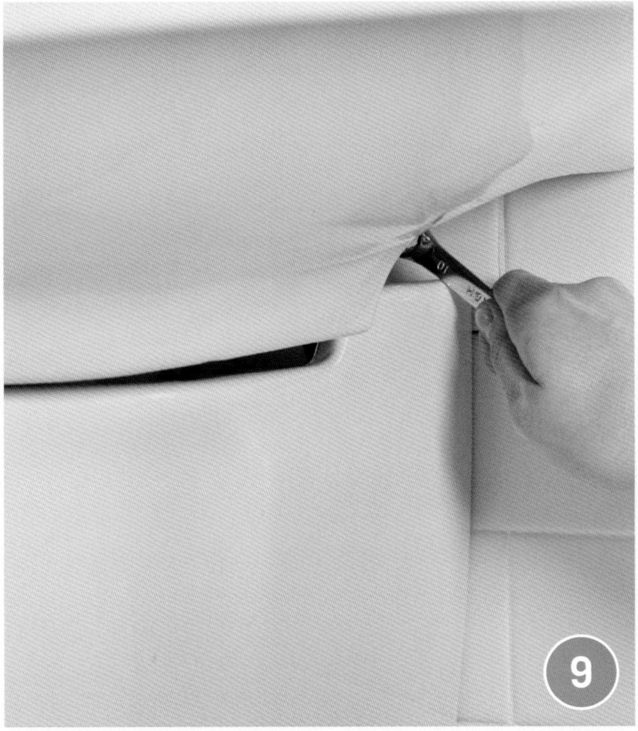

Slide the pedestal into place on the mounting studs. Working through the access space under the sink, use a wrench to tighten the mounting nut over the washer on the stud. Carefully tighten the nut until the pedestal is held securely in place. Be careful not to overtighten the nut.

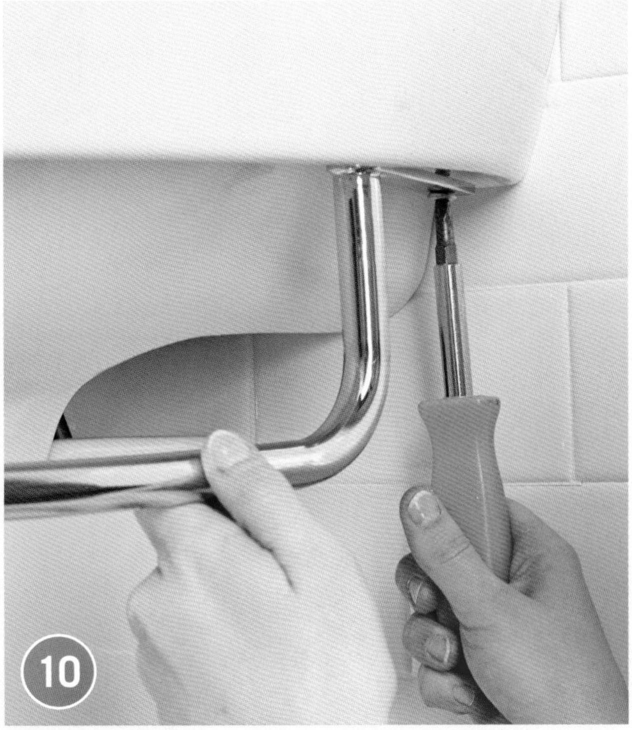

Attach the towel bar to the sink by first pushing the well nuts into the holes on the underside of the sink rim. Set the bar in place, and screw in the attachment screws on both sides, just until snug.

TOOLS & MATERIALS

- Pliers
- Wrench
- Vanity or countertop
- Vessel sink
- Pop-up drain
- P-trap and drain kit
- Faucet
- Eye and ear protection
- Work gloves

Vessel Sinks

The vessel sink harkens back to the days of washstands and washbowls. Whether it's round, square, or oval, shallow or deep, the vessel sink offers great opportunity for creativity and proudly displays its style. Vessel sinks are a perfect choice for a powder room, where they will have high visibility.

Most vessel sinks can be installed on any flat surface—from a granite countertop to a wall-mounted vanity to an antique dresser. Some sinks are designed to contact the mounting surface only at the drain flange. Others are made to be partially embedded in the surface. Take care to follow the manufacturer's instructions for cutting holes for sinks and faucets.

A beautiful vessel sink demands an equally attractive faucet. Select a tall spout mounted on the countertop or vanity top or a wall-mounted spout to accommodate the height of the vessel. To minimize splashing, spouts should direct flow to the center of the vessel, not down the side. Make sure your faucet is compatible with your vessel choice. Look for a centerset or single-handle model if you'll be custom-drilling the countertop—you only need to drill one faucet hole.

Vessel sinks are available in countless styles of materials, shapes, and sizes. Their one commonality is that they all need to be installed on a flat surface.

Vessel-Sink Options

This glass vessel sink embedded in a "floating" glass countertop is a stunning contrast to the strong and attractive wood frame anchoring it to the wall.

Vessel sinks come in many forms and colors, but a plain, curvy, brightwhite sink like this one is pleasing in almost any bathroom and with almost any faucet.

Vessel sinks don't have to be shaped like bowls. This rectangular tray sink is a cool alternative to a more common bowl shape and accents the chic, light wood vanity and cabinets in the room.

Vitreous china with a glazed enamel finish is an economical and durable choice for a vessel sink (although it is less durable than stone). Because of the flexibility of both the material and the glaze, the design options are virtually unlimited with vitreous china.

How to Install a Vessel Sink

Secure the vanity cabinet or other countertop that you'll be using to mount the vessel sink.

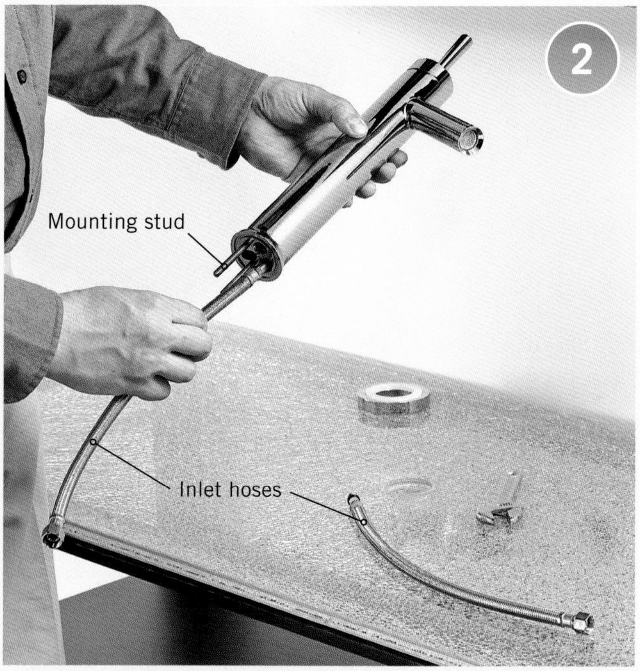

Begin hooking up the faucet. Insert the brass mounting stud into the threaded hole in the faucet base with the slotted end facing out. Hand-tighten, and then use a slotted screwdriver to tighten another half turn. Insert the inlet hoses into the faucet body and hand-tighten. Use an adjustable wrench to tighten another half turn. Do not overtighten.

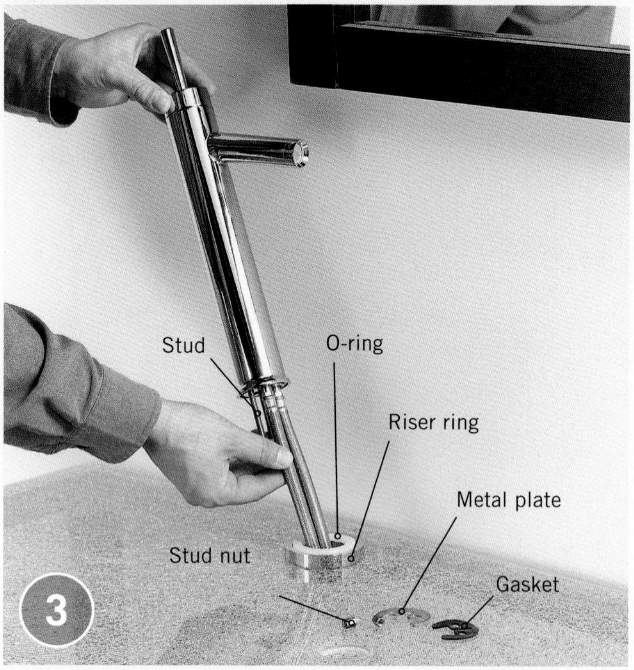

Place the O-ring on top of the riser ring over the faucet cutout in the countertop. From underneath, slide the rubber gasket and the metal plate over the mounting stud. Thread the mounting stud nut onto the mounting stud and hand-tighten. Use an adjustable wrench to tighten another half turn.

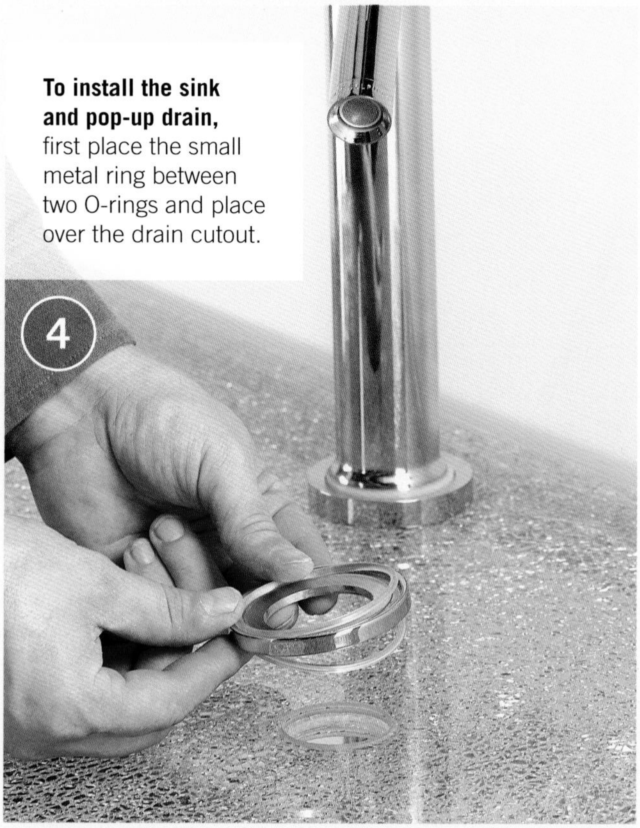

To install the sink and pop-up drain, first place the small metal ring between two O-rings and place over the drain cutout.

Place the vessel bowl on top of the O-rings. In this installation, the vessel is not bonded to the countertop.

Put the small rubber gasket over the drain hole in the vessel. From the top, push the pop-up assembly through the drain hole.

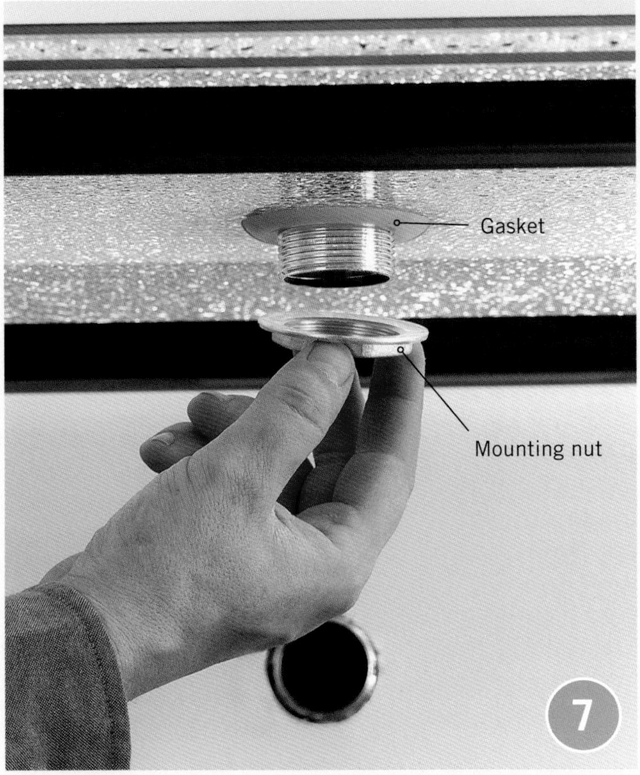

From underneath, push the large rubber gasket onto the threaded portion of the pop-up assembly. Thread the nut onto the pop-up assembly and tighten. Use an adjustable wrench or basin wrench to tighten an additional half turn. Thread the tailpiece onto the pop-up assembly.

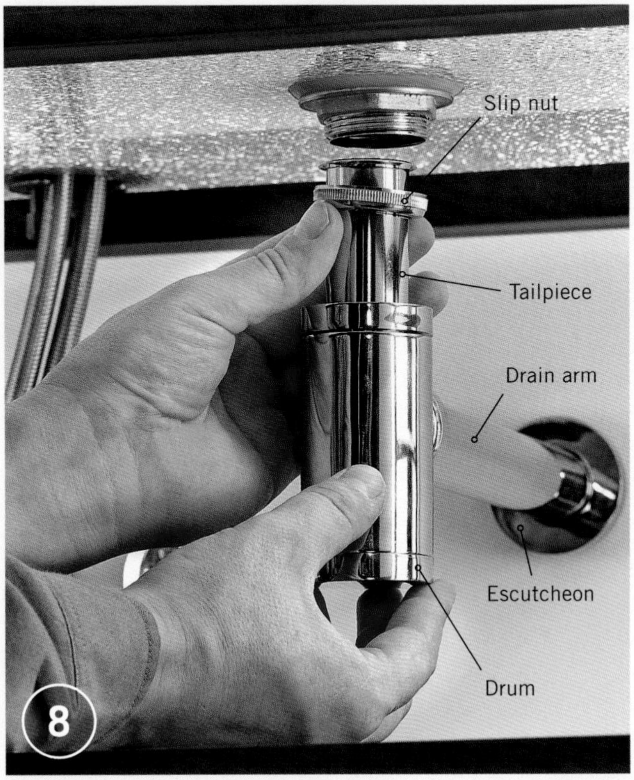

Install the drum trap. Loosen the rings on the top and outlet of the drum trap. Slide the drum-trap top hole over the tailpiece. Slide the drain arm into the side outlet with the flat side of the rubber gasket facing away from the trap. Insert the drain arm into the wall outlet. Hand-tighten the rings.

Traditional Vanity

Simple vanity bases are stages upon which much of the drama in a bathroom can play out. Because there are now so many sink and counter styles and materials, and ways of incorporating the two, a stable base that can be attractive in its own right is more important than ever.

Although vanity cabinet styles vary, the basic structure—such as incorporating a toe-kick—is common to the majority of them. The process outlined here covers the basic way that most vanities are secured in place to provide ample storage and sturdy foundation for sinks and countertops.

A traditional bathroom base cabinet serves to support an integral sink-countertop unit.

TOOLS & MATERIALS

Pencil	Basin wrench	Plumber's putty	Tub and tile caulk	Shims	Eye and ear protection
Carpenter's level	Cardboard	Lag screws	4' level	3" drywall screws	Work gloves
Screwdriver	Masking tape	Stud finder		Drill	

How to Install a Vanity Cabinet

Measure and mark the top edge of the vanity cabinet on the wall, then use an electronic level/stud finder to mark the stud locations and a level line.

Slide the vanity into position so that the back rail of the cabinet can later be fastened to studs at both corners and in the center. The back of the cabinet should also be flush against the wall. (If the wall surface is uneven, position the vanity so it contacts the wall in at least one spot and the back cabinet rail is parallel with the wall.)

Using a level as a guide, shim below the vanity cabinet until the unit is level.

VARIATION: To install 2 or more cabinets, set the cabinets in position against the wall, and align the cabinet fronts. If 1 cabinet is higher than the other, shim under the lower cabinet until the 2 are even. Clamp the cabinet faces together, then drill countersunk pilot holes spaced 12" apart through the face frames so they go at least halfway into the face frame of the second cabinet. Drive wood screws through the pilot holes to join the cabinets together.

At the stud locations marked on the wall, drive 3" drywall screws through the rail on the cabinet back and into the framing members. The screws should be driven at both corners and in the center of the back rail.

Run a bead of caulk along small gaps between the vanity and wall, and between the vanity and floor. For larger gaps, use ¼-round molding between the vanity and wall. Between the vanity and floor, install the same baseboard material used to cover the gap between the wall and floor.

Vanity Top with Integral Sink

An integral sink-countertop is the traditional match to a stock bathroom base cabinet.

Perhaps the easiest sink of all to install is one in which the countertop and sink are a single integrated unit that simply is attached to a standard vanity cabinet. These integrated sinks now come in hundreds of different styles and in a variety of materials, including premium solid-surface materials or synthetic stones. Gone are the days when integrated sinks were those plastic faux-marble units that looked as cheap as they were. Today's integrated bathroom sinks can be quite attractive as a design statement and are available in lots of different shapes and configurations.

What hasn't changed, though, is the ease with which they can be installed—a feature that makes them very attractive to DIYers. Since integral sinks are predrilled for faucet and drain hookups, installing one is really just matter of laying the unit on the vanity cabinet, leveling and attaching it, and making the plumbing connections.

TOOLS & MATERIALS

- Level
- Shims
- Faucet and drain fittings
- Wrenches
- Plumber's putty
- Silicone caulk
- Caulk gun
- Eye and ear protection
- Work gloves

How to Install a Vanity Top with Integral Sink

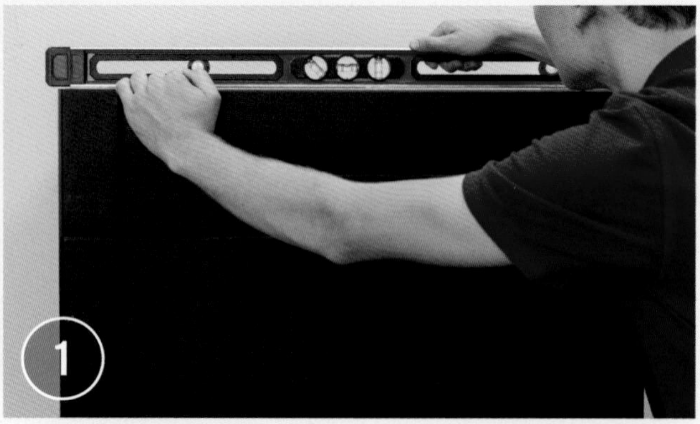

Check the vanity cabinet to make sure it is level. If not, you can place a shim under the base of the cabinet to bring it to level.

Test-fit the countertop-sink unit to make sure it fits solidly on the vanity. If it wobbles, or if the cabinet itself could not be leveled, you can level the countertop by placing shims between the bottom of the countertop and the top edge of the vanity cabinet.

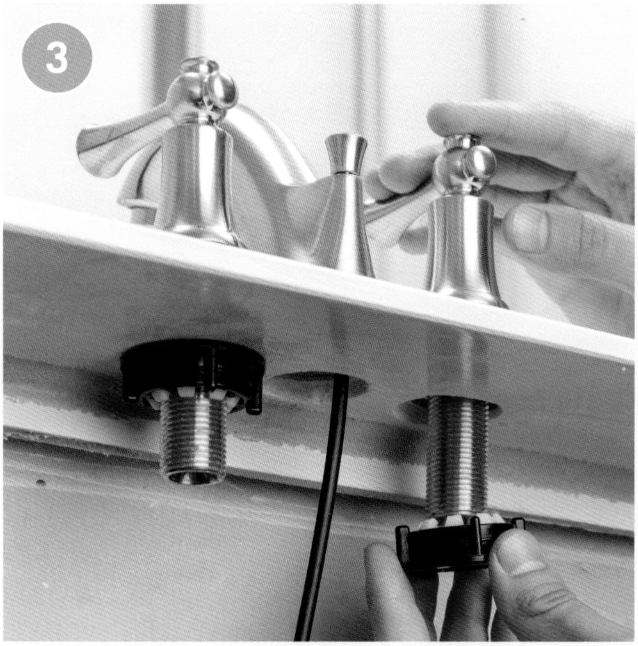

Remove the sink-countertop, place it on sawhorses, and then attach the faucet unit using the predrilled cutouts in the countertop. This is an easy matter of threading the mounting nuts onto the faucet tailpieces from below, but always make sure to follow the faucet manufacturer's directions. If you wish, you can also preattach the water-supply tubes to the bottom of the faucet tailpieces.

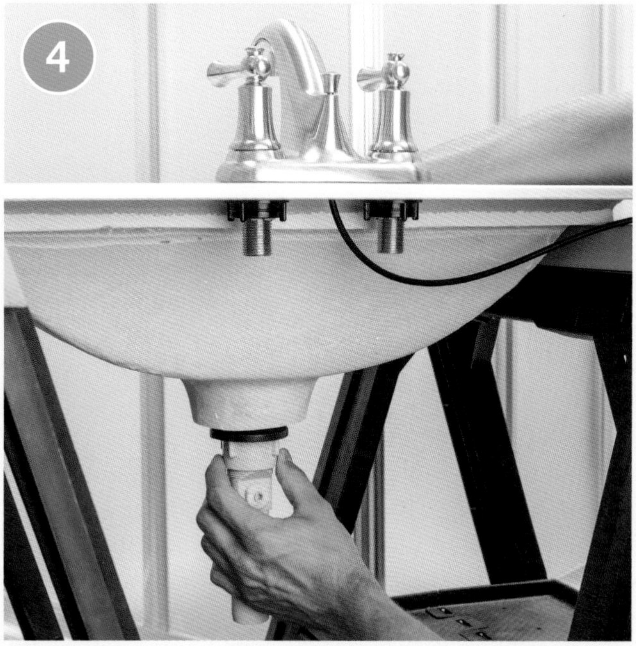

Begin installing the drain unit, again following the package instructions. Make sure to use plumber's putty or sealant between the sink surface and the bottom of the drain flange.

Finish up the drain installation by connecting the drain-stopper cable or lever to the pop-up drain fitting on the drain tailpiece.

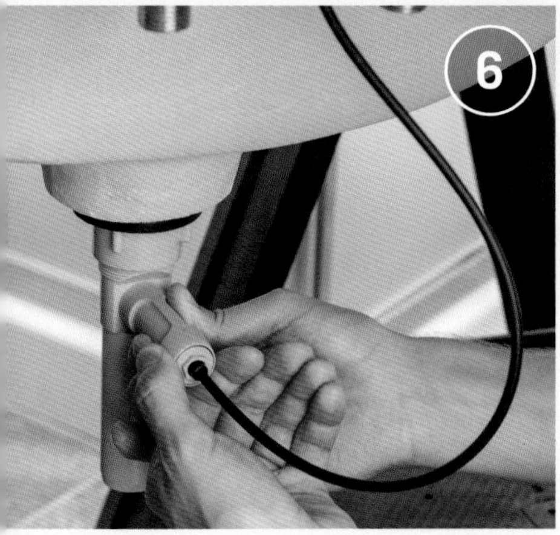

Apply a bead of silicone caulk around the top lip of the vanity cabinet. Silicone caulk has good adhesive properties, and no other fasteners are required. Set the sink-countertop unit onto the cabinet, and press down firmly to bond it to the cabinet. Let the caulk dry completely before completing the plumbing hookups.

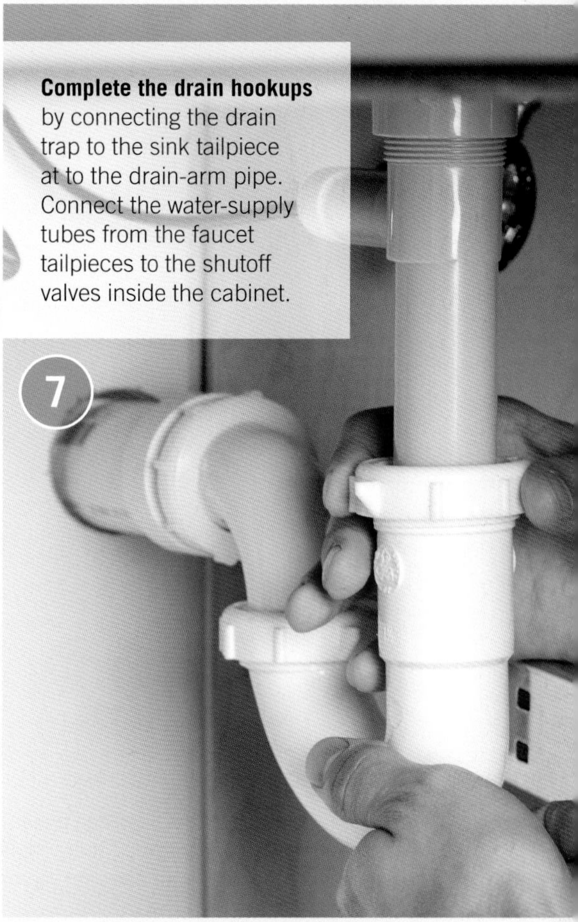

Complete the drain hookups by connecting the drain trap to the sink tailpiece at to the drain-arm pipe. Connect the water-supply tubes from the faucet tailpieces to the shutoff valves inside the cabinet.

Plumbing a Double-Bowl Vanity

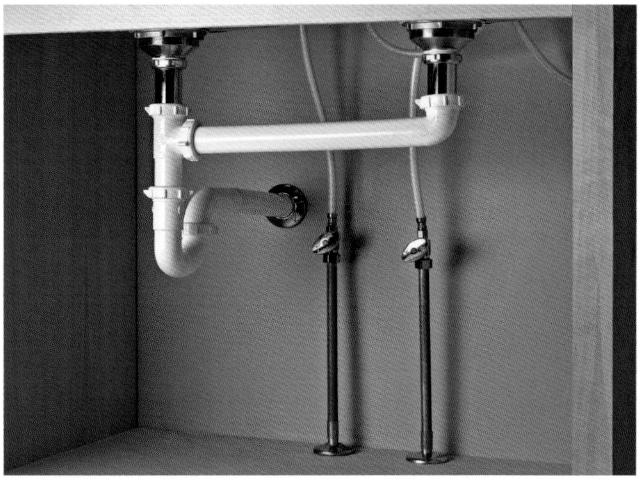

Double-bowl vanities have drain plumbing that's very similar to double-bowl kitchen sinks. In most cases, the drain tailpieces are connected beneath one of the tailpieces at a continuous waste T. The drain line from the second bowl must slope downward toward the T. From the T, the drain should have a trap (usually a P-trap) that connects to the trap arm coming out of the wall.

Side-by-side sinks are a bathroom luxury, especially for busy couples (which accounts for why they are called "his-and-her" sinks) or busy bathrooms. Although the basics of installing a vanity for a double sink are structurally the same as a single-bowl vanity, the plumbing requires modification to accommodate the extra fixture.

TOOLS & MATERIALS

- Carpenter's level
- Screwdrivers
- Stud finder
- Power drill and bits
- Basin wrench
- Adjustable wrench
- Hacksaw
- Silicone caulk
- Dual-outlet valves
- Braided-steel supply lines
- P-trap
- PVC connections
- Plumber's putty
- Eye and ear protection
- Work gloves

How to Plumb a Double Sink

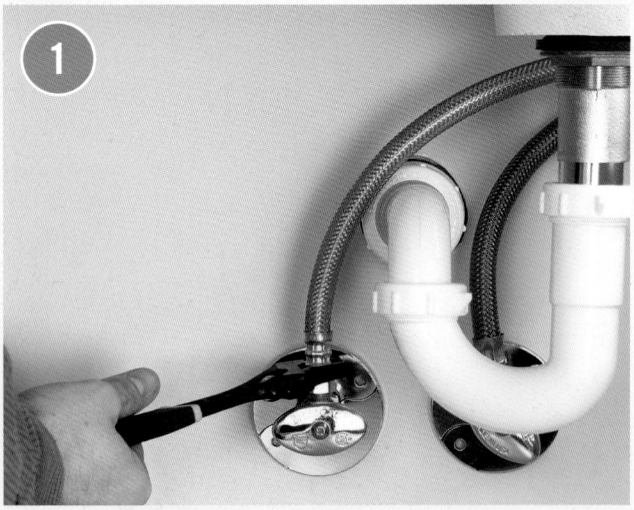

Shut off the supply valves located under the sink. Disconnect and remove the supply lines connecting the faucet to the valves. Loosen the P-trap nuts at both ends and remove the P-trap.

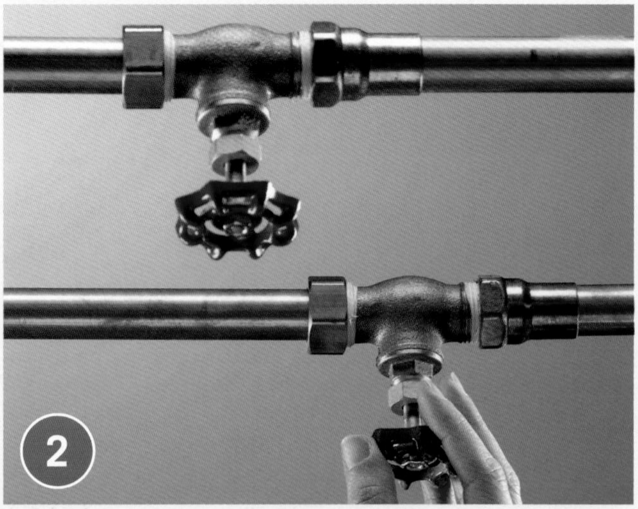

Remove the existing countertop and vanity. Turn off the house water supply at the main shutoff valve. Drain the remaining water by opening the faucet at the lowest point in the house. Use a hacksaw to remove existing undersink shutoff valves.

Slide the new dual-outlet valve onto the hot-water supply line, pass the nut and compression washer over the pipe, and tighten with a wrench. Install the dual-outlet valve on the cold supply line in the same way.

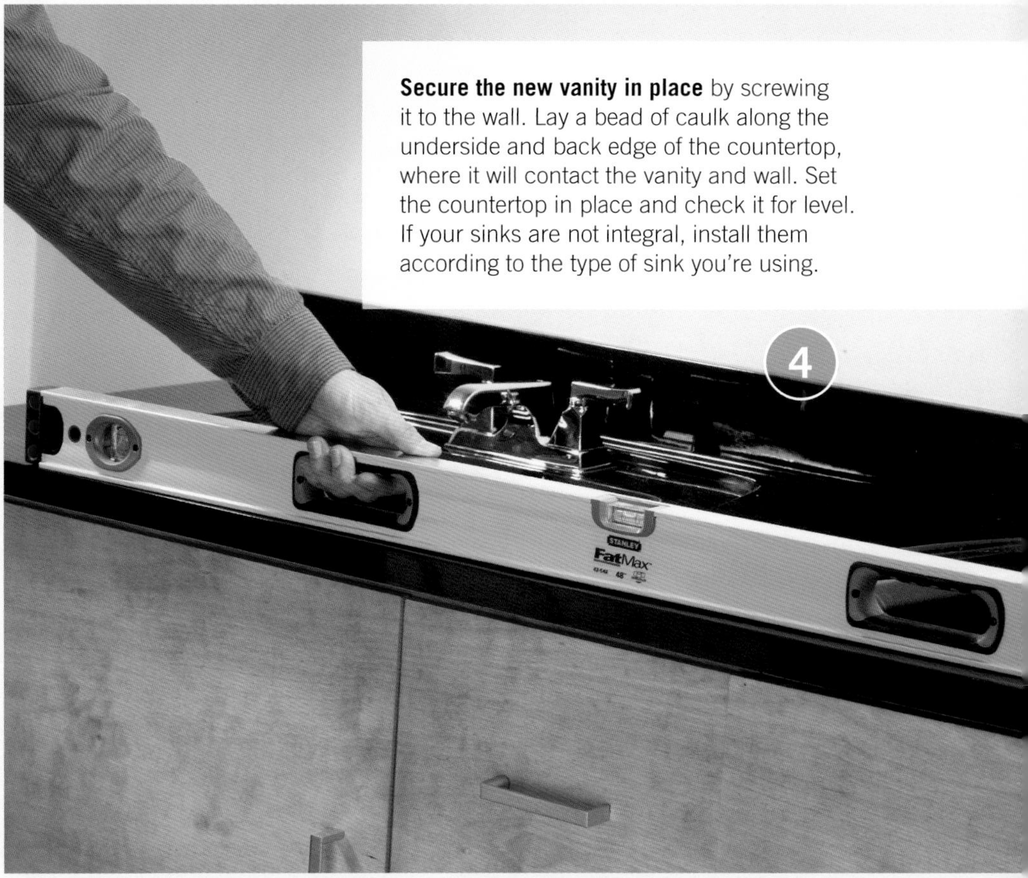

Secure the new vanity in place by screwing it to the wall. Lay a bead of caulk along the underside and back edge of the countertop, where it will contact the vanity and wall. Set the countertop in place and check it for level. If your sinks are not integral, install them according to the type of sink you're using.

Seat the faucets for the double sinks as you would for a single sink, by applying a bead of putty on the underside of the bases (unless they are to be used with gaskets instead of putty). Secure them in place by tightening the locking nuts on the underside of the faucets.

Connect a new PVC P-trap to the undersink drain pipe, and attach a T-connector to the trap. Extend PVC connections to the drain assemblies of both sinks.

Connect the pop-up stopper linkage. Connect the cold-water supply lines to the appropriate faucet tailpieces and repeat with the hot-water supply lines. Turn on the main water supply, remove the faucet aerator, and run the water in the sinks. Check for leaks and replace the aerator.

Lavatory Faucets

Bathroom faucets come in four basic mounting styles: centerset, single hole, wall mounted, and widespread. The type you choose depends largely on the sink or faucet body you are using—the new faucet may need to match the existing fixture. But in any case, the range of designs available in all mounting styles is astounding.

Widespread faucets have a clean, sophisticated look. They come in three pieces instead of one: a hot tap, a cold tap, and a spout. Each piece is mounted separately in its own hole in the sink. The hot and cold taps (valves) are connected to the spout with reinforced flexible hoses. If your lavatory doesn't have a predrilled flange, the great advantage to the widespread configuration is that you gain flexibility in locating your spout and handles (probably a bigger advantage for tubs than for lavatories). Even models made for bathroom lavatories, like the one you see here, offer many creative configuration options.

TOOLS & MATERIALS

Heatproof grease	Adjustable wrench
Teflon tape	Basin wrench
Measuring tape	Channel-type pliers
Loctite	Screwdriver
Pipe-joint compound	Standing flashlight
Plumber's putty	Eye and ear protection
New 3-piece faucet	Work gloves
Supply lines	

Single-body and centerset faucets are designed to fit into standard hole configurations. Make sure you know your sink's dimensions before buying the faucet: the most important dimension is the hole spread: 4 inches on center and 8 inches on center are most common.

An increasingly popular subset of single-hole faucets are touch faucets or motion-sensing faucets, such as the one shown here. Easy to install, these are also less challenging for anyone with motor-skill difficulties or serious disabilities to use.

BASIC LAVATORY FAUCET TYPES

Widespread faucets allow you to customize the locations and orientation of the faucets and spout in your sink deck.

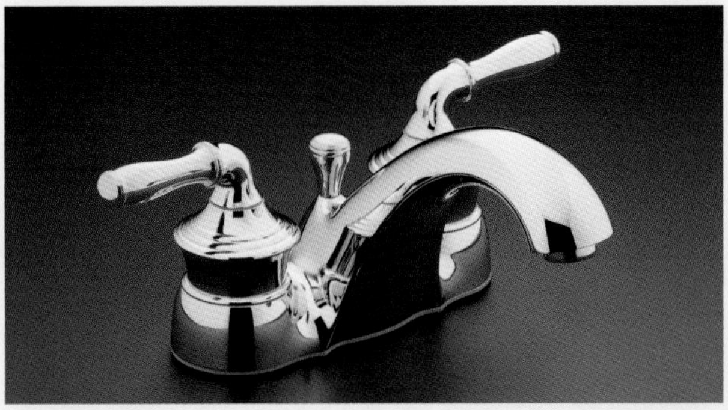

Single-body faucets are faster and easier to install and are extremely reliable.

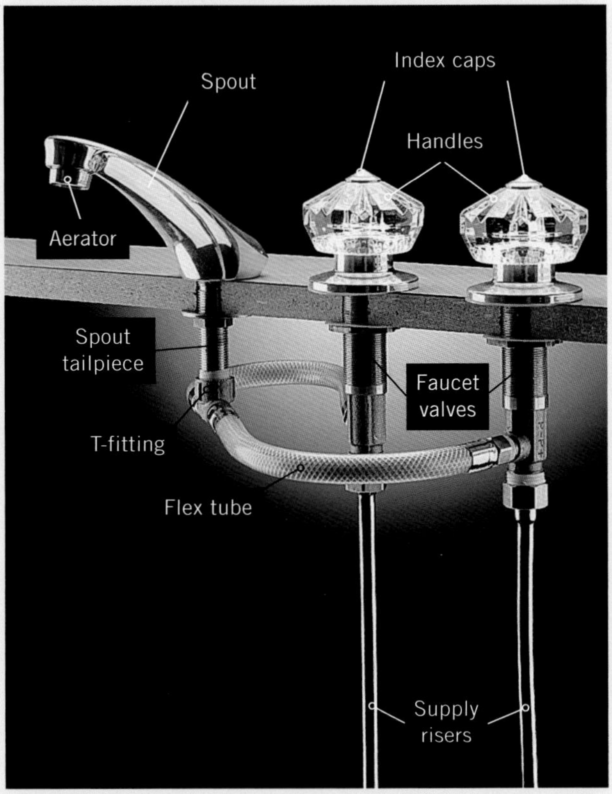

Widespread faucets come in three pieces, a spout and two valves. Supply risers carry hot and cold water to the valves, which are turned to regulate the amount of water going to the spout, where the water is mixed. Water travels from the valves to the spout through flex tubes, which in turn attach to the spout tailpiece via a T-fitting. Three-piece faucets designed to work with a pop-up stopper have a clevis and a lift rod. The handles attach with handle screws that are covered with index caps. An aerator is screwed on the faucet spout after debris is flushed from the faucet.

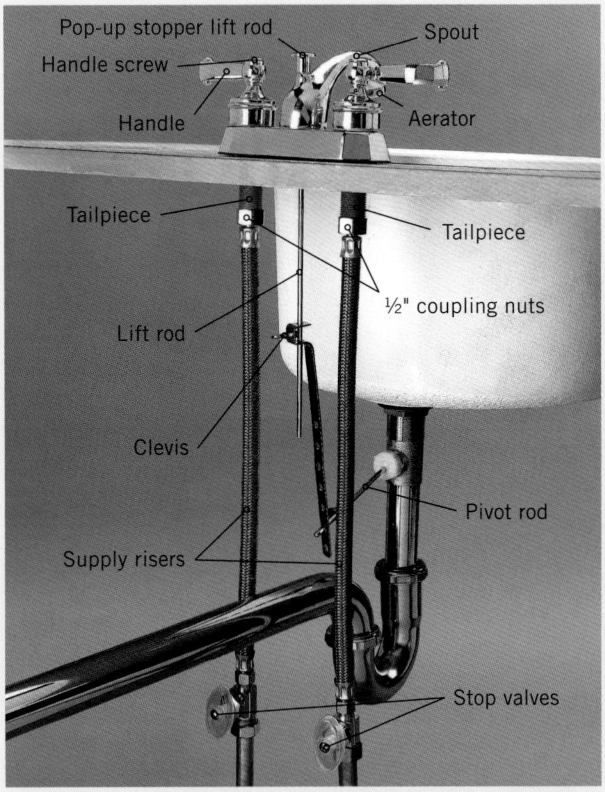

The tailpieces of a standard deck-mounted, one-piece bathroom sink faucet are 4" apart on center. As long as the 2 outside holes in the back of your sink measure 4" from center to center, and you have a middle hole for a pop-up stopper, you can put in any standard one-piece bathroom faucet with a pop-up stopper. The faucet is secured to the sink with mounting nuts that screw onto the tailpieces from below. Also get two flexible stainless-steel supply risers for sinks, long enough to replace the old tubes. These typically attach to the stop valves with ⅜" compression-sized coupling nuts and to the faucet with standard faucet coupling nuts. But take your old tubes and the old compression nuts from the stop valves to the store to ensure a match. The clevis, lift rod, and pivot rod are parts of the pop-up stopper assembly. The handles attach with handle screws that are covered with index caps.

How to Install a Widespread Faucet

Shut off the water to the existing faucet and open the valves to drain the water. Disconnect the water-supply tubes from the faucet, and remove the old faucet by unscrewing the mounting nuts.

NOTE: Removing the old faucet and installing the new one may be easiest if you remove the sink from the vanity.

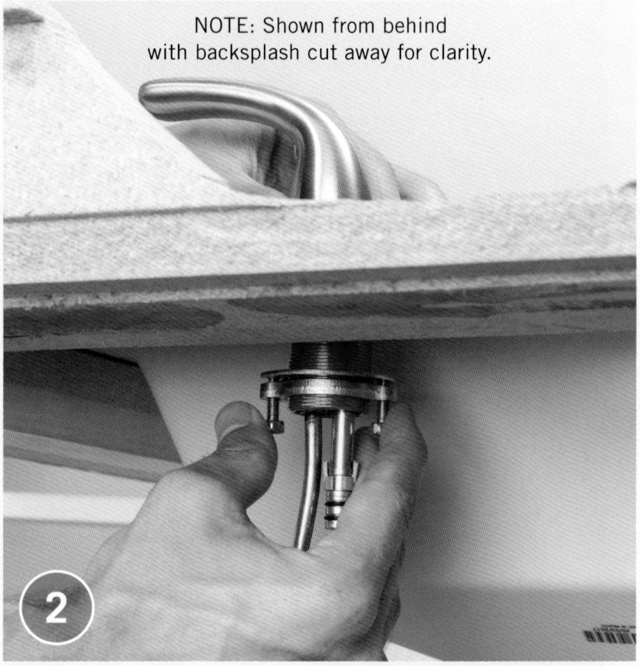

Clean away any existing plumber's putty or sealant from the surface of the sink, then lay a new bead of plumbers putty around each of the 3 openings. Install the 2 valves into the sink cutout openings by inserting the spout and valves and then threading the mounting screws onto the tailpieces from below the sink.

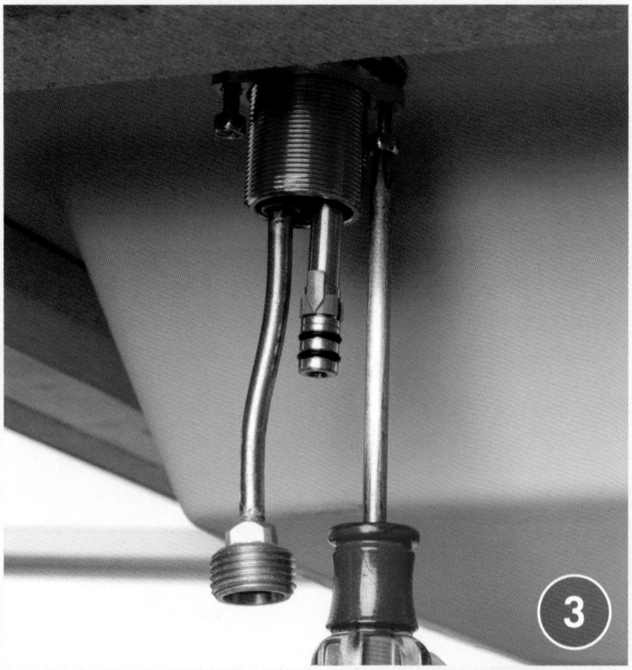

Exact mounting procedures vary; our faucet has retainer screws that are tightened after the mounting nut is threaded over the tailpieces. This secures the valves and spout tightly to the sink.

Repeat this procedure to install the center spout. Make sure the spout is aligned correctly to be perpendicular to the back of the sink.

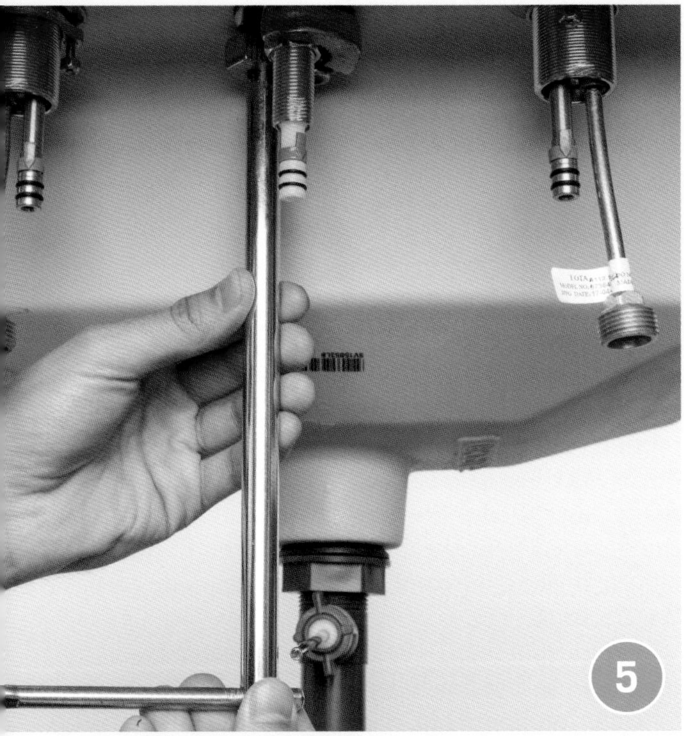

Tighten the spout mounting nut securely. A basin wrench will make this easier, since access to the mounting nut may be difficult.

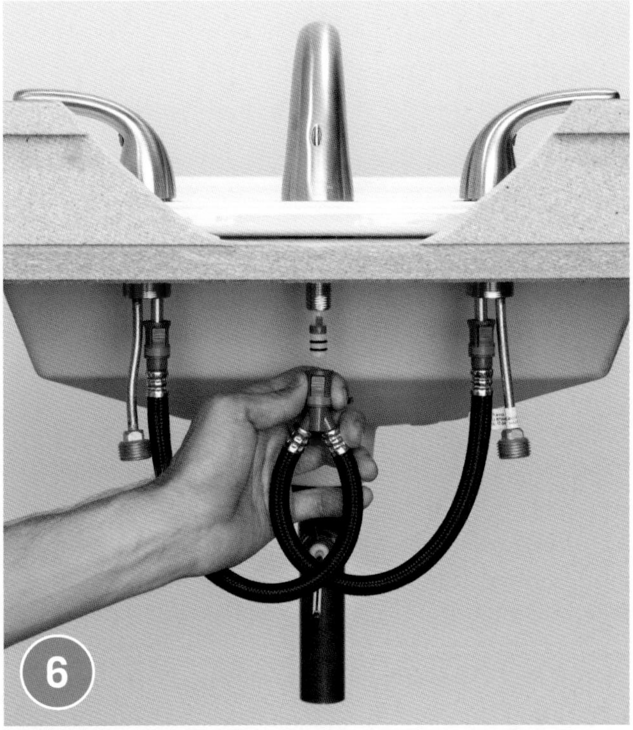

Attach the water connection tubes from the valve tailpieces to the spout tailpiece. Thread the mounting nuts by hand, then tighten slightly with channel-type pliers or an adjustable wrench (in tight quarters, this can also be done with a basin wrench).

Connect water-supply tubes from the water shutoff valves to the water-supply tubes on the faucet-valve tailpieces using an adjustable wrench (or basin wrench, where access is limited). In standard practice, the hot water normally connects to the left faucet valve and the cold water to the right. Turn on the water and test the faucet. If any fittings leak, tighten them slightly until they are watertight.

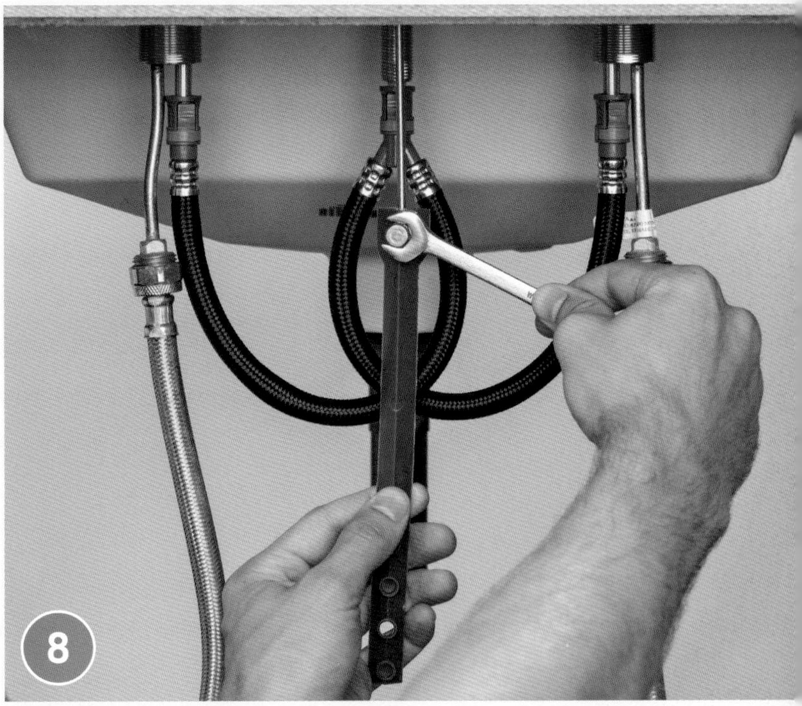

Attach the drain-stopper linkage to the push rod and to the stopper pivot lever.

TOOLS & MATERIALS

- Faucet and hardware
- Adjustable wrenches
- Channel-type pliers
- Teflon tape
- Flashlight
- Eye and ear protection
- Work gloves

Hands-Free Bathroom Faucets

If you've ever washed your hands in an airport bathroom, chances are you've already come across a hands-free faucet. Developed to conserve water and stop the spread of disease, these faucets have quickly become ubiquitous in commercial facilities across the country and around the world.

But now homeowners can enjoy the benefits of hands-free faucets in their own bathrooms. Although not as widely available as standard faucets, different hands-free units are beginning to appear in the aisles of large home centers and hardware stores nationwide. These feature varying technologies depending on the manufacturer.

The most common type of commercial hands-free bathroom faucet relies on an infrared motion sensor, much like those in home-security systems. When something solid passes within the sensor's range, the faucet turns on for a predetermined period of time. Home units operate a little differently. They include motion-sensing and "touch-on, touch-off" units. The model we selected for this installation project uses an electrical field sensor that reacts to the stored charge in every human body, called *capacitance*. Whether motion or touch activated, these home faucets rely on an electrical field created by a solenoid connected to the faucet body. When a human hand disrupts the electrical field, the faucet turns on or off. Touch faucets operate the same, but the faucet body itself is the electrical field.

For most of these types of faucets, water temperature and flow rate are set manually before the faucet is "programmed." Then it's a case of tapping the faucet body or waving a hand near it to start or stop the flow.

Although these faucets are pricier than standard manual models, they represent a leap forward for people with motor-skill difficulties, or for preventing disease spread between family members using a busy bathroom in a crowded house. The good news is that they are not much more challenging to install than a standard faucet—with the exception of units that are hardwired into the home's electrical system. Hardwired units should be installed by a licensed professional.

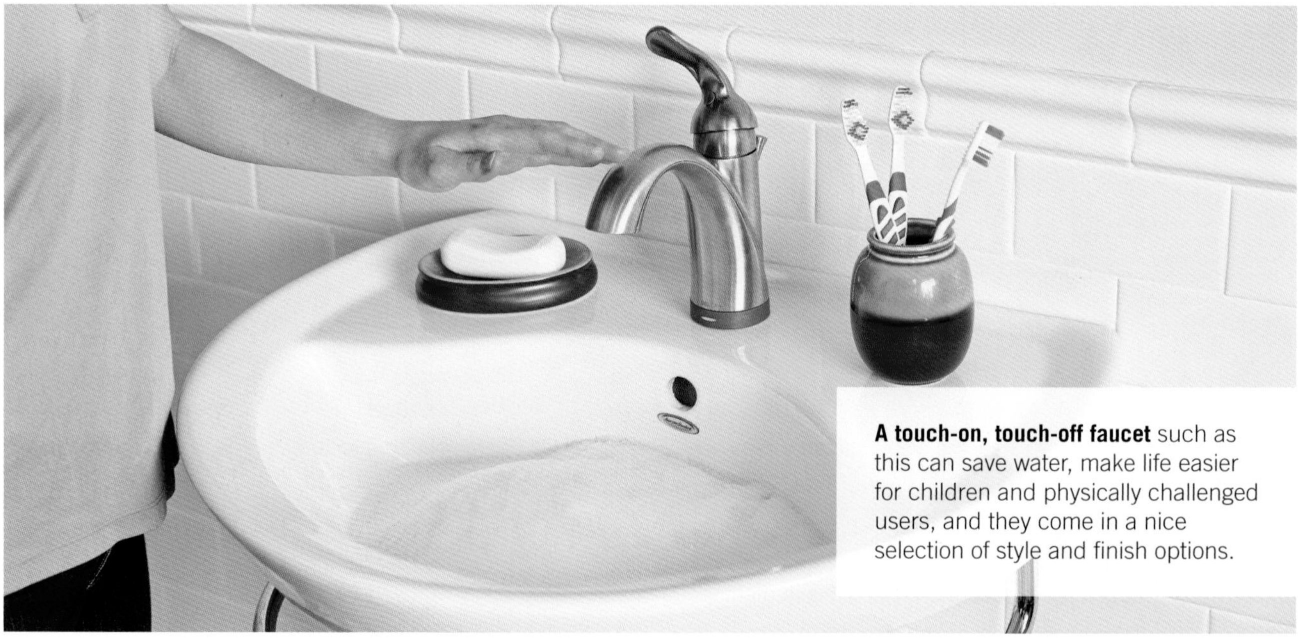

A touch-on, touch-off faucet such as this can save water, make life easier for children and physically challenged users, and they come in a nice selection of style and finish options.

How to Install a Hands-Free Faucet

Check the parts in the box against the instruction-sheet part list. Remove the center from the base gasket as necessary and thread the base's LED wire through the hole in the gasket. Seat the gasket into the groove in the insulator base and ensure that is snug and level.

NOTE: If your vanity deck has multiple holes, you'll need to use the supplied escutcheon plate. Run the LED wire through the escutcheon hole and seat the insulator base on top of the escutcheon (make sure the LED light is facing forward).

Slide the mounting bracket into place under the sink, on the mounting post. Be sure that the LED wire and supply lines are not crimped by the bracket. The mounting bracket needs to be oriented correctly; check the manufacturer's instructions to ensure it's situated in the right way and secured with the metal side down.

Ensure the LED wire is not crimped and thread the mounting-post nut on the mounting post. Hand-tighten. Check again that the faucet body is positioned correctly on the top of the sink and the LED light is facing forward. Tighten the mounting nut with a wrench, or with the tool supplied by the manufacturer, as shown here.

(continued)

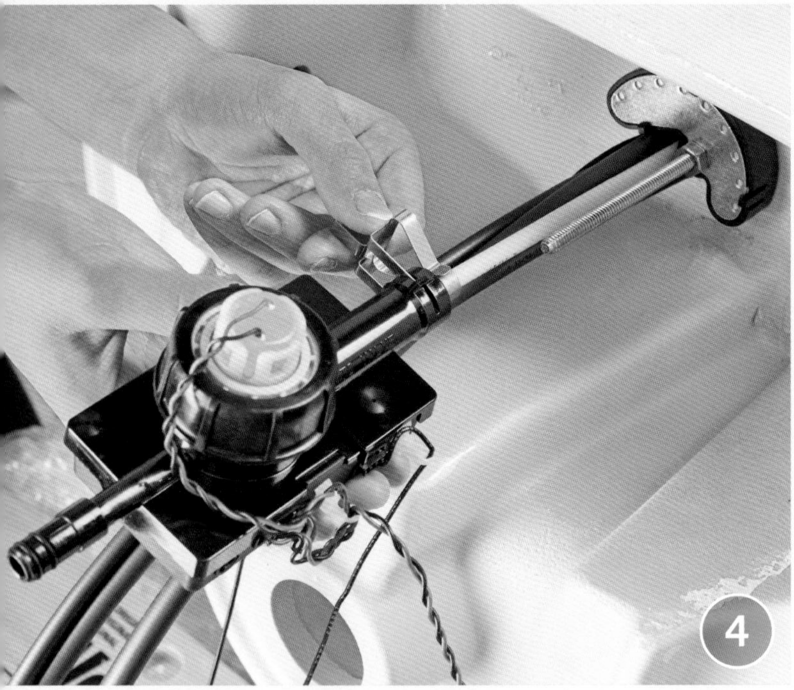

Insert the outlet tube into the top of the solenoid until it is snugly attached. Secure the tube in place with the metal clip provided. These clips can often be attached more than one way, so check the instructions to make sure you've installed the clip correctly. Then lightly pull on the solenoid to ensure the tube is firmly attached and won't come free under pressure.

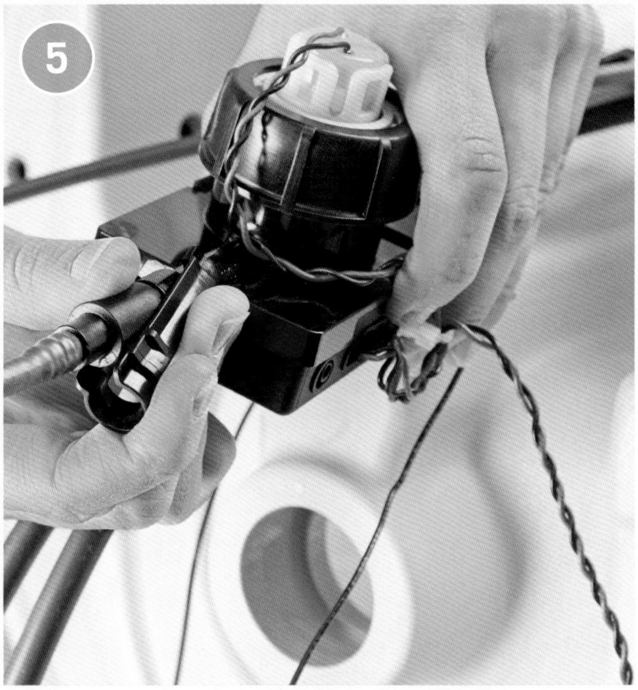

Slide the feeder hose into the bottom of the solenoid until it is snug. Snap the attachment clip in place to secure the hose, and again pull gently on the hose to make sure the clip is secure.

Touch the cold supply knob or another ground with your hand to dissipate any residual static charge. Remove the protective cap or endpiece from the end of the LED wire hanging from the faucet. Plug the prong of the wire into the hole in the solenoid. Make sure it is all the way in (on this model, you push until you hear a click).

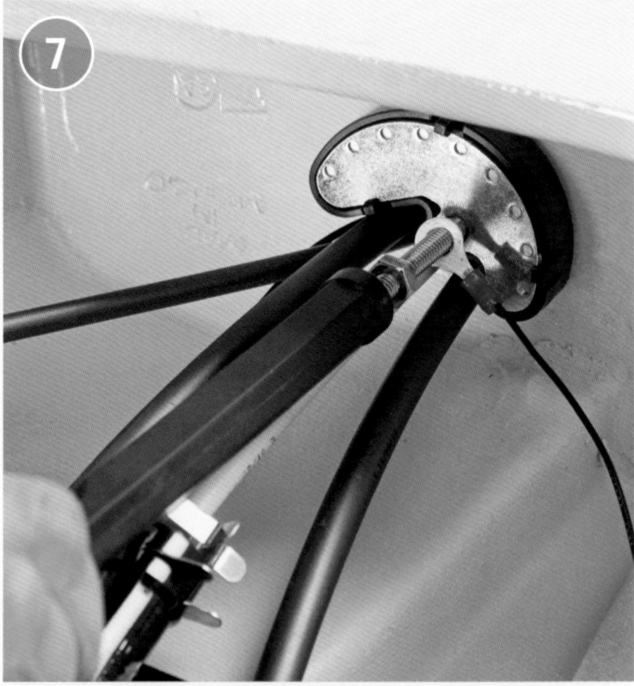

Slide the solenoid ground wire onto the mounting post and secure it in place with a nut. Tighten the nut with a wrench, ensuring that the wires don't twist together. Put the batteries in the battery box and then connect the wire from the solenoid to the connection on the battery box. Secure the battery box to the cabinet floor, wall, or underside of the sink according to the manufacturer's directions and the type of vanity you have.

HOOK UP AND TEST THE FAUCET

Connect the water lines for your hands-free faucet as you would with any faucet, using the supplied ferrules and check valves in place of the existing hardware on the stops. Insert the new ferrule and screw the check valve in place, hand tight. Then tighten the nut just one turn with a wrench. Attach the cold and hot lines to the proper check valves on the cold and hot stops—they must be connected to the appropriate stop (the ends of the faucet body supply lines will usually be marked as they are in this case—with either a color or other designation to signify which stop the supply line goes to). Attach the cold supply line to the check valve first, then repeat with the hot supply line. Snug to hand tight and then use a wrench to tighten one full turn more. Loop supply lines rather than cutting them.

Turn the faucet handle to the closed position and remove the aerator (use the manufacturer's supplied tool for this). Turn on both water supplies. Turn on the water for about 1 minute. Turn off the water and reinstall the aerator. Check the solenoid, stops, and faucet for leaks.

To set and test the touch feature, turn the handle on and leave it in the position that gives you the preferred temperature and flow rate. Touch the faucet body firmly and deliberately to turn the flow off. And then try tapping to turn it on. Tap at different areas around the body to turn the faucet on and off. If you've installed a motion-sensor faucet, you should be able to perform these functions just by moving your hand close to the faucet.

Lavatory Drains

Pop-up stoppers are chrome-plated, long-legged plugs in bathroom sinks that are opened and closed with a knob behind the spout. The stopper itself is just the visible part of a behind-the-scenes assembly that makes sure the stopper sits and stands on cue. New faucets come with their own pop-up stopper assemblies, assuming they use one, but you may also purchase one by itself. This will include everything from the stopper to the pipe that drops into the trap. Choose a pop-up stopper assembly that's heavy brass under the chrome finish. This will hold up better to time and abuse than a plastic or light-gauge metal model.

Installing a lavatory drain is a bit trickier than installing a kitchen-sink drain because most have a pop-up stopper with linkage.

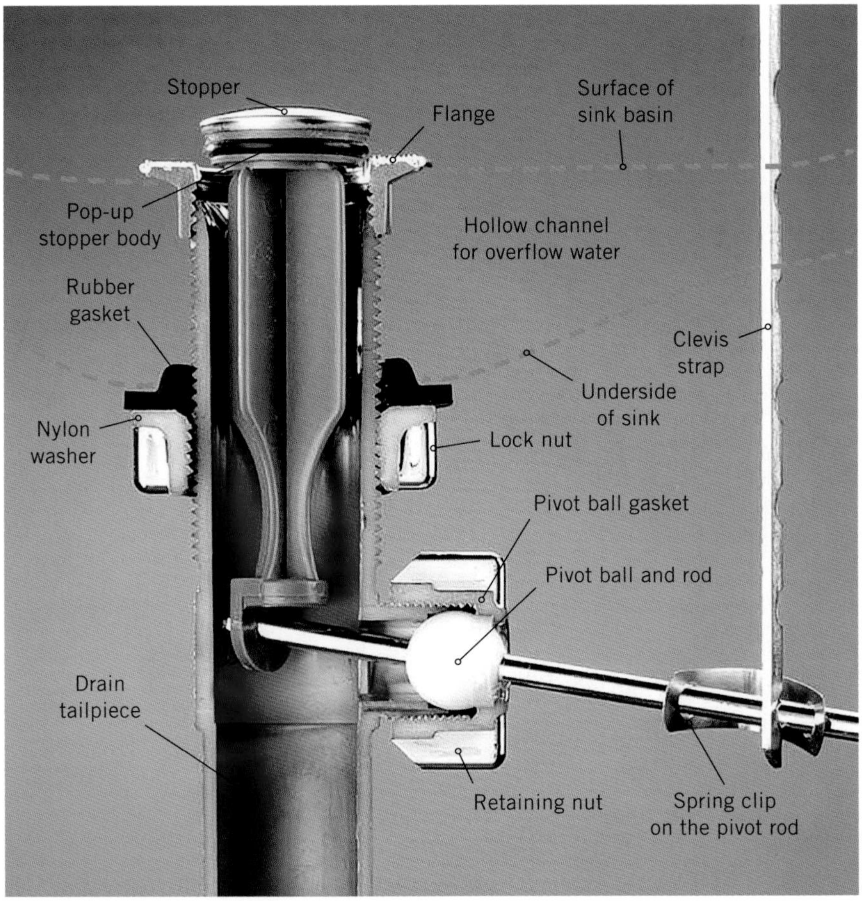

Pop-up stoppers keep objects from falling down the drain, and they make filling and draining the sink easy. When you pull up on the lift rod, the clevis strap is raised, which raises the pivot rod, which seesaws on the pivot ball and pulls the pop-up stopper down against the flange. This blocks water through the sink drain, but water may still overflow into the overflow channel drain through overflow ports in the pop-up body. This is a nice feature if you leave the water running in a plugged basin by mistake.

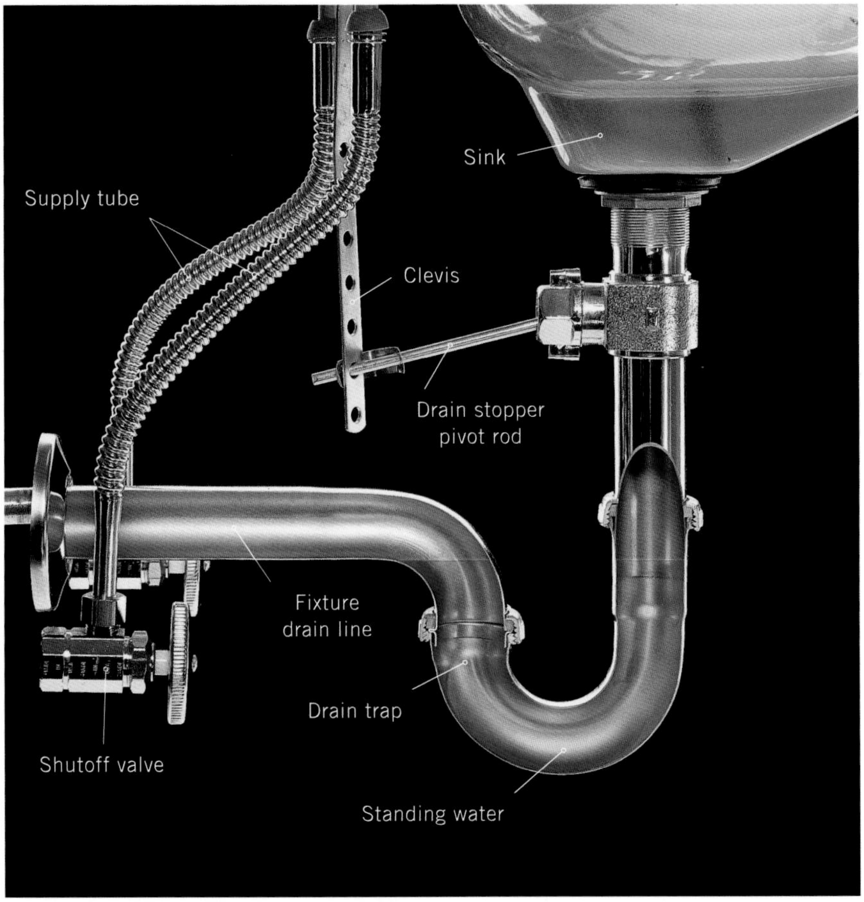

The lavatory drain trap holds water that seals the drain line and prevents sewer gases from entering the home. Each time a drain is used, the standing trap water is flushed away and replaced by new water. The shape of the trap and fixture drain line resembles the letter P, and sink traps are called P-traps.

How to Replace a Pop-Up Stopper

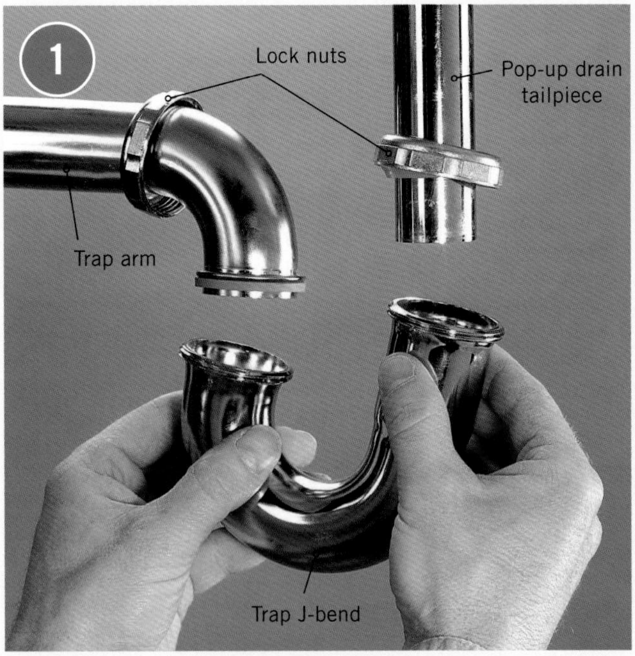

Put a basin under the trap to catch water. Loosen the nuts at the outlet and inlet to the trap J-bend by hand or with channel-type pliers and remove the bend. The trap will slide off the pop-up body tailpiece when the nuts are loose. Keep track of washers and nuts and their up/down orientation by leaving them on the tubes.

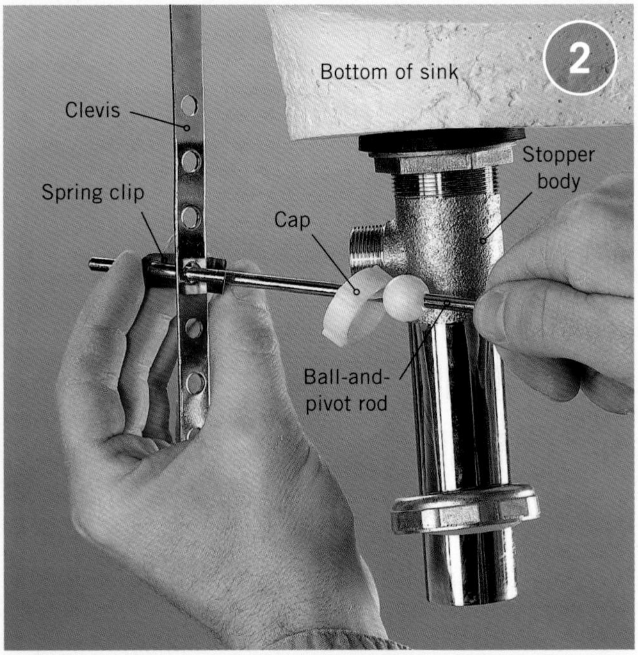

Unscrew the cap holding the ball-and-pivot rod in the pop-up body and withdraw the ball. Compress the spring clip on the clevis and withdraw the pivot rod from the clevis.

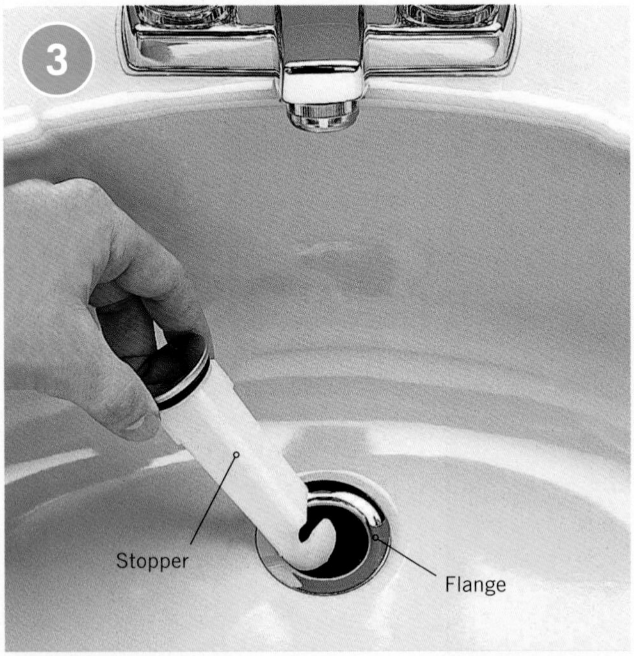

Remove the pop-up stopper. Then, from below, remove the lock nut on the stopper body. If needed, keep the flange from turning by inserting a large screwdriver in the drain from the top. Thrust the stopper body up through the hole to free the flange from the basin, and then remove the flange and the stopper body.

Clean the drain opening above and below, and then thread the locknut all the way down the new pop-up body followed by the flat washer and the rubber gasket (beveled side up). Wrap three layers of Teflon tape clockwise onto the top of the threaded body. Make a ½"-diameter snake from plumber's putty, form it into a ring, and stick the ring underneath the drain flange.

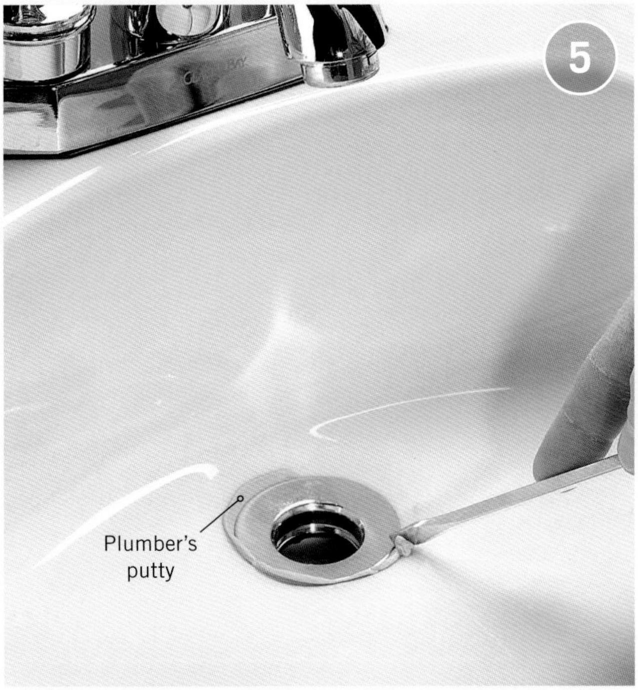

From below, face the pivot-rod opening directly back toward the middle of the faucet and pull the body straight down to seat the flange. Thread the locknut/washer assembly up under the sink, then fully tighten the locknut with channel-type pliers. Do not twist the flange in the process, as this can break the putty seal. Clean off the squeezeout of plumber's putty from around the flange.

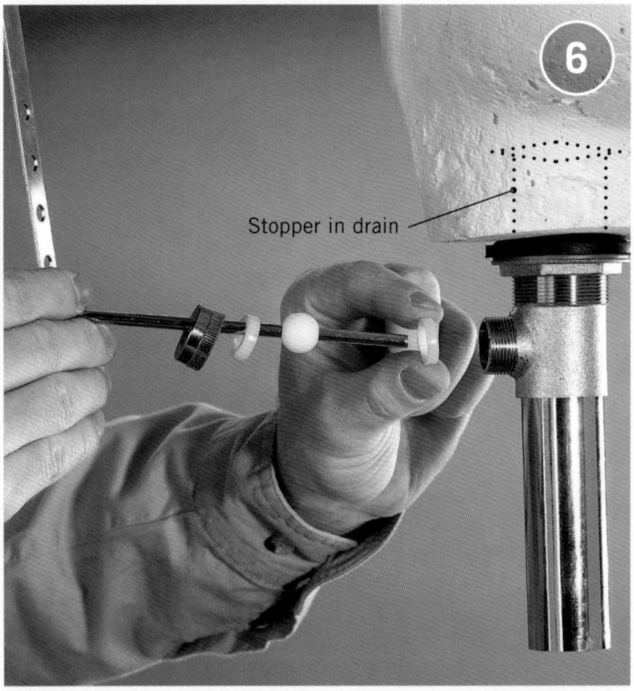

Drop the pop-up stopper into the drain hole so the hole at the bottom of its post is closest to the back of the sink. Put the beveled nylon washer into the opening in the back of the pop-up body with the bevel facing back.

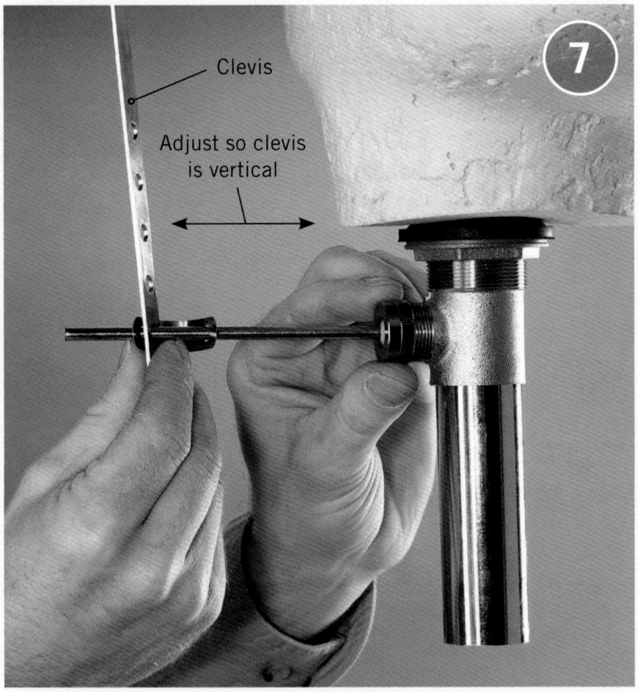

Put the cap behind the ball on the pivot rod as shown. Sandwich a hole in the clevis with the spring clip and thread the long end of the pivot rod through the clip and clevis. Put the ball end of the pivot rod into the pop-up body opening and into the hole in the the stopper stem. Screw the cap onto the pop-up body over the ball.

Loosen the clevis screw holding the clevis strap to the lift rod. Push the pivot rod all the way down (which fully opens the pop-up stopper). With the lift rod also all the way down, tighten the clevis screw to the rod. If the clevis runs into the top of the trap, cut it short with your hacksaw or tin snips. Reassemble the J-bend trap.

Toilets & Bidets

Modern toilet technologies have now given us toilets that contrast sharply to early low-flow models. Now they reliably flush, use precious little water, and are largely trouble free. Just the same, professionals estimate that half of all plumbing home-repair calls involve older toilets. That's why it's usually well worth the investment to install a new one.

Occasionally, American homes include a bidet, a fixture used in place or addition to toilet paper for personal hygiene. If you're opting for this European tradition, you'll want to match the bidet to the toilet. Today's marketplace offers a wealth of toilet and bidet styles, from traditional two-piece units to wall-mounted fixtures that work well in universal-design bathrooms, because they can be adjusted to whatever height is best for the user.

No matter what model you choose, it's likely your new toilet will help conserve water. All of today's toilets are low flow, complying with a 1992 federal law requiring that toilets use no more than 1.6 gallons of water per flush. Many toilets now are dual flush, giving you the option for a stronger flush when needed. So, really, your choice can be made almost entirely on looks.

In this chapter:

- Toilets
- Bidets

Toilets

Replace an older, inefficient, leaky, beat-up toilet with a new, high-efficiency, high-quality model and you've made an investment that will save you water and frustration. Especially if your existing toilet is a very old model.

Technology has evolved so that most new toilets have wide passages behind the bowl and wide, 3-inch flush-valve openings—features that facilitate short, powerful flushes. Manufacturers also developed dual-flush technology to give the homeowner more control of the toilet; you can choose between flushing options depending on what needs to be flushed. All that technological enhancement means few second flushes and fewer clogged toilets, which were the common complaints about the first generation of 1.6-gallon low-flow toilets.

Keep in mind that amidst all this technology, the styles of modern toilets have exploded. You'll find unibody models, tankless models, wall-mounted units, and more. Even if you're shopping for a traditional look and two-piece toilet, you'll have to decide whether you want a chair height, oval or round, or a short rough-in toilet. In addition to these choices, you have to find one that fits the look of your bathroom. But with a little bit of shopping and by asking a few questions, you're sure to find a toilet that will last you the next decade or more.

Sleek new toilet options offer attractive bathroom additions that are also more comfortable than ever before. This toilet features a compact design with a rough-in distance of 10 inches, translating to a lot of extra floor space in front of the toilet. The seat itself is positioned at chair height, making it extra comfortable for most users.

Buy a toilet that will fit the space. Measure the distance from the floor bolts back to the wall (if your old toilet has two pairs of bolts, go by the rear pair). This is your rough-in distance and will be either 10", 12", or approximately 14". Make note of the bowl shape, round or oval (long). Oval bowls (also called elongated bowls) are a few inches longer for greater comfort, but may be too big for your space. The safest bet is to buy a replacement with the same bowl shape. You can also opt for a wall-mounted unit. Although the installation is more involved, you can save up to a foot of floor space in front of the toilet—with the added bonus of being able to mount the toilet at whatever height works best for the primary users of the room.

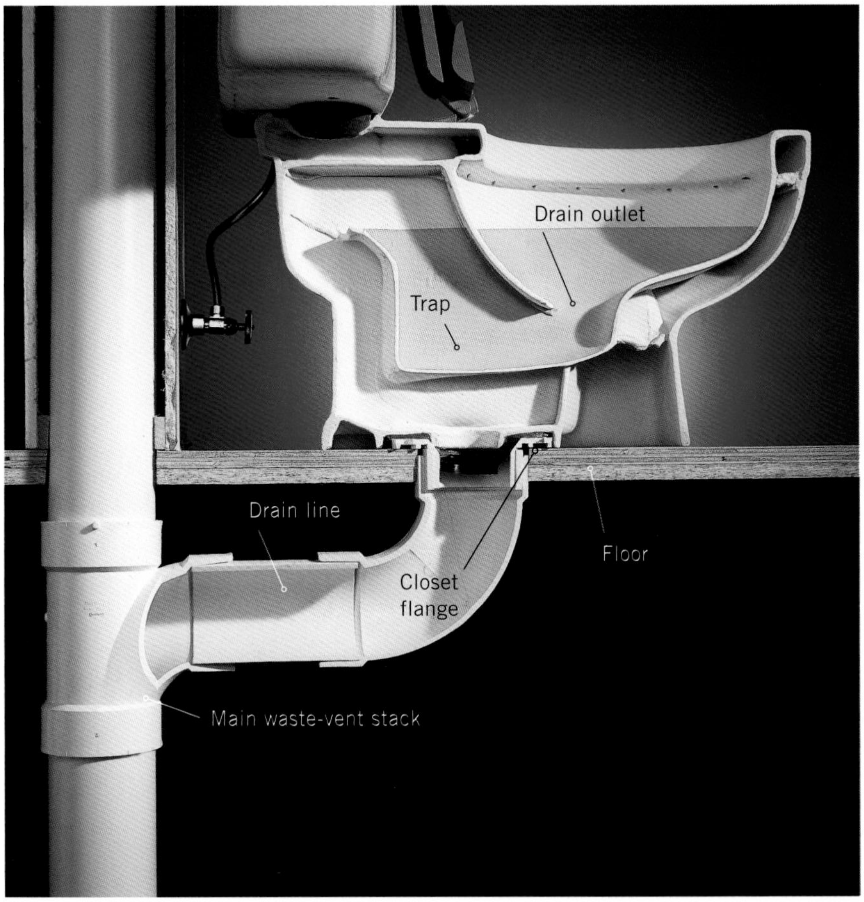

Knowing how a toilet works isn't essential to successful installation, but it helps. This cutaway photo features a pre-1.6-gallon-law model, so your new toilet will have a much smaller trap. When the flush handle on the tank is depressed, the water in the tank rushes out through the hole in the underside of the bowl rim. The onrushing water forces the contents of the bowl and the trap out through the closet flange and into the drain line, while the fresh tank water refills the bowl and trap.

How to Install a Toilet

Clean and inspect the old closet flange. Look for breaks or wear. Also inspect the flooring around the flange. If either the flange or floor is worn or damaged, repair the damage. Use a rag and mineral spirits to completely remove residue from the old wax ring.

REPLACING A FLANGE

If the old flange is solvent-welded to the closet pipe, cut the pipe flush with the floor. Dry-fit the new flange into the pipe. Turn the flange until the side cut-out screw slots are parallel to the wall. (Do not use the curved keyhole slots, as they are not as strong.) Attach the new flange with solvent glue.

Insert new closet bolts (don't reuse old ones) into the openings in the closet flange. Make sure the heads of the bolts are oriented to catch the maximum amount of flange material.

Remove the wax ring and apply it to the underside of the bowl, around the horn. Remove the protective covering. Do not touch the wax ring. It is very sticky.

Lower the bowl onto the flange, taking care not to disturb the wax ring. The holes in the bowl base should align perfectly with the tank bolts. Add a washer and tighten a nut on each bolt. Hand-tighten each nut and then use channel-type pliers to further tighten the nuts. Alternate back and forth between nuts until the bowl is secure. Do not overtighten.

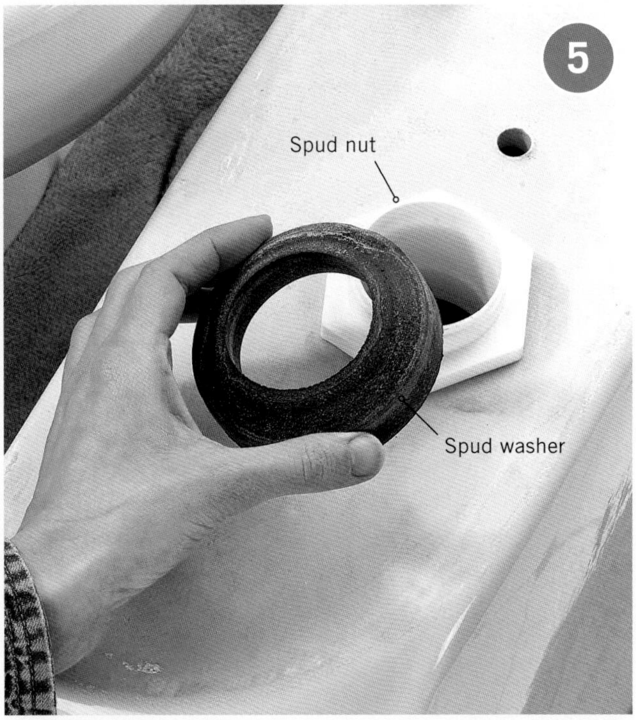

Attach the toilet tank. Some tanks come with a flush valve and a fill valve preinstalled, but if yours does not, insert the flush valve through the tank opening and tighten a spud nut over the threaded end of the valve. Place a foam or rubber spud washer on top of the spud nut.

Adjust the fill valve as directed by the manufacturer to set the correct tank water-level height and install the valve inside the tank. Hand-tighten the nylon lock nut that secures the valve to the tank (inset photo) and then tighten it farther with channel-type pliers.

With the tank lying on its back, thread a rubber washer onto each tank bolt and insert it into the bolt holes from inside the tank. Then, thread a brass washer and hex nut onto the tank bolts from below and tighten them to a ¼-turn past hand tight. Do not overtighten. *(continued)*

Position the tank on the bowl, spud washer on the opening, bolts through bolt holes. Put a rubber washer followed by a brass washer and a wing nut on each bolt and tighten these up evenly.

You may stabilize the bolts with a large slotted screwdriver from inside the tank, but tighten the nuts, not the bolts. You may press down a little on a side, the front, or the rear of the tank to level it as you tighten the nuts by hand. Do not overtighten and crack the tank. The tank should be level and stable when you're done.

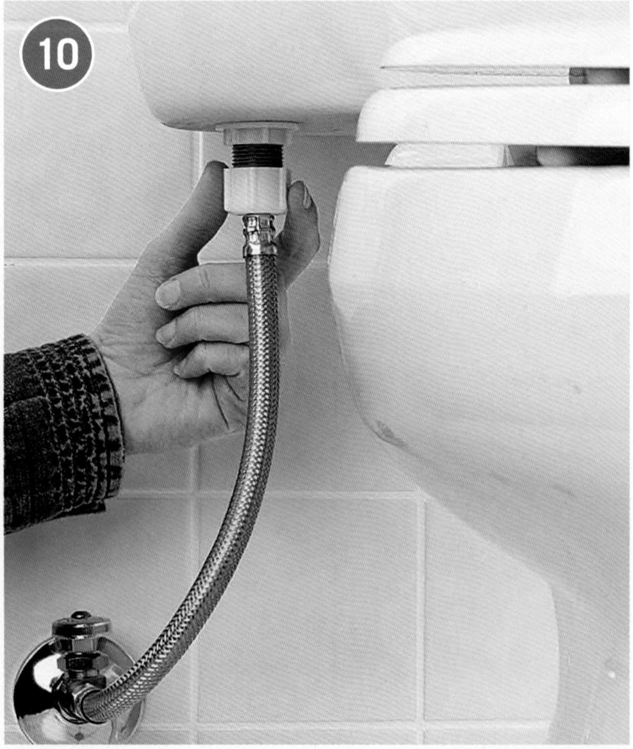

Hook up the water supply by connecting the supply tube to the threaded fill valve with the coupling nut provided. Turn on the water and test for leaks.

Attach the toilet seat by threading the plastic or brass bolts provided with the seat through the openings on the back of the rim and attaching nuts.

TOILET HEIGHT EXTENDERS

Although today's toilets are being made with higher seats than in the past, physically challenged and elderly people often find it difficult to use standard toilets, especially compact toilets (most of the more inexpensive toilets are compact). To address the problem of low toilet seats, you can retrofit your toilet with a seat riser or reinstall the toilet on a platform.

Hinged seat risers: By replacing your old toilet seat with a riser seat, you can raise the functional height of the toilet by 3" to 4". Look for models that are hinged or removable for easy cleaning. This is the least expensive option.

Wall-mounted toilets: If you're willing to spend significantly more, you can install a wall-mounted unit to whatever height is most comfortable for the user. These are especially effective in bathrooms used by someone who uses a wheelchair or walker.

Remove the old seat. If the nuts for the seat bolts are corroded, slip a hacksaw blade between the hinge plates and stool and cut the bolts.

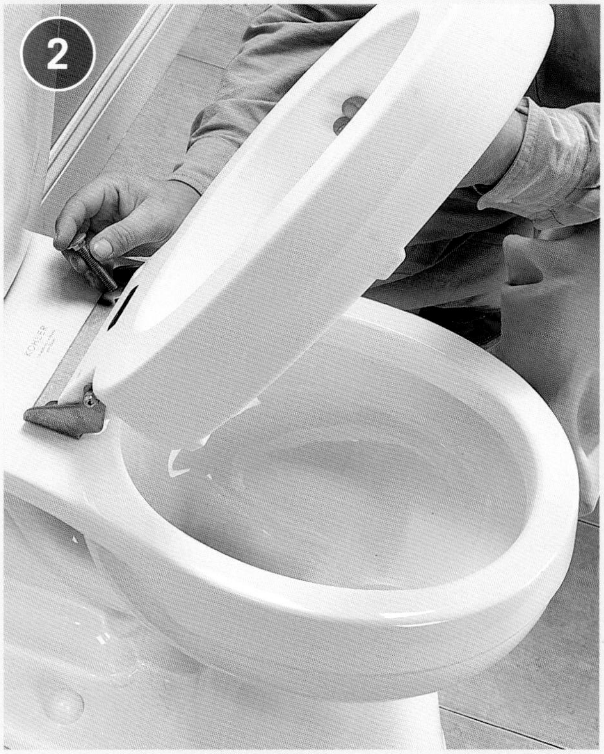

Install the new height extender by bolting it to the stool through the seat-bolt holes. Attach a standard toilet seat to the extender.

Bidets

TOOLS & MATERIALS

- Tape measure
- Drill
- Adjustable wrench
- Level
- Silicone sealant
- (2) ⅜" shutoff valves
- (2) ⅜" supply lines
- P-trap
- Tubing cutter
- Plumber's putty
- Thread tape
- Bidet
- Bidet faucet
- Marker
- Eye and ear protection
- Work gloves

Bidets are quite common in home bathrooms across Europe but less so in America. They are, however, worth considering if you have the physical space next to your toilet and the budget for one. The bidet takes the place of toilet paper and many people find the experience of a bidet cleaner and more satisfying.

With the trend moving toward larger and more luxurious bathrooms, many Americans are becoming intrigued by this personal hygiene appliance. The standard model features hot and cold faucets and either a movable nozzle located by the faucet handles or a vertical sprayer located near the front of the bowl. Most bidets are outfitted with a pop-up drain. You can also buy a combination toilet and bidet if space is an issue.

Installing a bidet is very much like installing a sink. The only difference is that the bidet can have the waste line plumbed below the floor, like a shower. But like sinks, bidets may have single or multiple deck holes for faucets, so be certain to purchase compatible components.

A bidet is a useful companion to a toilet, and it is a luxury item you and your family will appreciate. For people with limited mobility, a bidet is an aid to independent personal sanitation.

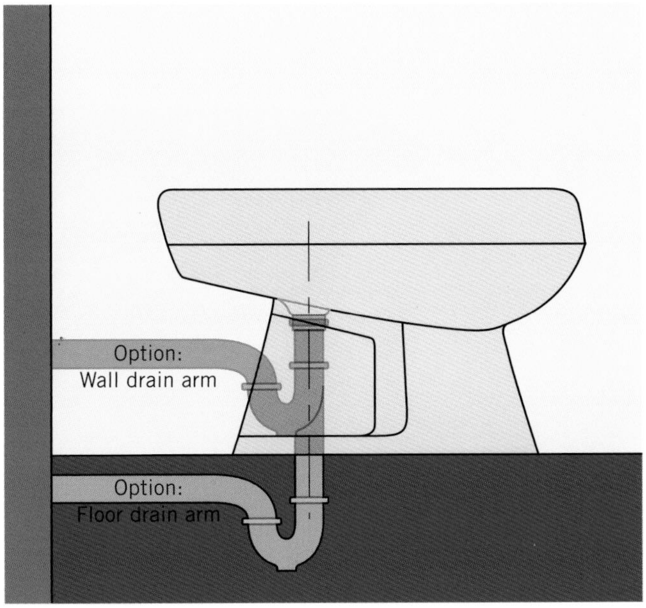

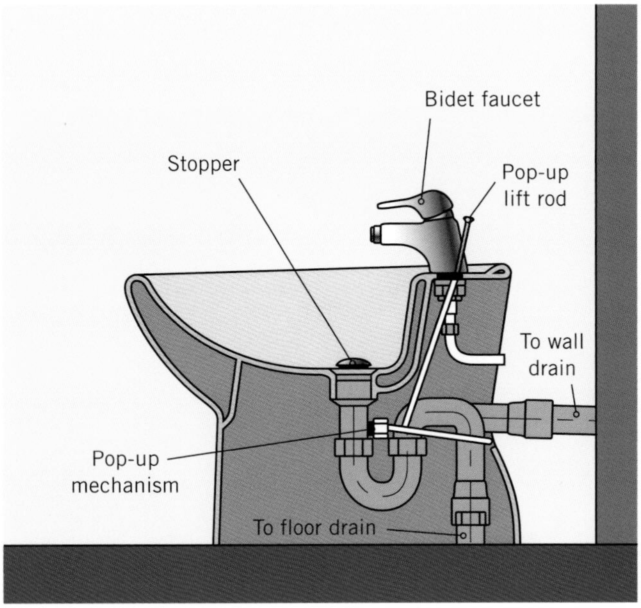

Bidet drains have more in common with sink drains than with toilet drains. Some even attach to a drain arm in the wall with a P-trap that fits between the fixture drain tailpiece and the arm. Other bidets drain into a floor-drain outlet with a trap that's situated between the tailpiece and the branch drain line.

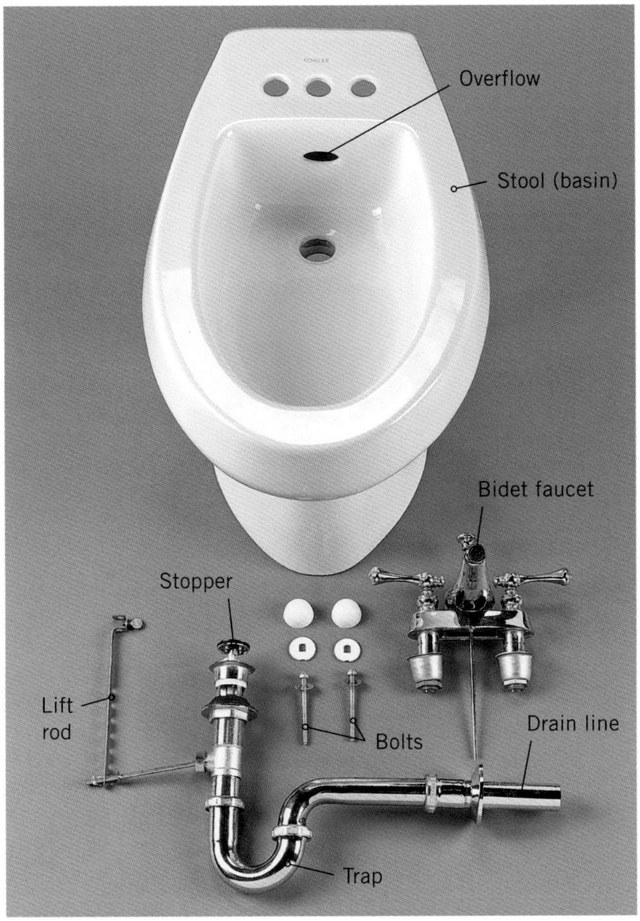

A bidet requires a special faucet that allows you to mix hot and cold water to a temperature you find comfortable. It has a third knob to control the water pressure. The aerator and spout pivot to allow you to adjust the spray to a comfortable height.

You can get all the features of a bidet on your existing toilet with a number of aftermarket bidet seats. These seats feature heaters, sprayers, and dryers in basic or deluxe versions. Installation takes less than an hour, and no additional space is needed.

How to Install a Bidet

Rough-in the supply and drain lines according to the manufacturer's specifications. If you do not have experience installing home plumbing, hire a plumber for this part of the job. Apply a coil of plumber's putty to the base of the bidet faucet, and then insert the faucet body into the mounting holes. Thread the washers and locknut onto the faucet-body shank and hand-tighten. Remove any plumber's putty squeezeout.

Apply a coil of plumber's putty around the underside of the drain flange. Insert the flange in the drain hole, place the gasket and washer, and then thread the nut onto the flange. Do not fully tighten.

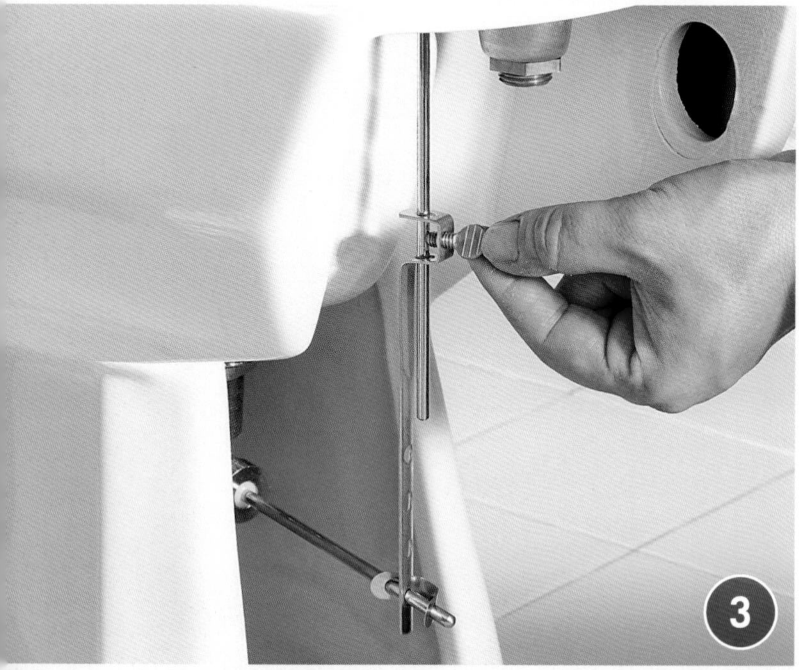

Install the pop-up drain apparatus according to the manufacturer's instructions.

Place the bidet in its final location, checking that supply and drain lines will be in alignment. Mark the locations of the two side-mounting holes through the predrilled holes on the stool and onto the floor.

Remove the bidet and drill 3⁄16" pilot holes at the marks on the floor. Drive the floor bolts (included with the bidet basin) into the holes. Position the bidet so the floor bolts fit into the bolt holes in the base. Tighten nuts onto the floor bolts.

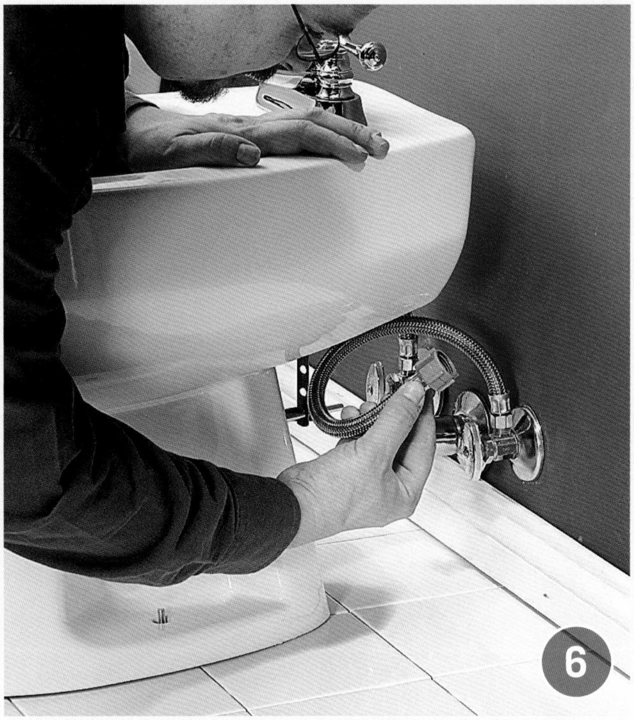

Connect the water-supply risers to the bidet faucet using compression unions. Make sure to hook the hot and cold risers up to the correct ports on the faucet.

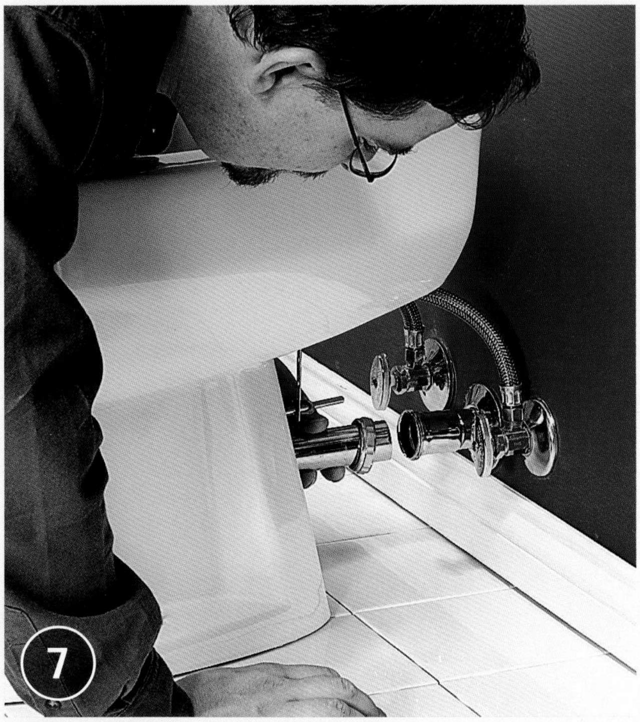

Hook up the drain line by attaching the P-trap to the drain tailpiece. The trap is then attached to a branch drain line coming out of the wall or floor in the same manner as a sink drain.

Remove the aerator so any debris in the supply line will clear and then turn on the water and open both faucets. Check for leaks in lines and fix, if found. Assemble the bolt caps and thread them onto the floor bolts.

NOTE: Do not dispose of paper in the bidet—return to the toilet to dry off after using the bidet for cleaning.

Lighting & Ventilaton

Lighting is the unsung hero of bathroom design. Think about it: the lighting in your bathroom accentuates every element of the design, adding to or subtracting from the look. More importantly, lighting is crucial to safety in a room where slips and falls are an ever-present danger.

As if that weren't enough, bathroom lighting, in and of itself, can be a decorative element. Just look at the great wealth of bathroom lighting fixtures at any home center or lighting store: they come in all sizes, shapes, and finishes as well as many different types. Want a sconce for the side of your vanity mirror? No problem—just be ready to choose from brushed nickel, chrome, brass, antiqued, or other finishes. Need a dimmable overhead light fixture? Okay—modern, Victorian, art deco, or plain? Enclosed ceiling light, light and fan, or chandelier? The choices go on and on.

The bulbs that the fixtures use represent even more options. Choose LEDs or halogens for bright, sharp, white light that brings out details. Or install more traditional incandescent fixtures for a warm, comforting light. Or split the difference with midrange compact fluorescent bulbs. You can even use different types of lights in different areas to suit your particular needs (such as a bright white halogen for a makeup desk and a soft yellow incandescent over a romantic drop-in jetted tub).

No matter what, your choice of bathroom lighting must always take into account the essential tasks that are done in the room, overall safety, and an understanding of how the light will play with features such as large mirrors, windows, and skylights.

In this chapter:

- Vanity Lights
- LED-Backlit Mirror
- Ceiling Lights
- Vent Fans

Vanity Lights

Vanity lights on the sides of the mirror provide ideal lighting for shaving, applying makeup, and other grooming tasks.

Many bathrooms have a single fixture positioned above the vanity, but a light source in this position casts shadows on the face and makes grooming more difficult. Light fixtures on either side of the mirror is a better arrangement.

For a remodel, mark the mirror location, run cable, and position boxes before drywall installation. You can also retrofit by installing new boxes and drawing power from the existing fixture.

The light sources should be at eye level; 66 inches is typical. The size of your mirror and its location on the wall may affect how far apart you can place the sconces, but 36 to 40 inches apart is a good guideline.

TOOLS & MATERIALS

Drywall tools	Circuit tester	Electrical boxes and braces	NM cable	Eye and ear protection
Drill	Screwdrivers	Vanity light fixtures	Wire connectors	Work gloves
Combination tool	Hammer		Drywall	

How to Replace Vanity Lights in a Finished Bathroom

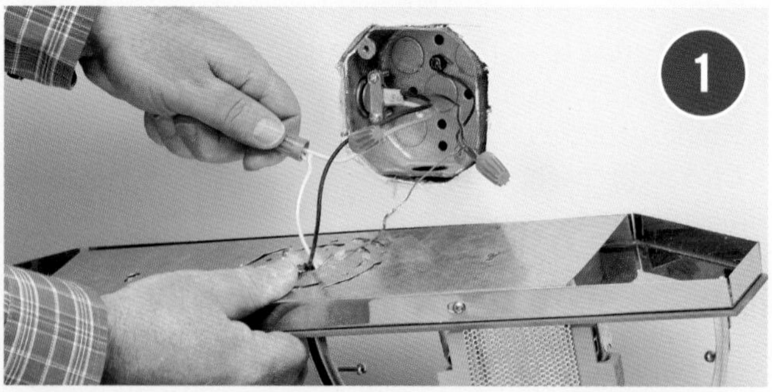

Turn off the power at the service panel. Remove the old fixture from the wall and test to make sure that the power is off. Then remove a strip of drywall from around the old fixture to the first studs beyond the approximate location of the new fixtures. Make the opening large enough that you have room to route cable from the existing fixture to the boxes.

Mark the location for the fixtures and install new boxes. Install the boxes about 66" above the floor and 18 to 20" from the centerline of the mirror (the mounting base of some fixtures is above or below the bulb, so adjust the height of the bracing accordingly). If the correct location is on or next to a stud, you can attach the box directly to the stud; otherwise you'll need to install blocking or use boxes with adjustable braces (shown).

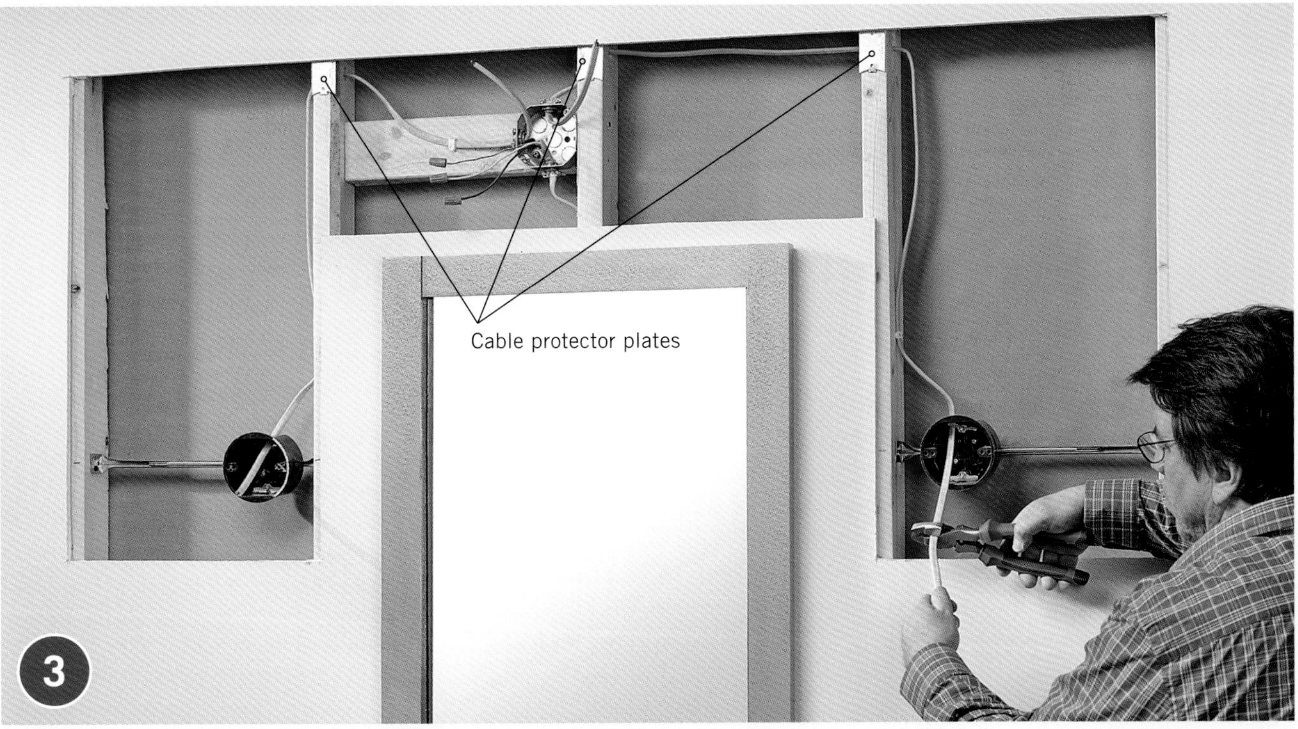

Open the side knockouts on the electrical box above the vanity. Then drill $\frac{5}{8}$" holes in the centers of any studs between the old fixture and the new ones. Run two NM cables from the new boxes for the fixtures to the box above the vanity. Protect the cable with metal protector plates. Secure the cables with cable clamps, leaving 11" of extra cable for making the connection to the new fixtures. Remove sheathing and strip insulation from the ends of the wires.

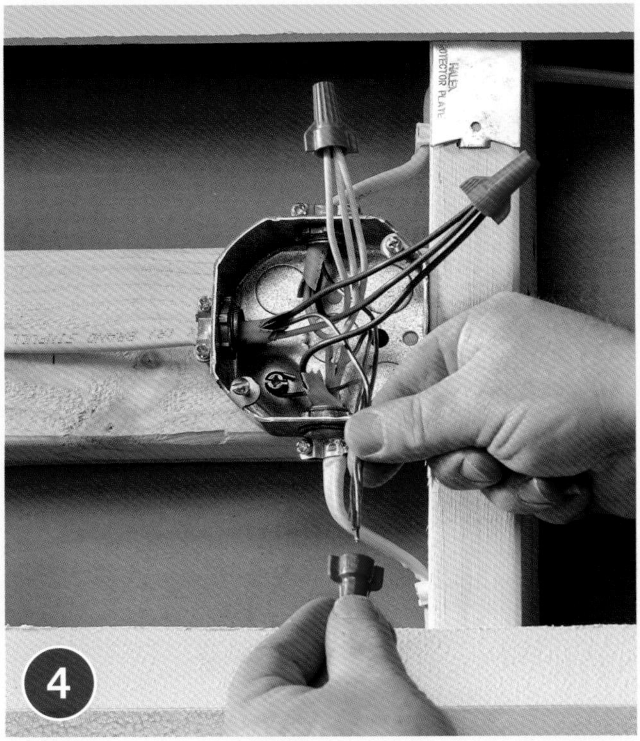

Connect the white wires from the new cables to the white wire from the old cable, and connect the black wires from the new cables to the black wire from the old cable. Connect the ground wires. Cover all open boxes and then replace the drywall, leaving openings for the fixture and the old box. (Cover the old box with a solid junction-box cover plate.)

Install the fixture mounting braces on the boxes. Attach the fixtures by connecting the black circuit wire to the black fixture wire and connecting the white circuit wire to the white fixture wire. Connect the ground wires. Position each fixture over each box, and attach with the mounting screws. Restore power and test the circuit.

LED-Backlit Mirror

An LED-backlit mirror adds a special element to a small—or even a large—bathroom, but the real benefit is a true-to-life representation in the mirror so you'll see exactly what other people will see.

Traditionally, the standard light source for smaller bathrooms and powder rooms is a light fixture above the mirror. This was often the only solution for vanity mirror lighting where there is little or no space on the sides of the mirror. Now, however, there is an interesting option: lighting that is emitted by the mirror itself.

LED-illuminated mirrors use a base that contains LED strips that provide backlight from around the edges of the mirror or an LED frame that actually shines through the mirror when turned on. This type of mirror is not particularly expensive, is fairly easy to install, and can add brilliantly useful lighting in cramped quarters.

The wiring for our mirror features an ordinary circuit plug that fits into a standard 115- or 120-volt outlet. Installation is quite easy if you happen to have a wall outlet located on the wall directly behind where your mirror will be installed. If not, then you will need to install (or have an electrician install) a standard wall outlet behind the mirror location. Our project assumes that this wall outlet already exists or has been preinstalled. You will need competent wiring skills if you expect to do this work yourself; if you are not skilled at such work, hire an electrician to run new cable and install the wall outlet.

TOOLS & MATERIALS

- Tape measure and bits
- Carpenter's pencil
- Stud finder
- Power drill and bits
- Torpedo level
- Eye and ear protection
- Work gloves

How to Install an LED-Illuminated Mirror

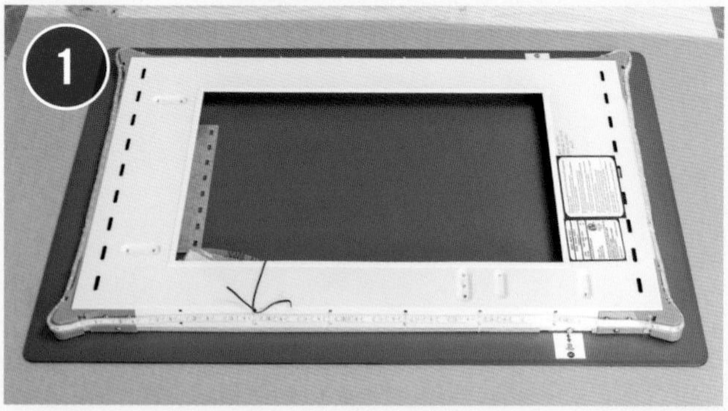

1

Unpack the LED mirror and place it face down on a flat surface. Examine the kit to make sure all parts are included. Make sure the necessary circuit wiring is done, based on the instructions with the LED kit. The following steps assume that the circuit wiring is complete before you continue. In our example, the assumption is that a simple circuit extension from the wall vanity light has been installed, so that the same switch that controls the wall light fixture will control the LED mirror.

2

Detach the mirror from the base by loosening the mounting screws. If your mirror has illuminated LED strips, there may also be wire connections running from the base to the mirror panel that need to be detached before you go any further.

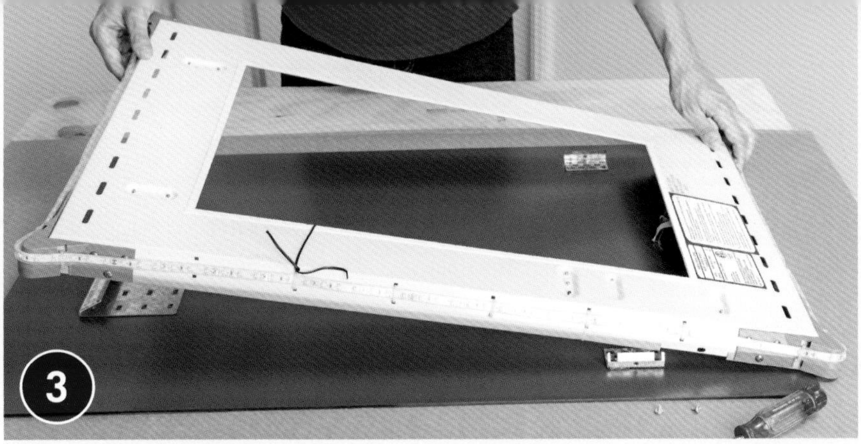

Remove the mirror base from the mirror panel. Establish a level line on the wall to mark where the bottom of the mirror will go. Installing a temporary ledger board along this line can help make installation easier.

Position the mirror base against the wall, and mark the location for the mounting holes on the wall. Ideally, you should be able to find locations over studs where you can mount the mirror base securely. Should this not be possible, you will need to attach plastic wall anchors to secure the mirror base or use toggle bolts to secure the mirror to the wall.

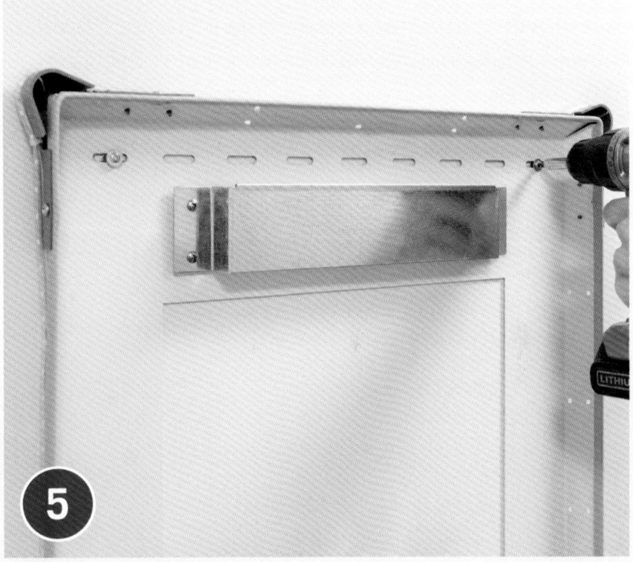

Secure the mirror base to the wall by driving mounting screws into wall studs, both at the top and bottom of the mirror on both sides. If you have access to wall studs on both sides, four screws driven near each corner should be sufficient to mount the mirror base securely. Plug in the electrical cord on the mirror base into the wall outlet.

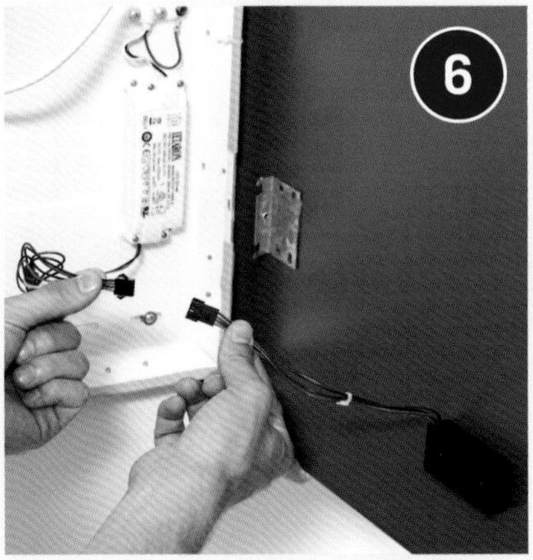

Holding the mirror panel in place, use the quick-fit connector to establish the electrical connection between the mirror panel and the base. This work is easiest if you have a helper hold the mirror panel as you plug in the wiring.

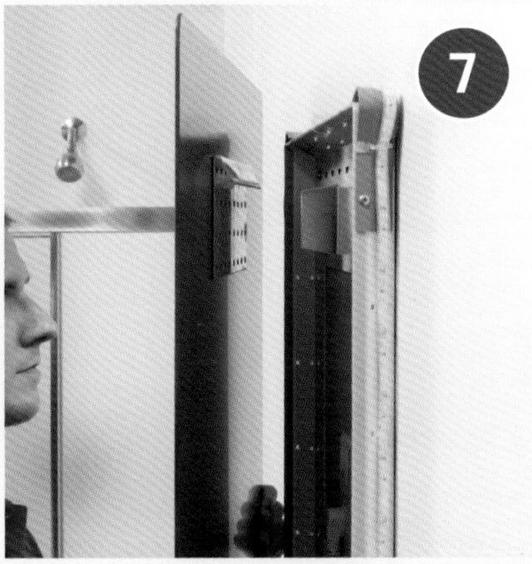

Carefully hang the mirror panel onto the mounting bracket on the base. Align the mirror panel so the mounting screws are properly positioned.

Secure the mirror panel to the base using the mounting screws included with the kit. Test the LED mirror to make sure it works properly.

Ceiling Lights

TOOLS & MATERIALS

Replacement light fixture
Combination tool
Voltage sensor
Insulated screwdrivers
Wire nuts
Eye and ear protection
Work gloves

Bathroom ceiling fixtures usually don't have moving parts, and their wiring is simple. So, other than changing bulbs, you're likely to enjoy decades of trouble-free service from a bathroom fixture. Although that sounds like a pure benefit, it means that the fixture will work fine long after the style of the fixture has become unfashionable. Thankfully, you don't really need a malfunction to use as an excuse for updating a bathroom lighting fixture. New fixtures are relatively inexpensive and easy to install, and they can be one of the most dramatic changes you make to a bathroom. You can even change the type of fixture—such as replacing a traditional incandescent fixture with a newer, energy-conserving halogen fixture. Whichever you choose, make sure it suits the room's décor.

Although most homeowners choose a general bathroom overhead fixture that complements and blends into the existing design style, you can always install a fixture that serves as a focal point itself. A small chandelier, like the one shown here, is an elegant and unusual addition.

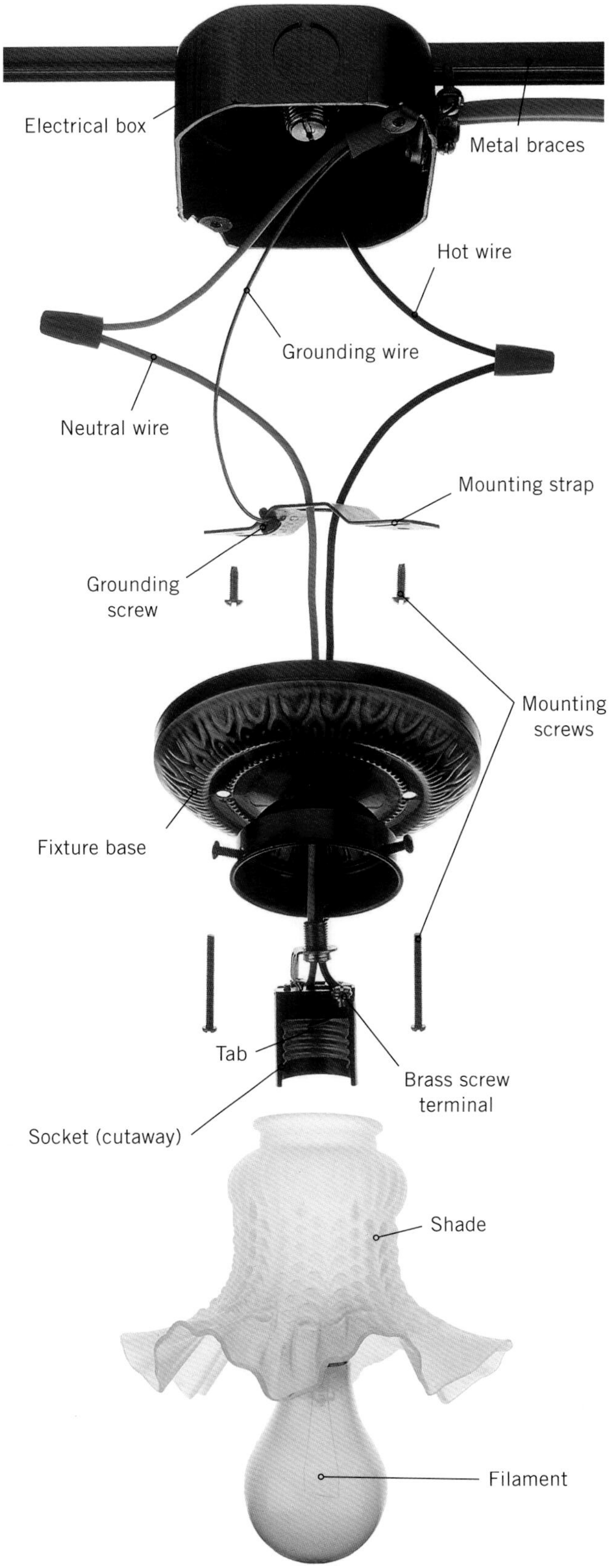

No matter what a ceiling light fixture looks like on the outside, they all attach in basically the same way. An electrical box in the ceiling is fitted with a mounting strap, which holds the fixture in place. The bare wire from the ceiling typically connects to the mounting strap. The two wires coming from the fixture connect to the black and the white wires from the ceiling.

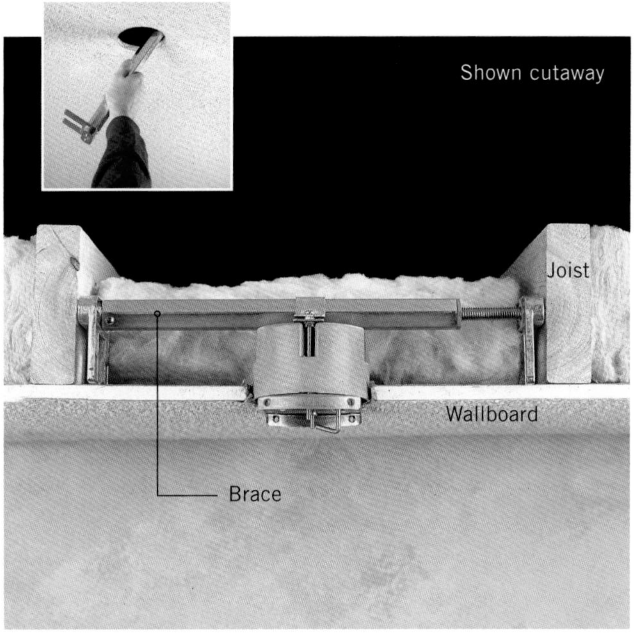

If the new fixture is much heavier than the original fixture, it will require additional bracing in the ceiling to support the electrical box and the fixture. The manufacturer's instructions should specify the size and type of box. If the ceiling is finished and there is no access from above, you can remove the old box and use an adjustable remodeling brace appropriate for your fixture (shown). The brace fits into a small hole in the ceiling (inset). Once the bracing is in place, install a new electrical box specified for the new fixture.

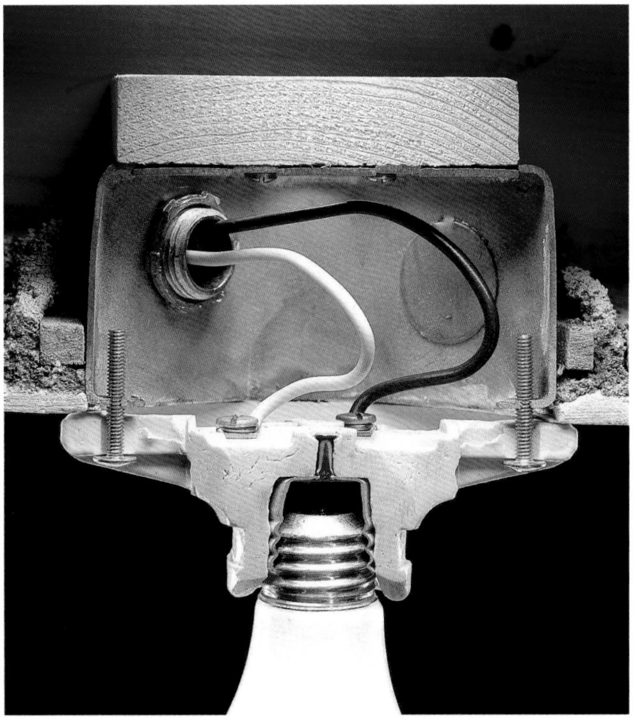

Inexpensive light fixtures have screw terminals mounted directly to the back side of the fixture plate. Often, as seen here, they have no grounding terminal. Some codes do not allow this type of fixture, but even if your hometown does approve them, it is a good idea to replace them with a better-quality, safer fixture that is UL approved.

How to Replace a Ceiling Light

Shut off power to the ceiling light and remove the shade or diffuser. Loosen the mounting screws and carefully lower the fixture, supporting it as you work (do not let light fixtures hang by their electrical wires alone). Test with a voltage sensor to make sure no power is reaching the connections.

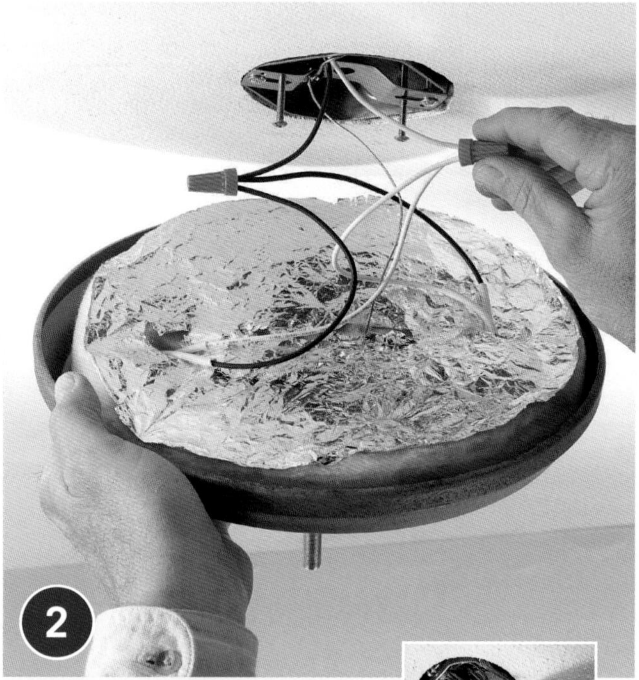

Remove the twist connectors from the fixture wires or unscrew the screw terminals and remove the white neutral wire and the black lead wire (inset).

Before you install the new fixture, check the ends of the wires coming from the ceiling electrical box. They should be clean and free of nicks or scorch marks. If they're dirty or worn, clip off the stripped portion with your combination tool. Then strip away about ¾" of insulation from the end of each wire.

Attach a mounting strap to the ceiling fixture box if there is not one already present. Your new light may come equipped with a strap; otherwise you can find one for purchase at any hardware store.

Lift the new fixture up to the ceiling (you may want a helper for this) and attach the bare copper ground wire from the power-supply cable to the grounding screw or clip on the mounting strap. Also attach the ground wire from the fixture to the screw or clip.

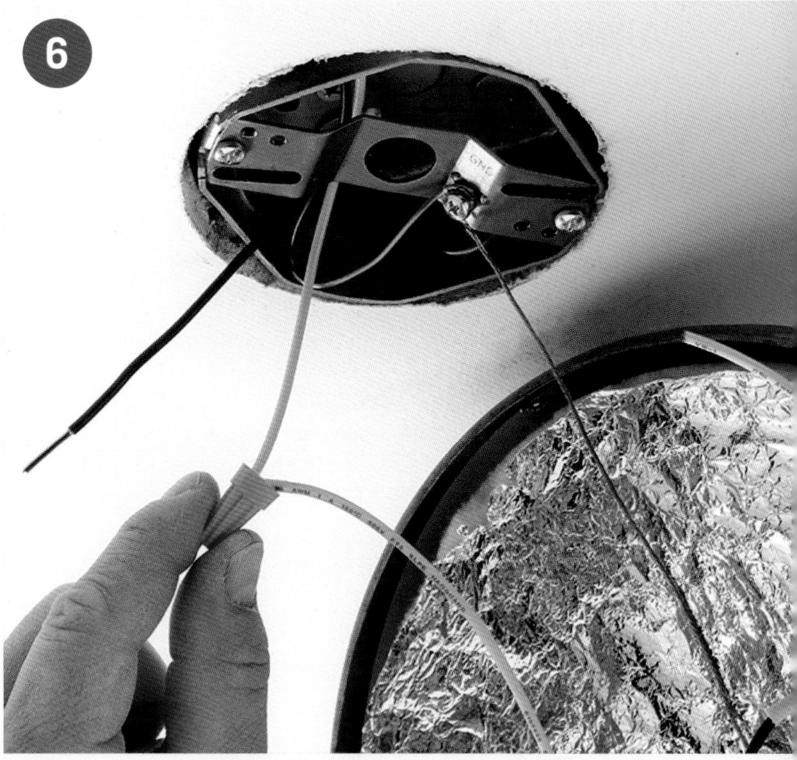

With the fixture supported by a ladder or a helper, join the white wire lead and the white fixture wire with a wire connector (often supplied with the fixture).

Connect the black power-supply wire to the black fixture wire with a wire connector.

Position the new fixture mounting plate over the box so the mounting-screw holes align. Drive the screws until the fixture is secure against the ceiling. Install light bulbs and attach the shade or diffuser.

Vent Fans

For most of us, a dream bathroom does not include foggy mirrors or unpleasant odors. Opening a window, if your bathroom is equipped with one, can help, but vent fans do the best job of clearing the air.

Most vent fans are installed in the center of the bathroom ceiling or over the toilet area. A fan installed over the tub or shower area must be GFCI protected and rated for use in wet areas. You can usually wire a fan with a light fixture into a main bathroom electrical circuit, but units with built-in heat lamps or blowers require separate circuits.

If the fan you choose doesn't come with a mounting kit, purchase one separately. A mounting kit should include a vent hose (duct), a vent tailpiece, and an exterior vent cover.

Venting instructions vary among manufacturers, but the most common options are attic venting and soffit venting. Attic venting routes fan ductwork into the attic and out through the roof. Always insulate ducting in this application to keep condensation from forming and running down into the motor. Carefully install flashing around the outside vent cover to prevent roof leaks.

TOOLS & MATERIALS

- Pencil
- Screwdrivers
- Jigsaw or drywall saw
- Reciprocating saw
- Power drill and bits
- Electrical tester
- Drywall screws
- Wire nuts
- Flexible dryer vent duct
- Dryer vent clamps
- Vent cover
- Drywall
- 4" hole saw
- Wire stripper or combination tool
- Fish tape
- Drywall tape
- Drywall compound
- Eye and ear protection
- Work gloves

Soffit venting involves routing the duct to a soffit (roof overhang) instead of through the roof. Check with the vent manufacturer for instructions for soffit venting.

To prevent moisture damage, always terminate the vent outside your home—never into your attic or basement.

You can install a vent fan while the framing is exposed or as a retrofit, as shown in this project.

A combination light/vent fan is a great product in powder rooms and smaller baths that to do not generate excessive amounts of air moisture. In larger baths with tubs and showers, install a dedicated vent fan with a CFM rating that's at least 5 CFM higher than the total square footage of the bathroom (inset photo).

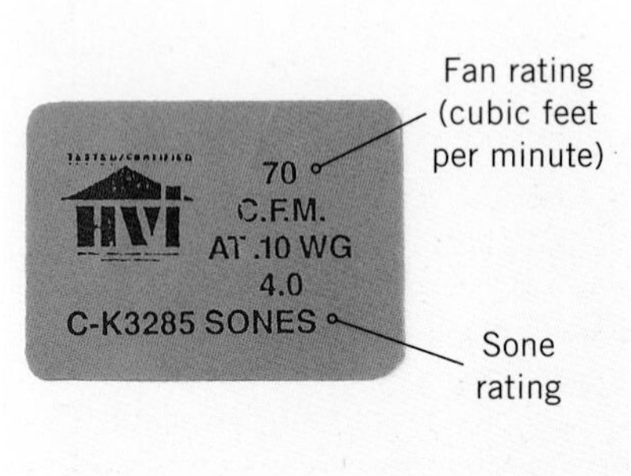

How to Replace an Overhead Light with a Light/Fan

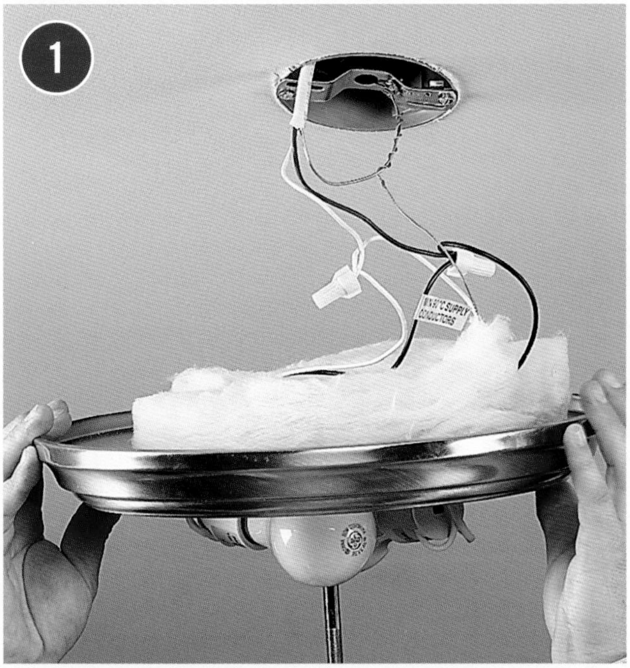

Shut off power to the ceiling light at the electrical service panel. Remove the globe and bulb from the overhead ceiling light, and then disconnect the mounting screws that hold the light fixture to the ceiling box.

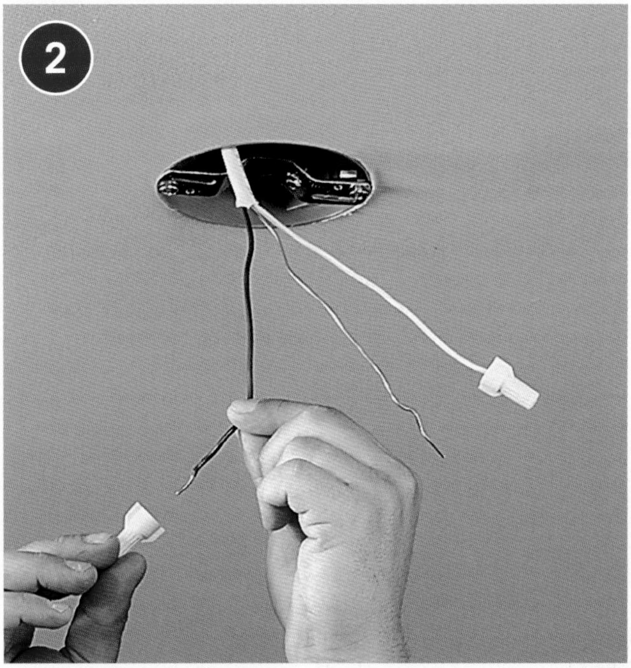

Test the wire connections with a current tester to make sure they are not live, and then disconnect the wires and remove the light fixture. Cap the wire ends.

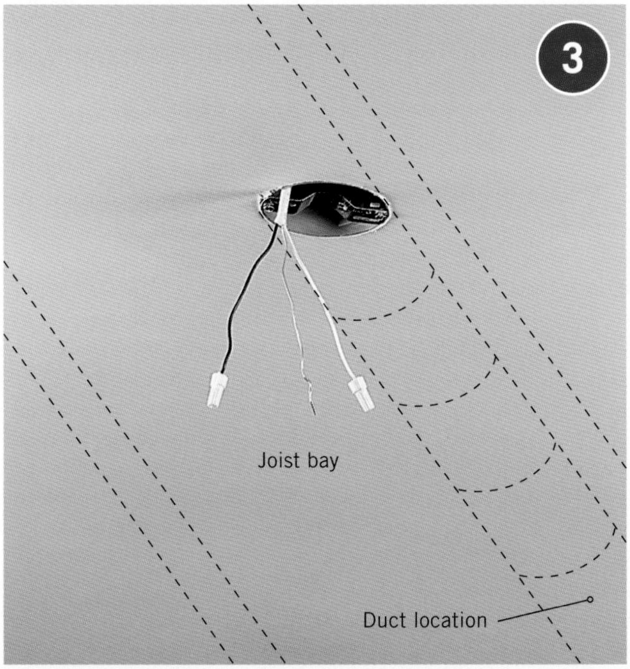

Plan your exhaust-pipe route. In most cases, this means determining the shortest distance between the fan and the outdoors. If the room is located at the top living level, venting through the roof is usually smartest. On lower levels and in basements, you'll need to go through an exterior wall. If you need to route through a wall in a room with a finished ceiling, choose a route that runs through a single ceiling joist bay.

Remove ceiling covering in the fan-unit installation area and between the joists at the end of the run, next to the wall. You'll need at least 18" of access. If you are running rigid vent pipe or the joist bay is insulated, you'll need to remove ceiling material between the joists for the entire run. Make cuts on the centerlines of the joists.

(continued)

Insert flexible vent tubing into one of the ceiling openings and expand it so the free end reaches to the ceiling opening at the wall. A fish tape for running cable through walls can be a useful aid for extending the tubing.

Draw a 4"-diameter circle on the wall framing at the end of the joist bay, marking the exit point for the duct. Choose a long, ¼"-diameter drill bit and drill a hole at the center of the circle. Drill all the way through the wall so the bit exits on the exterior side. This will mark your hole location outside.

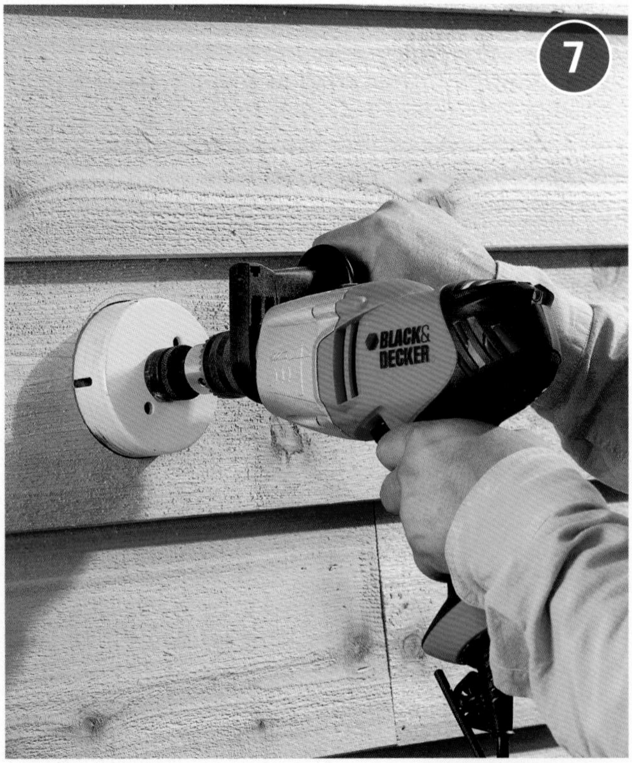

On the exterior, draw a 4"-diameter circle centered on the exit point of the drill bit. Cut out the opening for the vent cover with a reciprocating saw or a 4" hole saw.

Insert the vent-cover assembly into the opening, following the manufacturer's directions for fastening and sealing it to the house.

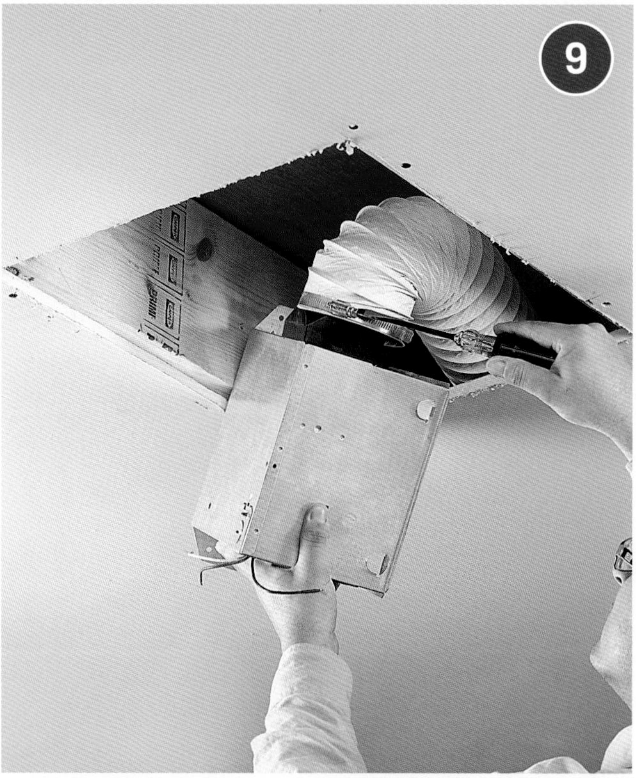

Attach the end of the vent tubing to the outlet on the vent-cover unit and secure it with a large pipe clamp.

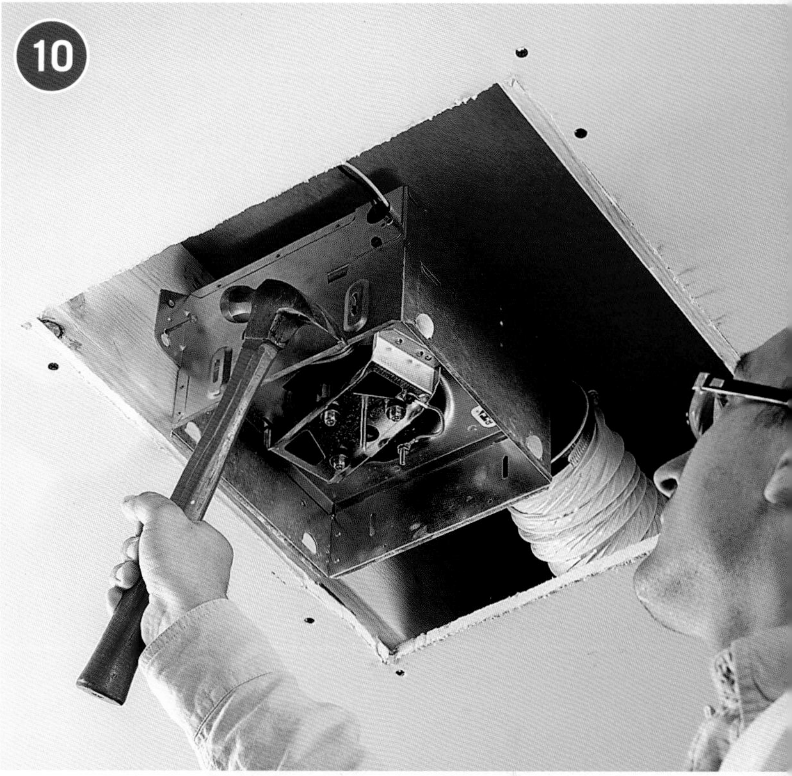

Nail the housing for the light/fan unit to the ceiling joist so the bottom edges of the housing are flush with the ceiling surface.

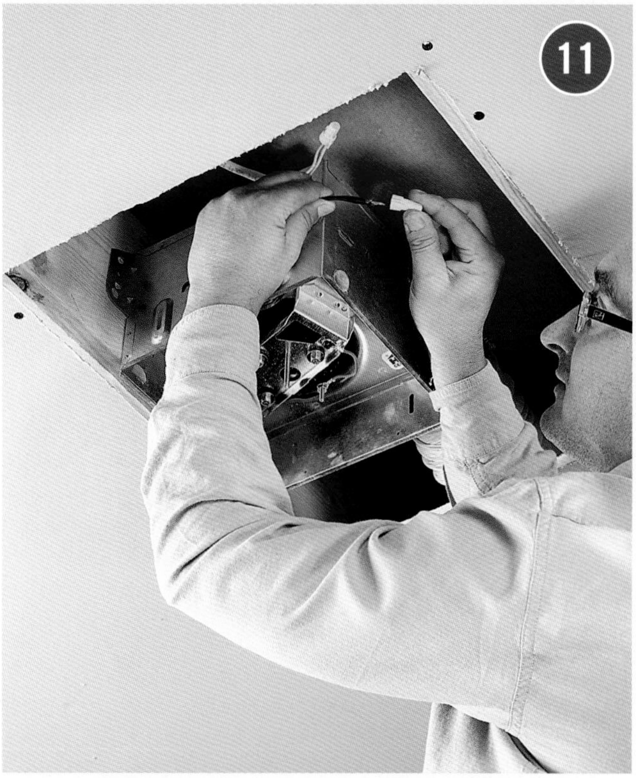

Make the wiring connections in the housing box according to the manufacturer's instructions. In just about every case you should be able to use the existing wires from the original light switch. Once you have connected the wires, restore the power and test the fan.

Patch and paint the wall and ceiling in the project area. Mount the light (the model we installed plugs into a receptacle in the fan box), grille, globe, and any other fixture parts.

Wall & Floor Projects

Bathroom walls and floors are easy to ignore because we tend to believe that only practical (and boring) surfaces can be used in bathrooms. After all, they need to be water resistant and easy to clean, right? Well, it's not that clear cut.

Yes, bathroom walls and floors should be water resistant, but that doesn't mean they have to be utterly impervious to moisture (unless, of course, they are in a shower stall). That said, you'll obviously want to avoid delicate or absorbent materials such as wallpaper, flat paint, or carpeting.

Even with those options out of the mix, though, you can pick from a growing list of wall and floor surfaces for your bathroom. Traditional choices such as ceramic and stone tile remain popular and present lots of looks, but you can also consider more contemporary alternatives, such as quartz composite surfaces, other solid-surface materials, and glass.

In this chapter:

- Installing Cementboard on Walls
- Wall Tile
- Tub Tile Surround
- Toilet Enclosure
- Radiant Floor
- Floor Tile

Installing Cementboard on Walls

TOOLS & MATERIALS

- Eye and ear protection
- Screw bit
- Stapler and staples
- Modified thinset mortar
- 4-mil clear poly sheeting
- 2" fiberglass mesh tape
- 1¼" cementboard screws
- 15# roofing felt
- ½" cementboard
- Work gloves
- Drill
- Tape measure
- 6" joint knife

Before you begin working, the wall and ceiling framing will need to be examined to make sure they meet the structural requirements for a backer-board installation. Studs, joists, and rafters, often referred to as framing members, should be spaced a maximum of 16 inches on center for wall applications.

In wet areas, the application of a moisture barrier, 15-pound roofing felt or polyethylene film, is required to protect the wall cavity from moisture intrusion. This is fastened directly to the framing members using staples or roofing nails. Polyethylene sheeting is commonly found in rolls that are wide enough to cover an entire wall in one piece. Asphalt roofing felt (also called building paper) is installed in lapped rows, starting from the bottom of the wall assembly. Subsequent rows should overlap the prior row by a minimum of 2 inches for horizontal seams and 6 inches for vertical seams and corners.

Attach ½"-thick cementboard to the framing members horizontally with the rough side facing out. Use 1¼" cementboard screws. Fasten screws every 6" on center for ceiling applications and every 8" on center for wall applications. Keep fasteners 2" away from each corner and no less than ⅜" from the panel edges.

Preparing the Wall

A moisture barrier consisting of 4-mil clear polyethylene sheeting can be stapled to framing members in damp areas before installing the cementboard.

Asphalt roofing felt (15# building paper) can also be used as a moisture barrier behind cementboard panels in damp areas.

How to Hang Cementboard on Walls

Fasten panels to the wall-framing members using 1¼" cementboard screws. Properly fastened, the head of each screw will sit flush with the surface of the panel. Make sure all seams fall at stud locations, and install the bottom course so the panels are around ¼" off the ground.

Fill the joints using a modified thinset mortar, and then embed fiberglass mesh tape into the mortar. Skim off excess mortar from the joint using a joint knife.

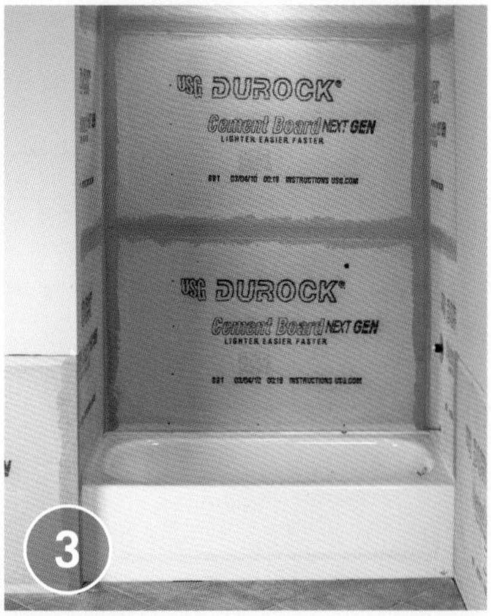

Complete the cementboard installation by applying thinset mortar over the tape and feathering out the edges. If you will be applying a waterproofing membrane over the cementboard surfaces, allow 24 hours for the thinset in the seams to dry.

Wall Tile

TOOLS & MATERIALS

Tile-cutting tools	Grout float	Straight 1 × 2	Tile grout with latex additive
Marker	Grout sponge	2 × 4	Tub and tile caulk
Tape measure	Soft cloth	Scrap 2 × 4	Alkaline a sealer
4' level	Caulk gun	Carpet	Cardboard
Notched trowel	Story stick/pole	Carpet scrap	Eye and ear protection
Mallet	Ceramic wall tile	Thinset tile mortar with latex additive	Work gloves
Small paintbrush or foam brush	Ceramic trim tile (as needed)		

Beautiful, practical, and easy to clean and maintain, tile walls are well suited to bathrooms. When shopping for tile, keep in mind that tiles that are at least 6 inches × 6 inches are easier to install than small tiles, because they require less cutting and cover more surface area. Larger tiles also have fewer grout lines that must be cleaned and maintained. Check out the selection of trim, specialty tiles, and accessories available to help you customize your project.

Most wall tile is designed to have narrow grout lines (less than ⅛ inch wide) filled with unsanded grout. Grout lines wider than ⅛ inch should be filled with sanded floor-tile grout. Either type will last longer if it contains, or is mixed with, a latex additive. To prevent staining, it's a good idea to seal your grout after it fully cures, then once a year thereafter.

You can use standard drywall or water-resistant drywall (called greenboard) as a backer for walls in dry areas. In wet areas, install tile over cementboard. Made from cement and fiberglass, cementboard cannot be damaged by water, though moisture can pass through it. To protect the framing, install a waterproof membrane, such as roofing felt or polyethylene sheeting, between the framing members and the cementboard. Be sure to tape and finish the seams between cementboard panels before laying the tile.

Tile is a practical, easy-to-maintain choice for bathroom walls. The variety of colors, shapes, patterns, and styles is nearly endless. Ceramic tile (right) remains a low-cost, versatile, and attractive option, but glass tile (below) adds shimmer to a room. Glass tiles can also offer a stunning contemporary edge with brilliant colors and patterns unlike any other material.

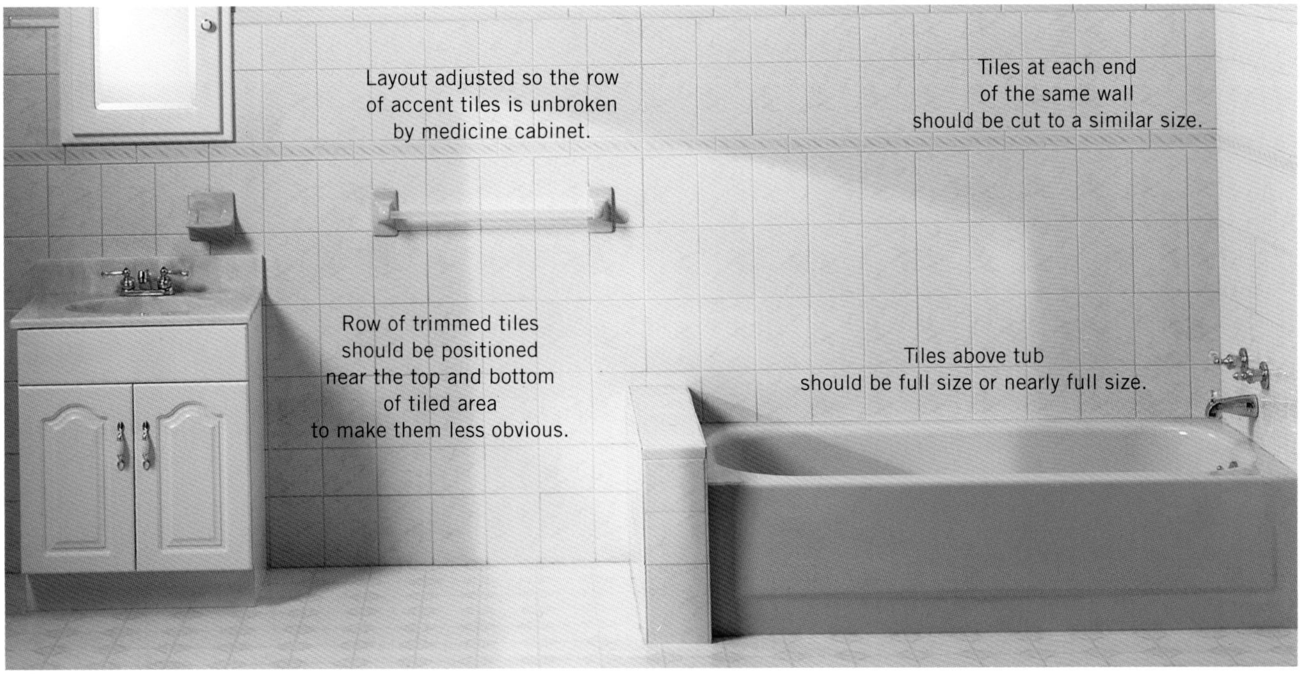

Tiling an entire bathroom requires careful planning. The bathroom shown here was designed so that the tiles directly above the bathtub (the most visible surface) are nearly full height. To accomplish this, cut tiles were used in the second row up from the floor. The short second row also allows the row of accent tiles to run uninterrupted below the medicine cabinet. Cut tiles in both corners should be of similar width to maintain a symmetrical look in the room.

How to Set Wall Tile

Design the layout and mark the reference lines. Begin installation with the second row of tiles above the floor. If the layout requires cut tiles for this row, mark and cut the tiles for the entire row at one time.

Mix a small batch of thinset mortar containing a latex additive. (Some mortar has additive mixed in by the manufacturer and some must have additive mixed in separately.) Cover the back of the first tile with adhesive using a ¼" notched trowel.

(continued)

VARIATION: Spread adhesive on a small section of the wall, then set the tiles into the adhesive. Thinset adhesive sets fast, so work quickly if you choose this installation method.

Beginning near the center of the wall, apply the tile to the wall with a slight twisting motion, aligning it exactly with the horizontal and vertical reference lines. When placing cut tiles, position the cut edges where they will be least visible.

Continue installing tiles, working from the center to the sides in a pyramid pattern. Keep the tiles aligned with the reference lines. If the tiles are not self-spacing, use plastic spacers inserted between tiles to maintain even grout lines. The base row should be the last row of full tiles installed. Cut tile as necessary.

As small sections of tile are completed, set the tile by laying a scrap of 2 × 4 wrapped with carpet onto the tile and rapping it lightly with a mallet. This embeds the tile solidly in the adhesive and creates a flat, even surface.

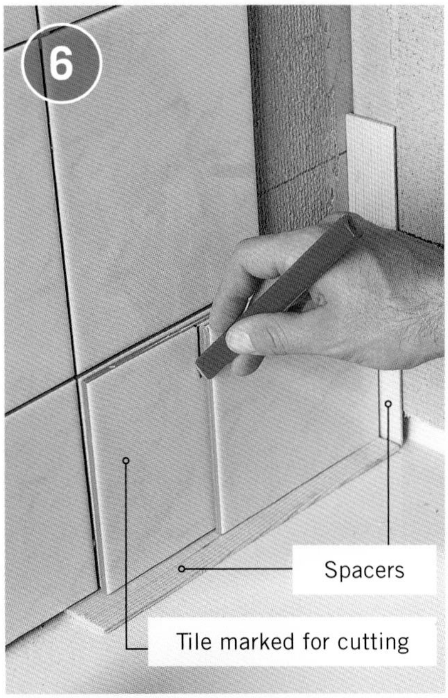

To mark bottom and edge row tiles for straight cuts, begin by taping ⅛" spacers against the surfaces below and to the side of the tile. Position a tile directly over the last full tile installed, then place a third tile so the edge butts against the spacers. Trace the edge of the top tile onto the middle tile to mark it for cutting.

Install any trim tiles, such as the bullnose edge tiles shown above, at border areas. Wipe away excess mortar along the top edges of the edge tiles. Use bullnose and corner bullnose tiles (with two adjacent bullnose edges) at outside corners to cover the rough edges of the adjoining tiles.

Let mortar dry completely (12 to 24 hours), then mix a batch of grout containing latex additive. Apply the grout with a rubber grout float, using a sweeping motion to force it deep into the joints. Do not grout joints adjoining bathtubs, floors, or room corners. These will serve as expansion joints and will be caulked later.

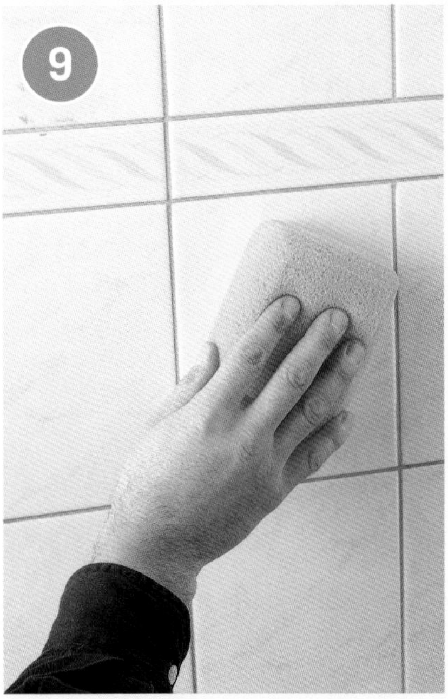

Wipe a damp grout sponge diagonally over the tile, rinsing the sponge in cool water between wipes. Wipe each area only once; repeated wiping can pull grout from the joints. Allow the grout to dry for about 4 hours, then use a soft cloth to buff the tile surface and remove any remaining grout film.

When the grout has cured completely, use a small foam brush to apply grout sealer to the joints, following the manufacturer's directions. Avoid brushing sealer on the tile surfaces, and wipe up excess sealer immediately.

Seal expansion joints at the floor and corners with silicone caulk. After the caulk dries, buff the tile with a soft, dry cloth.

Tub Tile Surround

With a nearly limitless selection of styles, colors, and sizes of tile to choose from, a tub tile-surround replacement is an ideal home-improvement project. It can transform your bathroom into a luxurious retreat, while increasing the value of your home.

Tub tile surrounds can be broken down into three basic components. The back wall is always tiled first. The towel-bar wall contains the optional posts and rod used for hanging bath towels. Lastly, the manifold wall contains the valve stems, shower head, and tub spout. Some tub surrounds are topped off with a low-hanging ceiling. If this is the case for your project, install the cementboard on the ceiling first and tile the ceiling after the walls have been tiled. Ceiling tile is often installed on a diagonal pattern to avoid alignment issues with the wall tile joints.

With proper care and maintenance, nearly any type of wall or floor tile can be used for a surround. Tiles that are rated vitrified or impervious, however, absorb less moisture and are better suited for wet areas. Unglazed tiles such as the tile installed in this project may be used, but be sure to seal them well with at least two coats of tile sealant.

While field tile is estimated and purchased by the total number of square feet, trim tile such as bullnose or cap tile is quantified in linear feet. If the tile you select isn't available with matching trim tile, consider making your own using a wet tile saw fitted with a bevel profile wheel. Through-body porcelain tile is an excellent choice for making custom trim because the surface color is uniform throughout the body of the tile. Most tiled surrounds include bath accessories such as a soap dish and towel bar fixtures. Some tile families offer these accessories in the same patterns and colors. In other cases, you'll have to choose a similar—or perhaps contrasting—style or color. Make sure the thickness of the base for these accessories matches the tile thickness.

To introduce a splash of color to an otherwise plain tile surround, consider adding one or more bands of contrasting tile into the installation. Some tile product lines are available in a variety of solid colors, allowing the installer to incorporate colored rows of similarly sized tiles into the installation without having to make special adjustments to the layout. For added effect, you can even match the trim color to the colored bands of tile or sprinkle some decorative accent tiles throughout the tile installation.

TOOLS & MATERIALS

- 1 × 2 furring strips
- 1¼" cementboard screws
- ½" cementboard
- 2" fiberglass mesh tape
- 4' level
- 4-mil polyethylene sheeting
- 6" joint knife
- Cardboard
- Caulk gun
- Drill
- Eye and ear protection
- Square notched trowel
- Modified thinset mortar
- Stapler and staples
- Carbide scoring tool
- Carbide hole saw bit
- Grout-release agent
- Grout float
- Grout
- Grout sponge
- Keyhole saw
- Latex tile caulk
- Tape measure
- Tarps
- Tile
- Tile-cutting tools
- Trim tile
- Work gloves
- Utility knife
- Screwdriver
- Hammer
- Wood blocking
- Tile spacers
- Small roller
- Pencil

A perfectly functional alcove bathtub surround (above) can be utterly transformed with tile (page opposite).

After

How to Install a Tiled Tub Surround

Remove the old fittings. To begin, remove the tub spout, faucet handles, and showerhead. Then, slice and remove the caulk from the corner joints. Existing ceramic fittings, such as soap dishes, should also be removed to prevent them from falling later and damaging the tub. Use a utility knife to remove old caulk, grout, and adhesive from around the lip of the tub. Finally, lay protective cardboard over the exposed surfaces of the tub and drape tarps over cabinets and toilets.

Cut out old surround panels or tiles. A keyhole or drywall saw can be used to safely cut through the drywall at the junction where it meets the surround. Use the edge of the tile or panel as a guide, taking care to feel for and avoid plumbing or other unseen obstacles hidden within the wall cavity.

Remove any drywall in the new tile-installation area. This will need to be replaced with cementboard. Remove all nails and debris from the framing members. If necessary, install additional wood blocking to accommodate the cementboard installation.

Install a moisture barrier. Fasten 4-mil clear polyethylene sheeting to the studs using staples. This step may be omitted if a waterproofing membrane will be applied over the surface of the cementboard later.

Install ½"-thick cementboard horizontally on the back wall first, and then on the side walls. Fasten the panels to the studs using 1¼" cementboard screws. To make straight cuts, score the panel using a carbide scoring tool, then snap the panel along the scored line. To make hole cuts for plumbing protrusions, use a drill fitted with a carbide hole-saw bit.

Fill the gaps between cementboard panels with thinset mortar, overlapping at least 2 to 3" on each side of the joint. Center and embed 2"-wide alkaline-resistant fiberglass tape over the joint and lightly skim thinset over the joint. If your local codes require it, apply a roll-on waterproofing membrane to the cementboard (see page 203).

Dry-lay tile for your surround on a flat surface, inserting ⅛" spacers between the tiles to set the gap. Lay out enough for roughly half the surround height and then measure the length of the dry-laid row to find the actual height of the tiles on the wall.

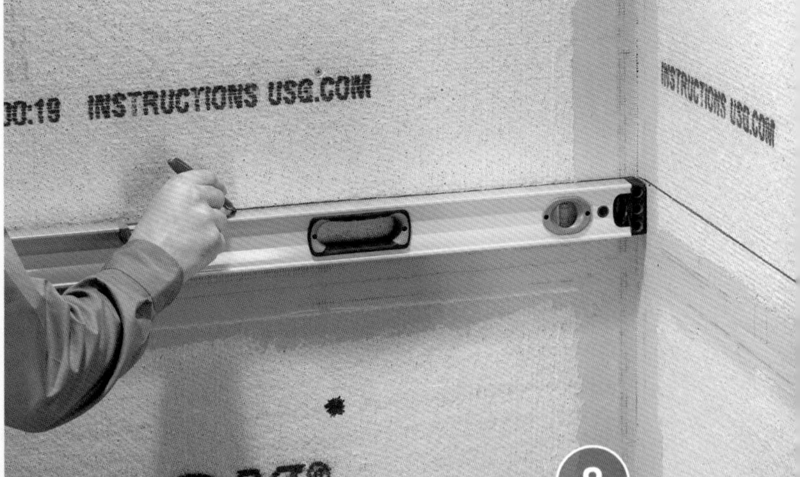

Draw horizontal reference lines on the wall using a 4' level to make sure the lines are level. Extend these reference lines to each side wall. Measure down from the horizontal lines to the tub at several points on all walls to make sure the tub deck and the lines are parallel. If they aren't, remeasure from the point where the tub deck is highest and transfer level lines all around from that point. *(continued)*

Draw a vertical reference line down the center of the back wall. To temporarily support the weight of the tile that will be installed above, align and fasten 1 × 2 furring strips just below the horizontal reference lines located in the midsection of the tub surround.

Set the first tiles. Mix a small batch of thinset mortar. Apply the thinset using a ¼" square-notched trowel held at a 45° angle. Spread the adhesive within the guidelines on the wall, aligning the ridges of the setting bed in a horizontal direction. Install tile on the back wall first, keeping tile aligned to the centered guide line.

Install two or three rows of tiles—here, a row of decorative accent tiles is installed as well.

To mark tiles for straight cuts, place a full tile directly on top of the field tile that is installed adjacent to the void. Position another full tile over the void, abutting the overhanging edge of the tile against a ⅛" spacer. Trace the edge of this tile to mark the underlying tile for cutting.

Complete the upper sections. After the top portion of the back wall is tiled, fill in the upper portions of each side wall. Leave out tiles as needed to accommodate tiled-in accessories such as a soap dish or towel rod.

Mark and cut tiles to fit around the valve stems and water pipes as required to install your tub spout, diverter, and showerhead (often, showerheads are installed above the tiles). Finish tiling the lower portions of the tile installation, then allow to dry for 24 hours.

TIP: Tape tiles together to prevent slippage while they dry.

Coat the tile surfaces with a sealer or other grout-release agent if they are not glazed by the manufacturer. This treatment will prevent grout from getting into places where it should not go.

Grout the tiles (see page 207). To apply grout, hold the grout float at an angle and force the mortar into the joints, skimming excess grout from the tile surface with each pass. Wipe tile clean using a damp grout sponge. After grouting, buff tile surfaces with a soft cloth to remove haze. Install fittings and hardware, and caulk around the tub deck.

Toilet Enclosure

TOOLS & MATERIALS

Prehung door unit	Drywall
Hammer	Handsaw
16d nails	Utility knife
Screwdriver	Wall compound
2 × 4 lumber	Interior door lockset
Drywall tape	Door trim
Wood shims	Silicone caulk
¼-round molding	Fiberglass insulation
Stud finder	Pencil
Circular saw	Eye and ear protection
Drill	Work gloves

One of the best ways to make a busy family bathroom more usable is to enclose the toilet in a room of its own. Toilet enclosures—originally called "water closets" after the cistern they enclosed—make a privacy compartment within the bathroom. This allows one person to shower while the other uses the toilet. It also effectively hides the fixture that most people think is the sore thumb of the bathroom.

Although toilet enclosures are basic structures comprising framed walls and a prehung door, they must be built to maintain adequate spacing around the toilet for maximum comfort and to meet local codes. As a general rule of thumb, you want to leave at least 15 inches from the center of the toilet bowl to the wall surface on either side, and at least 21 inches from the front of the bowl to the door. You may also want to add baffles or soundproofing inside the walls, to make the space as private as possible.

The enclosure shown here includes a combination lighting/ventilation fixture. Both are absolute musts for appropriate hygiene and comfort, even if they are not mandated by local codes. (A window can serve the ventilation function, but you'll still need to install lighting for nighttime use.)

When it comes to toilet enclosures, more room is always better. If you can dedicate extra space to the enclosure, you'll not only make the space more comfortable, you'll be able to add nice finishing touches such as a magazine rack or shelves for candles.

A full enclosure with a door offers the maximum in privacy, but it may be a more extreme solution than you require. A simple partition wall next to the toilet creates a sense of privacy without any claustrophobia.

How to Build a Toilet Enclosure

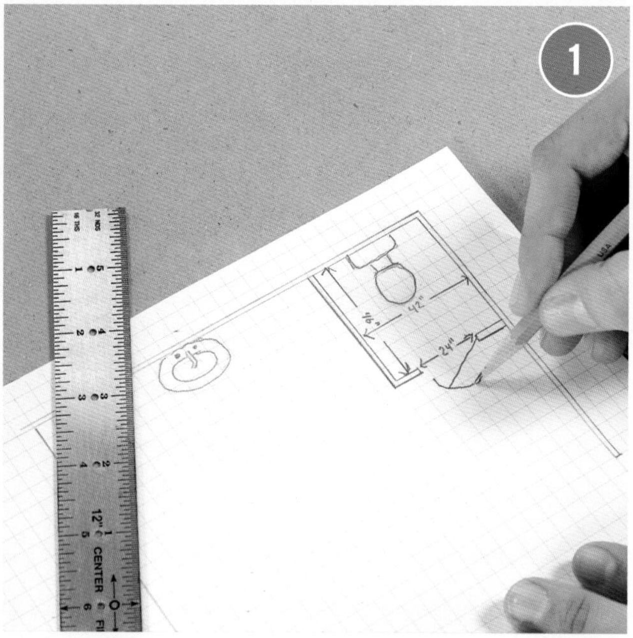

Carefully plan out the enclosure. Sketch your plans with exact dimensions to ensure that you allow proper space between toilet and walls, and to ensure door swing won't impede the shower, vanity drawers, or other fixtures.

Run wiring and ducting for lighting and ventilation as necessary. Install a box for an overhead fixture and run wire for the switch. We installed a combination light/vent fan (see page 196) connected to an interior wall switch placed just on the latch side of the enclosure wall. The fixture can be run off the light-switch circuit for the entire bathroom if that circuit has the capacity.

Check existing connection walls for plumb and square. Cut the sole and top plates accordingly, compensating as needed for any variances. Place top and sole plates side by side and mark stud locations, 16" on center.

Secure sole plates to the floor. Plates installed over resilient flooring, as shown here, can be nailed through to the subfloor. When installing over a tile floor, use a masonry bit to drill pilot holes and then screw through to the subfloor. (Over mosaic floors, it's best to remove the tiles from under the sole plate and secure the plate directly to the subfloor.)

Use a stud finder to locate ceiling joists, then nail the top plates into place. Frame out the walls by toenailing studs between top and sole plates as marked. Frame L-corner for walls, as shown (inset).

Frame the doorway with header, cripple studs, and jack studs (you should purchase your prehung door first, so that you can double-check the opening measurements against the actual door unit).

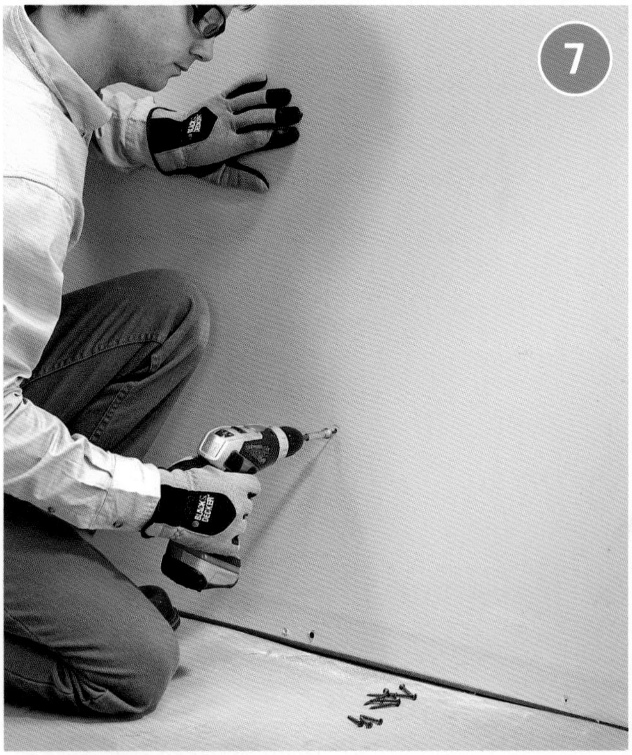

Hang drywall on the framed walls, inside and out. The enclosure here was clad with standard drywall rather than greenboard, because the walls won't be subjected to any direct moisture contact. If the enclosure abuts a shower or bath, use greenboard or cementboard. *(continued)*

Position the prehung door in place. Check that it is oriented correctly, to open out from the enclosure and against a wall, rather than blocking the central space or opening against the vanity.

Shim all around the jamb (specifically, behind hinges and lockset location) until the door unit is plumb and square in the opening and the door opens smoothly. Nail through the door jambs into the framing at the shim points.

Saw the shims off flush. Measure, cut, and nail the trim for the door in place. Putty and sand over the nail heads on jambs and casework.

USE THE WALL CAVITY

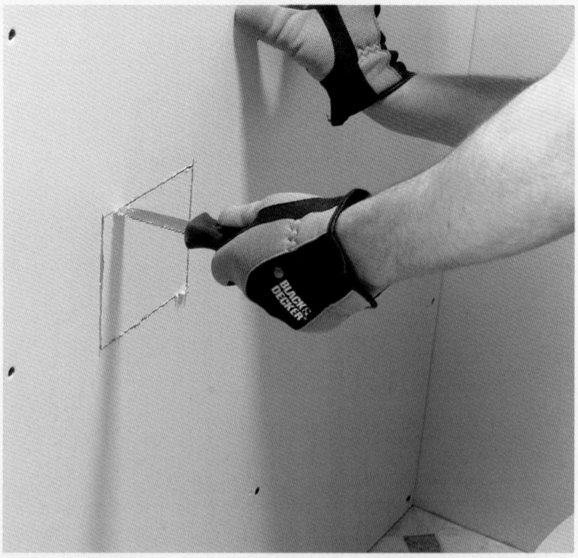

Because the partition wall you've built is essentially empty, it is a good candidate for installing niche fittings that are recessed into the wall. A recessed toilet tissue holder is one easy-to-install fitting. Space will be fairly tight in your enclosure, so using the wall space makes a lot of sense. A wall-niche magazine rack or niche shelving are just two additional ways you may use the wall cavity space.

Finish the drywall surfaces with tape and joint compound. Work as neatly as you can to minimize sanding. Seal the new drywall with drywall primer before you paint.

Paint the enclosure walls and add any additional elements, including paper holders, grab bars, and shelves or cabinets. The wall area behind the toilet tank is a good spot for installing shallow shelving, but keep it at least 3' above the tank lid.

Attach base ¼-round molding on the bottom of the walls, inside and out (or cove molding if you prefer). Apply a coat of silicone caulk to the bottom of the molding before nailing it in place.

Radiant Floor

Floor-warming systems require very little energy to run and are designed to heat tile floors only; they are not generally used as sole heat sources for rooms.

A typical floor-warming system consists of one or more thin mats containing electric resistance wires that heat up when energized, like an electric blanket. The mats are installed beneath the tile and are hardwired to a 120-volt GFCI circuit. A thermostat controls the temperature, and a timer turns the system off automatically.

The system shown in this project includes two plastic mesh mats, each with its own power lead that is wired directly to the thermostat. Radiant mats may be installed over a plywood subfloor, but if you plan to install floor tile you should put down a base of cementboard first and then install the mats on top of the cementboard.

A crucial part of installing this system is using a multimeter to perform several resistance checks to make sure the heating wires have not been damaged during shipping or installation.

Electrical service required for a floor-warming system is based on size. A smaller system may connect to an existing GFCI circuit, but a larger one will need a dedicated circuit; follow the manufacturer's requirements.

To order a floor-warming system, contact the manufacturer or dealer. In most cases, you can send plans to the manufacturer and they'll custom-fit a system for your project area.

TOOLS & MATERIALS

Vacuum cleaner
Multimeter
Tape measure
Scissors
Router/rotary tool
Marker
Electric wire fault indicator (optional)
Hot glue gun
Radiant floor mats
12/2 NM cable
Trowel or rubber float
Conduit
Thinset mortar
Thermostat with sensor
Junction box(es)
Tile or stone floor covering
Drill
Double-sided carpet tape
Cable clamps
Eye and ear protection
Work gloves

A radiant floor-warming system employs electric heating mats that are covered with floor tile to create a floor that's cozy underfoot.

INSTALLATION TIPS

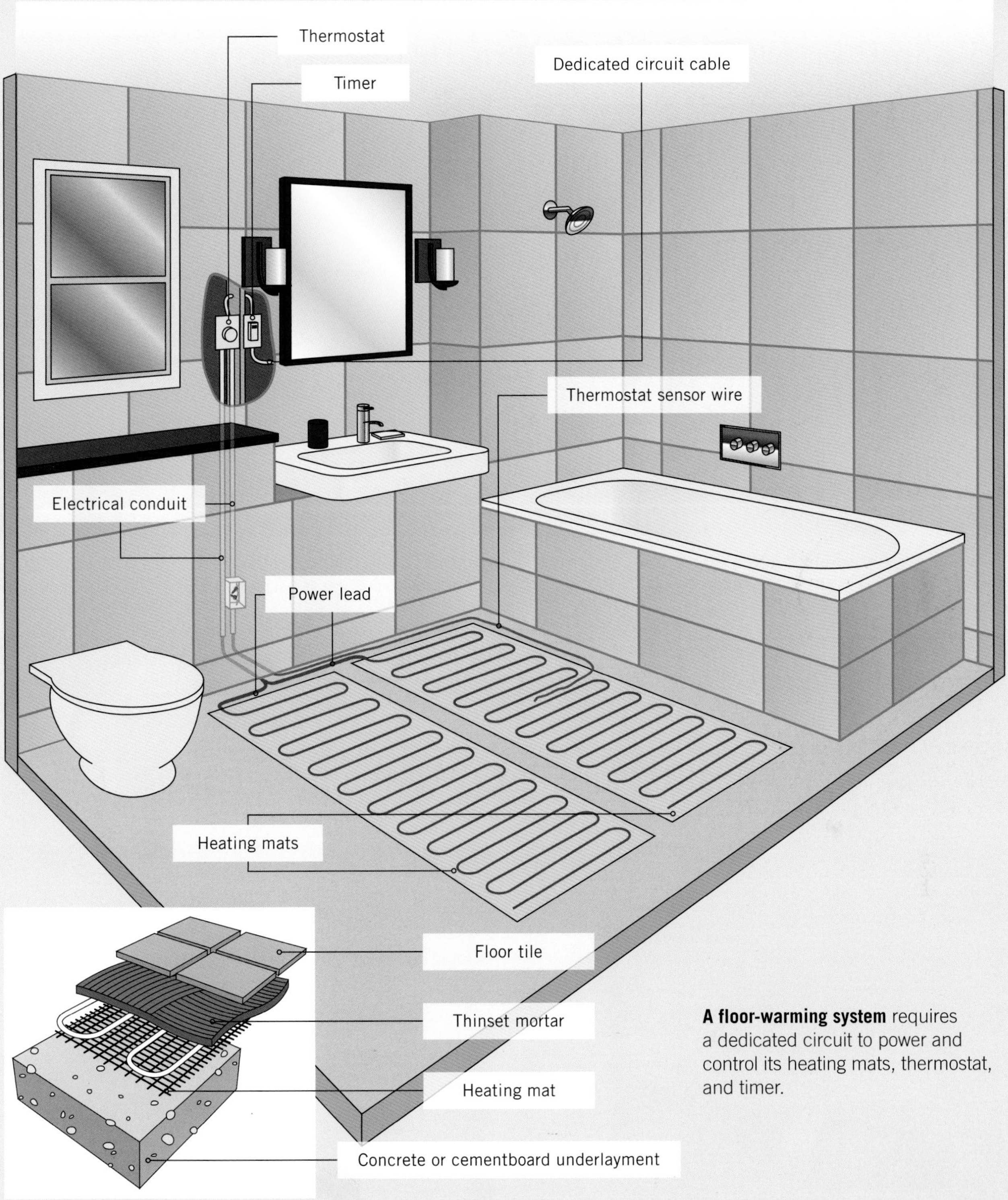

A floor-warming system requires a dedicated circuit to power and control its heating mats, thermostat, and timer.

- Each radiant mat must have a direct connection to the power lead from the thermostat, with the connection made in a junction box in the wall cavity. Do not install mats in series.
- Do not install radiant floor mats under shower areas.
- Do not overlap mats or let them touch.
- Do not cut heating wire or damage heating wire insulation.
- The distance between wires in adjoining mats should equal the distance between wire loops measured center to center.

Installing a Radiant Floor-Warming System

Floor-warming systems must be installed on a circuit with adequate amperage and a GFCI breaker. Smaller systems may tie into an existing circuit, but larger ones need a dedicated circuit. Follow local building and electrical codes that apply to your project.

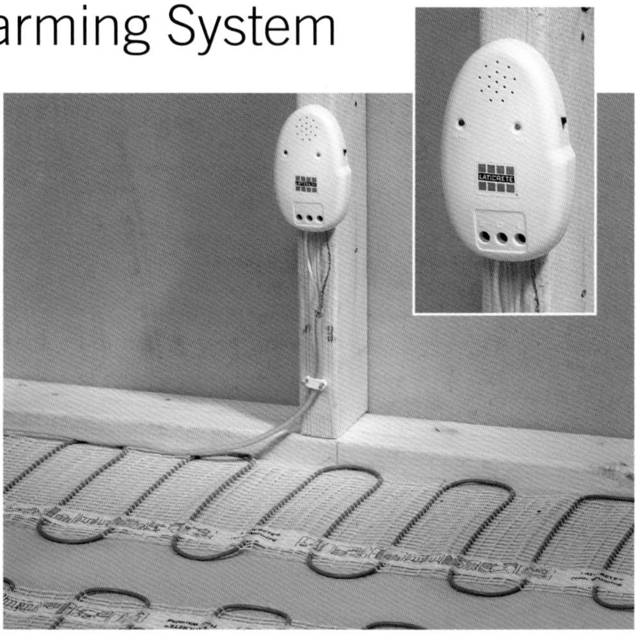

An electric wire fault indicator monitors each floor mat for continuity during the installation process. If there is a break in continuity (for example, if a wire is cut), an alarm sounds. If you choose not to use an installation tool to monitor the mat, test for continuity frequently using a multimeter.

How To Install a Radiant Floor-Warming System

Install electrical boxes to house the thermostat and timer. In most cases, the box should be located 60" above floor level. Use a 4"-deep × 4"-wide double-gang box for the thermostat/timer control if your kit has an integral model. If your timer and thermostat are separate, install a separate single box for the timer.

Drill access holes in the sole plate for the power leads that are preattached to the mats (they should be over 10' long). The leads should be connected to a supply wire from the thermostat in a junction box located in a wall near the floor and below the thermostat box. The access hole for each mat should be located directly beneath the knockout for that cable in the thermostat box. Drill through the sill plate vertically and horizontally so the holes meet in an L-shape.

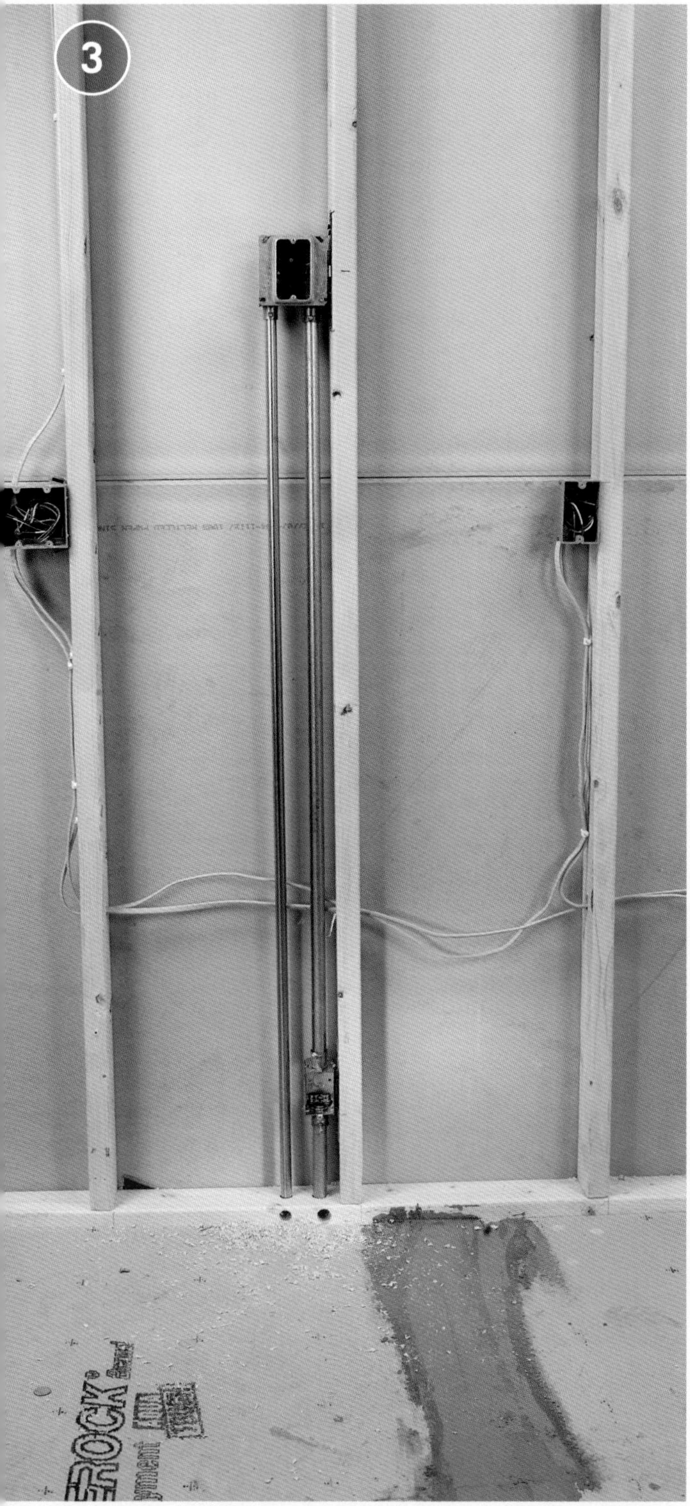

Run conduit from the electrical boxes to the sill plate. The line for the supply cable should be ¾" conduit. If you are installing multiple mats, the supply conduit should feed into a junction box about 6" above the sill plate and then continue into the ¾" hole you drilled for the supply leads. The sensor wire needs only ½" conduit that runs straight from the thermostat box via the thermostat. The mats should be powered by a dedicated 20-amp GFCI circuit of 12/2 NM cable run from your main service panel to the electrical box (this is for 120-volt mats—check your instruction manual for specific circuit recommendations).

Clean the floor surface thoroughly to get rid of any debris that could potentially damage the wire mats. A vacuum cleaner generally does a more effective job than a broom.

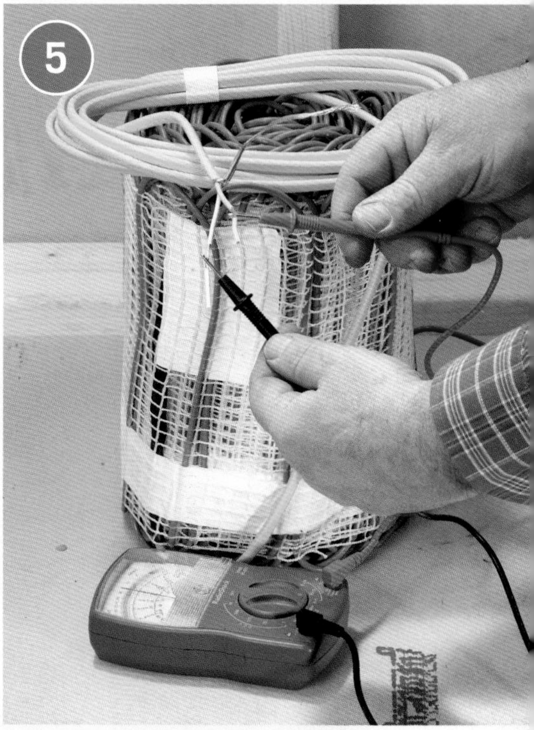

Test for resistance using a multimeter set to measure ohms. This is a test you should make frequently during the installation, along with checking for continuity. If the resistance is off by more than 10% from the theoretical resistance listing (see manufacturer's chart in installation instructions), contact technical support for the kit manufacturer. For example, the theoretical resistance for the 1 × 50' mat seen here is 19, so the ohms reading should be between 17 and 21.

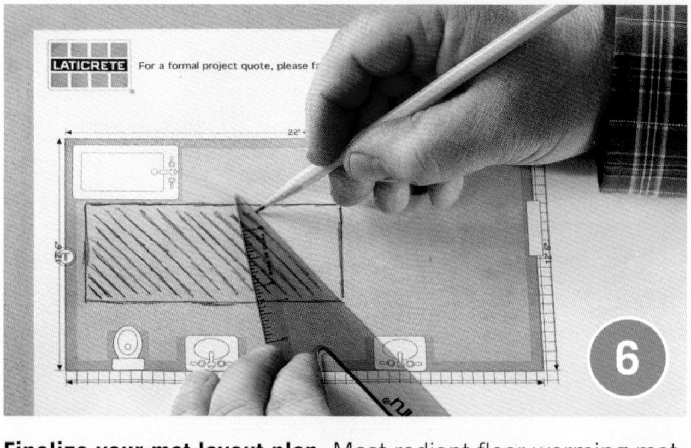

Finalize your mat layout plan. Most radiant floor-warming mat manufacturers will provide a layout plan for you at the time of purchase, or they will give you access to an online design tool so you can come up with your own plan. This is an important step to the success of your project, and the assistance is free.

(continued)

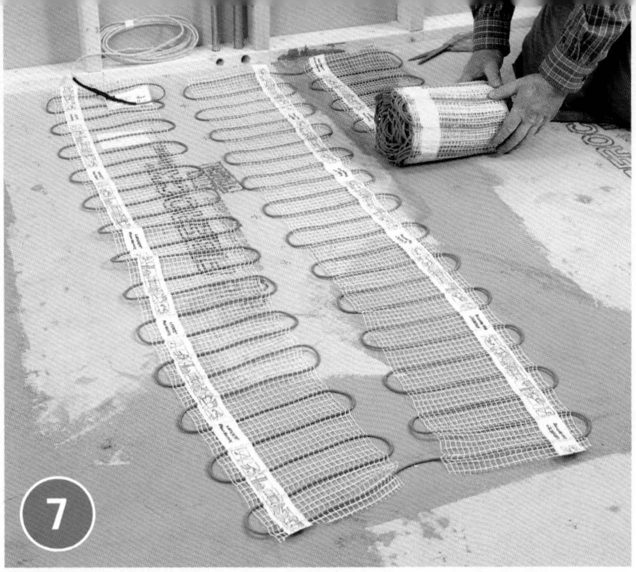

Unroll the radiant mat or mats and allow them to settle. Arrange the mat or mats according to the plan you created. It's okay to cut the plastic mesh so you can make curves or switchbacks, but do not cut the heating wire under any circumstances, even to shorten it.

Finalize the mat layout and then test the resistance again using a multimeter. Also check for continuity in several different spots. If there is a problem with any of the mats, you should identify it and correct it before proceeding with the mortar installation.

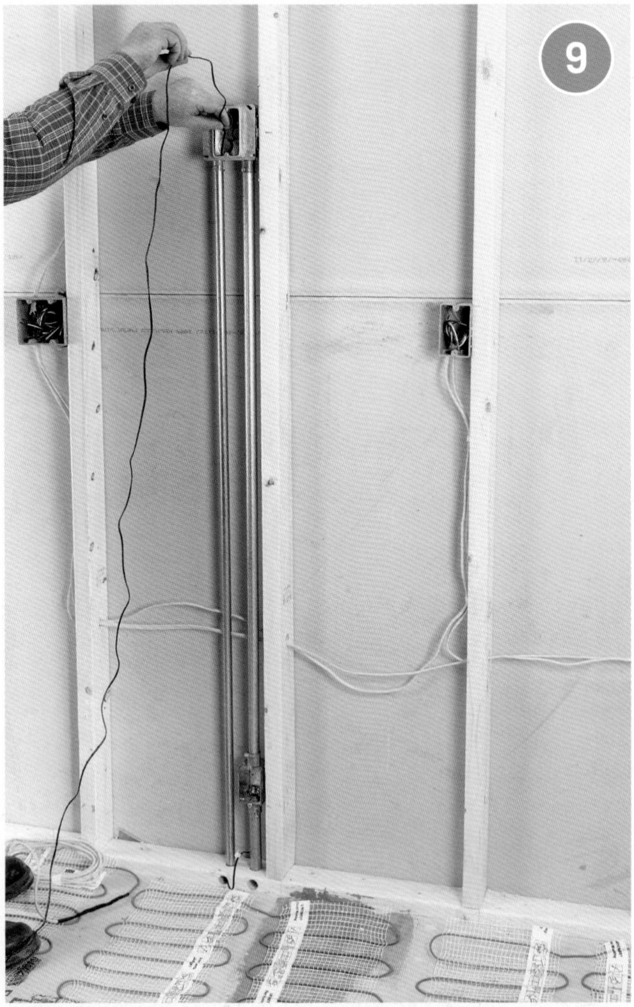

Run the thermostat sensor wire from the electrical box down the ½" conduit raceway and out the access hole in the sill plate. Select the best location for the thermostat sensor and mark the location onto the flooring. Also mark the locations of the wires that connect to and lead from the sensor.

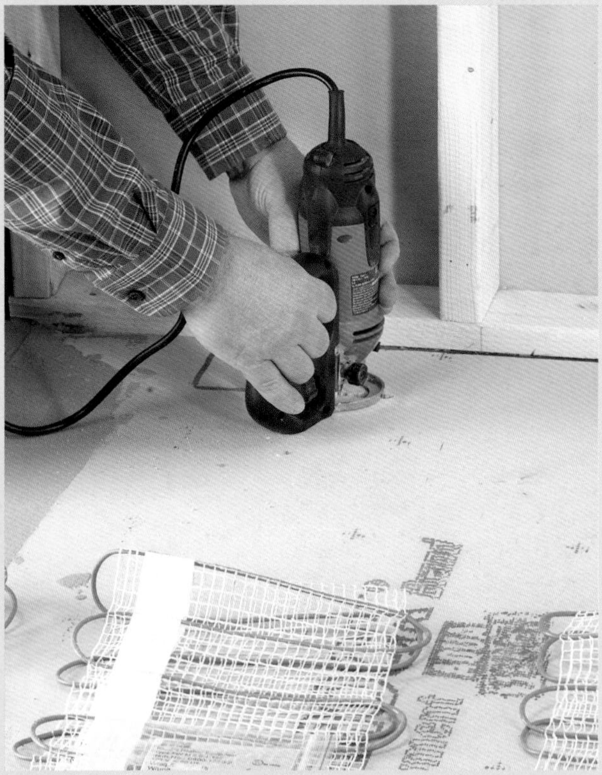

VARIATION: If your local codes require it, roll the mats out of the way and cut a channel for the sensor and the sensor wires into the floor or floor underlayment. For most floor materials, a spiral cutting tool does a quick and neat job of this task. Remove any debris.

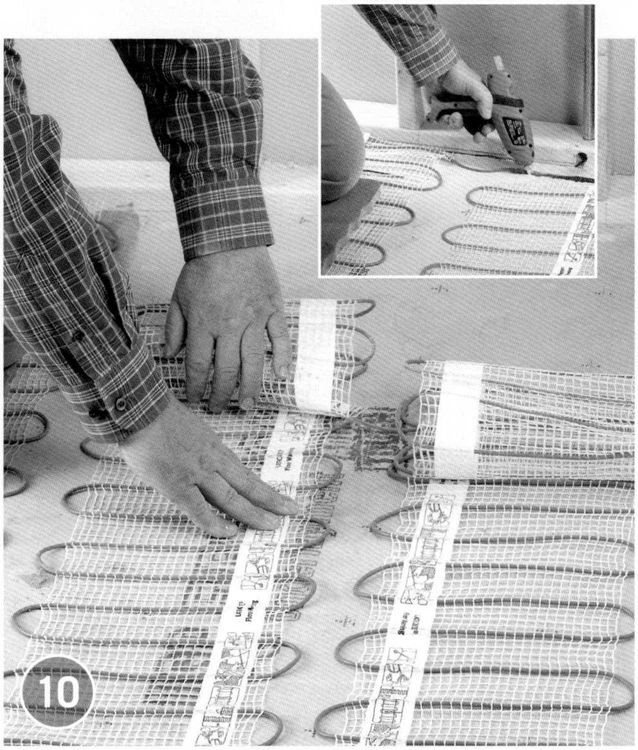

Bond the mats to the floor. If the mats in your system have adhesive strips, peel off the adhesive backing and roll out the mats in the correct position, pressing them against the floor to set the adhesive. If your mats have no adhesive, bind them with strips of double-sided carpet tape. The thermostat sensor and the power supply leads should be attached with hot glue (inset) and run up into their respective holes in the sill plate if you have not done this already. Test all mats for resistance and continuity.

Cover the floor installation areas with a layer of thinset mortar that is thick enough to fully cover all the wires and mats (usually around ¼" in thickness). Check the wires for continuity and resistance regularly and stop working immediately if there is a drop in resistance or a failure of continuity. Allow the mortar to dry overnight.

Connect the power supply leads from the mat or mats to the NM cable coming from the thermostat inside the junction box near the sill. Power must be turned off. The power leads should be cut so about 8" of wire feeds into the box. Be sure to use cable clamps to protect the wires.

Connect the sensor wire and the power-supply lead (from the junction box) to the thermostat/timer according to the manufacturer's directions. Attach the device to the electrical box, restore power, and test the system to make sure it works. Once you are convinced that it is operating properly, install floor tiles and repair the wall surfaces.

Floor Tile

Although the floor tiles shown in the steps that follow are porcelain, this process would be the same if you were installing ceramic or stone tiles. In all cases, a successfully tiled floor relies on proper preparation. That starts with laying down a stable, secure surface for the tile (see pages 70 to 75). But the most important step for the look of the finished floor is snapping the chalk lines and dry-fitting to determine the most visually pleasing tile placement. Beyond that, work carefully and steadily, using spacers throughout to maintain proper spacing, and be careful never to walk on a newly tiled floor. This means planning so that you never tile yourself into a corner. Plan carefully, pay attention when laying the tiles, and work within your own abilities and capacity, and you'll wind up with a long-lasting, beautiful tile floor.

Floor tile can be laid in many different patterns, but for your first effort, it's wise to stick to a basic grid. Generally, you'll combine the floor tile with a profiled base tile or cove molding, installed after the flooring is completely dry and set.

TOOLS & MATERIALS

¼" square-notched trowel
Rubber mallet
Tile cutter
Tile nippers
Handheld tile cutter
Needlenose pliers
Grout float
Grout sponge
Soft cloth
Thinset mortar
Tile
Tile spacers
Grout
Latex grout additive
Wall adhesive
2 × 4 lumber
Grout sealer
Tile caulk
Sponge brush
Cementboard
Chalk line
Tape measure
Drill
Paddle bit
Caulk gun
1¼" cementboard screws
Fiberglass-mesh wallboard tape
Utility knife or grout knife
Threshold material
Jigsaw or circular saw with a tungsten-carbide blade
Rounded bullnose tile
Eye and ear protection
Work gloves

How to Install Floor Tile

Screw the tile backer board down to the subfloor with 1¼" self-piloting screws driven every 2" around the edge. Tape the seams with fiberglass mesh tape and finish the backer board surface as described on page 203.

Draw reference lines and establish the tile layout. Check that the lines are square to each other using the 3-4-5 method. Dry-lay 2 half rows of tiles in place, running from the center in 2 directions out to the wall. Determine if the layout leaves less than ⅓ of a tile at either wall, and adjust your reference lines if it does.

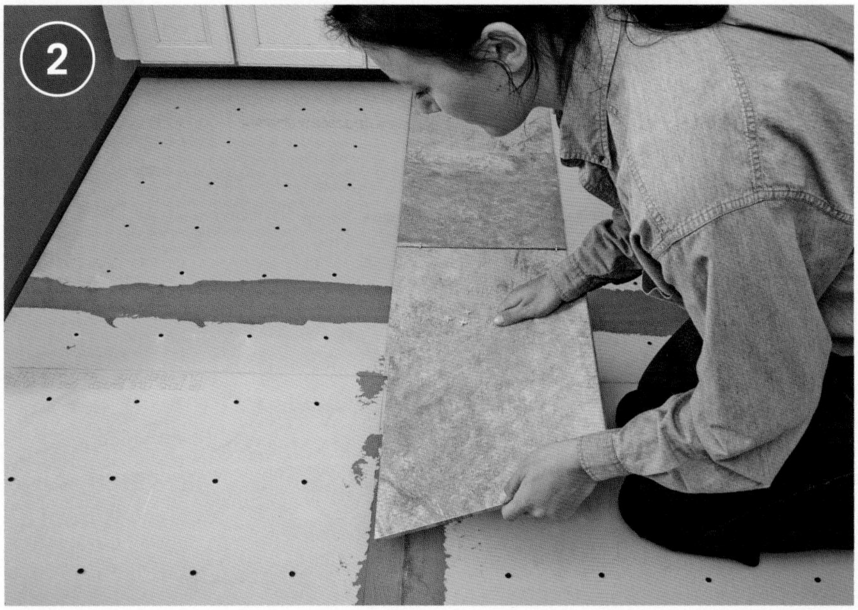

OPTION: Build a grid system of chalk lines based on the actual dimensions of your tiles, including the grout lines. A grid system ensures that you will stay on track and it helps you divide the project into small sections so you can apply the correct amount of thinset without guessing.

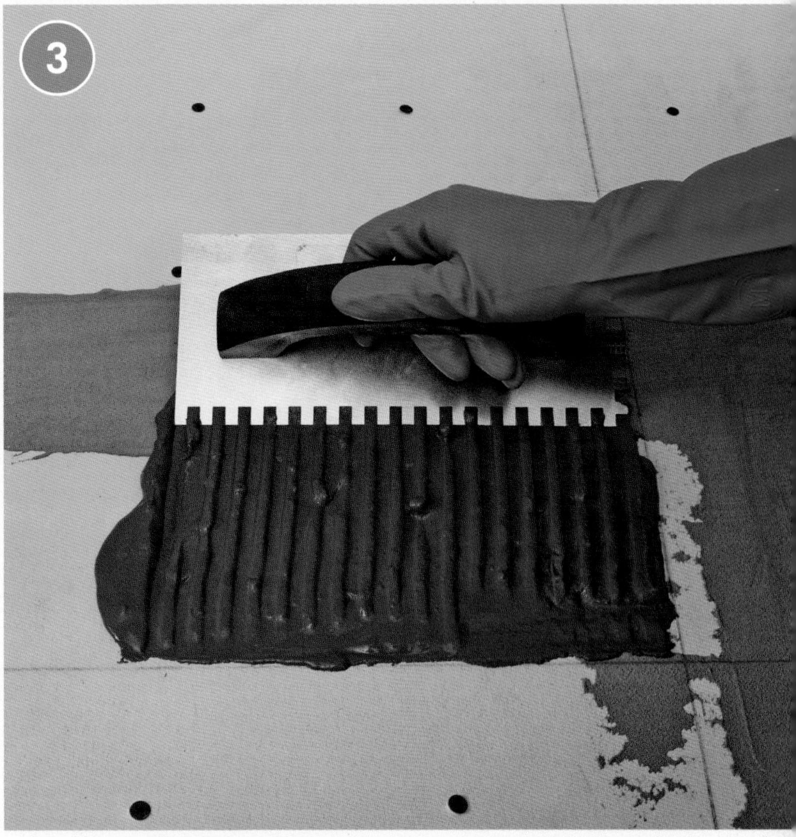

Mix a batch of thinset mortar and spread it evenly across a square along both reference lines of the quadrant. Use the notched edge to create furrows, being careful not to press down all the way to the backer board. *(continued)*

Press the first tile down into the mortar at the corner of the quadrant where the reference lines intersect. Twist it slightly and press down. Use a putty knife to pull the tile up to check that the mortar consistency is correct and coating all areas on the bottom of the tile. Press the tile back into position. Use a rubber mallet to gently tap the center area of the tile to set it properly.

VARIATION: For 16 × 16" or larger tiles or uneven stone, use a larger trowel with notches that are at least ½" deep.

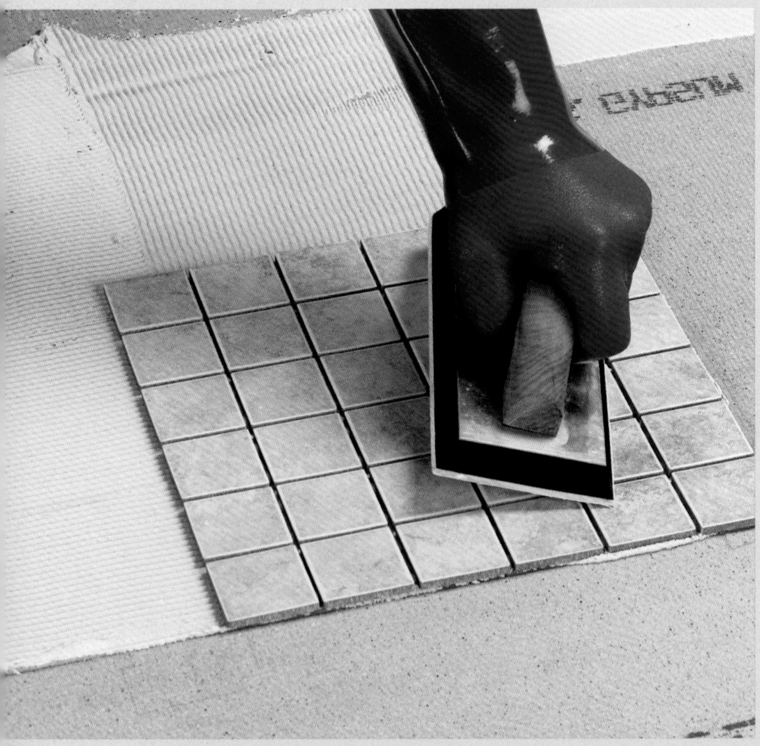

VARIATION: For mosaic sheets, use a 3⁄16" V-notched trowel to spread the mortar and a grout float to press the sheets into the mortar. Apply pressure gently to avoid creating an uneven surface.

Continue laying tiles along one row, using spacers to maintain spacing between tiles. Use the appropriate spacers for the size tile you are laying, and stand them upright; do not lay spacers flat at tile intersections because they will be impossible to remove from the mortar and can compromise the integrity of the grout lines.

To make sure tiles are level with one another, place a straight 2 × 4 across several tiles in a row and tap the top of the board with a rubber mallet.

TIP

Use a small, flat plastering trowel to scrape up any mortar squeezeout from the surface of the backer board around a set tile, so that you don't wind up with too much under the adjacent tiles. When you're ready to take a break or the mortar is starting to harden, clean up around the margins of the last tile you've laid with the same trowel.

As you work, clean up any mortar on the top of the tiles as soon as you detect it. Use a damp sponge to wipe up the mortar completely, to ensure it doesn't dry on the surface of the tile.

Lay the rest of the tile in the remaining area of the quadrant, repeating steps 2 through 7. Be careful to plan tile placement so that you don't tile yourself into a corner. Avoid stepping or kneeling on the laid tiles.

(continued)

In corners and against walls leave a gap of at least ¼" between the tiles and the walls or cabinets. Make sure the gap is still narrow enough that your base shoe molding or trim will cover it.

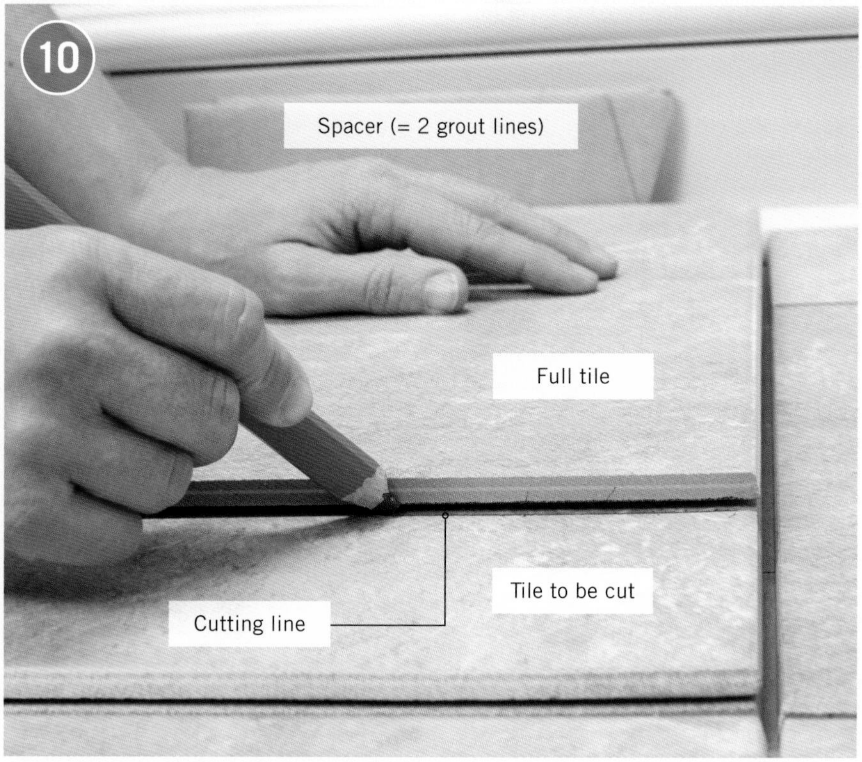

To mark tile for cutting so it will fit between the end or edge of a row and the wall, lay the tile to be cut directly on top of the full tile it will sit next to. Stand one or two tiles up flat against the wall as spacers (this will account for an expansion and the grout space between tiles) and lay another tile on top of the tile to be marked, with the edge butted against the tiles on the wall. Mark the second tile for cutting. Check the dry fit and then apply mortar for two partial tiles at a time and set them in place, leaving an expansion gap between the tile edge and the wall or obstruction.

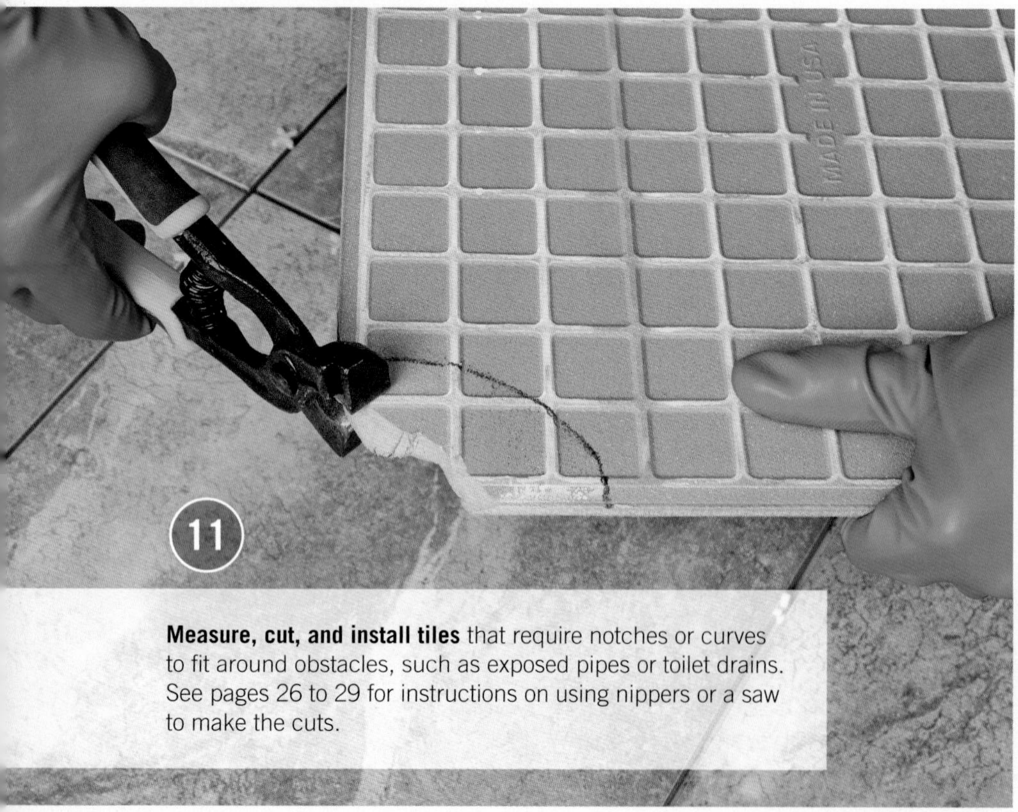

Measure, cut, and install tiles that require notches or curves to fit around obstacles, such as exposed pipes or toilet drains. See pages 26 to 29 for instructions on using nippers or a saw to make the cuts.

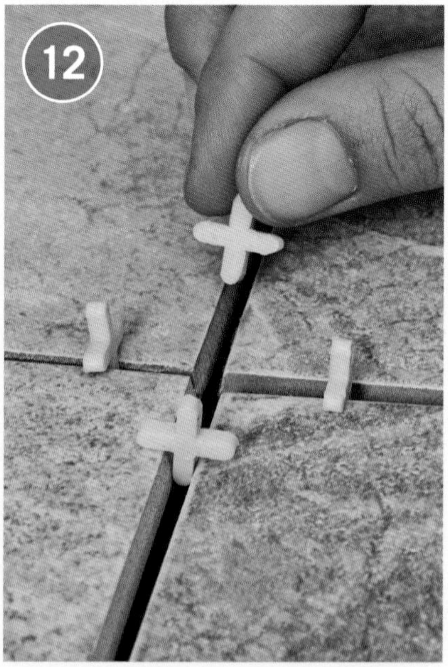

Continue laying tiles until the floor is complete. Allow 24 hours for the mortar to dry and then remove the spacers. To prepare for grouting, use painter's tape to protect any trim that abuts the tiled surface.

Mix the grout using the drill and paddle bit. Follow the instructions for the grout you're using.

NOTE: When mixing grout for porous tile, such as unsealed quarry or natural stone, include an additive with a release agent to prevent the grout from bonding to the tile surfaces.

Start in a corner and pour a small amount of grout onto the tiles. Use the float to spread the grout out from the corner, working in smooth arcs and pressing the grout into the spaces between tiles. Hold the float at about a 60° angle and work in a figure-eight motion. Work on 4-tile sections.

As you finish one small quadrant of tile, use the float and a small trowel to clean the excess grout off the surface of the tiles. Continue applying the grout at a 45° angle to the joints until you've finished about 25 sq. ft. of the floor.

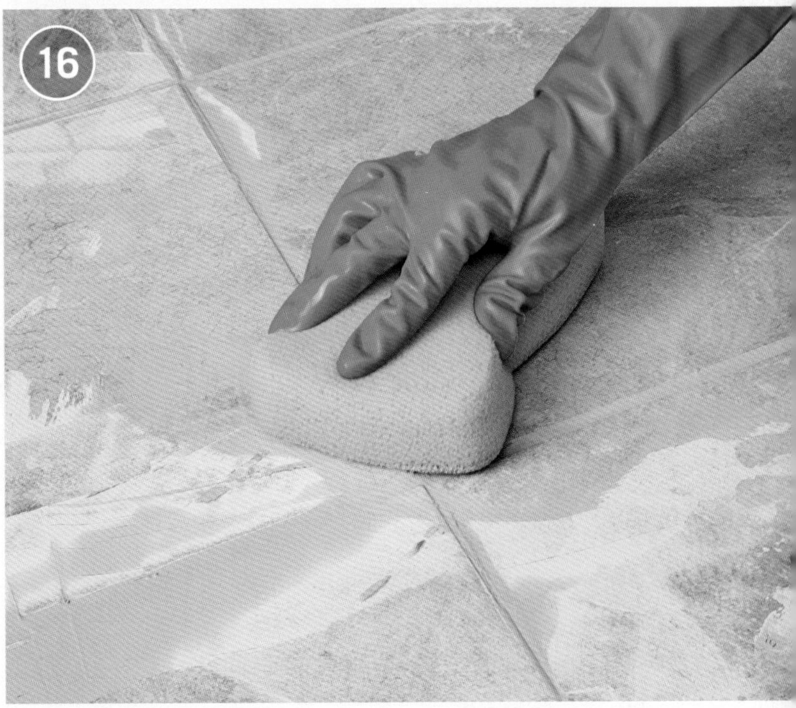

Wipe a damp grout sponge diagonally over about 2 sq. ft. of the floor to remove grout residue. Rinse the sponge in cool water between passes. Be careful not to press so hard you pull grout out of the joints, but use as many passes as necessary to clean the surface of the tiles. Change the rinse water frequently. *(continued)*

Allow the grout to dry for the recommended period (4 hours is a common drying time). Use a soft cloth such as folded cheesecloth to buff the tile surface and remove any remaining grout film. If any grout film remains, use a grout-remover solution.

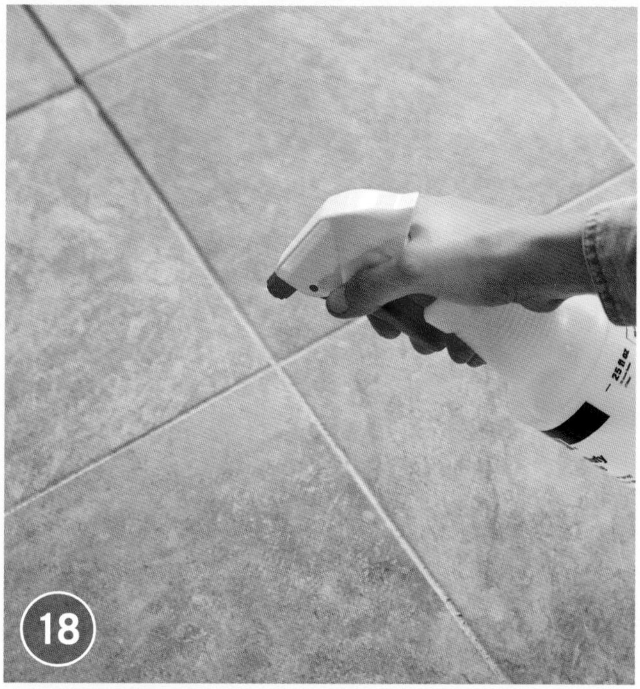

Ensure the integrity of the grout by misting it with water two to three times per day, for the first two or three days. This will help the grout cure evenly and completely and make it less likely to crack.

Apply grout sealer to all the grout lines. You can use an applicator bottle such as the one shown here, or you can use a formula meant to be applied with a small sponge or foam brush. Be careful to apply the sealer on the grout lines only.

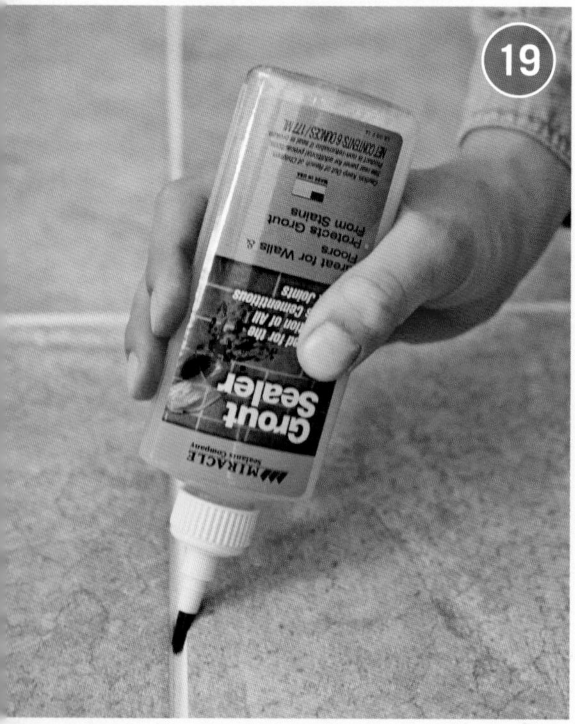

Install threshold transitions in doorways and between transitions to different flooring materials. If the threshold is too long for the doorway, cut it to fit with a jigsaw or circular saw equipped with a tungsten-carbide blade (if you are using a threshold made of tile). Depending on the type of threshold strip, either screw it down or set it in a bed of thinset mortar and allow 24 hours for the mortar to dry.

How to Install Bullnose Base Trim

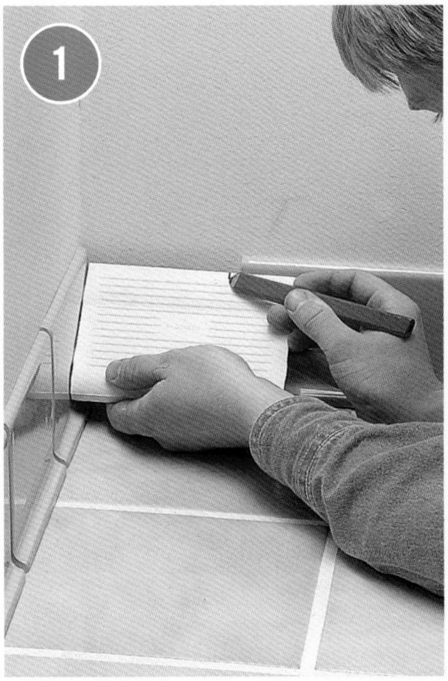

Dry-fit the tiles to determine the best spacing. Grout lines in base tile do not always align with grout lines in the floor tile. Use rounded bullnose tiles at outside corners, and mark tiles for cutting as needed.

Leaving a ⅛" expansion gap between tiles at corners, mark any contour cuts necessary to allow the coved edges to fit together. Use a jigsaw with a tungsten-carbide blade to make curved cuts.

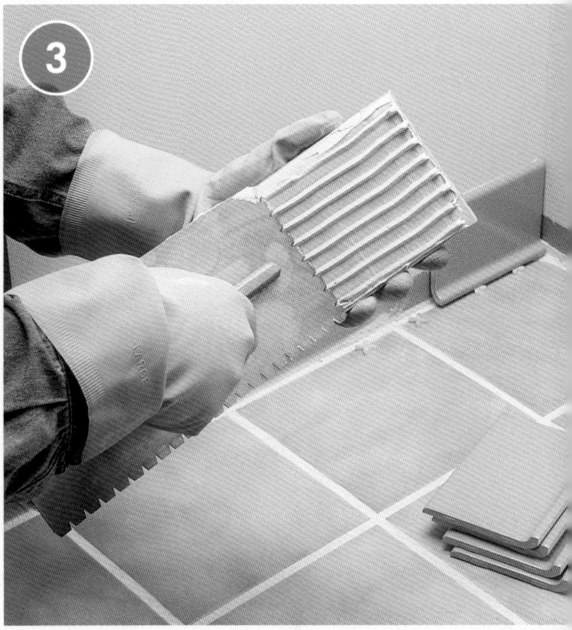

Begin installing base-trim tiles at an inside corner. Use a notched trowel to apply wall adhesive to the back of the tile. Place ⅛" spacers on the floor under each tile to create an expansion joint.

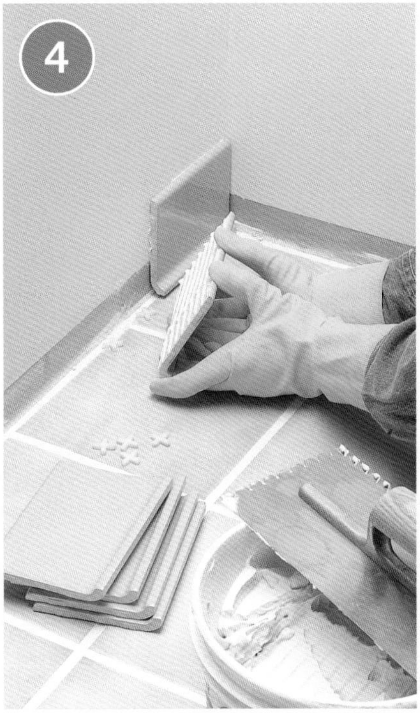

Press the tile onto the wall. Continue setting tiles, using spacers to maintain ⅛" gaps between the tiles and ⅛" expansion joints between the tiles and floor.

Use a double-bullnose tile on one side of outside corners to cover the edge of the adjoining tile.

After the adhesive dries, grout the vertical joints between tiles and apply grout along the tops of the tiles to make a continuous grout line. Once the grout hardens, fill the expansion joint between the tiles and floor with caulk.

Bathroom Accessories

The smaller accessories that you include in your bathroom's design can often make or break the look of the room. But more than that, the right accessory can make a bathroom more comfortable and enjoyable to use. Given that you use the room every day, and often multiple times during the day, the accessories you include have a big impact.

There are basically two types of bathroom accessories: little luxuries and practical essentials. The former include luxury medicine chests with overlarge mirrors and high-style towel bars and towel warmers. The more practical features include grab bars and other add-ons that make the room more accessible and welcoming to people with disabilities or mobility issues. These features also make bathrooms easier to use for the elderly and young children.

No matter what accessory you're adding, you'll never need to sacrifice the look of the room. Even the most practical accents—grab bars, for instance—now come in a full range of finishes and styles to suit any design vision. It's all a matter of mixing and matching needs and aesthetics to accessorize a bathroom that is as beautiful as it is easy to use.

In this chapter:

- Medicine Cabinets
- Grab Bars
- Glass Shelving
- Towel Warmers

Medicine Cabinets

Medicine cabinets were traditionally just shallow containers for pill bottles, with a mirrored door on the front. We've come a long way since then. Today, you can buy a medicine cabinet that includes power outlets for recharging your electric toothbrush, adjustable shelves, built-in LED lighting, and more. Whether you're ready to purchase a deluxe unit or just want to replace a flat mirror with some small-item storage, you'll choose between a surface-mounted unit and the more difficult-to-install recessed cabinet. The instructions for both are outlined here.

Medicine cabinets don't have to be frumpy. This sleek version has a simple knob handle and sleek aesthetic.

TOOLS & MATERIALS

Electronic stud finder	Drill	Framing square	2½" wood screws
Level	Circular saw	Duplex nails	Wood shims
Pry bar	Reciprocating saw	10d common nails	Cabinet
Hammer	Pencil	Finish nails	Eye and ear protection
Screwdriver	Bar clamp	1 × 4 lumber	Work gloves

How to Install a Surface-Mounted Medicine Cabinet

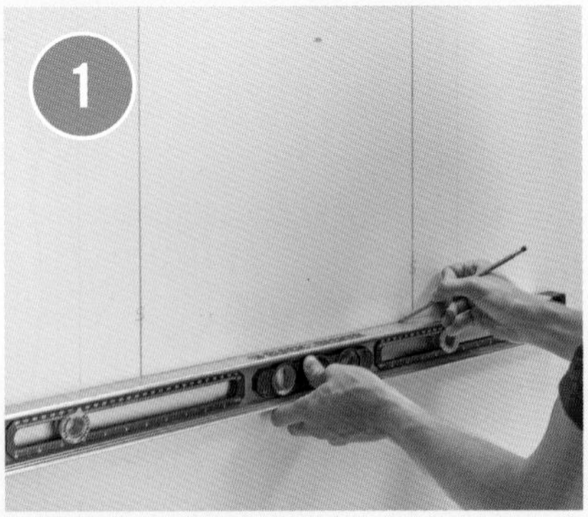

Locate the wall studs and mark them clearly on the wall surface. Draw a level line at the desired top height of the cabinet body, then measure and mark a second line to indicate the bottom of the cabinet.

Attach a temporary ledger board (usually 1 × 4) just below the lower level line using duplex nails. Rest the base of the cabinet on the ledger and hold it in place or brace it with 2 × 4s.

Attach the cabinet to the wall at the stud locations by drilling pilot holes and driving wood screws. Remove the ledger when finished, and patch the nail holes with drywall compound.

How to Install a Recessed Cabinet

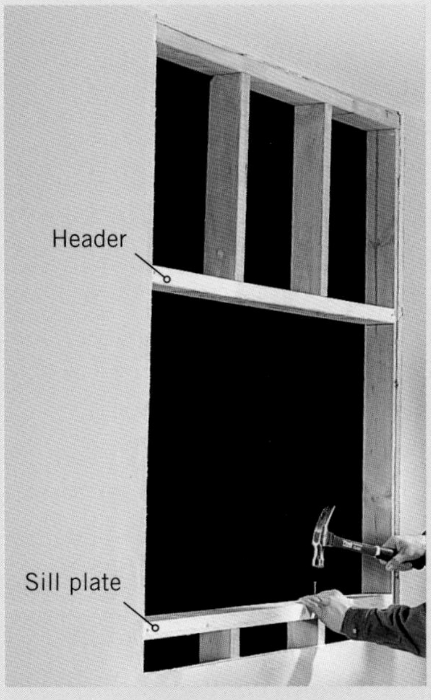

OPTION: Most recessed medicine cabinets sold today are sized in width to fit into the stud bay between standard studs that are 16" or 24" on center. If this lands the cabinet where you want it, you have a very easy job in front of you. But if you want the cabinet centered over a permanent furnishing, you may need to frame a new opening for the cabinet.

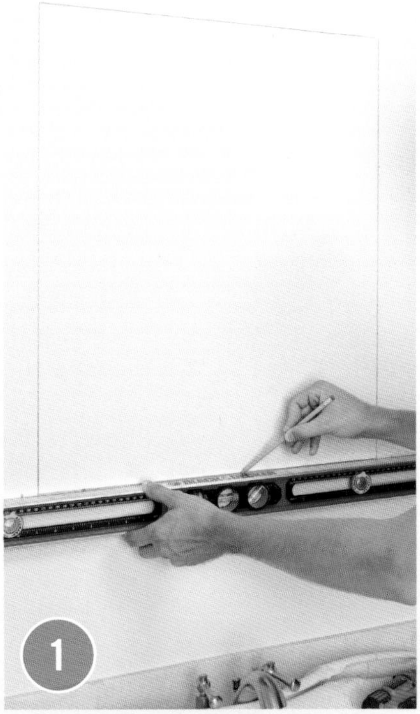

Use a stud finder to locate the wall-framing members and then draw an outline for the new cabinet, with the sides of the outline at the edges of the stud bay. (If you need to adjust the cabinet position or the cabinet you are installing is wider than the stud bay, see the option at left).

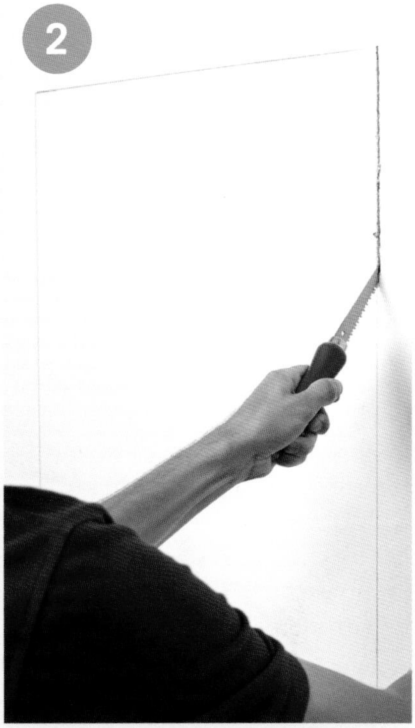

Shut off power at the main circuit panel in case there are any live wires in the stud cavity. Cut out the marked opening in the wall covering. A hand drywall saw will make neat work of this job.

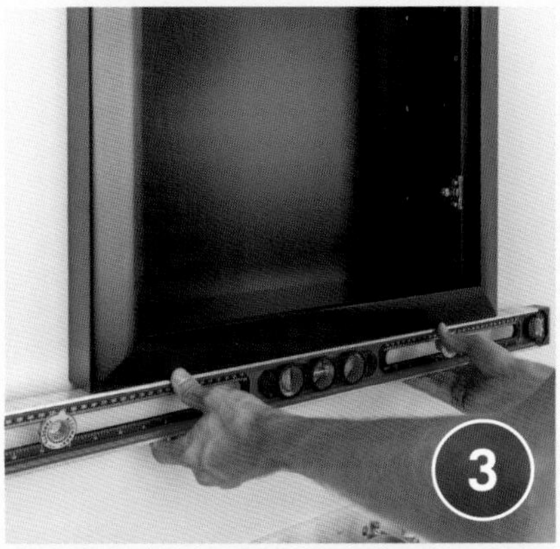

Remove the door/mirror from the cabinet and position the cabinet carcass in the opening. The opening should be slightly taller and wider than the cabinet. Set the height by resting the cabinet on a level and raising or lowering it. Tack the cabinet to a wall stud on one side with a nail driven through one of the screw access holes in the cabinet side.

Move the level to the cabinet side and adjust the cabinet until it is vertical. Tack it to the wall stud on the side opposite the first nail.

Drive a 2" drywall screw through one of the screw access holes on each side of the cabinet. Do not overdrive. Double-check for level and plumb, then add additional screws on each side until the cabinet is secure. Reattach the door/mirror.

Accessorizing for Universal Design

An increasing number of bathroom accessories are designed to make the room more usable for people with mobility limitations and motor-skill impairments—an important development as more consumers choose to stay in their homes as they age. These features are offered in many styles and finishes to complement just about any bathroom style. That means that there is really no reason not to include a set of grab-bar accessories in your bathroom.

The trick is to make sure these extras are installed correctly. They should be secured to studs or blocking to reliably support minimum weight requirements. But they also need to be installed at the correct heights. The following are the Americans with Disabilities Acts (ADA) requirements for grab-bar heights. The ADA is generally used as the basis for universal design and aging-in-place principles in bathrooms.

- **Toilets:** Grab bars behind toilets (centered over the tank, or bowl if no tank is present) should be a minimum of 36 inches long, mounted between 33 and 36 inches up from the floor. Grab bars on a wall alongside the toilet should be mounted 12 inches out from the back wall, 33 to 36 inches from the floor, and should be a minimum of 45 inches long. Where there isn't a side wall, you can use a swing-up or swing-away independent grab-bar unit with a supporting post and mounted with the same measurements as a wall-mounted bar.

- **Showers:** Back-wall (main-support) grab bars should be mounted 33 inches to 36 inches up from the shower floor and can be between 38 inches and 48 inches, depending on the space available in the stall. These can be used in conjunction with a permanent or fold-down seat mounted

This handsome bathroom is an example of ultimate accessibility, with a curbless shower that allows a wheelchair- or walker-using individual to easily take a shower (fold-down seat and grab bars assure stability). A roll-under sink is great for all users, and a toilet-side fold-down grab bar makes it simple for those with limited mobility to get on and off the essential fixture.

A stylish accent ring around the faucet controls in this tub doubles as a grip bar that helps bathers safely get into and out of the tub.

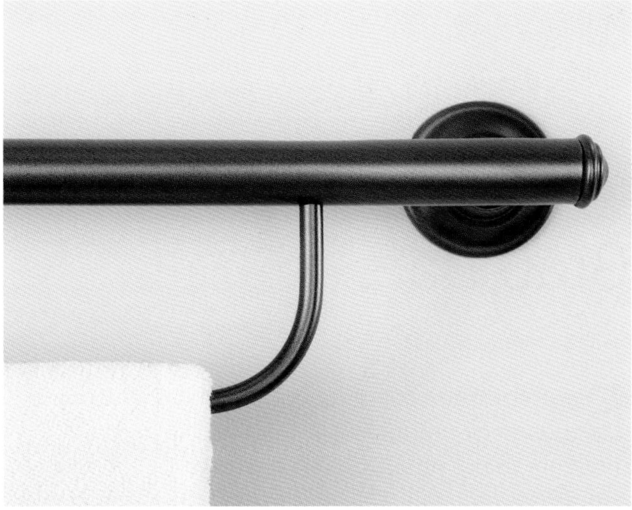

Why install just a towel bar, when you can add a safety feature with a combination towel-and-grab bar accessory? This one features a handsome rubbed-bronze finish, but you'll find these in a range of surface styles.

Combine stability with convenience by adding a simple shelf holder–grab bar combo like this one. The sleek curving style of this unit is just one of many forms and finishes available in this type of accessory.

Manufacturers continue to create accessible fixtures like this showerhead that is both a fixed and handheld unit. The head is easily removed from the stem—held in place by a magnetic connection. Once removed, a valve automatically redistributes the water to the head.

18 inches up from the shower floor. Side-wall grab bars should be a length that fits on the side wall, mounted 33 to 36 inches up from the shower floor.

- **Bathtubs:** As with other locations, all grab bars in a tub area should be mounted between 33 and 36 inches up from the floor of the bathroom. A back-wall grab bar should be a minimum of 48 inches long but should leave no more than 12 inches from the end of the grab bar to the head wall of the tub and no more than 15 inches from the back end of the grab bar to the foot wall of the tub. Head-wall grab bars should be a minimum of 24 inches long and should be mounted with the outer end flush with the outside edge of the head wall. A back-wall grab bar should be installed in the same way and should be a minimum of 12 inches long.

You can supplement these requirements with angled bars around shower stalls, offering variable heights at which the user can grab the bar. Use additional grab bars—such as those as part of a towel rack—to supplement these primary bars and make navigating the room easier.

Grab Bars

TOOLS & MATERIALS

- Measuring tape
- Pencil
- Stud finder
- Level
- Drill
- Masonry bit
- Grab bar
- Hollow-wall anchors
- #12 stainless-steel screws
- Silicone caulk
- Eye and ear protection
- Work gloves

Bathrooms are beautiful with their shiny ceramic tubs, showers, and floors, but add water and moisture to the mix and you've created the perfect conditions for a fall. The good news is that many falls in the bathroom can be avoided by installing grab bars at key locations.

Grab bars help family members steady themselves on slippery shower, tub, and other floor surfaces. Plus, they provide support for people transferring from a wheelchair or walker to the shower, tub, or toilet.

Grab bars come in a variety of colors, shapes, sizes, and textures. Choose a style with a 1¼- to 1½-inch diameter that fits comfortably between your thumb and fingers. Then properly install it 1½ inches from the wall with anchors that can support at least 250 pounds.

The easiest way to install grab bars is to screw them into wall studs or into blocking or backing attached to studs. Blocking is a good option if you are framing a new bathroom or have the wall surface removed during a major remodel (see Illustration A). Use 2 × 6 or 2 × 8 lumber to provide room for adjustments, and fasten the blocks to the framing with 16d nails. Note the locations of your blocking for future reference.

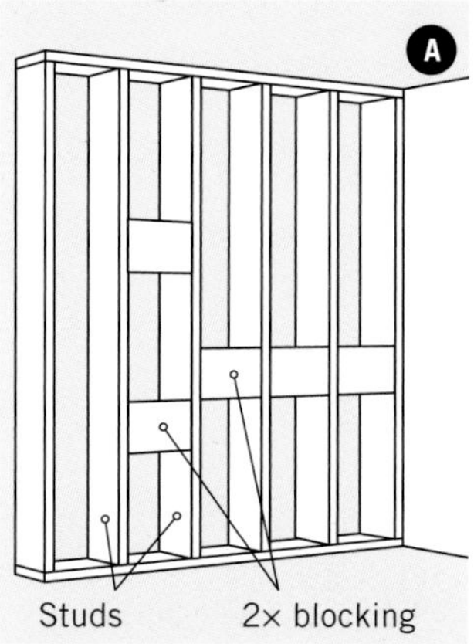

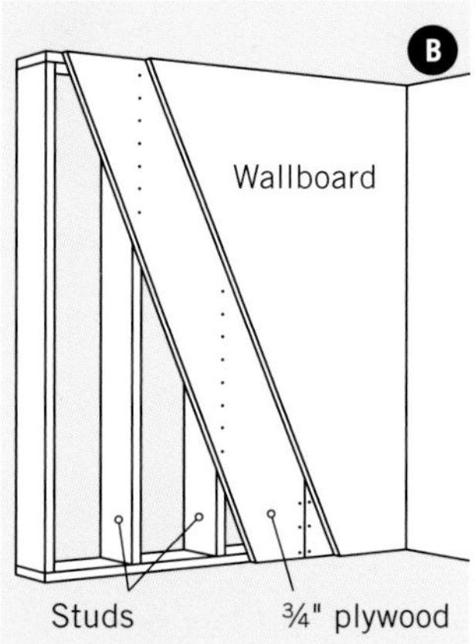

Blocking or backing is required for secure grab bars. If you know where the grab bars will be located, add 2× blocking between studs (Illustration A). You also can cover the entire wall with ¾" plywood backing, which allows you to install grab bars virtually anywhere on the wall (illustration B).

As an alternative, cover the entire wall with ¾-inch plywood backing secured with screws to the wall framing, so you can install grab bars virtually anywhere on the wall (see Illustration B).

Grab bars can be installed in areas without studs. For these installations, use specialized heavy-duty hollow-wall anchors designed to support at least 250 pounds.

Grab bars of different styles and configurations meet varied needs in any bathroom, and in different areas of the bathroom.

How to Install Grab Bars

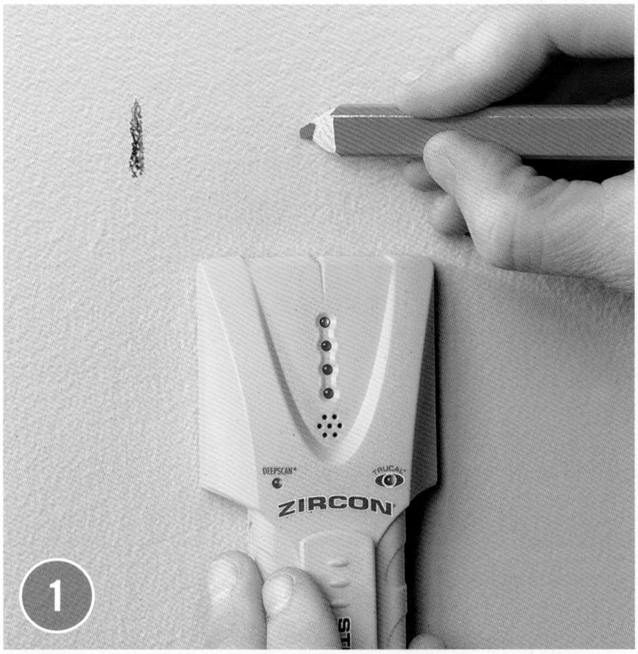

Locate the wall studs in the installation area using a stud finder. If the area is tiled, the stud finder may not detect studs, so try to locate the studs above the tile, if possible, then use a level to transfer the marks lower on the wall. Otherwise, you can drill small, exploratory holes through grout joints in the tile, then fill the holes with silicone caulk to seal them. Be careful not to drill into pipes.

Mark the grab-bar height at one stud location, then use a level to transfer the height mark to the stud that will receive the other end of the bar. Position the grab bar on the height marks so at least 2 of the 3 mounting holes are aligned with the stud centers. Mark the mounting-hole locations onto the wall.

Drill pilot holes for the mounting screws. If you are drilling through tile, start with a small bit (about ⅛"), then redrill the hole with the larger bit. For screws that won't hit studs, drill holes for wall anchors, following the manufacturer's directions for sizing. Install anchors, if necessary.

Apply a continuous bead of silicone caulk to the back side of each bar end (inset). Secure the bar to the studs using #12 stainless-steel screws (the screws should penetrate the stud by at least 1"). Install a stainless-steel screw or bolt into the wall anchors. Test the bar to make sure it's secure.

Glass Shelving

Glass shelving is unobtrusive so it can fit many styles of bathrooms—from sleek modern to elaborate Victorian. You can find a wide variety of shelving available in home stores and online.

Most glass shelves are held in place with metal mounts. How the shelves are secured to the mounts differs, and how the mounts are attached to the wall also differs. Most shelves have a hidden bracket that is secured to the wall. The mount then slips over the bracket and is secured with a setscrew. The most basic models may have mounts that are screwed directly into the wall with exposed screws. The directions here are for shelving that uses hidden brackets.

If you are installing shelves on a tiled wall, mount the brackets in grout lines if at all possible to minimize the possibility of cracking the tiles. Many glass shelves have some flexibility in the distance between the mounts.

TOOLS & MATERIALS

Level
Drill
Pencil
Glass shelves
Eye and ear protection
Work gloves

Glass shelves fit any style and size of bathroom. They are held in place with metal mounts, which can be decorative and attached to the wall.

How to Install Glass Shelves

Assemble the shelf and shelf holders (not the brackets). Hold the shelf against the wall in the desired location. On the wall, mark the center point of each holder, where the setscrew is.

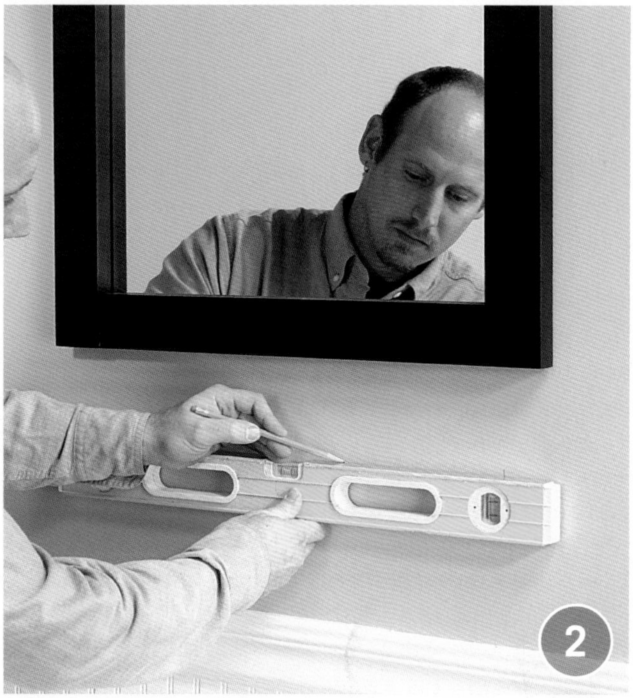

Remove the shelves and use the level to extend the mark into a 3" vertical line. Use the level to mark a horizontal line across the centers of these lines.

Center the middle round hole of the bracket over the intersection of the vertical and horizontal lines. Mark the center of each of the oblong holes. Put the bracket aside and drill a ¼" hole at each mark. Insert the included wall anchors in the holes. Replace the bracket, insert the screws into the wall anchors, and drive the screws. Repeat for the second bracket.

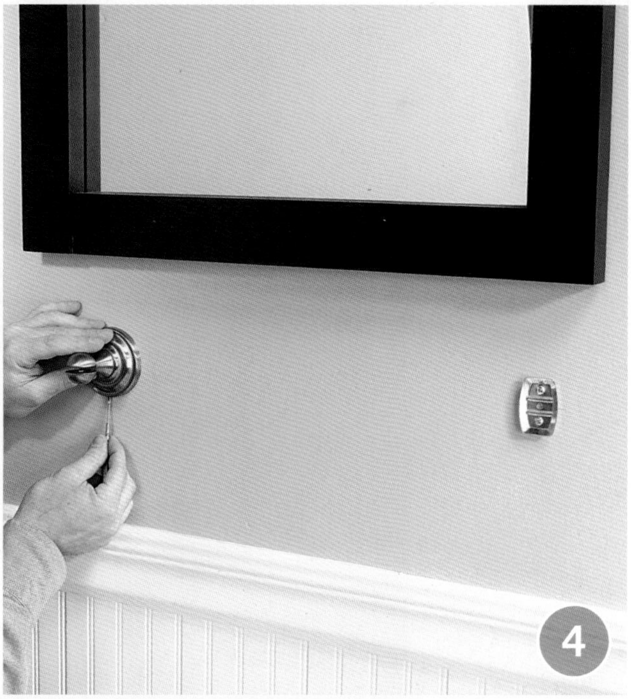

Remove the shelf from the holders. Slide a holder over a bracket, check that the shelf mount is level, and tighten the setscrew. Repeat with the other holder. Insert the shelf and fix in place. Check the shelf for level. If it's not level, remove one holder and loosen the bracket screws. Slide the bracket up or down to make the unit level. Replace the holder and shelf.

Towel Warmers

Here's a little bit of luxury that need not be limited to high-end hotel stays. You can have toasty towels in your own bathroom with an easy-to-install towel warmer. In a relatively cold room, this can make stepping out of the shower a much more pleasant experience.

Heated towel racks are available in a wide range of styles and sizes. Freestanding floor models as well as door- and wall-mounted versions can be plugged in for use when desired. Hardwired wall-mounted versions can be switched on when you enter the bathroom so your towels are warm when you step out of the shower. Although installing them requires some electrical skills, the hardwired models do not need to be located near wall receptacles, and they do not have exposed cords or extension cords hanging on the wall. However, if you locate the warmer directly above an existing receptacle, you can save a lot of time and mess by running cable up from the receptacle to the new electrical box for the warmer.

Before installing hardwired models, check your local electrical codes for applicable regulations. If you are not experienced with home wiring, have an electrician do this job for you or opt for a plug-in model.

TOOLS & MATERIALS

Drill
Level
Keyhole saw
Wiring tools
Phillips screwdriver
Stud finder
Retrofit electrical outlet box
Wire connectors
NM cable
Towel warmer
Pencil
Masking tape
Eye and ear protection
Work gloves

A hard-wired towel warmer offers the luxury of heated towels without the safety concerns of a plug-in device.

How to Install a Hardwired Towel Warmer

Use a stud finder to locate the studs in the area you wish to place the towel warmer. Mark the stud locations with masking tape or pencil lines. Attach the wall brackets to the towel warmer and hold the unit against the wall at least 7" from the floor and 3" from the ceiling or any overhang. Mark the locations of the wall-bracket outlet plate (where the electrical connection will be made) and the mounting brackets.

Shut off electrical power at the main service panel. At the mark for the wall-bracket outlet, cut a hole in the wall covering for a retrofit electrical box. Run NM cable from the opening to a GFCI-protected circuit (here, we ran cable down to a receptacle directly beneath it) or install a separate GFCI-protected circuit (you'll need to consult a wiring book or an electrician). Pull the cable through the hole in the retrofit box, then tighten the cable clamp. Place the box in the hole flush with the wall surface and tighten the mounting screw in the rear of the box. Cut the wires so about 5" extends into the box and strip the insulation off at ⅜" from the end of each wire.

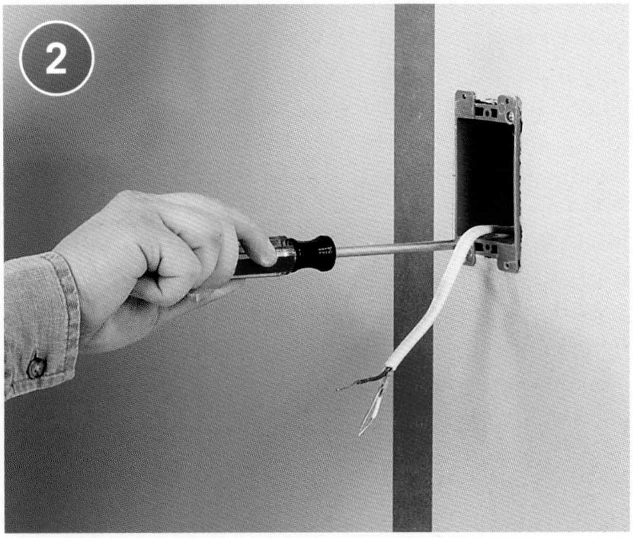

Position the towel warmer over the outlet box and mark the locations of the screw holes for the wall brackets. Make sure the appliance is level. Remove the warmer and drill ¼" pilot holes at the marked locations. If the marks are located over studs, drill ⅛" pilot holes. If not, push wall anchors into the holes. Thread the mounting screws through the brackets. Have a helper hold the towel rack in place and use wire connectors to connect the wires, including the ground wire, according to the instructions.

After the electrical connections are made, fasten the towel rack brackets to the wall. Turn on power and test the towel warmer. Finally, attach the electrical cover plate with integral on/off switch.

Appendix A: Plumbing Codes & Permits

The Plumbing Code is the set of regulations that building officials and inspectors use to evaluate your project plans and the quality of your work. Codes vary from region to region, but most are based on the National Uniform Plumbing Code, a highly technical, difficult-to-read manual. More user-friendly code handbooks are available at bookstores and libraries. These handbooks are based on the National Uniform Plumbing Code, but they are easier to read and include diagrams and photos.

Sometimes these handbooks discuss three different plumbing zones in an effort to accommodate state variations in regulations. Remember that local plumbing code always supersedes national code. Your local building inspector can be a valuable source of information and may provide you with a convenient summary sheet of the regulations that apply to your project.

As part of its effort to ensure public safety, your community building department requires a permit for most plumbing projects. When you apply for a permit, the building official will

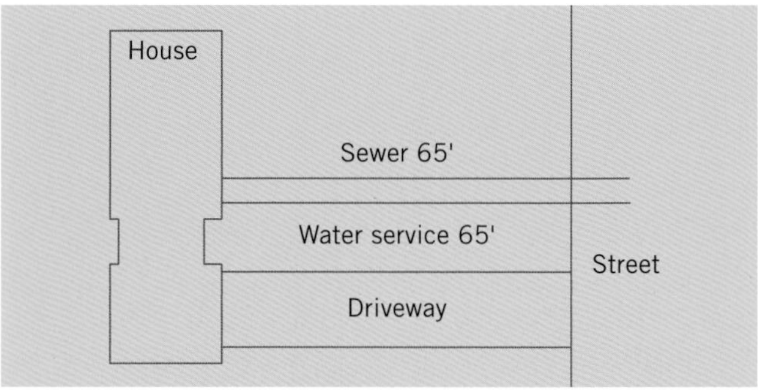

The site plan shows the location of the water main and sewer main with respect to your yard and home. The distances from your foundation to the water main and from the foundation to the main sewer should be indicated on the site map.

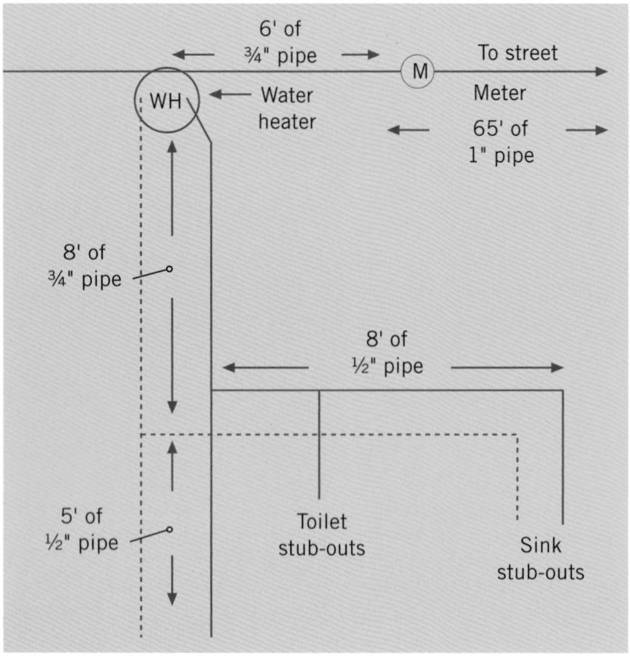

The supply-riser diagram shows the length of the hot and cold water pipes and the relation of the fixtures to one another. The inspector will use this diagram to determine the proper size for the new water-supply pipes in your system.

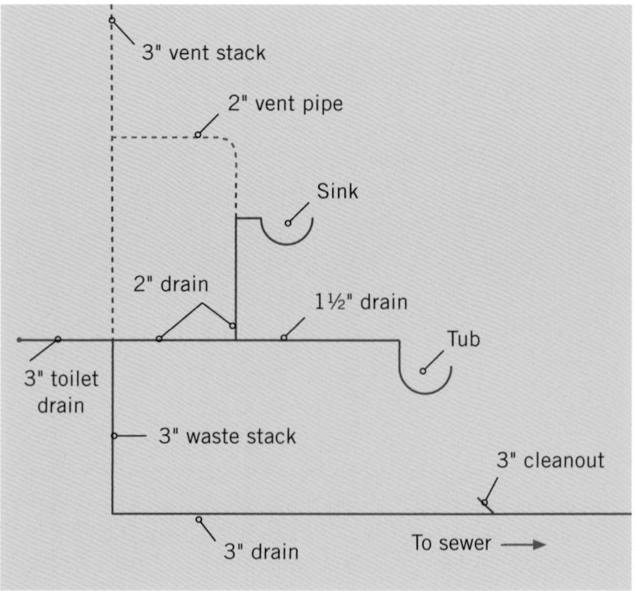

A DWV diagram shows the routing of drain and vent pipes in your system. Indicate the lengths of drain pipes and the distances between fixtures. The inspector will use this diagram to determine if you have properly sized the drain traps, drain pipes, and vent pipes.

want to review three drawings of your plumbing project: a site plan, a water-supply diagram, and a drain-waste-vent diagram (DWV). If the official is satisfied that your project meets code requirements, you will be issued a plumbing permit, which is your legal permission to begin work.

As your project nears completion, the inspector will visit your home to check your work.

NOTE: These specifications may not conform to all building codes; check with your local building department regarding regulations in your area.

FIXTURE SUPPLY PIPE & TRAP SIZES

FIXTURE	UNIT RATING	MINIMUM BRANCH-PIPE SIZE	MINIMUM SUPPLY-TUBE SIZE	MINIMUM TRAP SIZE
Toilet	3	½"	⅜"	NA
Vanity Sink	1	½"	⅜"	1¼"
Shower	2	½"	⅜"	2"
Bathtub	2	½"	½"	1½"

To determine the minimum size of supply pipes and fixture drain traps, you must know the fixture's unit rating, a unit of measure assigned by the plumbing code.

NOTE: Branch pipes are the water-supply lines that run from the distribution pipes toward the individual fixtures. Supply tubes carry water from the branch pipes to the fixtures.

SIZES FOR HORIZONTAL & VERTICAL DRAIN PIPES

PIPE SIZE	MAXIMUM FIXTURE UNITS FOR HORIZONTAL BRANCH DRAIN	MAXIMUM FIXTURE UNITS FOR VERTICAL DRAIN STACKS
1¼"	1	2
1½"	3	4
2"	6	10
2½"	12	20
3"	20	30
4"	160	240

Drain-pipe sizes are determined by the load on the pipes, as measured by the total fixture units. Horizontal drain pipes less than 3" in diameter should slope ¼" per 1' toward the main drain. Pipes 3" or more in diameter should slope ⅛" per 1'.

NOTE: Horizontal or vertical drain pipes for a toilet must be 3" or larger.

MAXIMUM HOLE & NOTCH SIZES

FRAMING MEMBER	MAXIMUM HOLE SIZE	MAXIMUM NOTCH SIZE
2 × 4 load-bearing stud	1⁷⁄₁₆" diameter	⅞" deep
2 × 4 nonload-bearing stud	2½" diameter	1⁷⁄₁₆" deep
2 × 6 load-bearing stud	2¼" diameter	1⅜" deep
2 × 6 nonload-bearing stud	3⁵⁄₁₆" diameter	2³⁄₁₆" deep
2 × 6 joists	1½" diameter	⅞" deep
2 × 8 joists	2⅜" diameter	1¼" deep
2 × 10 joists	3¹⁄₁₆" diameter	1½" deep
2 × 12 joists	3¾" diameter	1⅞" deep

The maximum hole and notch sizes that can be cut into framing members for running pipes is shown above. Where possible, use notches rather than bored holes to ease pipe installation. When boring holes, there must be at least ⅝" of wood between the edge of a stud and the hole and at least 2" between the edge of a joist and the hole. Joists can be notched only in the end ⅓ of the overall span; never in the middle ⅓ of the joist. When 2 pipes are run through a stud, the pipes should be stacked 1 over the other, never side by side.

PIPE SUPPORT INTERVALS

TYPE OF PIPE	VERTICAL SUPPORT INTERVAL	HORIZONTAL SUPPORT INTERVAL
Copper	6'	10'
ABS	4'	4'
CPVC	3'	3'
PVC	4'	4'
Galvanized Iron	12'	15'
Cast Iron	5'	15'

Minimum intervals for supporting pipes are determined by the type of pipe and its orientation in the system. Use only brackets and supports made of the same (or compatible) materials as the pipes. Remember that the measurements shown above are minimum requirements; many plumbers install pipe supports at closer intervals.

WET VENTING

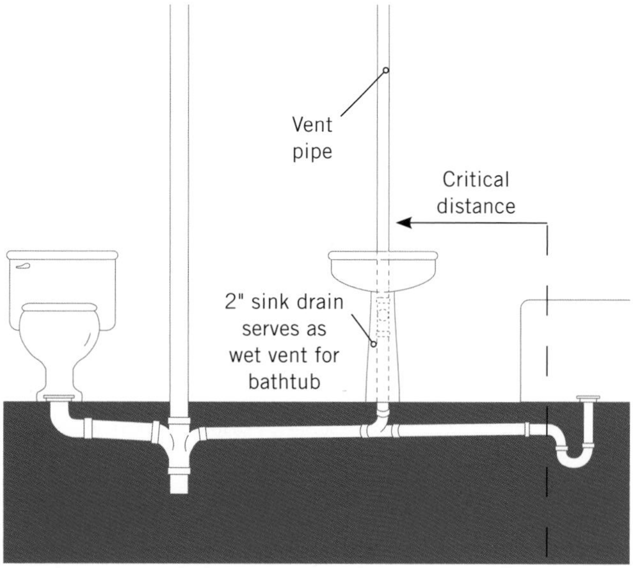

Wet vents are pipes that serve as a vent for 1 fixture and a drain for another. The sizing of a wet vent is based on the total fixture units it supports: a 3" wet vent can serve up to 12 fixture units; a 2" wet vent is rated for 4 fixture units; a 1½" wet vent for only 1 fixture unit.

NOTE: The distance between the wet-vented fixture and the wet vent itself must be no more than the maximum critical distance.

AUXILIARY VENTING

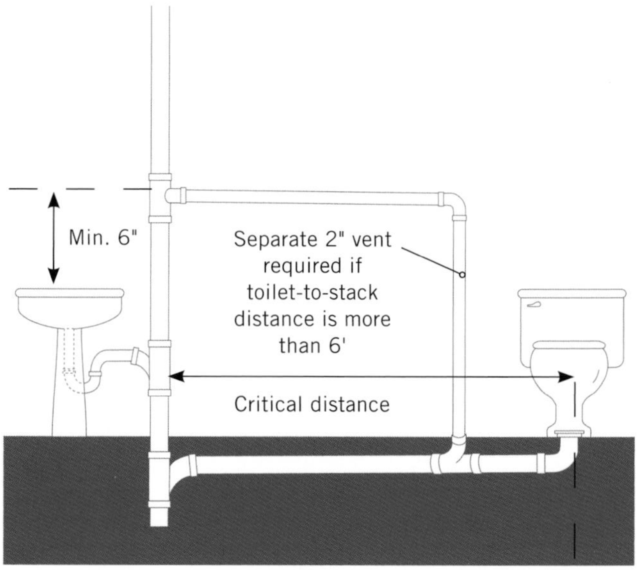

Fixtures must have auxiliary vents if the distance to the main waste-vent stack exceeds the critical distance. A toilet, for example, should have a separate vent pipe if it is located more than 6' from the main waste-vent stack. This secondary vent pipe should connect to the stack or an existing vent pipe at a point at least 6" above the highest fixture on the system.

VENT-PIPE SIZES & CRITICAL DISTANCES

SIZE OF FIXTURE DRAIN	MINIMUM VENT PIPE SIZE	MAXIMUM TRAP-TO-VENT DISTANCE
1¼"	1¼"	2½'
1½"	1¼"	3½'
2"	1½"	5'
3"	2"	6'
4"	3"	10'

Vent pipes are usually one pipe size smaller than the drain pipes they serve. Code requires that the distance between the drain trap and the vent pipe fall within a maximum critical distance, a measurement that is determined by the size of the fixture drain. Use this chart to determine both the minimum size for the vent pipe and the maximum critical distance.

VENT PIPE ORIENTATION TO DRAIN PIPE

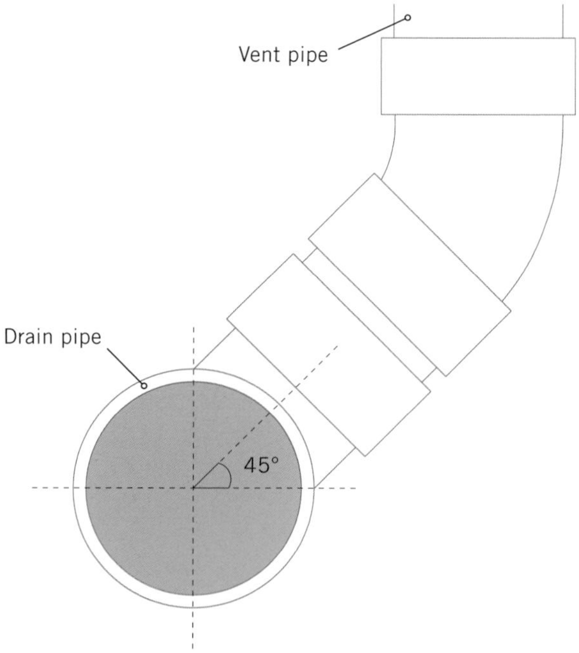

Vent pipes must extend in an upward direction from drains, no less than 45° from horizontal. This ensures that wastewater cannot flow into the vent pipe and block it. At the opposite end, a new vent pipe should connect to an existing vent pipe or main waste-vent stack at a point at least 6" above the highest fixture draining into the system.

Appendix B: Wiring Codes & Permits

To ensure public safety, every community requires that you get a permit to install new wiring and have the completed work reviewed by an appointed inspector. Electrical inspectors use the National Electrical Code (NEC) as the primary authority for evaluating wiring, but they also follow the local building-code and electrical-code standards.

As you begin planning new circuits, call or visit your local electrical inspector and discuss the project with him or her. The inspector can tell you which of the national and local code requirements apply to your job and may give you a packet of information summarizing these regulations. Later, when you apply to the inspector for a work permit, he or she will expect you to understand the local guidelines as well as a few basic NEC requirements.

The NEC is a set of standards that provides minimum safety requirements for wiring installations. It is revised every three years.

In addition to being the final authority of code requirements, inspectors are electrical professionals with years of experience. Although they have busy schedules, most inspectors are happy to answer questions and help you design well-planned circuits.

As with any project, if you are uncomfortable working with electricity, hire a professional electrician to complete new wiring installations and connections.

The bathroom requirements listed below are for general information only. Contact your local electrical inspector for specific wiring regulations:

- A separate 20-amp receptacle circuit for small appliances is required.
- All receptacles must be GFCI protected.
- Light fixtures and switches must be on a separate circuit (a minimum 15-amp circuit).
- All fixture and appliance switches must be grounded.
- There must be at least one ceiling-mounted light fixture.
- Whirlpools and other large fixtures or appliances are required to be on a dedicated circuit.

The manufacturers of some home-spa fixtures, such as saunas and whirlpools, may specify that a certified electrician make the electrical connections for their product. Make sure to follow these directions, as doing otherwise may result in the warranty being voided.

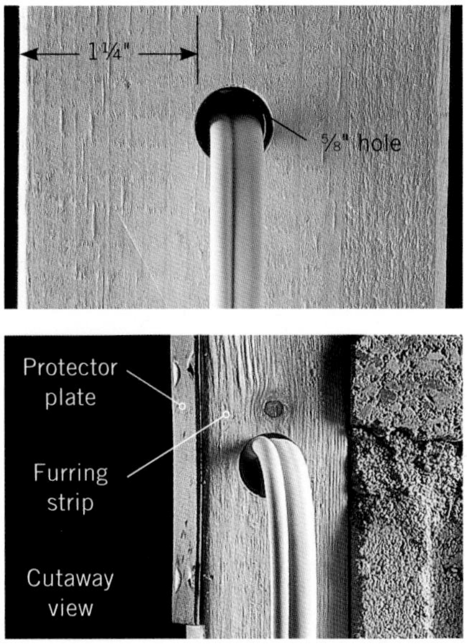

Cables must be protected against damage by nails and screws by at least 1¼" of wood (top). When cables pass through 2 × 2 furring strips (bottom), protect the cables with metal protector plates.

Kitchen and bathroom receptacles must be protected by a GFCI. Also, all outdoor receptacles and general-use receptacles in an unfinished basement or crawlspace must be protected by a GFCI.

Metric Conversions

ENGLISH TO METRIC

TO CONVERT:	TO:	MULTIPLY BY:
Inches	Millimeters	25.4
Inches	Centimeters	2.54
Feet	Meters	0.305
Yards	Meters	0.914
Square inches	Square centimeters	6.45
Square feet	Square meters	0.093
Square yards	Square meters	0.836
Ounces	Milliliters	30.0
Pints (US)	Liters	0.473 (Imp. 0.568)
Quarts (US)	Liters	0.946 (Imp. 1.136)
Gallons (US)	Liters	3.785 (Imp. 4.546)
Ounces	Grams	28.4
Pounds	Kilograms	0.454

TO CONVERT:	TO:	MULTIPLY BY:
Millimeters	Inches	0.039
Centimeters	Inches	0.394
Meters	Feet	3.28
Meters	Yards	1.09
Square centimeters	Square inches	0.155
Square meters	Square feet	10.8
Square meters	Square yards	1.2
Milliliters	Ounces	.033
Liters	Pints (US)	2.114 (Imp. 1.76)
Liters	Quarts (US)	1.057 (Imp. 0.88)
Liters	Gallons (US)	0.264 (Imp. 0.22)
Grams	Ounces	0.035
Kilograms	Pounds	2.2

CONVERTING TEMPERATURES

Convert degrees Fahrenheit (F) to degrees Celsius (C) by following this simple formula: Subtract 32 from the Fahrenheit temperature reading. Then multiply that number by 5⁄9. For example, 77°F - 32 = 45. 45 × 5⁄9 = 25°C.

To convert degrees Celsius to degrees Fahrenheit, multiply the Celsius temperature reading by 9⁄5. Then, add 32. For example, 25°C × 9⁄5 = 45. 45 + 32 = 77°F.

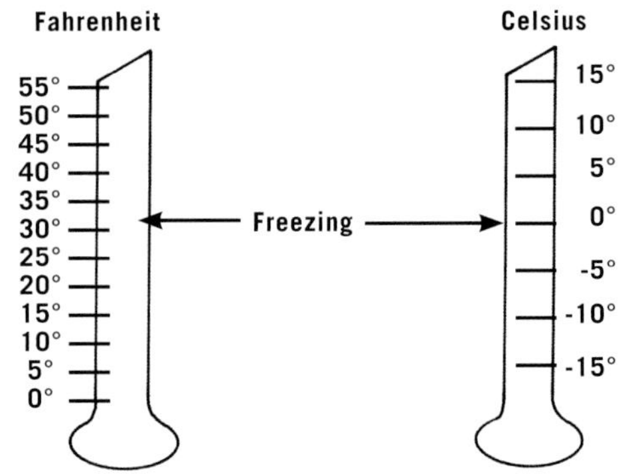

METRIC PLYWOOD PANELS

Metric plywood panels are commonly available in two sizes: 1,200 mm × 2,400 mm and 1,220 mm × 2,400 mm, which is roughly equivalent to a 4 × 8' sheet. Standard and Select sheathing panels come in standard thicknesses, while Sanded grade panels are available in special thicknesses.

STANDARD SHEATHING GRADE		SANDED GRADE	
7.5 mm	(5⁄16")	6 mm	(4⁄17")
9.5 mm	(3⁄8")	8 mm	(5⁄16")
12.5 mm	(½")	11 mm	(7⁄16")
15.5 mm	(5⁄8")	14 mm	(9⁄16")
18.5 mm	(¾")	17 mm	(2⁄3 ")
20.5 mm	(13⁄16")	19 mm	(¾")
22.5 mm	(7⁄8")	21 mm	(13⁄16")
25.5 mm	(1")	24 mm	(15⁄16")

LUMBER DIMENSIONS

NOMINAL - U.S.	ACTUAL - U.S. (IN INCHES)	METRIC
1 × 2	¾ × 1½	19 × 38 mm
1 × 3	¾ × 2½	19 × 64 mm
1 × 4	¾ × 3½	19 × 89 mm
1 × 5	¾ × 4½	19 × 114 mm
1 × 6	¾ × 5½	19 × 140 mm
1 × 7	¾ × 6¼	19 × 159 mm
1 × 8	¾ × 7¼	19 × 184 mm
1 × 10	¾ × 9¼	19 × 235 mm
1 × 12	¾ × 11¼	19 × 286 mm
1¼ × 4	1 × 3½	25 × 89 mm
1¼ × 6	1 × 5½	25 × 140 mm
1¼ × 8	1 × 7¼	25 × 184 mm
1¼ × 10	1 × 9¼	25 × 235 mm
1¼ × 12	1 × 11¼	25 × 286 mm
1½ × 4	1¼ × 3½	32 × 89 mm
1½ × 6	1¼ × 5½	32 × 140 mm
1½ × 8	1¼ × 7¼	32 × 184 mm
1½ × 10	1¼ × 9¼	32 × 235 mm
1½ × 12	1¼ × 11¼	32 × 286 mm
2 × 4	1½ × 3½	38 × 89 mm
2 × 6	1½× 5½	38 × 140 mm
2 × 8	1½ × 7¼	38 × 184 mm
2 × 10	1½ × 9¼	38 × 235 mm
2 × 12	1½ × 11¼	38 × 286 mm
3 × 6	2½ × 5½	64 × 140 mm
4 × 4	3½ × 3½	89 × 89 mm
4 × 6	3½ × 5½	89 × 140 mm

LIQUID MEASUREMENT EQUIVALENTS

1 Pint	= 16 Fluid Ounces	= 2 Cups
1 Quart	= 32 Fluid Ounces	= 2 Pints
1 Gallon	= 128 Fluid Ounces	= 4 Quarts

COUNTERBORE, SHANK & PILOT HOLE DIAMETERS

SCREW SIZE	COUNTERBORE DIAMETER FOR SCREW HEAD (IN INCHES)	CLEARANCE HOLE FOR SCREW SHANK (IN INCHES)	PILOT HOLE DIAMETER	
			HARD WOOD (IN INCHES)	SOFT WOOD (IN INCHES)
#1	.146 (9/64)	5/64	3/64	1/32
#2	¼	3/32	3/64	1/32
#3	¼	7/64	1/16	3/64
#4	¼	⅛	1/16	3/64
#5	¼	⅛	5/64	1/16
#6	5/16	9/64	3/32	5/64
#7	5/16	5/32	3/32	5/64
#8	⅜	11/64	⅛	3/32
#9	⅜	11/64	⅛	3/32
#10	⅜	3/16	⅛	7/64
#11	½	3/16	5/32	9/64
#12	½	7/32	9/64	⅛

NAILS

Nail lengths are identified by numbers from 4 to 60 followed by the letter "d," which stands for "penny." For general framing and repair work, use common or box nails. Common nails are best suited to framing work where strength is important. Box nails are smaller in diameter than common nails, which makes them easier to drive and less likely to split wood. Use box nails for light work and thin materials. Most common and box nails have a cement or vinyl coating that improves their holding power.

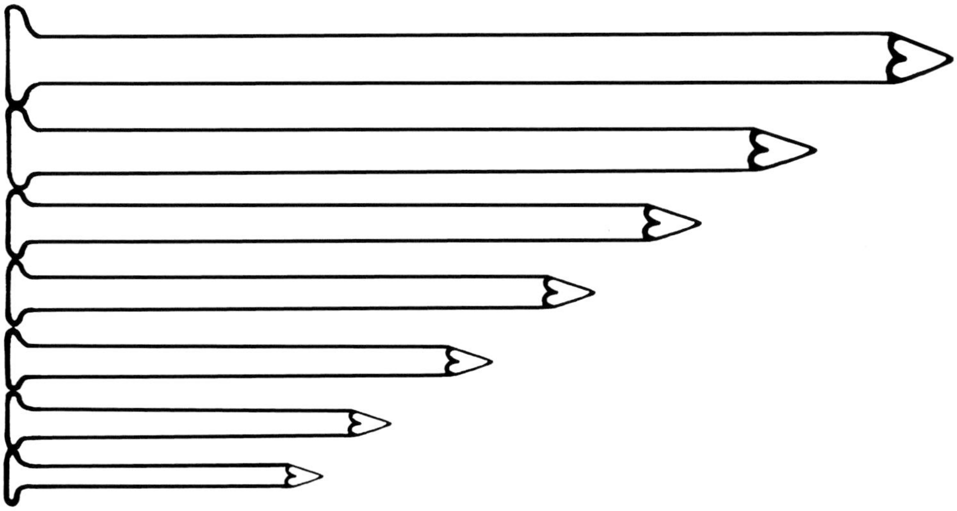

LBS.	MM	IN.
20d	102 mm	4"
16d	89 mm	3½"
10d	76 mm	3"
8d	64 mm	2½"
6d	51 mm	2"
5d	44 mm	1¾"
4d	38 mm	1½"

Resources

Accessibility Resource Center (ARC)
Shower and wet room kits, Aging in Place and accessibility accessories
715-743-2771
www.arcfirst.net

American Standard
Bathroom and kitchen fixtures
800-442-1902
www.americanstandard-us.com

BLACK+DECKER
Power tools and accessories
800-544-6986
www.blackanddecker.com

Duravit
Bathtubs, sinks, and bathroom furniture
www.duravit.us

Interstyle Glass and Ceramic
Ceramic glass and tiles
604-421-7229
www.interstyle.ca

Moen
Bathroom faucets, shower fixtures, safety and accessibility accessories
800-289-6636
www.moen.com

MTI
Tubs, shower bases, and enclosures, sinks, and accessories
800-783-8827
www.mtibaths.com

National Kitchen and Bath Association
Industry association offering advice and connection to professionals
800-843-6522
www.nkba.org

Plumbing, Heating, Cooling Contractors Association
Producers of the National Standard Plumbing Code
800-533-7694
www.phccweb.org

Robern
Bathroom cabinets, lighting, vanities, and mirrors
800-877-2376
www.robern.com

Photo Credits

ABF: 12 (bottom), 25 (bottom left)

American Standard: 13 (bottom), 28, 45 (top and bottom left), 67, 162, 239 (top left)

ARC: 78, 200, 234, 238, 240

Bain Ultra: 13 (top right), 37 (middle right)

Best Bath: 15 (top right)

Cambria: 12 (top), 176

Cosentino: 36 (top), 37 (bottom left), 41 (bottom), 144

Diamond Cabinets: 15 (bottom), 33 (top left and right)

Duravit: 31 (top), 153 (bottom left)

DVX: 21 (lower right)

Economic Mobility, Inc.: 44 (left)

Gail Owens: 6

Harrell Remodeling: 45 (top right)

Interstyle: 153 (top right), 204 (both)

Jacuzzi: 14 (bottom right), 15 (top left), 22

Kichler: 26 (left), 34 (bottom)

Kohler: 23 (both), 24 (left), 27 (top and middle), 29 (bottom left and right), 46 (both), 146 (both), 153 (bottom right), 214

Moen: 14 (top), 17 (bottom), 21 (top right), 24 (top), 31 (bottom), 42, 45 (bottom right), 104, 239 (lower right), 239 (top left and bottom left and right)

Mr. Steam: 17 (top)

MTI: 16, 25 (top and bottom right), 26 (right), 30, 34 (top), 37 (top), 41 (top), 114

Pyrolave: 13 (top left), 27 (bottom)

Robern: 10, 32, 33 (bottom), 36 (bottom)

Shutterstock: 20, 21 (top left), 29 (top right), 62, 78, 174, 192

Task Lighting: 40, 186

Walker Zanger: 14 (bottom left)

Index